The Business of Music

Liverpool Music Symposium

Liverpool Music Symposium 2

The Business of Music

edited by
Michael Talbot

LIVERPOOL UNIVERSITY PRESS

First published 2002 by
LIVERPOOL UNIVERSITY PRESS
4 Cambridge Street, Liverpool L69 7ZU

British Library Cataloguing-in-Publication Data
A British Library CIP record is available.

ISBN 0 85323 528 7 *cased*
ISBN 0 85323 538 4 *paper*

Typeset in Sabon with Gill Sans by
Northern Phototypesetting Co. Ltd, Bolton, Lancs.
Printed and bound in the European Union by
Bookcraft, Bath

Contents

Notes on Contributors

Judith Blezzard is a Senior Lecturer in Music at the University of Liverpool. Her areas of interest include manuscript studies, especially relating to choral and church music of the sixteenth and nineteenth centuries. Her publications include several editions and translations of choral works from European repertories, and she directs a local chamber choir.

Mike Brocken lectures at Liverpool John Moores University and Liverpool Hope. He is owner amd managing director of Mayfield Records, and as a broadcaster has just completed for the BBC a series of six documentaries on Liverpool venues in the 1970s.

Sara Cohen is a Senior Lecturer in the Department of Music at the University of Liverpool and a member of the editorial board of the journal *Popular Music*. She is the author of *Rock Culture in Liverpool* (Oxford University Press, 1991). Her most recent publications have focused on the diverse areas of popular music, gender and sexuality, and popular music and urban regeneration.

Cyril Ehrlich, Emeritus Professor of Social and Economic History at Queen's University, Belfast, specialises in the economic history of music. His books include studies of the piano, of the music profession, of the history of performing rights and of the Royal Philharmonic Society, and he has recently completed a history of the Wigmore Hall. He is currently Visiting Professor at Goldsmiths College.

Simon Frith is Professor of Film and Media Studies at the University of Stirling, and co-editor of the *Cambridge Companion to Rock and Pop*. He chairs the judges of the Mercury Music Prize.

Mike Jones is Course Director for the MBA in Music Industries at the University of Liverpool. His PhD research dealt with the industrial processes of music commodification. As a member of the group Latin Quarter, he released seven albums between 1984 and 1997, mainly for RCA Records.

Dave Laing is Reader in Music at the School of Communication and Creative Industries, University of Westminster. His many publications include *The Sound of Our Time* (1969) and *One Chord Wonders* (1985). His next book will be a study of the international music business.

Marion Leonard is a Lecturer at the Institute of Popular Music at the University of Liverpool. Her PhD research addressed issues of gender in the music industry. She has investigated and written on various subjects related to popular music that include ethnicity, gender, cultural policy and youth cultures.

Simon McVeigh is Professor of Music at Goldsmiths College, University of London. He has written extensively on the history of concerts in eighteenth- and nineteenth-century London (including *Concert Life in London from Mozart to Haydn*), and he is currently engaged on a project with Cyril Ehrlich entitled 'The Transformation of London Concert Life, 1880–1914'. He is also completing a study of the early-eighteenth-century Italian concerto.

Robert Orledge is Professor of Music at the University of Liverpool. A specialist in French music from 1850 to 1950, he has published books on Fauré, Debussy, Koechlin and Satie, as well as numerous related articles and editions. He is currently preparing a critical edition of Debussy's Poe opera *La Chute de la Maison Usher*.

Caroline Potter is a Senior Lecturer in Music at the University of Kingston. A specialist in French music since Debussy, she is the author of *Henri Dutilleux* (Ashgate, 1997). She is currently co-editing *French Music since Berlioz*, also for Ashgate, and writing a book on Nadia and Lili Boulanger.

Rob Strachan is currently completing a PhD at the University of Liverpool on the politics of independent record production. He teaches at the Institute of Popular Music, runs an independent record label and is an active musician. His research interests include cultural policy, taste cultures and the political economy of the music industry.

Recent publications include a chapter on the semiotics of music video in *Music and Manipulation* (Wesleyan University Press, 2001).

Michael Talbot is James and Constance Alsop Professor of Music at the University of Liverpool. A specialist in Venetian music of the late *Baroque*, he has produced books on Vivaldi, Albinoni and Vinaccesi. His most recent book is *The Finale in Western Instrumental Music* (Oxford University Press, 2001).

Introduction

Michael Talbot

The double meaning of the title for this volume, and for the symposium that preceded it, is of course intended. The first meaning, which one could paraphrase as 'What music is (or ought to be) about', contrasts with the second, which is: 'How music is produced and consumed, bought and sold'. But even if the two meanings are quite different, they are intertwined. No one is so naive as to imagine that the material circumstances of music's existence leave no mark whatever on its character. The important questions are, rather, whether such influences are (or should be) central or marginal and whether, on balance, they are good or bad.

No musical tradition is wholly unanimous about the answers. Where music produced in our own age is concerned, a kind of litmus test is provided by reactions to the description 'commercial' and its subtly different pair of antonyms, 'non-commercial' and 'uncommercial'. Within the Western art music tradition, commonly known as classical music, it would usually seem inadvisable, even improper, to apply the term 'commercial' to the music itself. Of course, everyone wishes for success (the composer and his or her performers must eat!) and for wide dissemination, even if, unexpectedly, to the *vulgus*. But in the view of the musicians most intimately involved, this success must appear almost accidental rather than engineered. If the community of practitioners and professional commentators describes a composition as 'good' or 'bad' according to its consensual aesthetic and technical standards, this quality remains unaffected by public success or failure and sticks to the work for as long as the experts remain in agreement.

The insulation of the concept of artistic value from survival in the marketplace is perhaps logical for a tradition that prizes durability and, almost uniquely among musical practices, likes to take the long-term view. Viewed in this light, the subsidy of classical music from the public or private purse is a great benefit, since it validates a distinction between artistic and commercial value: a *deus ex machina* plugs the gap between what concertgoers are willing to pay and how much composers, performers and venues need to earn in order to keep going. But such patronage is simply a different kind of commerce from the more familiar brand rather than a negation of commerce as such. Classical composers and ensembles nowadays compete for funding in the same way that others compete for market share.

It was not always so, of course. During the comparatively brief period when classical music, principally via publishing, the sale of musical instruments and the public concert, circulated among all European urban classes with little competition from other musical traditions – a period stretching from the middle of the nineteenth century to the end of the First World War – it possessed a vast 'popular' sector (of drawing-room ballads, piano miniatures, fashionable dances, etc.) that entered, and competed in, the marketplace like any other set of commodities.

Classical music is probably the only surviving musical tradition routinely to be funded, albeit only in part, by taxpayers and purchasers of consumer products who are not among its adherents. To give one example: a subscriber to a pension scheme who has no personal interest in classical music may nevertheless subsidise a symphony concert, unwittingly or even unwillingly, if his or her pension company decides to sponsor it. There are good arguments in favour of this apparently indefensible situation, provided that one is prepared (which not all defenders of classical music are) to grasp the nettle and stand up to, rather than to appease, those who make accusations of elitism. Ironically, it is the largely indirect support given to classical music by those who have no opinion about what it should be like that acts as the strongest guarantor of its vaunted non-commercial character: a negative (public indifference) creates a positive (artistic freedom).

On the surface, popular music (if one can use a single term to encompass such a huge variety of musical types) is, and has always been, 'commercial' in a perfectly orthodox way. Those artists who make the most money are deemed almost by definition to have deserved it. If the value-system of classical music seems at times to correlate musical worth (viewed in the light of eternity) inversely with audience appeal, the correlation is rarely other than brutally direct in the case of 'chart' music. Its dominant value-system could be expressed as an argument developed along the following lines:

1 Good music appeals to audiences.
2 The more people it appeals to, the more they invest their own money in it; the more money they invest in it, the more the artist earns.
3 The richer the artist, the better his or her music.

Naturally, there are counter-currents. Less successful artists in any popular genre often explain (or rationalise) their failure to make a breakthrough and win big audiences by employing arguments relating to artistic value similar to those heard in classical music. Indeed, there are two entire genres, jazz and folk, that are so ambivalent in general towards their marketplace status (in a way that classical music, with its guaranteed subsidies, does not need to be) that their adherents can rightly be accused of running with the hare while hunting with the hounds. They chase public funding and sponsorship while harbouring dreams of a mega-success that will put such humiliating necessities behind them. (It is perhaps because of this ambiguity rather than for any strictly musical reason that these two genres are accommodated so uncomfortably within the tent of popular music.)

Another complicating factor is that popular music, in most of its expressed forms (live concert, televised concert, video film, CD, etc.), is a composite entity made up not only of music but also of production features that include costume, lighting effects, choreographed movement on stage, ritualised banter with the audience and cover design. Whereas in classical music, with the notable exception of opera, every effort is made to standardise production features (such as concert dress) – to make them as conventional and unremarkable as possible in order to minimise any distraction from the music itself – in popular music their differentiation is vital to the artistic intention. Popular music does not invite its fans to unpack these components and assess them separately: it delivers integrated packages to be consumed and judged as a totality. Under these conditions, musical content, as a follower of classical music would understand it, becomes subordinated to something larger and more complex. The heterogeneity of the popular music event makes it easier to disguise or compensate for deficiencies of its individual components, musical or otherwise, and in that respect makes the product more malleable for commercial ends.[1]

If it is both too banal and too simple to say that modern popular music is commercial by design, whereas its classical counterpart is commercial by necessity, this formulation at least captures something of their difference. In practice, as the following chapters will show, convergences and parallelisms frequently arise. Mercantile and musical considerations are certainly different, but they are not necessarily antagonistic. In both camps, imaginative musicians and their supporting armies of publishers, record companies and publicists have tried, often with unexpected success, to reconcile the two imperatives. For the classical musician, the goal is to produce a music that, without compromise of taste or standards, wins public favour in the here and now and succeeds (or almost succeeds) in financing itself. For the popular musician, it is to produce a music whose appeal endures even after his or her career is over because of its originality, virtuosity and effective communication of feeling.

In Liverpool Music Symposium 1 (1998), which addressed the subject of the musical work and its definition, it emerged that something that was a cornerstone of one tradition (Western art music) was virtually ignored and sometimes even held in contempt by the other (Western popular music). The contrast pointed up fundamental differences between the two traditions that were not always obvious at first glance. This time, the difference is less stark, especially if classical music of the eighteenth and nineteenth centuries is taken into account. Indeed, some classical music is distinctly more 'commercial' in intention and result than some popular music. Irrespective of the type of music, once it has to move beyond the cosy world of family, neighbourhood or club, music is compelled to participate in social networks in which money changes hands. Because such transactions are anticipated, it is normally conceived with them already in mind, even if the passage of money occurs only towards the later stages of a long chain of events.

1. I owe the identification of the popular music event, rather than the popular music work (or number), as the basic 'unit of appreciation' operating within that tradition to David Horn's essay 'Some Thoughts on the Work in Popular Music', published in the proceedings of Liverpool Music Symposium 1 (*The Musical Work: Reality or Invention?*, ed. Michael Talbot, Liverpool, Liverpool University Press, 2000, pp. 14–34).

The contributors have wasted little space assessing from their own viewpoints whether the union of music and business is a good or a bad thing, although they do not fail to point out instances where the subjects of their investigations have found it uncomfortable. They take it as axiomatic that the conjunction takes place, and their concern is to show exactly how it comes about and what difference the commercial connection makes to the musical end-product, which we often consume today under circumstances very different from those that first brought it into being.

The chapters open with a contribution from myself that dissects, and relates to a wider context, the surviving contract signed in 1714 between the noble co-proprietors of a Venetian opera house and an obscure impresario. Over and above this document's relevance to the history of Venetian music and of early *Settecento* opera, and to the history of one particular theatre (the Teatro Sant'Angelo), it reveals some commercial aspects that we might recognise as surprisingly modern: how start-up capital for a season was raised by leasing some of the theatre's assets; how the distinct 'brand identity' that was developed for the theatre's productions fitted its modest economic circumstances; how ownership and control were scrupulously segregated; how a multi-level system of franchises simplified administration and spread the commercial risk more widely; how the state underwrote the operation as a guarantor of last resort.

For the chapters by **Judith Blezzard** and the joint authors **Simon McVeigh** and **Cyril Ehrlich,** we move to England in the late Victorian and Edwardian ages. Blezzard's focus is on choral music in the North of England (mostly east of the Pennines). She shows how a thriving culture of mostly amateur music-making in the late nineteenth century and beyond was sustained by local publishers, whose vast production, patchily preserved and even more patchily investigated in the past, contains items of real quality and great historical interest. The traditional emphasis, in studies of music publishing, on London – 'Novellocentricity', as one might call it – does a real disservice to English music during a period when the North, for once, shared in the rising prosperity and cultural aspirations of the South.

McVeigh's and Ehrlich's investigation is unapologetically metropolitan. They show how, around the turn of the century, concert life in London was rapidly transformed, becoming both more professional and more ambitious – to the extent that a 'crisis of overproduction' arose. Crucial to this transformation were the rise of the

West End as a shopping centre, the improved transport to and from the suburbs and the close involvement of sheet music publishers and musical instrument manufacturers in the building, ownership, management and repertory of concert halls. Such firms as Chappell and Bechstein acted, via their sponsorship of concert life, as the forerunners of the corporate giants of today. The rhythm of concert life changed, as the seasons grew longer and Sunday emerged as a legitimate, indeed preferred, day on which to hold events. By the time that the First World War imposed a brake on this hectic activity, London had gone far towards achieving a level of music-making commensurate with its exceptional size and economic power.

We then cross the Channel to look at French music in the same period and a little later in chapters by **Robert Orledge** and **Caroline Potter**. Orledge explores the relationship of a leading composer, Claude Debussy, and a leading publisher, Jacques Durand, bringing to the story of their close, though not always unproblematic, friendship and collaboration the fruits of new archival research. One learns to one's surprise that Debussy mapped out a programme of deliveries to his publisher (which he executed faithfully to a remarkable extent) years in advance, and that, in order to rescue his financial situation (often made precarious by alimony payments to his first wife and his own taste for luxury), the composer could always turn out a 'lollipop' for piano solo, achieving larger sales through an astute choice of picturesque title. Durand's generosity and careful attention to Debussy's needs, which reminds one a little of the all-round service that major record labels today offer to the artists in their stable, certainly paid off in the long run. Here, virtue and commercial acumen ran in parallel.

Potter examines a quite different area: that of the teaching of composition and music theory. Nadia Boulanger was the most celebrated *femme savante* of musical composition during the first half of the twentieth century, although, ironically, she composed very little herself. Another irony: Boulanger, as a female high-achiever, would have had every reason to ally herself with the feminist movement, but was disinclined to do so, perhaps influenced by her upper-class origins and lifestyle, and also by a feeling that through avoiding direct competition, as a composer, with her male pupils, she could increase her acceptability to them as a pedagogue-cum-confidante. Her financial strategy consisted in using modestly talented but rich pupils (mostly Americans) to cross-subsidise highly talented but poor ones. Once again, enlightened self-interest proved successful.

The chapters by **Dave Laing** and **Simon Frith** could be subtitled, respectively: 'View from the Gamekeeper's hut' and 'View from the Poacher's lair'. Both deal with the legalities of music as expressed in the various forms of 'right': copyright, intellectual property right, performing right, mechanical right, etc., in a highly complex situation not easily conducive to the understanding and acceptance of these rights, especially in an age of rapidly advancing technology. Laing, whose contribution marks the point of cross-over, in this volume, from the classical to the popular domain (though much of what he says remains equally relevant to classical music), argues on behalf of those, including struggling artists as well as large corporations, who stand to gain from enforcement of the law, while Frith considers the standpoint of those who can't pay, won't pay or don't even realise that they have to pay. Frith draws attention to the extreme difficulty, both conceptual and practical, of treating popular music as property protectable by law. The material itself is not amenable, and technical processes such as sampling blur the already weak boundaries between one piece and another. Moreover, identity politics, which implies the primacy of the individual or subcultural over the corporate or societal, encourages illegality as a way of 'getting back at' the System. Laing, for his part, shows via a series of case studies why an internationally recognised legal framework, however imperfect, is needed to ensure a minimum degree of orderliness in the music market – an orderliness that in the case of technical innovations serves the interest of consumers no less than that of producers. Interestingly, both chapters are rooted in the type of cultural criticism first introduced into Britain about forty years ago in the pages of *New Left Review*. They share a vocabulary, even if their perspectives are different; and both maintain the detachment proper to a commentator rather than a partisan.

Mike Brocken considers the present state of a 'scene' that once had an acknowledged home within youth culture but is today predominantly a refuge for the middle-aged and elderly: the folk revival. This once powerful post war movement was fuelled by sentiments of anti-imperialism and anti-capitalism, a fact that caused it to come adrift from its moorings at the end of the Cold War and in consequence of the steady decline of the traditional Labour Movement. Worse, the Leftist ideology and unbusinesslike temperament of the movement's most devoted adherents made it half-hearted, even ambivalent, about the related goals of making a commercial profit and building a larger audience share. Brocken sees chinks of light, however, in the growing pragmatism and diversification of the folk movement, and in the readiness of some within it no longer to cry 'sell-out!' at every musical innovation or successful marketing operation. Moreover, the 'Green' movement may well provide a secure mooring for it in the future.

A possible way forward for the folk revival in Britain is shown by the success of traditional music in Ireland, which enjoys both iconic cultural status, with all the access to public funding that this ensures, and a high degree of independent commercial success. However, in Ireland and Britain alike the real Cinderella of the public funding regime for music is the kind developed or encouraged by community organisations in areas of social deprivation. Drawing on evidence collected during a study of the music industry in Dublin, **Rob Strachan** and **Marion Leonard** argue for the social value (which may, of course, occasionally blossom into other kinds of value) of 'grassroots' musicmaking. Even though the benefits that arise from funding them cannot be measured in simple artistic or financial terms, community arts have a unique and irreplaceable function that should suffice to guarantee them a seat at the table of funding organisations. Strachan and Leonard also show, in passing, how simplistic attempts by public bodies to view different kinds of music as either aesthetically or economically desirable (but seemingly not both at once) come into conflict with the real situation, in which neither factor can ever be removed altogether from the equation.

Community music makes another appearance in the tragicomic account by **Sara Cohen** of attempts made in the 1980s and 1990s to enable music to contribute to, and profit from, large-scale projects aimed at the regeneration of Liverpool and its region. The familiar antitheses are all there: the triangular contest between the economic, the aesthetic and the social, and the many-sided tussles, punctuated by alliances of convenience, between practitioners (of several kinds), consultants, politicians and funding agencies. Cohen places special emphasis on what she calls the 'rhetoric of the local', which, in relation to the particular cases examined, includes civic pride and a strong sense of local belonging but also parochialism and xenophobic defensiveness. Her chapter is a chronicle of opportunities missed or insufficiently exploited, but, by laying bare the interests, ideologies and discourses of the interested parties, she points to ways in which more successful coalitions can be built in the future.

With **Mike Jones**, we move into the rapidly growing area of academic courses in music-industrial studies. There is already a broad consensus that such courses are timely and useful, but what character they should take remains a bone of contention. For the government, and for the industry itself, the operation is essentially about 'skilling' in order to turn out qualified operatives and executives. For higher education institutions, it is about education as traditionally conceived: knowing not only what things are but also why they are so – and even how they might be made otherwise. Jones argues, using the unsuccessful lawsuit of George Michael brought against Sony Music as a cautionary tale, that it is only by approaching the industry and its workings critically, with a clear understanding of its multi-faceted complexity and contradictions, that students can have a good prospect of making successful careers within it: skills alone do not suffice.

That brings our offerings to an end, appropriately with a chapter based partly on personal experiences gained in the home of the Symposium. Liverpool in 2001 is very different from Venice in 1700, but the path that we have traversed has, I think, thrown up enough common features and connections to make this volume cohere.

Finally, I would like to offer thanks on many sides: to the contributors for their enthusiasm and their patience with my demands; to Sarah O'Keeffe for organisational help; to the Faculty of Arts of the University of Liverpool for financial assistance; to Liverpool University Press for once again accommodating our proceedings; to the music publishing firms of J. Wood and Sons and Editions Durand for their kind permission to reproduce pages from documents in their archives as plates; and to my colleague John Williamson for volunteering to organise the next Liverpool Music Symposium, due to be held in autumn 2002.

I

A Venetian Operatic Contract of 1714

Michael Talbot

Contracts are useful documents for historical research, even if their significance is based more on inference than on fact. They do not say what happened, but they point unequivocally to what was feared might happen. Embedded in them is the memory of past mishaps and misunderstandings. They also illuminate, again obliquely rather than directly, the power relationship between the parties. Whoever sets the most conditions or exacts the heaviest penalties is likely to be the dominant party. Lastly, they can reveal a lot about the financial calculations underpinning the operations to which they refer: how much was spent, when it was spent, and who spent it.

Without doubt, opera has always been, ever since its creation shortly before 1600, the art form that is organisationally most complex, financially most problematic and artistically most diverse. It is the co-operative genre *par excellence*, depending as it does on the harnessing of several very distinct talents and roles. Any serious dissension between the major participants, and the whole project, affecting dozens of livelihoods, is imperilled. Crucial to the enterprise is the sharing out of risk, so that all the interested parties know that they have to sink or swim together. On the surface, a contract relating to opera may appear at times to place the two parties in an oppositional position, but at a deeper level it furthers solidarity by reinforcing their interdependence.

The present chapter takes the form of a detailed examination of a contract made on 11 December 1714 between the co-proprietors of the Venetian opera house known as the Teatro Sant'Angelo and the freelance impresario Pietro Denzio.[1] It begins with a citation of the

1. This contract, which is preserved in a manuscript in the Venetian State Archives (Inquisitori di Stato, Busta 914, *Case di gioco e teatri*, fascicolo 'S. Angelo'), is

entire document in English translation (a transcription of the original is given in Appendix A).[2] This is followed by a point-by-point commentary that makes frequent detours in order to build up a more complete picture of the operatic context as it existed in Venice in the early eighteenth century. The focus here is less on artistic matters than on economic, administrative and social ones.

The Contract

Laus Deo, 11 December 1714, Venice

At a meeting of the noblemen and noblewomen who are co-proprietors of the Theatre of Sant'Angelo,[3] comprising Zuanne Capello and his nephews; Polo Capello, son of the late Alvise Capello; Marietta Bolani, consort of Francesco Boldù; Pietro Zen, son of the late Vicenzo Zen; Anzolo Memo and his brothers, sons of the late Anzolo Memo; Giacomo Antonio Vettor Marcello, son of the late Alvise Marcello; Gerolemo Vettor Marcello, son of the late Francesco Marcello; and Ferigo Vettor Marcello Renier, son of the late Alvise Marcello Renier, all acting in accordance with their stake in the said theatre,[4] the undersigned, who constitute the majority of those

well known to specialists in the history of Venetian opera. Its first part (up to the list of boxes made over to the impresario) is transcribed complete in Francesco Mancini, Maria Teresa Muraro and Elena Povoledo, *I teatri del Veneto, II: Venezia e il suo territorio. Imprese privati e teatri sociali*, Venice, Fiore, 1996, pp. 41–42. The discussion of the Sant'Angelo theatre in this volume (pp. 3–62) is by far the fullest and most diligently researched of any to date, and I acknowledge my great indebtedness to it (for brevity, I will refer to it simply as 'Mancini (1996)' in later references). In its turn, the book's section on Sant'Angelo takes much of its information on the period in question from Gastone Vio, 'Una satira sul teatro veneziano di Sant'Angelo datata "febbraio 1717"', *Informazioni e Studi Vivaldiani*, Vol. 10 (1989), pp. 103–28. Few similar contracts relating to Venetian opera houses of the same period survive; the closest equivalent is one drawn up for the San Moisè theatre in 1708.

2. All translations into English are my own.

3. The titles 'Nobil Homo' (or 'Nobil Donna') and 'Ser' (Sir) are omitted from the translation for the sake of brevity. Names are left in their Venetian dialectal forms: thus 'Zuane' (or 'Zuanne') instead of 'Giovanni', 'Anzolo' instead of 'Angelo', 'Ferigo' in place of Federico', etc.

4. 'Stake' is the simplified translation I have used for the phrase 'porzioni, attioni, ragioni, e rappresentanze', which means more precisely 'portions, claims, ownerships and surrogacies'.

present, have agreed the following terms for managing and hiring out the theatre:

With the present private contract, which is to have the same legal force as if it had been drawn up by a public notary of this city of ours [Venice], the same persons give and hire out for the coming year, starting on the first day of Lent 1715 and finishing on the last day of Carnival 1716, the above theatre in their ownership to Signor *Pietro Denzio*, who is granted its lease and management in accordance with the agreements, modalities, terms and conditions set out below, namely:

1 That the said impresario, as he has promised and undertaken to the noble co-proprietors, shall put on in that theatre two or more operas in the Autumn and ensuing Carnival of that year [1715/16] in good and creditable form throughout the period of the present lease and management.

2 That if, through his fault, the performances fail to take place and, consequently, the lessees of the boxes refuse to pay the normal annual rental so that the said nobles do not realise the income from the unlet boxes, the impresario shall be obliged to indemnify the latter in full and also pay them damages, this being an express condition of the present lease. However, if there is a general public ban on the performance of operas or if a fortuitous event such as fire or plague (which God forbid) should prevent the said impresario from putting on the performances in the said theatre, he is exempted from the requirement to pay an indemnity and damages.

3 That he shall not, under any pretext, sublet the theatre to others without the previous assent and written permission of the said noble co-proprietors.

4 That he shall be bound, once Carnival ends, freely to give up the said theatre and the use of the [associated] house to the same [noble co-proprietors] when he is asked to do so, and to leave them in good order and in the same state in which he found them.

5 That the said impresario shall have complete freedom of action in all matters concerning the theatre, the operas and the performances, and that the said noble co-proprietors undertake not to become involved in anything to do with them, no exceptions being allowed.

6 That the noble co-proprietors shall grant to the said impresario for the stated period of one year full authority over, and sole right to the proceeds of, ticket sales and door receipts and to the income earned by subcontracting the right to sell food and drink and to hire out chairs in the said theatre.

7 That they shall make over and assign to the said impresario free of charge for his use and profit the upper circle of the theatre with its boxes for the stated period of one year, except for the central box which is enjoyed by Signor Agostin Rosa, the theatre's general manager and solicitor.

8 That they shall likewise assign to him free of charge box no. 7 at ground level, which is customarily occupied by the *protettore*, and also the new box next to the proscenium on the side of the ticket office, which is customarily used for the accommodation of the singers.

9 That the impresario shall receive this coming Lent all the scenery, materials and other items used for operas and kept in the theatre, which are to be listed in an inventory in the customary manner, and which the said impresario will maintain, preserve, restore and return together with the other materials, pieces of scenery and anything else of use to the stage, making over everything to the said theatre and its owners, the said noble co-proprietors, and renouncing all claim to anything; at the conclusion of the performances, these new or returned items shall be checked against the accounts and inventories at the request of the said noble co-proprietors, or whenever the general manager demands it, without hindrance or delay.

10 That throughout the stated period the impresario shall have the enjoyment and the use for rehearsals and, if necessary, for the accommodation of the singers who come to perform in the said theatre, of the house belonging to them next to the same theatre, which is likewise made over to him on condition that he restores and returns it in the same good order in which he finds it.

11 That the said noble co-proprietors, each contributing according to the shares and stakes he holds in the said theatre, shall grant and make over (as, in making the present contract, they effectively grant, make over, assign and yield) to the said impresario the lump sum of 640 ducats current, each valued at 6 *lire* 4 *soldi*, in the form of rental from boxes and of unlet boxes, which will be listed below with details of the portions and ownership of each. Each co-

proprietor shall make over and yield to him his due share of the whole without accepting any responsibility for the ease or difficulty with which he will be able to benefit from it, giving him full authority to make use of it as if it were his own, to keep the annual rent from the boxes that are let, and to rent out or to have rented out those that are not let, within the period of one year as per the present contract.[5] He shall be able to rent them out evening by evening if he desires and may make whatever kind of arrangements he prefers in regard to payment, keeping an account of money received and issuing receipts. In cases of the non-payment of rent the impresario shall be permitted to have recourse to all legal means to obtain payment in the name of the said noble co-proprietors. This will be done at his own expense but with legal assistance from Signor Agostin Rosa, the theatre's solicitor.

12 That the said noble co-proprietors and their noble ladies and gentlemen and other members of their households, as well as the advocate Zuanne Alberti and the solicitor Agostin Rosa, who are both in the service of the theatre, together with members of their households, shall have free admission to the opera on all occasions without ticket or charge, the impresario having no obligation to issue them with red tickets as other impresarios did previously, no kind of regulation or special pass for anyone else being permitted.

13 That the observance, maintenance and strict execution of everything contained in the present agreement, interpreted in its most correct, solemn and general manner, shall be binding on all the noble co-proprietors in respect of the interest, shares, present and future goods and heirs proper to each, and similarly on the impresario, his heirs and estate. And there will be two signed copies made of the present contract for retention by each of the parties.

Particulars of the leases follow

Herewith follow particulars of the leases of the boxes and of the unlet boxes made over to the impresario as stated above

Representing the share of Zuanne Capello and his nephews	d101	g7
From Antonio Molin, son of the late ..., for box 6 in tier 3	d25	g–
From Zuanne Bernardo for half of box 7 in tier 3	d12	g12

---

5. The translation of this sentence and of the three following it (originally part of the same sentence) has been somewhat curtailed and simplified, the style of expression being even more verbose and convoluted than usual.

From Count Francesco Cusina for box 11 in tier 3	d25	g–
From Silvestro Valier for half of box 18 in tier 4	d10	g–
Half of box 3 in tier 4, unlet	d10	g–
All of box 7 in tier 4, unlet	d20	g–
	d102	g12
To be reimbursed to him on receipt of the payments	d1	g5
Balance	d101	g7
Representing the share of Polo Capello, son of the late Alvise	d101	g7
From Pietro Benzon for the ground-level box marked F	d20	g–
From Vettor Grimani for ground-level box 27	d20	g–
From Ferigo Barbarigo and his brothers for half of box 10 in tier 3	d12	g12
From Zuanne Battista Grimani, son of the late Zuanne, for box 13 in tier 3	d25	g–
From the heirs of the late Nicolò Resio for box 9 in tier 4	d20	g–
In cash at the conclusion of the performances	d3	g19
	d101	g7
Representing the share of Marietta Bolani Boldù	d42	g10
All of box 5 in tier 4, unlet	d20	g–
Half of box 1 in tier 4, unlet	d10	g–
Half of the ground-level box 4, unlet	d10	g–
In cash at the conclusion of the performances	d2	g10
	d42	g10
Representing the share of Piero Zen	d42	g10
From Messer Nicolò Sagredo, Procurator of St Mark's, for half of box 8 in tier 2	d12	g12
Half of the ground-level box 4, unlet	d10	g–
Half of box 1 in tier 4, unlet	d10	g–
Half of box 2 in tier 4, unlet	d10	g–
	d42	g12
To be reimbursed to him on receipt of the payments	d–	g2
	d 42	g 10
Representing the share of Anzolo Memo and his brothers, sons of the late Anzolo	d32	g14
From Costantin Renier for the use [?] of Piero Venier for half box 6 in tier 2	d12	g12
From Count Piero Lion for half the above box 6 in tier 2	d12	g12
From Francesco Antonio Farsetti, Kavalier, for half of box 4 in tier 3	d12	g12
	d37	g12
To be reimbursed to him on receipt of the payments	d4	g22
	d32	g14
Representing the share of Giacomo Antonio Vettor Marcello, son of the late Alvise	d148	g20
Gerolemo Giustinian, Procurator of St Mark's, for a sixth of the ground-level box 26	d3	g8

From Tomaso Querini for a third of box 18 in tier 2, at present held by the most-serene Electress of Bavaria	d8	g8
From Francesco Morosini, Kavalier, and his brother, in place of the [late] Doge Morosini, for box 20 in tier 2	d25	g–
From Nicolò Contarin, son of the late Aurelio, for half of box 24 in tier 2	d12	g12
From Gerolemo Michiel, son of the late Nicolò, and his brothers for half of box 23 in tier 3	d12	g12
From Gerolimo Foscarini, son of the late …, for half of box 26 in tier 3	d12	g12
A third of the unlet half of the ground-level box 20	d3	g8
A third of box 21 in tier 4, unlet	d10	g0
A third of box 27 in tier 4, unlet	d10	g0
Half of proscenium box D in tier 4, unlet	d10	g0
All of box 22 in tier 4, unlet	d20	g0
All of box 26 in tier 4, unlet	d20	g0
In cash at the conclusion of the performances	d1	g8
	d148	g20
Representing the share of Gerolemo Vettor Marcello, son of the late Francesco	d144	g12
From Pietro Duodo and his brothers for half of the ground-level box 19	d10	g–
From Carlo Pisani for half of the ground-level box 22	d10	g–
From Gerolemo Canal, Procurator, for the portions belonging to him according to the division of the ground-level box marked G	d12	g12
From Tomaso Querini for a third of box 18 in tier 2, at present held by the most-serene Electress of Bavaria	d8	g8
From the heirs of the late Zuanne Grimani for half of box 22 in tier 2	d12	g12
From Francesco Morosini, Kavalier, for a quarter of box 27 in tier 2	d6	g6
From Almorò Dolfin for box 25 in tier 2	d25	g0
Box 25 in tier 4, unlet	d20	g0
Proscenium box B in tier 4, unlet	d20	g0
Box 27 in tier 4, unlet	d10	g0
Half of proscenium box D in tier 4, unlet	d10	g0
	d144	g14
To be reimbursed to him on receipt of the payments	d–	g2
	d144	g12
Representing the share of Ferigo Vettor Marcello Renier	d26	g16
From Gerolemo Giustinian, Procurator of St Mark's, for a third of the ground-level box 26	d6	g16
From Tomaso Querini for a third of box 18 in tier 2, at present held by the most-serene Electress of Bavaria	d8	g8
From the heirs of the late Don Nicolò Passalaqua for half of box 15 in tier 4	d10	g0
A third of the unlet half of the ground-level box 20	d3	g8

	d28	g8
To be reimbursed to him on receipt of the payments	d1	g16
	d26	g16
[Total]	d640	

[followed by the signatures of the eight co-proprietors]

Commentary

The contract is written in a neat secretarial hand on two nested bifolios, neither of which is foliated or paginated. The outer bifolio contains the contract proper, the inner bifolio the itemised list of boxes and fractions of boxes made over to the impresario (beginning at 'Herewith follow particulars' in the translation and at 'Seguono li affitti' in the original text).[6] As the last sentence of the final clause (numbered 13) makes clear, this was only one of three identically worded examples of the contract. The example that has survived was lodged with the authorities (an essential precaution against 'tampering'), and the two others, probably no longer extant, were held by the two parties to the contract.

In the second paragraph the contract is described as a private one drawn up 'as if' by a public notary, but in fact without employing any legal help. Just as it is possible in modern Britain to write one's own will without employing a solicitor by basing the text on established formulae taken from a template or from an earlier version of the same kind of document, so, too, in eighteenth-century Venice, many legal documents of a routine kind were prepared in this manner. The same paragraph fixes the duration of the impresario's tenancy: from the first day of Lent 1715 (6 March) to the last day of Carnival 1716 (25 February). In other words, the tenancy is to begin one day after the premises are vacated by the previous impresario and to end one day before the next impresario takes possession.

The two opening paragraphs identify the parties to the contract. On one side we have the eight co-proprietors of the theatre;[7] on the other, the impresario Pietro Denzio.

---

6. To simplify matters, the outer bifolio is identified, in the transcription given in Appendix A, as fols 1–2, the inner bifolio as fols 3–4. This numbering reflects the sequence in which the folios are intended to be read.
7. In two cases (Zuanne Capello and Anzolo Memo), the person named represents family members in addition to himself.

In the original Italian text all the co-proprietors are identified by prefixed titles as members of the Venetian patriciate.[8] As Venetian nobles go, they belong neither to the highest nor to the lowest echelon. In 1714 the total number of male patricians, including minors, was computed as 2,851, divided into 667 families (*case*) belonging to 216 clans sharing a surname (*famiglie*).[9] In a total population for the city of some 140,000 (half of which was female) this amounted to only about four per cent. Despite its small size in both relative and absolute terms, the Venetian patriciate was able, until the extinction of the republic in 1797, to retain its monopoly of political power and, to a large extent, also its economic power, which was based above all on ownership of land and buildings (and not on manufacturing, as in former times).

Simplified accounts of early opera often draw a sharp distinction between 'court opera', as represented by Monteverdi's *L'Orfeo*, given in Mantua at the Gonzaga court in 1607, and 'public opera', as represented by the same composer's *L'incoronazione di Poppea*, given at the Venetian theatre of SS Giovanni e Paolo in 1642. The antithesis is not entirely false, since the audience at a court opera was essentially an invited one, whereas that at a public opera was admitted (subject to a dress code) simply on production of a previously purchased ticket. It does, however, tend to obscure the fact that until the nineteenth century Italian opera houses, and in fact theatres of any kind, were owned and ultimately controlled by the nobility, irrespective of the degree of public access they granted. Just as hunting was an essential ingredient of the nobility's lifestyle in the country-

8. The prefix consists, in the case of males, of the abbreviation N. H. (for 'Nobil Huomo', or nobleman) followed by a special form of the letter 'S' (standing for 'Ser', or Sir). In the plural N. H. becomes N.N.H.H. The corresponding female form is N. D. (for 'Nobil Donna'). Most of the male nobles are identified further by a patronymic (introduced by 'fù de' – the 'fù' is used when the father is already dead). This is no mere courtesy: several given names were used preferentially by certain Venetian noble families (making it more difficult to distinguish individual members belonging to different generations), and many of the older families had splintered into different branches that operated quite independently, thus multiplying the possibility of confusion. Quoting a patronymic had the same usefulness as quoting a middle name today.

9. Vincenzo Coronelli, *Nomi, cognomi, età e blasoni ... de' veneti patrizi viventi e de' genitori loro defonti ... matrimonii e figli di essi nel libro d'oro registrati*, Venice, Tommasini, 1714, p. 252.

side, operagoing was seen as a necessary part of its social life in the cities. In his brilliant study of the world of the impresario in Italian opera of the eighteenth and nineteenth centuries John Rosselli has demonstrated the extent to which a theatre, especially one in which opera played, fulfilled the function of a clubhouse to which 'the leading families of the town were coming pretty regularly night after night and occupying their boxes'.[10] Yet for all its indispensability to the social fabric (Rosselli describes it as a substitute for a parliament and free press),[11] opera was rarely profitable and often ruinous. Whoever promoted it had to be prepared to underwrite its almost inevitable losses. In the words of an anonymous pamphleteer: 'these promoters are ordinarily upper-class persons, rich persons, who, banding together, consider it an honour to make a sacrifice for the entertainment of their fellow citizens. If they break even, it is most often on account of the games of chance for which they act as bankers and which are tolerated during those periods.'[12] Only the nobility had the ample funds and the overriding motive to take on this role. Whatever profits were made from a season accrued not so much to the owner of the theatre as to impresarios, concessionaires, boxholders and others operating at lower levels of the enterprise.

A noble proprietor of a theatre and the consortium of subscribers (described as *caratadori*, or shareholders) he gathered around him thus regarded themselves first and foremost as public benefactors, not entrepreneurs. In the early eighteenth century nearly all Venetian theatres were owned by individual families, coming under the control of whichever member was head of the family at the time. The largest, grandest and most socially distinguished was that of San Giovanni Gristostomo, owned by the Grimani family. (It should be mentioned at this point that Venetian theatres were customarily named after the parish in which they were located, after the family that owned them or after both simultaneously.) During the period under consideration it hosted only operas, never comedies. It opened almost every Carnival season (i.e. Carnival proper, running from 26 December to Shrove

---

10. John Rosselli, *The Opera Industry in Italy from Cimarosa to Verdi: The Role of the Impresario*, Cambridge, Cambridge University Press, 1984, p. 10.
11. Ibid., p. 4.
12. *Réflexions d'un patriote sur l'opéra françois, et sur l'opéra italien, qui présentent le parallèle du goût des deux nations dans les beaux arts* (Lausanne, 1754).

Tuesday, and its preceding Autumn season, beginning at the end of November and continuing up to 14 December).[13]

The same family also owned the small San Samuele theatre. In Autumn and Carnival this was generally employed for comedy.[14] From 1720 onwards, however, San Samuele was the theatre used most regularly for the short season coinciding with the city's annual Ascensiontide fair.[15]

Second largest and second most prestigious of Venice's theatres was that of San Cassiano, owned by the Tron family. This hosted operas for preference, but in many seasons, doubtless largely for economic reasons, comedy was substituted.[16]

The smallest of the principal theatres (I omit all mention of theatres whose involvement with opera was ephemeral or non-existent during this period) was that of San Moisè, which in 1700 was in the hands of the Zane family but in 1715 reverted to its original owners, the Giustinian family (San Barnaba branch). Like San Cassiano, San Moisè

13. During the period covered by Appendix B (1700–40) San Giovanni Grisostomo was closed only in 1714/15 (when, to replace it, the Grimani family opened its other large theatre, SS Giovanni e Paolo, which had otherwise lain unused since 1699 and reverted to that state immediately afterwards) and 1736/37. Until 1699, when the Council of Ten (the most powerful legislative body of the Venetian state) decreed the closure of all theatres during the Novena of Christmas, Autumn and Carnival effectively formed a unbroken 'long season', and even after then they are most appropriately treated as a single unit. Important for our purpose is that impresarios were appointed, and singers engaged, for Autumn and Carnival combined or (should no Autumn opera be planned) for Carnival alone, but never for Autumn separately. Since even without its Autumn preface Carnival straddled two years, it is clearest to refer to the season as the juncture of two years (e.g. '1714/15', as above) rather than to use the later year alone. Venetian theatres opened for stage plays (not only the semi-improvised *commedia dell'arte* but also fully scripted comedies) already in early October, but Autumn operas, for which audience size was more critical, had to wait until the Venetian nobility had returned from its second vacation of the year and the Great Council (*Maggior Consiglio*) reconvened.
14. Between 1700 and 1740 opera replaced comedy only in the following seasons: 1710/11, 1713/14, 1731/32, 1736/37 and 1738/39.
15. It missed a season only in 1721 (when no Ascension operas were given in Venice) and 1727.
16. The seasons given over to comedy were those of 1713/14–1716/17, 1718/19–1726/27, 1730/31–1733/34, 1735/36 and 1737/38–1739/40 (all dates inclusive).

oscillated between opera and comedy, but with a bias towards the second.[17]

The remaining theatre is the one that interests us, Sant'Angelo. Its ownership was different in nature from that of its sister theatres, and, as we shall see, this held important consequences for not only its management but also its artistic policy (if one may employ so modern an expression). This theatre, intermediate in size between San Moisè and San Cassiano, was erected in 1676 by the scenographer Francesco Santurini on land owned jointly by two noble families, Marcello and Capello. According to the surviving contract signed by the entrepreneur and by representatives of the two families, Santurini was to build the theatre and run it for his sole profit for seven years (1677–83), after which time it would revert to the two families, each of which owned an equal share in it.[18] The project proceeded entirely according to plan, except that Santurini requested, and was granted, an extension of two years, relinquishing the theatre finally in 1685. Because of the shared ownership of the theatre, it was clear from the start that it could not be managed by a single entrepreneurial owner in the manner of the Grimani, Tron and Giustinian theatres. This situation was only reinforced by the continuing fragmentation of ownership, as generation succeeded generation, through inheritance or by the acquisition of dowries.[19]

What happened was that the co-proprietors constituted themselves as a consortium of *caratadori* whose financial stake in each season was calculated in accordance with the proportion of the theatre (and in particular of its boxes, representing its most valuable asset) that each owned. The management of Sant'Angelo was entrusted, season by season, to an impresario, who was given an initial *dote* (endowment)

17. The Autumn–Carnival seasons devoted to opera were 1703/04, 1715/16–1717/18, 1719/20–1724/25, 1726/27–1731/32 and 1733/34. San Moisè did, however, host Ascension operas in 1720, 1726, 1728 and 1731 – as if to re-establish its operatic credentials after a Carnival season devoted to comedy.
18. Venice, Archivio di Stato, Sezione Notarile, Atti notaio Bianconi, Busta 1103, fols 97–99.
19. The Venetian system of inheritance, based on Roman law, did not privilege primogeniture, with the result that patrimonies tended to be dispersed with the passage of time. It was for this reason that the Venetian patriciate (misguidedly, from a demographic viewpoint) restricted marriage among its sons and packed a good proportion of its daughters into convents.

to meet some of his immediate costs and then left more or less to fend for himself. In the other theatres ownership and management were more closely intertwined. As Rosselli aptly observes: 'Where members of the upper classes controlled theatres there was a standing temptation for them to take part in the running of a season even if a professional impresario held the contract.'[20] From Vivaldi's correspondence of the late 1730s and from Goldoni's Memoirs, for example, we know how attentively Michele Grimani watched over the affairs of San Giovanni Grisostomo and San Samuele.[21] At Sant'Angelo, in contrast, none of the co-proprietors had the authority or, one suspects, the desire to adopt such a hands-on approach, except when their financial interests were threatened. For some of the younger nobles, the co-ownership of one theatre out of the several they patronised must have seemed a mere historical accident.

But who were these impresarios and what were their qualifications? The title of the second chapter of Rosselli's book, 'A Profession of Sorts', sums up the situation well, as does a contemporary description of them as 'speculators with little capital and no real estate'.[22] Those who took the plunge to become impresarios had invariably once been on the receiving end of dealings with members of that profession as singers, players, composers, librettists, choreographers, scenographers or some other kind of person necessary to the operatic enterprise. There was no formal apprenticeship or career path: experience was the only teacher, and track record the only prerequisite for continuing in the career. If we examine the names of impresarios provided in Appendix B, we discover those of two violinists (Antonio Madonis, Giovanni Battista Vivaldi), a composer (Antonio Vivaldi), a singer (Pietro Ramponi), a choreographer (Giovanni Galletto) and two librettists (Pietro Chechia and Bartolomeo Vitturi). In the case of Antonio Vivaldi, we can be certain, in the perspective of surviving correspondence and contemporary observations, that the urge towards an impresarial role (pursued concurrently with composing, violin-playing and musical direction) stemmed from a near-paranoid desire for total control allied to the dream of making a fortune. In other instances, especially concerning singers, the motivation may have been to escape from a career in decline while continuing to work

20. Rosselli (1984), p. 20.
21. See Michael Talbot, *Vivaldi*, London, Dent, 1993, 61–64.
22. Rosselli (1984), p. 6.

in the world of opera (one is reminded of the solo performers who today 'reinvent' themselves unexpectedly as conductors).

Impresarios were normally pleased to remain in the shadows, hoping (more often than not in vain) that their name would not become more widely known as a result of litigation. Most of the names of impresarios listed in Appendix B come from dedications to librettos that they signed. A printed libretto, which served the audience as a literary text that could be studied and appreciated in its own right as well as a souvenir programme, was produced under conditions that we could liken to 'vanity' publishing today. Whoever paid the printer's bill received all the copies, whose cost was recouped partly from sales at the door to operagoers, partly from a gratuity (*regalo*) received from the noble person to whom the libretto was dedicated. If a libretto was newly written, the author himself customarily dealt with the printer, penned the dedication and handled sales. When an old libretto was reprinted (usually with modifications), it might be left to the impresario to market it and concoct a dedication.[23]

Identifying the impresario is made harder by the practice, especially prevalent in Venice at that time, of joint management and subcontraction. In the manner of today's pyramid sellers, holders of posts delegated tasks or reassigned privileges wholesale. Such descriptions as *concessionario*, *procuratore*, *agente*, *appaltatore* and *fattore*, all of which are used to describe persons acting on behalf of others or holding franchises from them, occur extremely often in documents dealing with operatic affairs. It is therefore sometimes hard to ascertain whether a person executing a managerial role is a lone impresario, an impresario acting in association with others or only a subordinate.

What Pietro Denzio, to whom the co-proprietors entrusted Sant' Angelo in 1714, did before he became an impresario is unknown. He is certainly related in some way to two Venetian singers with the same surname, Antonio Denzio (born c.1690, last mentioned in 1763) and Elisabetta (Isabetta) Denzio (c.1695–1716), since their paths often cross.[24] One suspects that he, too, was trained as a singer, although he

---

23. There also exist a few cases where it appears that the printer himself took over the author's role. The sale price of a libretto ranged upwards from one *lira* ten *soldi* (see Appendix C for a description of the Venetian monetary system).
24. On the members of the Denzio family and their interactions see Daniel E. Freeman, *The Opera Theater of Count Franz Anton von Sporck*, Stuyvesant, NY, Pendragon Press, 1992, *passim*. See also my article on Antonio Denzio in *The New*

is not recorded as such in Claudio Sartori's compendious libretto dictionary.[25]

His first known appearance as an impresario was in Ferrara, at the theatre of Santo Stefano, in the summers of 1711, 1712 and 1713. There is no confirmation that he honoured his undertaking to manage Sant'Angelo in 1715/16, for in that very season we find him at the side of the seasoned impresario Giovanni Orsatto at San Moisè, where Antonio Denzio was making his debut as a tenor. In 1715/16 Antonio Vivaldi, who had managed (and directed the music of) Sant'Angelo in the two previous seasons, likewise moved over to San Moisè, although he returned to work – as a composer – for Sant'Angelo in 1716/17. Reinhard Strohm has astutely pointed out that the sudden conversion of San Moisè from comedy to opera in 1715/16 could be related to a shift in the opposite direction by San Cassiano in 1713/14 (coupled, perhaps, with uncertainty over the reopening of San Giovanni Grisostomo?).[26] At all events, there was a major shake-up in Venetian operatic life in 1715 that may have caused Pietro Denzio to think twice about taking over Sant'Angelo. Of course, one cannot rule out the possibility that he acted simultaneously as principal impresario at Sant'Angelo and assistant impresario at San Moisè. There is certainly nothing unusual in the operas programmed at Sant'Angelo in 1715/16 to suggest any crisis or change of plan.

Thereafter, we soon lose track of Pietro Denzio. He was back in Ferrara at Santo Stefano in the summer of 1718, and we last hear of him in Mantua and Verona at the end of 1726. Circumstantial evidence suggests that he co-operated again with Orsatto at San Moisè in 1719/20, where both Carnival operas, *La pace per amore* and *Il Filindo*, were ones revived by him in 1726. To have acted as an impresario over a period of at least sixteen years implies that he enjoyed at least some success, but the fact that he worked mostly in the provinces and was content repeatedly to serve up the same few works reveals him to have been only a small-time operator.[27]

      Grove Dictionary of Opera, ed. Stanley Sadie, London, Macmillan, 1992, Vol. 1, p. 1126.

25. Claudio Sartori, *I libretti italiani a stampa dalle origini al 1800*, Cuneo, Bertola & Locatelli, 1991, 7 vols.

26. Reinhard Strohm, *Essays on Handel and Italian Opera*, Cambridge, Cambridge University Press, 1985, p. 144.

27. His war-horse was *La fede tradita e vendicata* (poetry by Francesco Silvani, music by Francesco Gasparini), presented at Ferrara in 1711, Venice in 1715 and Bergamo in 1726.

Clause 1

The impresario's first obligation is to put on a minimum of two operas during Autumn and Carnival. As Appendix B shows, in the period 1700–14 it was most normal at Sant'Angelo for one opera to be given in Autumn and another in Carnival. In 1701/2 both operas were given, exceptionally, in Carnival, perhaps on account of a delay in the preparation of the first. In four seasons, however, a single Autumn opera was followed by two Carnival operas, and in two others both Autumn and Carnival held two operas.[28] The reason for the addition of extra operas was usually not, as one might innocently suppose, because the season was going well, but quite the reverse. In Venice, productions ran strictly consecutively:[29] the season began with one opera, which was repeated almost nightly until the planned run ended or it was thought appropriate to take it off and replace it by another. The unfavourable public reception of a scheduled opera would often cause an impresario to put another into rehearsal with the hope of rescuing the season by a substitution.[30] We have to recognise here a major difference in operagoing habits between the eighteenth century and our own age. Nowadays, we attend an opera as we do any other kind of musical performance, attempting to assimilate and appreciate it at one sitting. The opera house becomes, in effect, a concert hall. In the eighteenth century, however, an opera was treated more like a floor show at a night club. The expectation was that patrons would come to it several times in the season and assimilate it in stages (along-side such other activities as eating, gambling and gossiping). Indeed, patrons often visited more than one theatre in the same evening before ending up, as likely as not, at the *ridotto* (casino).[31] For an

28. The 1 + 2 pattern occurred in 1702/3, 1706/7, 1708/9 and 1712/13, the 2 + 2 pattern in 1709/10 and 1711/12.
29. This was a different pattern from that employed on the London stage, where performances of plays or operas commonly alternated.
30. Conversely, but much more rarely, an unexpectedly successful opera could hold the stage beyond its planned duration and hold up its successor. Giovanni Carlo Bonlini's register of Venetian operas *Le glorie della poesia e della musica con-tenute nell'esatta notitia de teatri della città di Venezia* (Venice, Buonarrigo, 1730) contains on p. 169 an annotation relating to the production of Giovanni Alberto Ristori's *Orlando furioso* at Sant'Angelo in Autumn 1713 that states that the opera was given over forty performances. It is likely in these circumstances that the run 'spilled over' into Carnival, as certainly happened at the same the-atre with Tomaso Albinoni's and Giovanni Porta's *La Mariane* in 1724/25.
31. A typical opera, into which comic intermezzos or ballets might be inserted as entr'actes, lasted between four and five hours.

opera to be successful, and for an impresario to sell an adequate number of entrance tickets, the public had to visit it repeatedly, not just once. This pattern of attendance (i.e. relatively few people making relatively frequent visits) is already implied by the practice of booking boxes for a whole season in advance.

In those seasons with more operas than the norm, one can often detect a crisis merely from the nature of the programmed works: the replacement opera may be a *pasticcio* (a patchwork opera assembled from old and new components) stitched together by the season's musical director or a work dredged up from old repertoire. Strangely, the variable length of the Carnival season (Shrove Tuesday can fall on any day between 3 February and 9 March) seems not to have been an important factor in determining the number of operas performed.

In 1714/15 Sant'Angelo enters a new phase in which two Carnival operas, not one, become the standard. The reason for this is unclear, but it parallels a change that had already occurred at San Cassiano and was soon to occur also at San Giovanni Grisostomo. Perhaps it merely reflects an increasing thirst for novelty on the public's part. Once again, there are occasional 'supernumerary' operas in either Autumn or Carnival. Particularly interesting are those occurring in seasons – 1714/15, 1726/27, 1733/34 and 1737/38 – when Antonio Vivaldi was acting (with others) as impresario. Here, one suspects that the additions were pre-planned and not necessarily a reaction to the failure of programmed operas. As a rare specimen of an impresario who was also a musical director able to compose new works (or arrange old ones) extremely quickly, Vivaldi may have been tempted to adopt a 'scatter-gun' policy – to come armed with a surplus of operas in the hope that at least one of them would win public favour.

The contract also requires of the operas that they be 'in good and creditable form'. Francesco Mancini and his fellow authors are right to protest, in *I teatri del Veneto*, against an entrenched tradition among historians of Venetian opera that sees this theatre as second-rank in its artistic pretensions, the cheap and cheerful counterpart to San Giovanni Grisostomo.[32] About the cheapness, admittedly, there can be no argument. Right from its inception under Santurini's management its ticket prices for operas were designed to undercut those of the other theatres (San Moisè sometimes excepted). In the period

32. Mancini (1996), Vol. 2, p. 219.

of the contract Sant'Angelo was still charging only one *lira* and eleven *soldi* (a quarter ducat) for nightly entry to the theatre, as compared with the three *lire* and six *soldi* at San Giovanni Grisostomo.[33] Other charges were correspondingly lower. Hire of a chair at the front of the pit cost (at 1721 prices) one *lira* and ten *soldi*, as compared with one *lira* and sixteen *soldi* at the other theatre;[34] the cheapest seasonal rent for a box (in the *pepian*, or ground-level tier) was 124 *lire* (twenty ducats), as compared with 310 *lire* (fifty ducats).[35]

33. Price levels at San Cassiano tended to be intermediate, those at San Moisè the same as at Sant'Angelo or slightly higher. At Sant'Angelo, and probably at all the other theatres, a block of tickets could be purchased in advance at a discount. From the household accounts of the patrician Girolamo Ascanio Giustinian (1697–1749) preserved in the Venetian State Archives (Ospedali e luoghi pii diversi, Registro 1004, opening 240) we learn that in 1727 Giustinian paid Vivaldi sixty-two *lire* for an unspecified number of tickets; in 1728 he paid the new impresario, Gerolemo Gentillini, the same sum to obtain '52 tickets for all the nights'.

34. These chairs were arranged in rows, ten to twelve deep, at the front and centre of the pit. They were favoured over boxes by that part of the audience (including some of the nobility) that took the performance seriously and wished to see and hear the performance clearly. Unfortunately, the occupants of the chairs were favourite targets for the occupants of the boxes (particularly those sitting in the higher tiers), who during a performance customarily rained down on them spittle, orange peel, apple cores and other missiles; those who tried to read the libretto by candlelight as the performance proceeded were singled out for special attention. At the sides and back of the pit the audience, formed by members of the lower classes, remained standing. Noisiest and cheekiest of all the plebeians were reckoned to be the gondoliers, whose clapping, hissing and shouting often drowned the music. See Joachim Christoph Nemeitz, *Nachlese besonderer Nachrichten von Italien*, Leipzig, Gleditsch, 1726, pp. 74–76, and Eberhard Preussner, *Die musikalischen Reisen des Herrn von Uffenbach*, Kassel and Basel, Bärenreiter, 1949), p. 65–68. Nemeitz, a court official from Saxony, visited Venice in 1721, Uffenbach, a jurist from Frankfurt am Main, in 1715. Nemeitz's travel guide is an especially valuable witness to Venetian operatic life because it provides precise comparative data, while Uffenbach's journal is of great interest to students of Vivaldi and of Sant'Angelo since its author visited that theatre twice and recorded his impressions vividly. Uffenbach notes that, learning from his experience in the pit at SS Giovanni e Paolo, he took care to occupy a box at Sant'Angelo – and (he confesses with some embarrassment) to retaliate for his earlier discomforts.

35. Boxes were cheaper to rent in Ascension, when the season was much shorter, or when comedy played instead of opera. At San Moisè in the 1720s and 1730s 155 *lire* were charged for seasons of opera but only 124 *lire* for comedy.

However, eye-witness accounts generally speak as highly of the quality of performance and production at Sant'Angelo as at any of the houses with which it competed. Even the scenery and costumes, for which a much smaller budget was available than at the larger theatres, sometimes came in for praise.

Despite the constant turnover of impresarios, it is possible to identify a Sant'Angelo 'brand identity' predicated on the theatre's small stage, limited financial resources and constant need to hold its own against its rivals in order to survive. In many ways this identity resembles that of a successful minor label in today's CD market. Sant'Angelo specialised in discovering, nurturing and retaining (for as long as its resources permitted) new talent and in inaugurating new trends. The composers of merit who were introduced to Venetian opera audiences via Sant'Angelo included, besides the obvious and well-known case of Vivaldi, Johann David Heinichen, Giovanni Alberto Ristori, Fortunato Chelleri, Baldassarre Galuppi and Giuseppe Antonio Paganelli, not to speak of successful 'relaunches' of composers who had fallen silent for some years (Giuseppe Boniventi and Giovanni Maria Ruggieri are the two salient instances). Other composers received – and apparently squandered – their early opportunities at Sant'Angelo (examples are Agostino Bonaventura Coletti and Giacomo Rampini). Among the librettists, the name of Grazio Braccioli (1682–1752) stands out. Braccioli was a doctor of civil and canon law, in which he lectured at the university of his native city, Ferrara. From 1711/12 to 1715/16 he was so dominant a presence at Sant'Angelo that he deserves almost to be called its 'house librettist'.[36] He specialised in reworking episodes taken from Renaissance epic poetry (Boiardo, Ariosto, Tasso), and his disregard for the Aristotelian unities and the concept of verisimilitude in his dramas opposes them to the dominant current represented by those of Apostolo Zeno. One might well term his typical creations 'magic operas': they are tailor-made for colourful orchestral and scenographic effects. Although he ceased to work for Sant'Angelo after 1716 (the remake of his Orlando furioso for Autumn 1727 was probably undertaken without his participation), Braccioli left a lasting imprint on its image and character. Among the scenographers we also find some significant names:

36. Bartolomeo Vitturi acted for Sant'Angelo in a similar capacity during the 1730s. He was an arranger of older librettos quite as much as an original librettist, and undoubtedly receives too little credit for this activity in Appendix B.

Bernardo Canale, later joined by his sons, one of whom was the famous painter Antonio Canale detto [nicknamed] Canaletto, in the 1710s; Antonio Mauro in the 1720s and 1730s.

It seems that at Sant'Angelo what one might term informal con-stellations of composers (including arrangers of the music of others), librettists (including arrangers of the dramas of others) and scenogra-phers – to whom we could surely add, had we more information, ballet masters, costumiers, stage technicians and other significant col-laborators in whom the music historian is less interested but who cer-tainly meant a great deal to contemporary audiences – maintained the traditions of the theatre almost independently of the impresarios, who came and went with great frequency. Like the theatre's owners, those impresarios who were not themselves practitioners of any of these arts (and many were) probably had no strong feelings about artistic policy, allowing what had worked well in the recent past to continue. They were doubtless easily persuadable by the 'old hands' who had served their predecessors.

The innovations pioneered at Sant'Angelo were several, but not all of them proved sustainable at that theatre. A case in point was the independent comic intermezzo (as distinct from comic scenes inserted into an otherwise serious opera), the first examples of which date from 1706. San Cassiano introduced a set of comic intermezzi in Car-nival 1706, followed by Sant'Angelo in the Autumn of the same year. But whereas San Cassiano persisted with the genre, Sant'Angelo seems for a while to have abandoned it, apparently preferring to retain the traditional ballets. In Autumn 1711 Sant'Angelo brought out another novelty: a comic opera entitled *Elisa* (libretto by Domenico Lalli, music by Giovanni Maria Ruggieri). Giovanni Carlo Bonlini noted approvingly in his opera register: 'This drama repre-sents a genuine musical comedy, the first in its genre that the Venetian stage ever witnessed.'[37] Once again, however, the innovation was not followed up.

Vivaldi's activity at Sant'Angelo in the mid-1710s brought in new ideas about the treatment of the orchestra. He had already embraced the idea of including a cadenza for a solo instrument (the violin, played by himself) at the end of an aria in his first opera, *Ottone in villa* (Vicenza, 1713).[38] This practice was evidently continued at Sant'

37. Bonlini (1730), p. 164.
38. This aria, 'Guarda in quest'occhi', is the penultimate one in the third act.

Angelo, since we find Uffenbach referring to it with a mixture of amazement and delight in his account of a performance of *Nerone fatto Cesare* (Carnival 1715). In general, Vivaldi fostered the use, albeit only in a small minority of arias, of obbligato instruments and special orchestral effects such as pizzicato and muting.

In the 1722/23 season we find at Sant'Angelo, for the first time in Venice, an opera by a member of the newer Neapolitan school of composers: Leonardo Leo.[39] Reinhard Strohm has commented that the importation of Leo was probably connected with the presence at the theatre of the librettist Domenico Lalli, who, as a Neapolitan by birth, could be expected to favour a countryman.[40] Be this as it may, Neapolitan opera, which in the following seasons conquered the other major Venetian theatres, failed to take root at Sant'Angelo for many years. Not until 1731/32 do we find another Neapolitan composer, Nicola Porpora, and the first use of a libretto by Pietro Metastasio, doyen of the librettists associated with the new wave. In fact, Sant'Angelo retrenched for many years, falling back on younger Venetian composers such as Galuppi and Pescetti or providing opportunities available nowhere else in Venice for local composers of a older generation (Albinoni, Vivaldi), who might, by the 1730s, have contemplated final relegation to the provincial circuit.[41]

This retrenchment probably had economic causes. Operas by a Leo, Vinci or Porpora on a Metastasio libretto were undoubtedly more expensive to mount because they required especially expert and appropriately trained singers – and the Neapolitan 'invasion' of the 1720s coincided with an explosion in the fees paid to the leading exponents of the new style, many of whom fell outside the price

39. The opera was *Timocrate*. According to Strohm, at least two arias by Leo were inserted into the score of the second Carnival opera, *I veri amici*, attributed in the libretto to Andrea Paulati (who may have been the musical director) but based on a setting by Albinoni performed in Munich in 1722.
40. Reinhard Strohm, *Dramma per musica: Italian Opera Seria of the Eighteenth Century*, New Haven and London, Yale University Press, 1997, p. 67.
41. Albinoni's two last operas, *Candalide* (Carnival 1734) and *Artamene* (Carnival 1741), received their first and only performances at Sant'Angelo (between those years even the provinces heard nothing by him). Vivaldi's *Feraspe* (Autumn 1739) was the last opera he composed. Unlike Albinoni, Vivaldi sometimes had the opportunity to prolong his life as a composer of operas by taking over the reins as impresario and/or musical director and giving commissions to himself, which he did at Sant'Angelo in 1733/34 and 1737/38.

bracket affordable by Sant'Angelo. Let us first hear Bonlini, digressing on this subject in the middle of his listing of the Carnival operas for 1720:

> Since operas have become a commercial business in Venice, more than anywhere else in Italy, to observe the number of major theatres presenting them reduced, in these present times, to only one, San Giovanni Grisostomo, would give one cause to believe that the customary profits are slow to arrive. And in truth expenditure has started to exceed income from the time when our coffers opened wide to secure the services of a single singer of some reputation. Once it was considered unusual to pay more than a hundred *scudi* for a reasonably good voice, and the first singer to be paid a hundred and twenty *scudi* was the object of marvel and passed into folk legend. But what comparison can there be with the present time, when it has become almost routine to pay the exorbitant fee of over a thousand sequins to someone who can claim to be better than his peers? This example has raised to an immoderate level the demands of every singer, and the result cannot but be that the interested parties [i.e. the theatres] suffer the dire consequences if they pay the asking price, as they all too often do.[42]

Bonlini did not exaggerate. In January 1726 the *Mercure de France* published (on pp. 96–97) an account of the fees paid to the leading singers for the 1724/25 seasons at San Giovanni Grisostomo, San Cassiano and Sant'Angelo. The figures are these:

San Giovanni Grisostomo

Faustina Bordoni	1,200 sequins	= 26,400 *lire*
Antonia Merighi	1,900 ducats	= 11,780 *lire*
Carlo Scalzi	2,000 ducats	= 12,400 *lire*

San Cassiano

Marianna Benti Bulgarelli	3,000 ducats	= 18,600 *lire*
Nicola Grimaldi	2,500 ducats	= 15,500 *lire*
Domenico Gizzi	1,500 ducats	= 9,300 *lire*

Sant'Angelo

Rosaura Mazzanti	1,500 philips	= 12,750 *lire*

---

42. Bonlini (1730), pp. 182–83. It is unclear whether Bonlini is referring to the year 1720 or to 1730, when his catalogue came out. There is in fact no year between 1710 and 1730 when San Cassiano, Sant'Angelo and San Moisè (all of which are surely 'major' in Bonlini's terms) were all closed over Carnival. In 1719, certainly, San Cassiano offered no opera, but Sant'Angelo (and San Fantino, an even smaller theatre) proceeded normally. See Appendix C for information on the value of the sequin and the *scudo*.

| Giovanni Paita | 1,200 philips | = 10,200 *lire* |
| Giovanni Carestini | 2,000 philips | = 17,000 *lire* |

And these were only the three highest-paid singers in a solo cast of six or more! It is obvious which theatre had the most, and which the least, money to spend. The hike in singers' fees during the 1720s was undoubtedly stimulated by the continuing 'globalisation', as one might call it, of Italian opera. London, favoured by England's greater prosperity, paid the most generously of all. There, Faustina could command a fee of £2,000, equivalent to about 80,000 *lire*.

Clause 2

Because the co-proprietors were also the owners of the boxes (a situation that was not the case, or not fully so, in theatres with a single owner), they had a massive stake in realising the expected income from each of them. It was not the impresario's task to let out the boxes (other than those that came to him by way of endowment), since the owners did this in their own right, but, were the season to be cancelled, each of them would be the poorer, to say nothing of the annoyance caused to their fellow nobles and their own loss of face. This is an appropriate moment to describe the layout of the boxes in 1714 in so far as this can be gleaned from various forms of evidence, most of it gathered by Mancini and his colleagues.

The boxes, five tiers high, were wrapped in an oval or, better, horseshoe shape around the pit. This was a classic Italian design shared, with no important deviations, by all the other Venetian theatres. The last two columns of boxes, at the tips of the horseshoe, were known as proscenium boxes since they flanked the front of the stage itself. The boxes at the two extremities (which, exceptionally, were only four tiers high and therefore totalled eight) were known as the 'new proscenium boxes', having been added in 1702 by Francesco Santurini, who had proposed them to the co-proprietors. In a deal resembling in miniature that for the construction of the theatre itself twenty-five years previously, Santurini was given the right, in return for constructing the boxes without charge, to keep the rental income from them for the first season.[43] It would appear from the list of boxes

---

43. Venetian State Archives, Sezione Notarile, Atti Valerio de Boni, Busta 450, atto 51, transcribed in Mancini (1996), Vol. 2, p. 40. In fact, the two ground-level boxes could not be let, since they were earmarked for the use of the singers, but the co-proprietors offered Santurini two other boxes in lieu. Mancini is mis-

made over to Denzio that in 1714 the new proscenium boxes bore no individual identification numbers or letters, although in a plan of the theatre's boxes dating from c.1792–94 the boxes in each column are designated 'X' and 'Z', respectively.[44] The two columns immediately inside those just described were known as the proscenium boxes (without the 'new'), and these were lettered. Next to these, but evidently just beyond the proscenium, was another column of lettered boxes. It is probable that neither of these lettered columns extended to a fifth tier; in the plan one sees enclosures labelled *forni* (literally, 'bakeries'– equivalent to what Covent Garden calls 'slips') above the three last boxes on each side.[45]

The main group of boxes is a loop of twenty-seven in each tier bearing numbers (in an ascending sequence from right to left as viewed from the stage). In the plan there are only two irregularities: the *pepian* box 14, centrally placed at the back of the auditorium, is replaced by an entrance to the pit, and the fifth tier (the *soffitta*, or upper circle, 'amphitheatre') runs not from 1 to 27 but from 1 to 26 following a box designated 'C', which was perhaps added at a point when the numbering of the boxes in this tier was too well established to alter.[46]

There were thus 158 boxes in all, as can be verified from the diagram presented as Table 1. Since all of those in the *soffitta* were by custom made over to the impresario, the theatre's owners were left with a maximum of 131 of which to dispose. In practice, of course, some would be conceded in whole or part to the impresario as part of his endowment, while a few others, as the contract specifies, would be given free of charge to named persons. The owners themselves kept a

taken, I believe, in identifying Santurini on p. 5 as the impresario for the 1702/3 season, for this was Giovanni Orsatto; Santurini's proposal was doubtless connected with his normal activity as a scenographer and theatre architect.

44. The plan in reproduced in Mancini (1996), Vol. 2, p. 18. It appears, from all the other evidence, to correspond remarkably closely to the layout of the boxes in 1714.

45. The term is still current in Italian.

46. Mancini (1996) accepts as a general rule that boxes identified by letter instead of number were ones owned personally (rather than rented) by their occupants. Whatever the general truth of this, it cannot apply to Sant'Angelo, where, so far as one knows, there were no independent boxholders. Besides, it would be very odd if such boxholders were able to acquire boxes only at the outer fringes of the seating.

Table 1: Plan of the boxes at Sant' Angelo, c.1792–94 (as viewed from the stage)

soffitta	forni	box numbers	'slips'	circle
soffitta	forni	26 25 24 23 22 21 20 19 18 17 16 15 14 13 12 11 10 9 8 7 6 5 4 3 2 1 C		
3° ordine	Z D B	27 26 25 24 23 22 21 20 19 18 17 16 15 14 13 12 11 10 9 8 7 6 5 4 3 2 1	A C X	tier 4
2° ordine	Z D A	27 26 25 24 23 22 21 20 19 18 17 16 15 14 13 12 11 10 9 8 7 6 5 4 3 2 1	O C X	tier 3
1° ordine	Z D B	27 26 25 24 23 22 21 20 19 18 17 16 15 14 13 12 11 10 9 8 7 6 5 4 3 2 1	A C X	tier 2
pepian	Z H G	27 26 25 24 23 22 21 20 19 18 17 16 15 13 12 11 10 9 8 7 6 5 4 3 2 1	F C X	tier 1

Notes

The *palchi proscenici nuovi* (new proscenium boxes) are the outside columns (Z and X).

The *palchi proscenici* (prosccenium boxes) are the columns one place from the outside (D, H, C).

The entrance to the pit lies between boxes 15 and 13 at ground level (tier 1).

few boxes for their private use. The standard rental of a box for a combined Autumn and Carnival season was twenty ducats for a box in the *pepian* tier or in the fourth tier (known as the third 'order', since the former was not numbered), twenty-five ducats for a box in the second or third tier (first or second 'order'). The price differential, mirrored in all the other Venetian theatres, reflected a perception that the cheaper tiers were less favourably located. A description of Venetian theatres by the French visitor Chassebras de Cramailles published in the *Mercure galant* of March 1683 explained that the *pepian* boxes were less popular since they were closer to the pit and because the necks of the theorbos in the orchestra (which project upwards even further than the necks of double basses) obstructed vision.[47]

On the most conservative estimate, there were over 2,000 ducats to be made collectively by the owners of Sant'Angelo from letting out their boxes each season. This is hardly more than the *primo uomo*, Carlo Scalzi, earned at San Giovanni Grisostomo in 1724/25, but represents nevertheless a tidy sum. One therefore understands the owners' insistence on being indemnified by the impresario if the season collapses. Naturally, they make an exception in the case of *force majeure*, such as the compulsory closure of the theatre by the authorities in response to plague or civil commotion, or fire damage.[48]

The Venetian state, too, had a strong interest in ensuring the completion of an operatic season, once contracted. This was a matter not only of civic – indeed, national – pride but also of satisfying the tourist trade. (The term is not anachronistic, since Venice already depended economically on the influx of visitors from other Italian states and the whole of northern Europe, which 'peaked' at the times of year when the theatres were open.) If the Council of Ten got word from a complainant that a theatre was in financial trouble and threatened to close prematurely, it had the power to remove the impresario and appoint its own administrator, who took over the box-office and attempted to satisfy all creditors, *pro rata* if not in full, by the end of the season. We know of three occasions during the period 1700–40 when this

---

47. *Le Mercure galant*, March 1683, pp. 230–309, transcribed in Eleanor Selfridge-Field, *Pallade veneta: Writings on Music in Venetian Society, 1650–1750*, pp. 346–52, at p. 347.

48. Venice did not, however, close its theatres for a whole season as an act of public mourning (say, for the death of a doge), thus avoiding what, in many cities, was the greatest hazard.

occurred at Sant'Angelo. In 1712 the impresario Cristoforo Frigieri had to make way for an administrator only about a week before the season ended.[49] In 1712/13 Giovanni Orsatto fell out with his associate Gabriel Faggia, and both were replaced by an administrator, Bortolo Pugnai.[50] This was the season when Heinichen, the young German composer, made his Venetian debut as an operatic composer at Sant'Angelo, and it is interesting to compare the evidence of Venetian documents (which deal only with the financial aspects) with the account of the episode given in Heinichen's autobiography as relayed several decades later by Johann Adam Hiller.[51] This account centres on the decision of the unnamed impresario to take off one of the German's operas after only two performances, withholding the fee for it, and to replace it by one of a native composer – a move thwarted by the unexpected public outcry. For all the embroidered, anecdotal quality of its telling, Hiller's story is doubtless true in substance, but it remains to be established whether personal rivalries were the cause or the effect of the financial crisis.

In the 1716/17 season the debacle was even greater. As a result of a dispute with his impresario, the composer of the first Carnival opera, Fortunato Chelleri, who was to direct performances from the harpsichord, walked out of the theatre on 28 December (possibly the opening night) with his score just as the performance was about to begin. That the dispute concerned overdue payment is made clear from the prose introduction to a 48-stanza satire commemorating the episode.[52] *Penelope la casta* was rescued a few days later by the Council of Ten, which compelled Chelleri to release the score (without which the performances could not proceed) but imposed an administrator. Feelings ran so high that there was an attempt on Chelleri's life. On 8 January Alexander Cunningham, British Resident in Venice, reported in separate letters to the British government officials Robert Pringle and Sir Paul Methuen that the composer had received two or three serious stab wounds, delivered by two would-be assassins, as he was delivering the singer Anna Maria Fabri (*seconda donna* in

49. Mancini (1996), Vol. 2, p. 37.
50. Ibid., pp. 37–38.
51. Johann Adam Hiller, *Lebensbeschreibungen berühmter Musikgelehrten und Tonkünstler neuerer Zeit*, Leipzig, Dykische Buchhandlung, 1784, pp. 128–46, at pp. 132–36.
52. Venice, Museo Civico Correr, Ms. Cicogna 1178. In Vio (1989) the satire is transcribed complete on pp. 103–8, the introduction on pp. 118–19.

Penelope) to her gondola. Cunningham surmised that the attack was in retaliation for the failure of the opera, which (in his words to Methuen) 'was damned the second and third night'.[53] Chelleri recovered well enough to try his luck again at Sant'Angelo two seasons later, having evidently made his peace with the theatre in the meantime.

Doubtless, the three seasons when we know that an administrator had to step in at Sant'Angelo form only the tip of an iceberg. Opera was a precarious business.

Clause 3

It has already been remarked that subcontraction and partnership were a Venetian way of life. This clause does not forbid the practice: it merely requires the impresario to seek the prior agreement of the co-proprietors. By mentioning the possibility, in fact, it anticipates it.

Clause 4

That the impresario, on expiry of his lease, should leave the theatre as he found it stands to reason. The direct beneficiary would be not the owners of the theatre but the next impresario. This clause mentions the house attached to the theatre. Sant'Angelo, which abutted the Grand Canal, was accessed by land from a small square then called Corte dell'Albero ('Tree Court': today known as Ramo e Campiello del Teatro), and in this same square, adjoining the theatre, stood a house that was placed at the impresario's disposal.[54] It was used primarily to accommodate visiting singers, hold rehearsals and store equipment. The possession of such a house was normal for all theatres – by a strangely apt act of fate, Vivaldi ended his days in a similar house in distant Vienna.

Clause 5

This clause, which is the first to address the interests of the impresario rather than those of the owners, gives explicit force to a situation that

53. London, Public Record Office, SP 99/61, fols 285v–286r (Cunningham) and fol. 298r (Methuen).
54. If one visualises the Grand Canal as a reversed letter S, Sant'Angelo (no longer standing) stood on the right-hand side as one follows the line downwards, a short distance before the start of the lower bend (the *volta*, in Venetian parlance).

has already been described as peculiar to Sant'Angelo: the guarantee of non-interference by the latter in artistic and practical matters. This meant, for example, that none of the nobles could compel the impresario to engage a singer of whom he was the patron or to accept a libretto that he had himself written. The impresario's success is to be measured, in the final analysis, by the 'bottom line' alone.

Clause 6

The sale of entrance tickets, which had to be bought by all patrons of the theatre, regardless of whether they stood, sat in the pit or sat in a box, was the impresario's main source of revenue. Extra income from the hire of chairs and the provision of refreshments (both at stalls and by ambulant vendors) was not inconsiderable – one might draw a parallel with the sale of ice cream and popcorn in modern cinemas – but these activities were normally franchised by the impresario to others.

Clause 7

The value to the impresario of the boxes in the *soffitta* is hard to gauge, since we do not know how much was charged for their rental (quite possibly, they were hired out only on a nightly basis). The central box, which is termed a *palco pergolo* ('balcony box') on account of its projection into the auditorium, is reserved free of charge for the solicitor Agostin Rosa, the general manager of the theatre. Rosa's central location is well in keeping with his central role, since he was the point of contact, in disputes and otherwise, between the impresario and the co-proprietors.

Clause 8

This clause identifies two ground-level boxes that are reserved for particular people without charge. One is no. 7, which is customarily occupied by the *protettore*. The identity and function of the person so described is rather mysterious. The term is most commonly used with the sense of 'benefactor' or 'patron'. Star singers, for example, had *protettori*. Mancini and his fellow authors, while admitting to a difficulty with the interpretation of the word, are inclined to equate it with an anonymous patron of the theatre itself, a kind of perpetual guarantor.[55] However, such an important person would hardly be

---

55. See, for example, Mancini (1996), Vol. 2, p. 41 n.45.

accommodated in the *pepian* tier. Moreover, the implication, through the use of the word 'solito', that this *protettore* occupied his box only by custom, not (like Rosa) by right, suggests to me that he is a person of interest to the impresario rather than to the co-proprietors. Perhaps he was the 'sugar daddy' of the *prima donna*.[56] The destination of the other box is unambiguous: the cast. Not by chance is their box positioned next to the stage, enabling them to slip in and out of it inconspicuously.

Clause 9

Despite the value set on originality and surprise in stage design, the stereotypical situations demanded by *opera seria* allowed a huge amount of recycling. A theatre therefore built up a stock of basic sets corresponding to the most frequently encountered stage directions. For example, part of the scenery used for the temple to Pluto in Vivaldi's *Orlando finto pazzo* (Autumn 1714) might well have seen life again in the temple to Vulcan in the same composer's *Arsilda, regina di Ponto* (Autumn 1716), and the 'remote place' of the first might easily have become the 'solitary retreat' of the second with little alteration. Because of the value of this operatic stock-in-trade, the theatre's owners need to make sure that the impresario does not damage it or walk off with it at the end of the season, hence the inventories and final verification.

Clause 10

This merely confirms the impresario's tenancy of the house next to the theatre and his requirement to keep it in good order.

Clause 11

This long clause explains the form taken by the endowment to the impresario. Rather cunningly, the co-proprietors provide it not in cash (as sometimes happened at other theatres) but in kind. No money is provided 'up front', and the impresario has the onus of realising, through letting, the value implicit in the boxes and part-boxes that constitute this endowment. In principle, boxes were to be paid for in advance, so that most of the endowment could be used by the

---

56. It is interesting that Santurini's contract of 1702 with the theatre's owners (see note 11, above) allows two boxes for the use of the singers. Perhaps one is equivalent to the box of the *protettore* in the 1714 contract.

impresario as start-up capital. In practice this was easier said than done, since the nobles who rented the boxes (usually the same box year after year) were apt to be tardy in making payment. This is very evident from the household accounts of Girolamo Ascanio Giustinian, who rented boxes every year at all the major theatres. These accounts reveal a jumble of boxes duly paid for in advance and others paid for in arrears, sometimes long after the season had closed. At Sant'Angelo the situation may have been especially difficult, since the impresario, not a noble himself, could put less pressure on a noble box-tenant than one of the latter's confrères could. The contract anticipates this difficulty, promising Denzio the full support of the co-proprietors and the practical assistance of Rosa in extracting payment. Luckily, not only the impresario's income but also his outgoings were staggered; singers (whose fees constituted about half of his total expenditure) were customarily paid in several instalments as specified in their contracts.[57]

The manner in which the 640 ducats making up the endowment (or rather, their value as expressed in boxes) are distributed among the co-proprietors is interesting (it emerges from the list that follows). The fraction of this sum that each of the eight nobles has to contribute, proportionate to his or her share of ownership, is first worked out. It can be seen from the list that the fifty–fifty division between the original Marcello and Capello families still survives, since the first five nobles (two Capellos, a Bollani, a Zen and a Memo) provide exactly 320 ducats, while the remaining three (two Marcellos and a Marcello Renier) muster the same amount. Otherwise, the fractions are extremely complex and testify to complex transfers of ownership in the years since 1676. Only the portion donated by Ferigo Vettor Marcello Renier – 26 ducats and 16 *grossi*, which is exactly a twenty-fourth part – has a transparent relationship to the total, although one can assume that all the fractions were calculated with meticulous accuracy.

On the assumption of a standard rental for each box (20 ducats for boxes in the pepian and fourth tiers, 24 for those in the second and third tiers), each owner represents his contribution as accurately as possible in terms of whole boxes or fractions (half, a third, a quarter,

---

57. The contract of Vivaldi with the singer Lucrezia Baldini to sing in the second Carnival opera at Sant'Angelo in 1727 is well known. Her fairly modest fee of 200 ducats was to be paid in three instalments: the first on the opening night; the second mid-way through the run; and the third on *giovedì grasso*, the last Thursday before Lent.

even a sixth) thereof. Where small discrepancies remain, either the impresario or the owner, as appropriate, has to settle up in cash at the end of the season.

The fractions into which boxes are divided give us a clue to the number of seats that each contained. Their division into thirds and even into sixths makes it virtually certain that six was the normal number of seats. A division into quarters occurs only once, in connection with box no. 27 in the second tier (i.e. the first *ordine*), rented by Francesco Morosini. Presumably, this box, which was close to the proscenium, where one would not be surprised to find space more limited than elsewhere, had only four seats.[58]

The owners give Denzio a free hand in his exploitation of the boxes. He can let them for the full season or on a nightly basis; he can let them as wholes or break them up into fractions. After all: it is his own money he is playing with, and they trust him to act efficaciously in pursuit of his interests.

Clause 12

If no action were taken, the co-proprietors and their dependants would have to purchase entrance tickets to access their own boxes. This clause promises them unrestricted free access to the inside of the theatre without the need even to acquire special passes (the 'bolettini rossi' to which the original text refers), which a former impresario had presumed to issue. Besides the owners, Agostin Rosa and the advocate Zuanne Alberti enjoy this privilege. The impresario is not permitted, however, to admit any other persons without a ticket.

Clause 13

This clause makes the contract binding not only on its signatories but also on their heirs. It mentions the preparation of duplicate copies for each of the parties.

Conclusion

The details of the persons renting the boxes to be made over to Denzio furnish plenty of interesting material for historians of the

---

58. The statistics given in Mancini (1996) for the total capacity of the boxes in each theatre (including Sant'Angelo) appear to assume that each held only four persons. This may need revision.

Venetian patriciate. They should banish the idea that Sant'Angelo was, socially speaking, of second rank in comparison with any Venetian theatre besides San Giovanni Grisostomo. Among the tenants are three procurators of San Marco (the highest dignity after that of doge): Nicolò Sagredo, Girolamo Ascanio Giustinian (his first given name transmuted into its Venetian form, Gerolemo) and Gerolemo Canal. Present, too, is the Electress of Bavaria, Kunigunde von Wittelsbach, who settled permanently in her beloved Venice after the death in 1726 of her husband, Max II Emanuel. The essential point is that the Venetian nobility patronised *en masse* all their local theatres as a matter of course: they knew that none held a monopoly on good productions, and they did not want to miss any enjoyable experience, in whatever house it occurred. For this reason, it would be fruitless to try to identify a distinctive Sant'Angelo audience. Because of two important protection mechanisms – the willingness of patrician owners to subsidise opera generously and the readiness of the state to intervene in situations of crisis – no rental of a box or advance purchase of entrance tickets was likely to result in total disappointment. As Bonlini sagely commented, opera was indeed a business at which Venice excelled. Venice's military defences were fragile; its merchant shipping was being driven out of the Mediterranean by British and French fleets; its manufactures were outmoded and uncompetitive in relation to those of northern countries; but its tourist industry, with opera as its central attraction, prospered and even boomed in the eighteenth century. The primacy of the service sector is certainly no recent invention.

Viewing Sant'Angelo in a wider historical context, it is interesting to find evidence for practices that we commonly think of as modern: the spreading of risk among several parties; the outsourcing of ancillary services; state intervention to rescue a tottering enterprise of national importance; a continuity of artistic policy despite frequent changes of management; a system of staggering payments in order to balance the inflows and outflows of cash; a flexible method of charging that caters for both regular attenders and casual visitors; an escalation of artists' fees beyond the economically rational; a concern for forward planning (terms were agreed while the preceding season was in progress). We even find on occasion what looks like 'thematic' programming – 'Armida' operas in 1707/08 and 'Orlando' operas in 1714. Certain other features may appear archaic but are in fact quite modern if we choose the most appropriate comparators for them.

Take, for example, the strange marginalisation (in terms of public awareness) of the contribution made by composers, whose names sometimes do not appear even in the librettos. Such casualness would be inadmissible in a modern opera house but not in a night club, to which, in this context and a few others, the eighteenth-century venue better corresponds.

In a curious way, the Sant'Angelo of 1714 is more, not less, 'businesslike' than its present-day counterpart. Its mission is entertainment (perhaps with a little moralising thrown in), not high culture. The Great and the Good hold the ultimate purse strings but do not impose any conditions on the enterprise except that it be respectful of church, state and the established order – and, if possible, solvent. Librettists, composers, scenographers and performers interweave their talents in ways that rely on the tried and tested, leaving little room for experimentation. Each party to the collaborative effort works for a success that is immediate, repeatable and lucrative: masterworks for posterity are on no one's agenda. It is my belief that historians of opera before the nineteenth century have a lot to learn from students of today's popular public culture, notably from the way in which forms of commerce and art can, in the right circumstances, be made to interact in fruitful and entirely non-antagonistic ways.[59]

59. I would like to make acknowledgement here to Carlo Vitali, who read and made very helpful comments on an earlier draft of this chapter.

Appendix A

Transcription of the contract (Archivio di Stato di Venezia, Inquisitori di Stato, Busta 914, *Case di gioco e teatri*, fascicolo 'S. Angelo')

[f. 1r] L[aus] D[eo] Adi 11 Decembre 1714 Venezia

Ridottosi li Nob[ili] Ho[mini] Consorti Comp[ad]roni del Teatro di S. Angelo che sono li Nob[ili] Ho[mini] S[er] Zuane, e nipoti Capello, il N[obil] H[omo] S[er] Polo Capello fù de S[er] Alvise, la N[obil] D[onna] Marietta Bolani Con[sort]e del N[obil] H[omo] S[er] Fran[ces]co Boldù, il N[obil] H[omo] S[er] Pietro Zen fù de S[er] Vicenzo, li N[obili] H[omini] S[er] Anzolo, e fr[ate]lli Memo fù de S[er] Anzolo, il N[obil] H[omo] Giacomo Antonio Vettor Marcello fù de S[er] Alvise, il N[obil] H[omo] Gerolemo Vettor Marcello fù de S[er] Fran[ces]co, et il N[obil] H[omo] Ferigo Vettor Marcello Renier fù de S[er] Alvise, cadauno di essi p[er] le proprie porzioni, attioni, ragioni, e rapp[resen]tanze, che in d[ett]o Teatro tengono, et delli radunatisi, li sottosc[rit]ti che compongono la mag[gio]r parte, Havendo stabilita la Condotta, et affitanza del Teatro sud[dett]o nel modo infras[crit]to

Perciò con la p[rese]nte privata sc[rittu]ra, che valer debba, come se fatta fosse p[er] atti di Pub[lic]o Nod[ar]o di q[ue]sta Città n[o]st[r]a da' med[e]mi dato et in affitto concesso, come dan[n]o, et in affitto concedono per an[n]o uno prossimo venturo che principierà il primo giorno della Quadragesima prossima ventura 1715, e terminerà l'ultimo giorno di Carnevale dell'an[n]o 1716 il Teatro sud[dett]o di loro ragione al Signor *Pietro Denzio*, che in affitto, e condotta lo riceve, et accetta con li patti, modi, forme, e conditioni, et obligationi infra dichiarite cioè

P[ri]mo Che d[ett]o Conduttor habbi, come così promette, et s'obliga verso essi N[obili] H[omini] Comp[ad]roni a far seguir in esso Teatro le Recite di due, o più Opere in Musica nell'Auttuno, et Carnevale susseguente di d[ett]o an[n]o in buona, e laudabil forma p[er] tutto il tempo, che durerà la p[rese]nte Condotta, et affittanza.

2°   Che se p[er] sua colpa andassero in difetto le recite, et p[er] ciò venisse dalli affittuali de Palchi ricusata la solita an[n]ual corrisponsione delli affitti e se non consequissero essi N[obili] H[omini] Comp[ad]roni le utilità de loro Palchi inaffittati, resti, e sia obligato esso Conduttore al rissarcim[en]to, et satisfazione intiera degl'affitti tutti, e dan[n]i, che p[er] tal causa essi N[obili] H[omini] rissentissero, così per patto espresso, senza di che non sarebbero condescesi alla p[resen]te Locatione; Con dichiaraz[ion]e però, ch'in caso di vietto Pub[li]co g[e]n[era]le, che proibiscesse le Recite dell'opere, ò d'altro accidente fortuito d'incendio, ò Peste (ch'il Sig[no]r Iddio tenga [f.1v] lontano), p[er] il che restasse impedito a d[ett]o Conduttor il poter far seguire le recite in d[ett]o Teatro, in tali casi non abbi à soccomber à tal rissarcimento, e dan[n]o.

3°   Che non possa sotto qual si sia pretesto sublocar ad altri il Teatro stesso senza il previo assenso, e permissione in scritto de detti N[obili] H[omini] Comp[ad]roni.

4°   Che sia tenuto, terminato il Carneval, ogni volta sarà ricercato[,] rilasciar liberam[ent]e a' med[e]mi, et à loro disposiz[ion]e il Teatro s[tesso] et uso d[e]lla Casa in conzo, e colmo, e nel stato, che le resta consegnato. Senza che abbi a precedere alcuna notizia, o Cognito, caso che non si concordasse di provogar la p[rese]nte, derogandosi, et espressam[en]te renonciandosi in ciò ad ogni legge, ò uso, che vi fosse in contrario, così fermam[en]te stabilitosi.

5°   Che à d[ett]o Conduttor resti l'intiera, e total assoluta libertà, disposiz[ion]e, e direzione independente in tutti gl'interessi, et affari d[e]l Teatro, Opere, e recite, con che d[ett]i N[obili] H[omini] Comp[ad]roni non abbino, ne possano ingerirsi, come cosi promettono in cosa alcuna im[m]aginabile à ciò attinente, ò dipendente, niuna eccettuata.

6°   Che d[ett]i N[obili] H[omini] Comp[ad]roni concedono a d[etto] Conduttore il Jus, Patronia, et utilità proveniente dalla dispensa de Boletini, e Porta, et d'affittar Bettola, Scaletter, Scagni, et altro in d[ett]o Teatro, cosi che tutto sia, e resti di prop[ri]o conto, et rag[ion]e di esso Cond[utto]re p[er] il sud[ett]o tempo di an[n]o uno.

7°   Li concedono, et assegnano ad esso Cond[utto]re la soffita del Teatro med[esim]o con li palchi in q[ue]lla esistenti a disposiz[ion]e, et utilità d'esso Cond[uttor]e p[er] il sud[ett]o tempo d'an[n]o uno, eccettuato il Palco Pergolo di mezo goduto del Sig[no]r Agostin Rosa, Agente, et Interv[enien]te del Teatro, quale resta à sua disposiz[ion]e senz'obligo di veruna contribuzione.

8°   Le assegnano pure il Palco No. 7 à pepian, sive il godim[en]to di q[ue]llo solito servir p[er] il Protettore, e cosi il Palco Proscenio novo, che è dalla parte del Buso de Bolettini, solito servir à com[m]odo de Musici, senza haver quello à contribuir cosa veruna.

9°   Resterà consegnato à d[ett]o Cond[utto]r nella Quadragesima pross[im]a ventura le scene tutte, materiali, et altro inservienti all'opere, che vi saran[n]o nel Teatro stesso, dà esser descritte nell'Inventario giusto l'ordinario, quali d[ett]o Conduttore dovrà mantenir e conser[f. 4r]var, e restituir, et reconsegnar assieme con tutti gl'altri Materiali, Scene, et altro, ch'esso facesse di vantaggio, solito praticarsi, ad uso d[e]lla Scena, lasciando il tutto in benefizio, e dote del Teatro sud[ett]o, e dominio d'essi N[obili] H[omini] Comp[ad]roni, senza pretender

p[er] quelli cos'alcuna, quali consegne, e reconsegne doveran[n]o farsi
con gl'incontri necessarij, et Inventarij, subito terminate le recite, ad
ogni richiesta d'essi N[obili] H[omini] Comp[ad]roni, e quando sarà
ricercato dall'Agente del Teatro senza verun'ostacolo, o dilazione.

X°   Che p[er] tutto il d[ett]o tempo le resti il com[m]odo, et uso p[er] far
le prove, e ponervi ad abitar, occorendogli, Musici che veniran[n]o à
recitar in d[ett]o Teatro, della Casa an[n]essa al Teatro med[esim]o di
loro rag[ion]e, quale le resta pure consegnata per restituirla, e recon-
segnarla in conzo [e] in colmo, come s'attrova.

XI°   Che li sud[ett]i N[obili] H[omini] Comp[ad]roni cadauno d'essi p[er]
le loro porzioni, e Caratti, che tengono in d[ett]o Teatro cedino, et con-
segnino, come con la p[rese]nte effetivam[en]te cedono, consegnano,
assegnano, et rinonciano à d[ett]o Sig[no]r Cond[utto]re, come sopra
à titolo di regalo ducati seicento, e quaranta cor[ren]ti dà £6 4s p[er]
d[et]to an[n]o, in tanti affitti de Palchi, et palchi in[n]affittati, che
saran[n]o qui sotto registrati, delle porzioni, et rag[io]ni di cadauno
d'essi, cedendogli, et rinonciandogli cad[aun]o d'essi p[er] la prop[ri]a,
et contingente sua porzione à com[m]odo, et incom[m]odo però d'esso
Conduttore quanto sia all'esigibilità, mantendolo nella realtà ponen-
dolo ne medemi in ogni loro loco, stato[,] ragion, et essere constituen-
dolo in quello loro Proc[urato]re irrevocabile, come in cosa propria,
libera, et espedita, dandole percio piena, et ampla [sic] facoltà, et aut-
torità di quelli ceder, renonciar, et assegnar, et à suo piacere riscuoter
dagl'affituali di quelli affitati l'annual affitto, e di quelli non affittati,
affittarli, et farli affittare, p[er] il sud[ett]o tempo di an[n]o uno d[e]lla
p[rese]nte Condotta, et anco di sera in sera, co[f. 4v]me più le piacerà
p[er] conseguirne gl'affitti, e utilità de med[e]mi, e del scosso, essatto,
et cesso farne le debite ricevute[,] cauzioni, e quietanze, et in caso di
renitenza degl'affituali nel pagam[en]to astringerli, et farli astringer,
praticando l'esecuzioni, et atti occorressero p[er] via di Giust[izi]a anco
con il nome de med[e]mi N[obili] H[omini] Comp[ad]roni a spese però
d'esso Conduttore con l'assistenza degl'atti giudiziarij del Sig[no]r
Agostin Rosa Interv[enien]te d[el] Teatro stesso.

XII°   Che ad essi N[obili] H[omini] Comp[ad]roni, et loro Gentildon[n]e, e
Gentiluomeni et altri de loro Casa, et cosi all'Ecc. D. Zuan[n]e Alberti
Av[voca]to, et Agostin Rosa Interv[enien]te del Teatro stesso, et suoi di
propria Casa resti libera, et franca la porta, et introito p[er] andar all'
Opera, quando sarà in loro piacere, senza Bolettini, ne aggravio
alcuno, senz'obligo al Conduttore di consegnarli à verun di essi Bolettini rossi, come facessero altri Conduttori antecedentj, vietato restando
qualunque ordine, ò Viglietto p[er] altri.

XIIJ° Che all'osservanza, e mantenzione, et essecuzione inalterabile di tutto
ciò, che nella p[rese]nte si contiene obligano tutti N[obili] H[omini]

Comp[ad]roni, cadauno d'essi però p[er] il proprio interesse, e contingenti porzioni respettivam[en]te p[er] se, et heredi tutti, e cadauni loro beni presenti, et futuri, et cosi s'obliga esso Sig[no]r Conduttore p[er] se heredi, et confini suoi p[resen]ti nella piu valida, solen[n]e, e general forma; Et della presente ne saran[n]o due simili sottosc[rit]te p[er] restarne una p[er] parte.

Seguono li affitti

[f. 2r] Seguono li affitti de Palchi, et Palchi in[n]affittati come sopra cessigli

Per la porzione delli N[obili] H[omini] S[er] Zuan[n]e, e Nepoti Capello	d101	g7
Dal N[obil] H[omo] S[er] Antonio Molin fù de S[er] ... per il Palco No. 6 in 2° ordine in 2° ordine	d25	g–
Dal N[obil] H[omo] S[er] Zuan[n]e Bernardo p[er] mezo il palco No. 7 in 2. ordine	d12	g12
Dal Sig. Co. Fran[ces]co Cusina p[er] il palco No. 11 in 2° ordine	d25	g–
Dal N[obil] H[omo] Silvestro Valier p[er] mezo il palco No. 18 in 3° ord[in]e	d10	g–
Mezo il Palco No. 3 in 3° ordine inaffittato	d10	g–
Tutto il Palco No. 7 in 3° ordine inaffittato	d20	g–
	d102	g12
Dà restituirgli dal Cond[utto]r fatti le riscossi[o]ni	d1	g5
P.C.	d101	g7
Per la porzione del N[obil] H[omo] Polo Capello fù de S[er] Alvise	d101	g7
Dal N[obil] H[omo] Pietro Benzon p[er] il palco pepian seg[na]to F	d20	g–
Dal N[obil] H[omo] Vettor Grimani p[er] il palco No. 27 à pepian	d20	g–
Dalli N[obili] H[omini] Ferigo, e Fra[te]lli Barbarigo p[er] mezo il palco No. 10 in 2° ordine	d12	g12
Dal N[obil] H[omo] S[er] Z[uanne] Bat[tis]ta Grimani fu de S[er] Zuan[n]e p[er] il palco No. 13 in 2° ordine	d25	g–
Dagl'heredi d[e]l q[uonda]m Ecc[ellentissimo] Nicolò Resio p[er] il palco No. 9 in 3° ordine	d29	g–
In contanti terminate le recite	d3	g19
	d101	g7
Per la porzione della N[obil] D[onna] Marietta Bolani Boldù per	d42	g10
Tutto il palco No. 5 in 3° ordine in[n]affittato	d20	g–
Mezo il palco No. 1 in 3° ordine in[n]affittato	d10	g–
Mezo il palco No. 4 à pepian inaffittato	d10	g–

In contanti terminate le recite	d2	g10
	d42	g10
Per la porzione del N[obil] H[omo] Piero Zen per	d42	g10
Dal N[obil] H[omo] M[esse]r Nicolò Sagredo P[rocurato]r di		
S. Marco p[er] mezo il Palco No. 8 in p[rim]o ordine	d12	g12
Mezo il palco No. 4 à pepian in[n]affittato	d10	g–
Mezo il palco No. 1 in 3° ordine in[n]affittato	d10	g–
Mezo il palco No. 2 in 3° ordine in[n]affittato	d10	g–
	d 42	g 12
Dà restituirgli fatte le riscossioni	d–	g2
	d42	g10

[f. 2v]
Per la porzione delli Nob[ili] Ho[mini] S[er] Anzolo, e fra[te]lli

Memo fù de S[er] Anzolo per	d32	g14
Dal N[obil] H[omo] S[er] Costantin Renier, p[er] aga il N[obil]		
H[omo] Piero Venier P[er] mezo il palco No. 6 in p[rim]o ordine	d12	g12
Dal N[obil] H[omo] Co. Piero Lion p[er] mezo il Palco sud[ett]o		
No. 6 in p[rim]o ord[in]e	d12	g12
Dal N[obil] H[omo] S[er] Fran[ces]co Ant[oni]o Farsetti K[avalie]r		
p[er] mezo il palco No. 4 in 2° ordine	d12	g12
	d 37	g12
Dà restituirgli fatte le riscossioni	d4	g22
	d32	g14

Per la porzione d[e]l N[obil] H[omo] S[er] Giac[om]o Ant[oni]o		
Vettor Marcello fù de S[er] Alv[is]e p[er]	d148	g20
Dal N[obil] H[omo] S[er] Gerol[em]o Giustinian Proc[urato]r di		
S. Marco per il 6° del Palco No. 26 a pepian	d3	g8
Dal N[obil] H[omo] S[er] Tomaso Querini p[er] il 3° d[e]l Palco		
No. 18 in primo ord[in]e ora tenuto dalla Ser[enissi]ma Elettrice		
di Baviera	d8	g8
Dalli N[obili] H[omini] S[er] Fran[ces]co K[avalie]r e f[rate]llo		
Morosini in loco del Ser[enissi]mo Morosini p[er] il palco No. 20		
in p[rim]o ordine	d25	g–
Dal N[obil] H[omo]S[er] Nicolò Contarin fù de S[er] Aurelio		
p[er] mezo il palco No. 24 in primo ordine	d12	g12
Dalli N[obili] H[omini] S[er] Gerol[em]o, e fra[te]lli Michiel fù		
de S[er] Nicolò p[er] mezo il palco No. 23 in 2° ordine	d12	g12
Dal N[obil] H[omo] S[er] Gerolimo Foscarinj fù de S[er] …		
p[er] mezo il palco No. 26 in 2° ordine	d12	g12
Il terzo d[e]lla metà del Palco No. 20 à pepian in[n]affittato	d3	g8
Mezo il Palco No. 21 in 3° ordine in[n]affittato	d10	g0
Mezo il Palco No. 27 in 3° ordine in[n]affittato	d10	g0
Mezo il Palco Proscenico D in 3° ordine in[n]affittato	d10	g0

	d	g
Tutto il Palco No. 22 in 3° ordine in[n]affittato	d20	g0
Tutto il Palco No. 26 in 3° ordine in[n]affittato	d20	g0
In contanti terminate le recite	d1	g8
	d148	g20
Per la porzione del N[obil] H[omo] Gerolemo Vettor Marcello fù de S[er] Francesco p[er]	d144	g12
[f. 3r]		
Dalli N[obili] H[omini] Pietro, e fra[te]lli Duodo p[er] mezo il palco No. 19 à pepian	d10	g–
Dal N[obil] H[omo] S[er] Carlo Pisani p[er] mezo il palco No. 22 à pepian	d10	g–
Dal N[obil] H[omo] S[er] Gerol[em]o Canal P[rocurato]r p[er] le porzioni à lui tangenti giusto le divisioni del palco seg[na]to G à pepian	d12	g12
Dal N[obil] H[omo] S[er] Tomaso Querinj p[er] il 3° del Palco No. 18 in p[rim]o ordine ora tenuto dalla Ser[enissi]ma Elettrice di Baviera	d8	g8
Dà her[ed]i q[uonda]m N[obil] H[omo] S[er] Zuan[n]e Grimani p[er] mezo il palco No. 22 in p[rim]o ordine	d12	g12
Dal N[obil] H[omo] S[er] Fran[ces]co Morosinj K[avalie]r p[er] il 4° d[e]l palco No. 27 in p[rim]o ordine	d6	g6
Dal N[obil] H[omo] S[er] Almorò Dolfin p[er] il palco No. 25 in p[rim]o ord[in]e	d25	g0
Il palco No. 25 in 3° ordine in[n]affittato	d20	g0
Il palco proscenico B. in 3° ordine in[n]affittato	d20	g0
[Mezzo] Il palco No. 27 in 3° ordine in[n]affittato	d10	g0
Mezzo il palco Prosc[enic]o D. in 3° ord[in]e in[n]affittato	d10	g0
	d144	g14
dà restituirgli fatte le riscossioni	d–	g2
	d 144	g 12
Per la porzione d[e]l N[obil] H[omo] S[er] Ferigo Vettor Marcello Renier p[er]	d26	g16
Dal N[obil] H[omo] Gerolemo Giustinian P[rocurato]r di S. Marco p[er] il 3° del palco No. 26 à pepian	d6	g16
Dal N[obil] H[omo] Tomaso Querini p[er] il 3° di palco No. 18 in p[rim]o ordine ora tenuto della Ser[enissi]ma Elettrice di Baviera	d8	g8
dà her[edi] d[e]l q[uonda]m D[on] Nicolò Passalaqua p[er] mezo il palco No. 15 in 3° ordine	d10	g0
Il 3° d[e]lla mettà del palco No. 20 à pepian in[n]affittato	d3	g8
	d28	g8
Dà restituirgli fatte le riscossioni	d1	g16
	d26	g16
	d 640	

[followed by the signatures of the eight co-proprietors]

Appendix B

Repertory of Sant'Angelo, 1699/1700–1739/40

Season	Carnival 1699/1700[60]
Autumn opera	*Rosane, imperatrice degli Assiri*
Librettist/composer	A. Aureli/various
Carnival opera	*L'oracolo in sogno*
Librettist/composer	F. Silvani/various
Season	Carnival 1700/1
Autumn opera	*Diomede punito da Alcide*
Librettist/composer	A. Aureli/T. Albinoni
Carnival opera	*L'inganno innocente*
Librettist/composer	F. Silvani/T. Albinoni
Season	Carnival 1701/2
Carnival opera 1[61]	*La vittoria nella costanza*
Librettist/composer	F. Passarini/G. Boniventi
Carnival opera 2	*Tiberio, imperadore d'Oriente*
Librettist/composer	G. D. Pallavicino/F. Gasparini
Season	Carnival 1702/3
Impresario	G. Orsatto
Autumn opera	*Demetrio e Tolomeo*
Librettist/composer	A. Marchi/A. Pollarolo
Carnival opera 1	*Gli amanti generosi*
Librettist/composer	G. B. Candi/B. Vinaccesi
Carnival opera 2	*Almansorre in Alimena*
Librettist/composer	G. M. Giannini/C. F. Pollarolo
Season	Carnival 1703/4
Autumn opera	*Farnace*
Librettist/composer	L. Morari/A. Caldara
Carnival opera	*Pirro*
Librettist/composer	A. Zeno/G. Aldrovandini

60. In this appendix 'Carnival', as applied to a whole season, includes also the preceding Autumn.
61. The sequence of operas produced in the same season follows the order in which they appear in the published registers of Bonlini (1730) and Antonio Groppo (1755), both of which appear normally to list productions in their true chronological order. (This is verifiable by cross-checking against printing licences, news sheets, diaries, the dates of dedications and other independent data.)

Season	Carnival 1704/5
Autumn opera	*Virginio consolo*
Librettist/composer	M. Noris/A. Giannettini
Carnival opera	*Artaserse*
Librettist/composer	A. Zeno and P. Pariati/ A. Giannettini
Season	Carnival 1705/6
Autumn opera	*Creso tolto a le fiamme*
Librettist/composer	A. Aureli/G. Polani
Carnival opera	*La regina creduto re*
Librettist/composer	M. Noris/M. A. Bononcini
Season	Carnival 1706/7
Autumn opera	*Paride in Ida*
Librettist/composer	F. Mazzari/A. B. Coletti after C. Manza[62]
Carnival opera 1	*Ifigenia*
Librettist/composer	A. Aureli after P. Riva/A. B. Coletti
Carnival opera 2	*La fede tra gl'inganni*
Librettist/composer	F. Silvani/T. Albinoni
Season	Carnival 1707/8
Autumn opera	*Armida abbandonata*
Librettist/composer	F. Silvani/G. M. Ruggieri
Carnival opera	*Armida al campo*
Librettist/composer	F. Silvani/G. Boniventi
Season	Carnival 1708/9
Impresario	C. Frigieri
Autumn opera	*Arrenione*
Librettist/composer	F. Silvani/various, including G. M. Ruggieri
Carnival opera 1	*Il tradimento tradito*
Librettist/composer	F. Silvani/T. Albinoni
Carnival opera 2	*Edvige, regina d'Ungheria*
Librettist/composer	T. Malipiero/various
Season	Carnival 1709/10
Autumn opera 1	*Il tradimento premiato*

62. 'After' will be used to identify composers and librettists whose work is arranged or supplemented by others. Obviously, some arrangements are light and others heavy, but no attempt will be made here to distinguish between different degrees of intervention.

Librettist/composer	G. B. Candi/G. Polani
Autumn opera 2	*Endimione*
Librettist/composer	F. Mazzari/G. Boniventi
Carnival opera 1	*Arato in Sparta*
Librettist/composer	F. Mazzari after N. Minato (?)/G. M. Ruggieri[63]
Carnival opera 2	*Berengario, re d'Italia*
Librettist/composer	M. Noris/G. Polani
Season	Carnival 1710/11
Autumn opera	*Non sono quella è la difesa*
Librettist/composer	G. A. Falier/G. M. Ruggieri
Carnival opera	*Circe delusa*
Librettist/composer	G. A. Falier/G. Boniventi
Season	Carnival 1711/12
Impresario	C. Frigieri
Autumn opera 1	*Armida in Damasco*
Librettist/composer	G. Braccioli/G. Rampini
Autumn opera 2	*Elisa*
Librettist/composer	D. Lalli/G. M. Ruggieri
Carnival opera 1	*La costanza in cimento con la crudeltà*
Librettist/composer	G. Braccioli/G. M. Ruggieri
Carnival opera 2	*Arsinoe vendicata*
Librettist/composer	G. Braccioli/G. M. Ruggieri
Season	Carnival 1712/13
Impresario	G. Orsatto, with G. Faggia
Autumn opera	*La gloria trionfante d'amore*
Librettist/composer	G. Braccioli/G. Rampini
Carnival opera 1	*Calfurnia*
Librettist/composer	G. Braccioli/J. D. Heinichen
Carnival opera 2	*Le passioni per troppo amare*
Librettist/composer	M. Noris/J. D. Heinichen
Season	Carnival 1713/14
Impresario	A. and G. B. Vivaldi
Musical Director	A. Vivaldi

63. The tentative attribution of the libretto by Bonlini and other early writers to Benedetto Marcello is unfounded. The libretto is signed 'F. M.', which suggests Francesco Mazzari, but there is evidence that Nicolò Minato was the original author.

Autumn opera	*Orlando furioso*
Librettist/composer	G. Braccioli/G. A. Ristori
Carnival opera	*Rodomonte sdegnato*
Librettist/composer	G. Braccioli/M. A. Gasparini
Season	Carnival 1714/15
Impresario	A. and G. B. Vivaldi
Musical Director	A. Vivaldi
Autumn opera 1	*Orlando finto pazzo*
Librettist/composer	G. Braccioli/A. Vivaldi
Autumn opera 2	*Orlando furioso*
Librettist/composer	G. Braccioli/G. A. Ristori with additions by A. Vivaldi
Carnival opera 1	*Lucio Papirio*
Librettist/composer	A. Salvi/L. A. Predieri
Carnival opera 2	*Nerone fatto Cesare*
Librettist/composer	M. Noris/various, arranged A. Vivaldi
Season	Carnival 1715/16
Impresario	P. Denzio (?)
Autumn opera	*Alessandro fra le Amazoni*
Librettist/composer	G. Braccioli/F. Chelleri
Carnival opera 1	*L'amor di figlio non conosciuto*
Librettist/composer	D. Lalli/T. Albinoni
Carnival opera 2	*Il più fedel fra i vassalli*
Librettist/composer	F. Silvani/F. Gasparini
Season	Carnival 1716/17
Impresario	P. Ramponi
Musical Director	A. Vivaldi (?)
Autumn opera	*Arsilda, regina di Ponto*
Librettist/composer	D. Lalli/A. Vivaldi
Carnival opera 1	*Penelope la casta*
Librettist/composer	M. Noris/F. Chelleri
Carnival opera 2	*L'incoronazione di Dario*
Librettist/composer	A. Morselli/A. Vivaldi
Season	Carnival 1717/18
Autumn opera 1	*L'innocenza riconosciuta*
Librettist/composer	T. Malipiero/C. F. Pollarolo
Autumn opera 2	*Il vinto trionfante del vincitore*
Librettist/composer	A. Marchi/various
Carnival opera 1	*Meleagro*

Librettist/composer   P. A. Bernardoni/T. Albinoni
Carnival opera 2   *Cleomene*
Librettist/composer   V. Cassani/T. Albinoni

Season   Carnival 1718/19
Autumn opera   *L'amor di figlia*
Librettist/composer   G. A. Moniglia/G. Porta
Carnival opera 1   *Amalasunta*
Librettist/composer   G. Gabrieli/F. Chelleri
Carnival opera 2   *Il pentimento generoso*
Librettist/composer   D. Lalli, S. A. Fiorè

Season   Carnival 1719/20
Autumn opera   *La caduta di Gelone*
Librettist/composer   F. Rossi/G. M. Buini
Carnival opera 1   *La sorte nell'amore*
Librettist/composer   F. Silvani/various
Carnival opera 2   *Armida delusa*
Librettist/composer   G. M. Buini/G. M. Buini

Season   Carnival 1720/21
Musical director   A. Vivaldi
Autumn opera   *La verità in cimento*
Librettist/composer   G. Palazzi/A. Vivaldi
Carnival opera 1   *Filippo, re di Macedonia*
Librettist/composer   D. Lalli/A. Vivaldi and G. Boniventi
Carnival opera 2   *Antigona*
Librettist/composer   B. Pasqualigo/G. M. Orlandini

Season   Carnival 1721/22
Autumn opera 1   *Cimene*
Librettist/composer   B. Pasqualigo/various
Autumn opera 2   *La fede ne' tradimenti*
Librettist/composer   G. Gigli/various
Carnival opera 1   *L'innocenza difesa*
Librettist/composer   F. Silvani/F. Chelleri
Carnival opera 2   *Gli eccessi della gelosia*
Librettist/composer   D. Lalli/T. Albinoni

Season   Carnival 1722/23
Autumn opera   *Arminio*
Librettist/composer   A. Salvi/C. F. Pollarolo
Carnival opera 1   *Timocrate*

Librettist/composer	D. Lalli after A. Salvi/L. Leo
Carnival opera 2	*I veri amici*
Librettist/composer	D. Lalli after F. Silvani/A. Paulati after T. Albinoni (?)
Season	Carnival 1723/24: Comedy
Season	Carnival 1724/25
Impresario	A. and G. B. Madonis
Autumn opera	*La Mariane*
Librettist/composer	D. Lalli/G. Porta after T. Albinoni
Carnival opera 1	*Seleuco*
Librettist/composer	A. Zeno and P. Pariati/G. Zuccari
Carnival opera 2	*Ulisse*
Librettist/composer	D. Lalli/G. Porta
Season	Carnival 1725/26
Impresario	A. Biscione (or Bissone)
Musical director	A. Vivaldi
Autumn opera	*L'inganno trionfante in amore*
Librettist/composer	M. Noris/A. Vivaldi
Carnival opera 1	*Turia Lucrezia*
Librettist/composer	D. Lalli/A. Pollarolo
Carnival opera 2	*Cunegonda*
Librettist/composer	A. Piovene/A. Vivaldi
Carnival opera 3	*La fede tradita e vendicata*
Librettist/composer	F. Silvani/A. Vivaldi
Season	Carnival 1726/27
Impresario	A. Balletti, assisted by A. Vivaldi
Musical director	A. Vivaldi
Autumn opera	*Dorilla in Tempe*
Librettist/composer	A. M. Lucchini/A. Vivaldi
Carnival opera 1	*Medea e Giasone*
Librettist/composer	G. Palazzi/G. F. Brusa
Carnival opera 2	*Farnace*
Librettist/composer	A. M. Lucchini/A. Vivaldi
Season	Carnival 1727/28
Musical director	A. Vivaldi
Autumn opera 1	*Orlando*
Librettist/composer	G. Braccioli/A. Vivaldi
Autumn opera 2	*Farnace*

Librettist/composer	A. M. Lucchini/A. Vivaldi
Carnival opera 1	*Rosilena e Oronta*
Librettist/composer	G. Palazzi/A. Vivaldi
Carnival opera 2	*Gl'odi delusi dal sangue*
Librettist/composer	A. M. Lucchini/G. B. Pescetti and B. Galuppi
Season	Carnival 1728/29: comedy
Impresario	G. Gentillini
Season	Carnival 1729/30
Autumn opera	*I tre difensori della patria*
Librettist/composer	A. Morselli/G. B. Pescetti
Carnival opera 1	*L'odio placato*
Librettist/composer	F. Silvani/B. Galuppi
Carnival opera 2	*Elenia*
Librettist/composer	L. Bergalli/T. Albinoni
Carnival opera 3	*Statira*
Librettist/composer	A. Zeno and P. Pariati/T. Albinoni
Season	Carnival 1730/31
Impresario	G. Tonini
Musical director	A. Galeazzi (?)
Carnival opera 1	*L'odio vinto dalla costanza*
Librettist/composer	A. Marchi/A. Galeazzi after A. Vivaldi
Carnival opera 2	*Il trionfo della costanza in Statira vedova di Alessandro*
Librettist/composer	B. Vitturi after F. Silvani/A. Galeazzi
Season	Ascension 1731
Impresario	Pietro Chechia
Ascension opera	*Gli sponsali d'Enea*
Librettist/composer	F. Passarini/B. Cordans
Season	Carnival 1731/32
Autumn opera	*Annibale*
Librettist/composer	F. Van Strypp/N. Porpora
Carnival opera 1	*Nino*
Librettist/composer	V. Cassani after I. Zanelli/F. Courcelle
Carnival opera 2	*Alessandro nell'Indie*
Librettist/composer	P. Metastasio/G. B. Pescetti

Season	Ascension 1732
Ascension opera 1	*Chi non fa non falla*
Librettist/composer	G. M. Buini/G. M. Buini
Ascension opera 2	*L'Ortolana contessa*
Librettist/composer	G. M. Buini/G. M. Buini
Season	Carnival 1732/33
Impresario	G. Orsatto
Autumn opera 1	*Ardelinda*
Librettist/composer	B. Vitturi/T. Albinoni
Autumn opera 2	*La caduta di Leone, imperator d'Oriente*
Librettist/composer	C. P. Cesa/G. A. Paganelli
Carnival opera 1	*Argenide*
Librettist/composer	G. Giusti/B. Galuppi
Carnival opera 2	*Tigrane*
Librettist/composer	B. Vitturi/G. A. Paganelli
Season	Ascension 1733
Impresario	G. Grandini
Ascension opera	*L'ambizione depressa*
Librettist/composer	G. Papis (?)/B. Galuppi
Season	Carnival 1733/34
Musical director	A. Vivaldi
Autumn opera	*Motezuma*
Librettist/composer	G. Giusti/A. Vivaldi
Carnival opera 1	*Candalide*
Librettist/composer	B. Vitturi/T. Albinoni
Carnival opera 2	*Dorilla in Tempe*
Librettist/composer	A. M. Lucchini/A. Vivaldi
Carnival opera 3	*L'Olimpiade*
Librettist/composer	P. Metastasio/A. Vivaldi
Season	Carnival 1734/35
Impresario	C. Garganti
Autumn opera	*Tamiri*
Librettist/composer	B. Vitturi/B. Galuppi
Carnival opera 1	*Lucio Vero*
Librettist/composer	A. Zeno/F. Araja
Carnival opera 2	*Cajo Fabrizio*
Librettist/composer	A. Zeno/J. A. Hasse

Season	Carnival 1735/36
Impresario	G. Galletto
Autumn opera	*L'inganno scoperto*
Librettist/composer	G. Giusti/various
Carnival opera 1	*Elisa, regina di Tiro*
Librettist/composer	A. Zeno and P. Pariati/B. Galuppi
Carnival opera 2	*Mandane*
Librettist/composer	B. Vitturi/I. Fiorillo

Season	Carnival 1736/37
Impresario	C. Garganti
Autumn opera	*Ergilda*
Librettist/composer	B. Vitturi/B. Galuppi
Carnival opera 1	*Ciro riconosciuto*
Librettist/composer	P. Metastasio/various
Carnival opera 2	*Artaserse Longimano*
Librettist/composer	P. Metastasio/G. A. Pampani

Season	Carnival 1737/38
Impresario	C. Garganti, replaced by A. Vivaldi
Autumn opera	*Ezio*
Librettist/composer	P. Metastasio/ G. B. Lampugnani
Carnival opera 1	*L'oracolo in Messenia*
Librettist/composer	A. Zeno/A. Vivaldi
Carnival opera 2	*Rosmira*
Librettist/composer	S. Stampiglia/various, arranged by Vivaldi
Carnival opera 3	*Armida al campo d'Egitto*
Librettist/composer	G. Palazzi/A. Vivaldi

Season	Carnival 1738/39
Impresario	B. Vitturi
Autumn opera	*Argenide*
Librettist/composer	G. Giusti/B. Galuppi
Carnival opera 1	*Achille in Sciro*
Librettist/composer	P. Metastasio/P. Chiarini

Season	Carnival 1739/40
Impresario	G. F. Dini
Autumn opera	*Feraspe*
Librettist/composer	F. Silvani/A. Vivaldi
Carnival opera 1	*Candaspe, regina de' Sciti*
Librettist/composer	B. Vitturi/G. B. Casali

Carnival opera 2   *Cleonice*
Librettist/composer   B. Vitturi after Metastasio/J. A. Hasse
Carnival opera 3   *Tullo Ostilio*
Librettist/composer   A. Morselli/G. B. Pescetti

Appendix C

A Note on the Venetian Monetary System

Because the value of coins fluctuated according to the market value of the metals (gold, silver, etc.) they contained, and because coins minted at different times and in different states were in circulation, it was necessary to make a distinction between the 'ideal' money – money of account – used in bookkeeping and the 'real' money in the form of coinage changing hands in transactions. In relation to this 'ideal' money, the 'real' money (particularly the coins made of precious metal) resembled – to make a modern comparison – a foreign currency floating up or down (generally the first, on account of inflationary pressures) in accordance with market conditions.

In the eighteenth century Venice used two moneys of account: (1) the *lira di piccoli* comprising the *lira* (pound), divided into twenty *soldi* (shillings), each of which was made up of twelve *piccoli* (pence); (2) the *lira di grossi* comprising another, much more valuable kind of *lira*, divided into ten ducats current (equivalent to florins), each of which was subdivided into twenty-four *grossi*. Of the two moneys, the first was by far the more commonly used in everyday transactions. The ducat current, which was a tenth part of the *lira di grossi*, had a value of six *soldi*, four *piccoli*, as expressed in *lire di piccoli*.

There is no need here to discuss further aspects of the system, which included an *agio* (bank rate) by which money used in bank transactions increased in value by a given percentage, except to list the coins mentioned in the article and give their values in *lire di piccoli*.

The difficulties of finding a meaningful modern equivalent for old currencies are well known. But just to give a rough indication: in 1791 a guide for British travellers in Italy estimated that a single male tourist could subsist for a year in Venice on £70 sterling, or just over 450 ducats. This sum included an allowance of approximately 135 ducats for a manservant's pay.[64]

Filippo (philip)	A coin worth 8 *lire*, 10 *soldi*.
Scudo	A silver coin, whose value climbed steadily from 9 *lire* in 1630 to 12 *lire* 8 *soldi* in 1733.

---

64. Thomas Martyn, *A Tour through Italy containing Full Directions for Travellers in that Interesting Country*, London, Kearsley, 1791, p. ix.

Zecchino (sequin)   A gold ducat, whose value climbed steadily from 16 *lire* in 1643 to 22 *lire* in 1717, at which level its value was finally pegged.

2

What Choirs Also Sang: Aspects of Provincial Music Publishing in Late-nineteenth-century England

Judith Blezzard

Publishing and the Music Trade

A conspicuous feature of nineteenth-century English musical life was the establishment of a large number of firms trading in music, offering items and services as diverse as a burgeoning market for music demanded. There were sellers and repairers of musical instruments, many of whom manufactured their own instruments for sale, organ builders and firms dealing solely with the manufacture, sale and maintenance of pianos. There were 'professors of music', which in the present context means persons who professed, or taught, music. These professors sometimes organised themselves into commercial groups, perhaps under the title of 'Academy', and many of them also held positions as church organists. Any, or all, of these types of individual or organisation could (and often did) publish music. In addition, there were booksellers, printers and stationers, whose main activities concerned the written word but who were also sometimes commissioned to print or sell items of music. In the early part of the century, therefore, the concept of the music publisher as a specialist principally in that single area was almost non-existent. Even in the second half of the century, well after the establishment of such large London firms as Novello (1810), Chappell (1811) and Boosey (c.1816) and the mid-century advances in music-printing technology, this multiplicity of functions continued for the most part to prevail. It did so for much of the twentieth century, too, and some such firms are still in existence, for example Banks of York and Forsyth of Manchester.

For the present-day investigator of music publishing, whose principal sources of evidence include sheet music, catalogues and advertisements, as well as trade directories, in which classifications are unfortunately seldom sufficiently precise or accurate, the concept of the music publisher in the nineteenth century can sometimes be uncomfortably vague. An interest in enhancing personal fame or fortune from music in print seems here to have been the determining factor, rather than a particular function in the process of producing or disseminating it. For example, in one instance the composer of a piece of music might be recorded as its publisher, because this single person had carried out every stage in the music's creation and dissemination except the act of printing it. In another, a commissioning body might be recorded as the publisher, although this organisation might nowadays more commonly be termed the sponsor or promoter. An example of this usage is provided by the firm of William Creamer and Company of Liverpool, named as the publisher, in 1887, of a celebratory piano piece for Queen Victoria's Golden Jubilee. The absence of this firm from the handful of music traders listed for that year in Liverpool at first led me to believe that it must have been a very small concern. Later, however, William Creamer and Company were revealed to have been a firm of furriers in the fashionable thoroughfare of Bold Street, which had apparently sponsored and circulated the piece.[1]

Many firms were very short-lived, sometimes to the extent of publishing only a single musical work, which was perhaps composed by an individual who was the firm's sole proprietor. Among the slightly larger, more enduring firms, the progression (then as now) seems to have been away from a large number of small undertakings towards a small number of large ones. Again as at present, this pattern does not seem to have deterred new firms from entering the market, sometimes for special groups of customers such as Welsh speakers or brass band musicians. However, later in the nineteenth century the increasing use of rail freight transportation made it cheaper to buy music of many kinds from London than to produce it locally. Similar considerations applied to imports of sheet music and of scores from Europe and elsewhere. These economic considerations became increasingly important

---

1. G. Jacobi, *The Queen's Jubilee Parade: March, for Piano*, William Creamer and Co., Liverpool, 1887, recorded under the obsolete shelfmark DQ3460 in an old card catalogue of Liverpool City Library, but otherwise untraced. I am grateful to Mrs Sally Drage of the Colchester Institute for drawing my attention to the existence of this catalogue, and to the staff in the Local History section of Liverpool City Library for making available to me this catalogue and other material from the archives.

as corporate music-making joined domestic musical activity: for example, the choral group (for which multiple copies would be required) as distinct from the pianist.

Growth Areas in Music Publishing

Particularly at the start of the nineteenth century, numerous publishers in London and elsewhere supplied a market eager for music that could be performed by capable amateurs, principally in domestic surroundings but also in church and in connection with special events. Not surprisingly, piano music and songs featured strongly in publishers' lists. Dances, often for a small instrumental ensemble including a piano and possibly a guitar, flute or violin, were also represented. Other ensemble and solo piano music included arrangements, sets of variations or pot-pourris on well-known or fashionable tunes (sometimes described as 'celebrated melodies'), descriptive pieces, marches and didactic music. There were also collections and series of pieces such as songs, studies, glees for small vocal ensemble, and certain types of dance such as quadrilles. Almost all these pieces, together with their composers, performers and publishers, are forgotten today. Even the composers of ballads that enjoyed phenomenal popularity over a number of years often passed into near-oblivion as a result of changing fashion: Sir Henry Rowley Bishop, whose ballad *Home Sweet Home* came out in 1823 and was still being republished as late as 1922, is a case in point, for no other work from his prolific output springs readily to mind. Any familiar names are likely to be ones of renowned composers such as Haydn, extracts from whose most popular works were arranged for the domestic musical market – which was the only way to reproduce such pieces before the advent of mechanical and recorded music. Much of this music is lost. A glimpse of music publishers' activities in this period is offered by two important reference works: that by Frank Kidson, which breaks off at 1830, and the more comprehensive but sometimes less detailed book by Charles Humphries and William C. Smith, which goes only up to about 1850.[2] Both books are organised by geographical location, adopting an inclusive approach to what

2. Frank Kidson, *British Music Publishers, Printers and Engravers from Queen Elizabeth's Reign to George the Fourth's*, London, W. E. Hill & Sons, 1900; Charles Humphries and William C. Smith, *Music Publishing in the British Isles from the Earliest Times to the Middle of the Nineteenth Century*, London, Cassell, 1954.

constitutes music publishing and listing numerous (though not all) publishers active in the repertories described above. However, although the authors of both books include Irish and Scottish locations and firms, they leave out Welsh ones altogether – a curious omission for which they offer no explanation.

A further important area in which publishers of music in early-nineteenth-century England were active was that of church music, particularly settings of psalms and (typically somewhat later) hymns. Sometimes these were intermixed in collections, which could also include settings of canticles or other devotional texts, all in metrical form. It is important to remember that, even though numerous psalters and hymnals were published in the early nineteenth century, much material of this kind still circulated in manuscript. For example, Francis Roads is currently studying the west gallery psalmody preserved in the Colby manuscripts used in the Isle of Man and dating from about 1810.[3] I have recently been shown a manuscript collection of metrical psalm and hymn settings from a church near Haworth, West Yorkshire, possibly dating from the 1850s and intended for local use. At Durham Cathedral the last official transcriber, Matthew Brown, whose distinctive hand graces sets of partbooks in the Cathedral Library, ceased work as late as 1869. From this date the choir at Durham Cathedral began to use only printed copies.[4] A similar date for this change applies also to Westminster Abbey and apparently to Chester Cathedral (where my study of this aspect of the Cathedral's music holdings is still in progress), a fact which suggests a general pattern.

Sometimes, it was more practical and cheaper to make customised manuscript copies, so to speak, than to buy a printed music publication. For the mid nineteenth century, we find observations that enthusiastic musicians would sometimes club together to buy a single copy of a collection or a piece of music they liked, such as Handel's *Messiah*, and sit up all night by candlelight after a day at work, copying (and possibly arranging) extracts they wanted to use.[5] The reference works by Kidson, Humphries and Smith do not, of course, take

3. University of Liverpool, PhD dissertation in progress, title forthcoming.
4. Brian Crosby, 'Church Music in Durham Cathedral in the Nineteenth Century', paper presented at the Second Biennial Conference on Music in Nineteenth-century Britain, University of Durham, July 1999.
5. David Russell, *Popular Music in England, 1840–1914: A Social History*, Manchester, Manchester University Press, 1987, p. 154.

account of manuscript copies, but for all geographical areas they list numerous publishers, booksellers and engravers with books of psalmody on their lists, some overtly didactic, others described as collections of the most useful tunes or the newest tunes. A further reflection of this remarkable degree of activity concerning psalms, hymns and associated material can be found in a monumental recent study by Nicholas Temperley, which indexes hymn-tune publications (and therefore, by implication, some psalmody books) up to 1820 and lists their publishers, who operated in numerous locations, large and small, in the British Isles and the USA.[6]

From the 1830s onwards the establishment and growth of choral societies, particularly in northern England, provided a lucrative and expanding market for music publishers eager to supply multiple copies to choral groups large and small. This new market emerged alongside that centred on domestic music, which continued to flourish. Many choral societies were established in connection with other institutions, such as churches, chapels, temperance societies and working men's clubs. The convergence of music and religious expression in the nineteenth century was characterised by ambivalent views on the purpose, function and power of music in the context of an established Anglican church embattled by factions within and beyond it and in particular by rising Nonconformism.[7] One positive factor in the popularity of oratorio in this period (on which music publishers gleefully capitalised) was that it transcended denominational boundaries. Another was its perceived role as a respectable religious experience that did not, however, compel attendance at a church service: people would rather listen to an aria than to a sermon. A third factor was its potential embrace by enthusiastic amateur performers including, notably, women, for whom participation in oratorio (as distinct from opera) was acknowledged as a respectable pursuit.[8]

But the history of choral music publishing in this period is not just the history of oratorio. There was much more besides. As well as

6. Nicholas Temperley, *The Hymn-tune Index: A Census of English-language Hymn-tunes in Printed Sources from 1535 to 1820*, Oxford and New York, Clarendon Press, 1997, 4 vols, Vol. 1, pp. 377–408.
7. Jim Obelkevich, 'Music and Religion in the Nineteenth Century', in *Disciplines of Faith*, ed. Jim Obelkevich, Lyndal Roper and Raphael Samuel, London, Routledge, 1987, pp. 550–65.
8. Ronald Pearsall, *Victorian Popular Music*, Newton Abbot, David & Charles, 1973, pp.12–15, 138–43.

church service-settings and large oratorios, there were numerous shorter works: cantatas, anthems, partsongs, glees, festival pieces and pieces for special occasions. Although music on sacred texts and subjects lay at the heart of the choral movement, much music was published that would have found no place in a sacred context, being more at home in the concert room or at convivial or festival gatherings. As for the character of the music, which is often maligned nowadays because of changes in fashion, there are possible social reasons, such as a desire to conform to expected parameters, to explain the relative conservatism of what is sometimes regarded as second-rate output. The Tonic Sol-fa movement, commendable though it was for teaching sight-singing to large numbers of people who were not innately musical, may well have been a factor in encouraging the composition and promotion of unimaginative music.[9] The longer works by famous composers (ones perhaps remembered nowadays) were, so to speak, the tip of an iceberg: the smaller, less well-known and less enduring works provide a musical backdrop to the relatively small canon of established works that has emerged from nineteenth-century England.

Publishers and their Markets

In the second half of the nineteenth century the larger music publishing houses sponsored performances of their own material, even to the extent of financing the building of concert halls, supplying pianos for them, presenting concerts and engaging performers. A combination of corporate, civic and personal prestige drove the market, in particular that for choral music. Increasingly, publishers began to specialise. This was the case with regional publishers as much as with the London firms, although the influence of the latter on music-making in other regions grew rapidly during this period.

Leaving aside the very smallest and shortest-lived publishing concerns, many regional firms continued to prosper, often reflecting the promotional activities of the London houses, albeit on a smaller scale. For example, the music firm of Forsyth in Manchester was active in promoting concerts and selling instruments as well as in publishing

9. Patrick Joyce, *Visions of the People*, Cambridge, Cambridge University Press, 1991, pp. 230–55; Pearsall (1973), pp. 117–20.

music. It was founded in 1857 by the brothers James and Henry
Forsyth. Much of its success in publishing was the result of collaboration between James Forsyth and other local businessmen aimed at
promoting Manchester as a centre of musical culture. By this time Sir
Charles Hallé (1819–95), a pianist and conductor of German birth,
had settled in Manchester and established a series of orchestral concerts employing a group of musicians that was later to form the basis
of the Hallé Orchestra. Clearly, he and the Forsyth brothers had a
common interest in fostering musical activity. Co-operation is evident
in some items published by Forsyth at the end of the century. For
example, in 1884, standing out conspicuously from the usual run of
English composers' songs, piano pieces, small sacred and choral items
and so forth issued by Forsyth and other publishers, we encounter a
series of thirty pieces for piano solo for sale at two shillings each and
entitled *Hallé's Musical Library*. This collection consists almost
entirely of sonatinas (significantly, not sonatas), rondos and descriptive pieces by such older German composers as Hiller, Hummel and
Kalkbrenner. The degree of co-operation between Forsyth and Hallé
cannot easily be ascertained: it is not known whether Hallé chose the
pieces himself, perhaps even having a hand in the editorial process (if
any), or whether he merely agreed to 'front' the series as a distinguished musical name. By this stage, also, Forsyth had opened a
branch in London. A smaller Manchester firm, Hammond, also
included a few pieces by German composers in its list of the same
year, but it operated on a much smaller scale than the Forsyth enterprise. The vast majority of composers whose works were published
provincially and in London were English.[10]

It is clear from trade directories and similar publications that many
music firms were short-lived. One of the more enduring (but possibly
only because it underwent several transformations of function and,
within one family, of ownership) was the firm of Hime in Liverpool.
It was established in the 1780s by the brothers Humphrey and Maurice Hime and passed out of Hime family ownership only in 1879.
One reason for this firm's prosperity was its proximity to, and family

10. Margaret Cranmer, 'Forsyth', in *The New Grove Dictionary of Music and Musi-
     cians*, ed. Stanley Sadie, London, Macmillan, 1980, Vol. 6, p. 720; Michael
     Kennedy, 'Hallé, Sir Charles', ibid., Vol. 8, pp. 54–55; Michael Kennedy, 'Man-
     chester', ibid., Vol. 11, pp. 594–98; 'The Music Publishers' Association Cata-
     logue, The Musical Times', Vol. 25, 1884, p. 668.

connections with, Ireland, where Maurice Hime established a music business in 1790, printing and selling music in Dublin. Although copyright protection laws applied to books and music registered with the Stationers' Company by virtue of increasingly restrictive Acts of Parliament from 1709, in particular those of 1814 and 1842, this protection did not apply in Ireland. Maurice Hime was thus able to print music cheaply in Dublin for export to England, to be sold at advantageous rates.[11] Apart from this material, the firm of Hime published music mostly of the kinds mentioned earlier that reflected domestic amateur taste, contracting out much of the printing work to a local engraver, William Dixon. Hime published very little choral or church music. There was certainly nothing to suggest Hime's adoption of a cumulative publishing strategy in these fields. This is perhaps surprising, considering the proximity of Liverpool to Wales and the emerging choral culture in these places in the nineteenth century. The Liverpool firms James Smith & Son and William Wrenshall & Son's Music Academy apparently specialised in sacred music during the late nineteenth century but published very little. In all, there were thirty-two printers and publishers of music active in Liverpool in the nineteenth century. Several published only one or two pieces, and many seem to have published music only incidentally – for example, as an adjunct to the printing of concert programmes. The lack of prolific music publishers in Liverpool by the end of the nineteenth century may reflect the relative cheapness and ease with which copies of music could be obtained from London.[12]

Similar patterns of provincial publishing emerged elsewhere, with regional specialisms such as the Hallé connection in Manchester or the Irish connection in Liverpool influencing aspects of the output but not determining it entirely. By the end of the nineteenth century, and probably considerably earlier, Welsh-language editions of choral music, both by Welsh composers and by other composers in translation, were being produced by Gwynn in Llangollen and Snell in

11. Gavin McFarlane, 'Copyright', in *The New Grove Dictionary of Music and Musicians*, ed. Stanley Sadie, London, Macmillan, 1980, Vol. 4, p. 736; Frank Kidson, William C. Smith and Peter Ward Jones, 'Hime', ibid., Vol. 8, p. 571.
12. Monica W. Felton, *Music Printing, Publishing and Selling, and the Musical Instrument Trade in Liverpool in the Eighteenth and Nineteenth Centuries*, unpublished dissertation, MA in Librarianship, University of Sheffield, 1969, pp. 9, 13–16, 26–74.

Swansea, as well as by other, smaller firms in Wrexham and elsewhere.[13] Some Welsh and diglot editions were published in London
and other places in England. In these cases, the use of a language
other than English in the editions indicates a separate, specialised
market unlike the apparently more general markets sought by provincial music publishers in England.

In York the music publishing firm of Banks & Son succeeded
Thomas Haxby, who, though primarily an organ builder, was also the
proprietor of one of about twenty music businesses trading in York in
the early nineteenth century. A ledger from Banks & Son covering the
period 1829 to 1870 shows that throughout this period the firm was
fulfilling orders for its publications from traders large and small,
including such substantial London firms as Augener, Boosey, Novello
and Schott. A folder of samples and catalogues, probably dating from
the late nineteenth and early twentieth centuries and perhaps com-
piled for use by the firm's travelling representatives, reveals the existence of a wide range of publications by Banks & Son, including
songs, piano tutors and salon pieces. There is also an extensive choral
list that rivalled, but clearly did not eclipse, the one offered by J.
Wood and Sons, of Bradford, which is discussed in more detail below.
If we discount Banks & Son, little publication of music seems to have
taken place in York in the nineteenth century. The number of traders
appears actually to have decreased over that time, but this may be a
reflection more of the changing organisation of categories in trade
directories than of an actual contraction of activity.[14]

Leeds, Bradford, Halifax and Huddersfield were at the centre of
the nineteenth-century upsurge in choral music. This situation was
reflected to some extent in music publishers' output – though, again,
not to the exclusion of other genres. In Leeds, for example, the firms
of J. Broadbent & Son and Blackburn & Company published series of
choral leaflets. The Blackburn list was particularly enterprising,
including the *Yorkshire Glees and Partsongs* series, *The Free Church
Choir Album* (the adjective applied to the church, not to the singers
or the music!) and the *Phlox* series in Tonic Sol-fa notation. The above

13. I am grateful to Mr Glyn Môn Hughes for information on Welsh nineteenth-cen-
    tury music publishers.
14. *Kelly's Directory of York and Hull, 1897*, London, Kelly & Co. Ltd, 1897, pp.
    95, 104; *Robinson's Yorkshire Business Directory*, Leeds, J. & D. Robinson Ltd,
    1904, pp. 350–51, 585.

two firms seem to have been the main publishers of choral music, but they and other publishers in the city also produced music of the kinds previously described: psalmody, songs, dances, piano music and solo instrumental items. Educational music also featured increasingly. The fortunate survival of a single copy (no further copies are known) of a directory published in Leeds in 1894 sets the relatively small specialism of music publishing in the wider context of the business of music. Publication of the directory itself must have been one such enterprise, supportive of the parallel activity of the publishing firm as an artists' concert agency. Individuals who wished their names to appear in the directory or to place advertisements in it had to pay a fee of at least one shilling. This particular venture appears to have been unsuccessful, since no further issues were published. However, the 1894 publication is remarkable – not only for the huge number of music practitioners it lists but also for the diversity of what they could offer. As well as the predictably large categories of (for example) vocalists, teachers and 'professors' of music, and music sellers, there are elocutionists, handbell ringers, comedians, a phrenologist, a (male) 'humourist and lady impersonator', and even a *prestidigitateur*.[15]

Halifax and Huddersfield present similar profiles to Leeds and other provincial northern cities, though on a smaller scale. However, there is one conspicuous exception here. The Huddersfield firm of Wood & Marshall, founded by Joseph Wood in 1850 and trading also as J. Wood and Sons, dealt in all kinds of musical instruments including organs and pianos, offering special imports, tuning, maintenance, repair, tuition and sheet music. It was also extremely active in publishing music, largely through its main outlet in Bradford, which opened in 1877. Numerous other music dealers traded in the city, but no publishing enterprise and few retail ones in Bradford or the towns and cities nearby matched Wood's for scale or endurance. In both Huddersfield and Bradford the firm was well established and apparently active in some or all of these retail, tuition and publishing areas from 1850 until the end of the century. Although it is difficult to ascertain the dates of several of the Wood publications, some can be dated with certainty to the 1880s and others to as late as 1913.

---

15. *Hanson's Directory of the Musicians, Music Traders, Dancing Masters, Elocutionists, and Entertainers in Yorkshire for 1894*, Armley, Leeds, West Riding Advertising Agency, 1894. I acknowledge with gratitude the help of the staff at Leeds City Library in helping me gain access to this unique volume.

Further Wood publications may either antedate or postdate these. It seems that, like Forsyth in Manchester and Banks in York, Wood in Bradford was exceptional for a provincial firm not only in its longevity but equally in the volume and diversity of its catalogue. Like Forsyth and Banks, it survives to the present day but, uniquely among the three firms, it is still owned and run by members of the founding family. Again, the overall profile of the output from Wood typifies that of provincial publishers of the period, but Wood cultivated a specialism in the form of small-scale choral music more conspicuously, in relation to the rest of its output, than did the two others.

At first encounter, this is hardly surprising. As a growth area in music publishing, choral music in the northern textile towns seems to have had enormous potential not only for commercial exploitation but also for musical development. Although the Wood enterprise seems to have been the largest in the area and one that was commercially successful (judging partly from proclamations, on reprints, of the number of copies of particular pieces sold), there is very little evidence of the music's performance or of its place in the lives of those who bought, sang or heard it. Scrutiny of programmes of the period for the area's choral societies reveals the usual enthusiasms for such composers as Handel, Haydn and Mendelssohn, besides further composers whose works were published by Novello. Given this picture, it would be all too easy to dismiss the Wood enterprise as a regional sideline purveying a succession of worthless ephemera for amateurs to sing. But that would be to discard a more balanced and accurate view of choral activity that took account of this music alongside material that has lasted in the choral repertory. Moreover, much Wood and similar material is genuinely worthwhile, not least because it provides a tangential view of popular choral developments of mainstream styles. It was clearly not intended to cater only for Yorkshire choirs or audiences. Perhaps the chief factor militating against a balanced view of material published provincially is the spectacular rise of London music publishers in the late nineteenth century and the consequent omnipresence of their publications (particularly those of Novello) in the choral market and the higher incidence of surviving material concerning these firms or published by them. Many of these larger publishing enterprises (unlike Wood and a few others) survived the First World War. The contrast in scale of operation and (largely as a result of this) in accessibility of material is probably the principal feature distinguishing the London publishers from their provincial counterparts.

The Predominance of London Music Publishers

All music publishers in the nineteenth century faced problems brought about by the spectacular growth of the industry and by rapid changes in musical fashion. In cases where seller and publisher were not one and the same person or organisation, reciprocal mistrust was apt to develop. This was a result of the 'novelty' system, whereby publishers' travellers declined to supply local dealers with stock unless they also took a number of novelties (new pieces of music for special promotion). Once the novelties had been sold and if they had achieved popularity – partly, of course, as the result of the dealer's effort – those same pieces would be made available to the dealer again, but only at a higher price and on acceptance of a further allocation of novelties. Another problem that undermined the legitimate music trade was piracy, particularly as visited on popular songs written by such composers as Ciro Pinsuti; the repeated seizure by the police of pirate copies from street traders was ineffective as a deterrent. Organisations of music sellers were formed in London and the provinces (with particularly high profiles in Leeds and Liverpool) to try to combat piracy, but the problem persisted until the passing of the 1906 Copyright Act, with further measures following in 1911 and 1914. Small publishers and dealers, particularly in the provinces, were particularly at risk from the novelty system and piracy, which probably helps to explain why so many of them did not last long.[16]

The spectacular growth of the music publishing industry in nineteenth-century London outstripped similar activity in the provinces and, since music from the large London establishments was cheap and ever easier to obtain, probably contributed to its relatively low profile. It is no accident that a commentary on music publishing in nineteenth-century Britain published as recently as 1981 amounts to a discussion of London publishers' activity, acknowledging the existence of provincial music publishers only as an aside in a single sentence. The same commentary gives some annual totals of music copyrights. Although for various reasons the figures may not be completely accurate, the trend is clear: 159 in 1800, 1,142 in 1850, 7,114

---

16. James Coover, *Music Publishing, Copyright and Piracy in Victorian England*, London, Mansell, 1985, pp. vii–x, 65–70, 81, 103–8; Percy Scholes, *The Mirror of Music*, 2 vols, London, Novello and Oxford University Press, 1947, Vol. 2, pp. 754–55.

in 1900, rising to 11,436 in 1914 – an almost hundredfold increase in the course of just over a century. In the case of choral music, where the principal publisher was Novello, it is arguably true that this firm's policy of publishing a high volume of music very cheaply contributed to the 'freezing' of the classical music repertory around the corpus of established masterworks.[17]

The firm of Novello started up in 1810 as a small publishing business, but in the 1840s Alfred Novello initiated a period of expansion by capitalising on the need for didactic choral material on the part of the increasingly popular sight-singing classes. Shortly afterwards, the firm began to issue cheap editions of popular oratorios, including, of course, Handel's *Messiah*. Part of Novello's success was the result of the firm's policy of using the latest music-printing technologies and working practices to produce clear and reliable copies at prices that were progressively reduced, thereby facilitating participation in choral music by members of the less wealthy social classes. This trend was accelerated by a change in the system of taxation on materials and activities relating to publication. The abolition of Newspaper Stamp Duty in 1855, of Advertisement Duty in 1857 and of Paper Duty in 1861, brought about largely by Alfred Novello's efforts, meant that such publishers as Novello were freed from significant burdens of cost and administration. In 1844 the monthly periodical then entitled *The Musical Times and Singing Class Circular* (later to become *The Musical Times*) was established by Novello; in every issue of this journal a separate, detachable choral piece, such as an anthem, was given away free. Novello took over other, smaller firms and expanded its range of merchandise to include hymnals, opera and orchestral scores, and handbooks. It is probably safe to say that every choral singer active in England up to about 1970 will have sung music published by Novello, and that most will be familiar with their brown-covered oratorio editions, in which extracts from the huge Novello choral catalogue are listed in small print on the back pages. Some idea of the range of oratorios on offer can be gained from lists abstracted from *The Musical Times*, which show works performed in 1846–47, 1886–87 and 1926–27.[18] The catalogue ran to many hundreds of pieces – not only oratorios and other large-scale works but also anthems, motets, glees,

17. Donald W. Krummel, 'Music Publishing', in *Music in Britain: The Romantic Age 1800–1914*, ed. Nicholas Temperley, Oxford, Clarendon Press, 1981, pp. 46–59, especially pp. 49–50, 58.
18. Scholes (1947), Vol. 1, pp. 144–47, and Vol. 2, pp. 751–53.

partsongs and cantatas. A particularly notable feature was the inclusion of madrigals written in the nineteenth century as well as some from the sixteenth and seventeenth centuries. A handful of nineteenth-century composers, including Samuel Wesley and Robert Lucas Pearsall, were largely responsible for a brief revival of the madrigal and its associated styles of choral composition. In addition there were arrangements. These were not only written for particular groupings such as high-voice choir but also derived from music beyond the most likely sources. Adapted polyphony was thus given a wider dissemination for use in church. For the same purpose, the more recent continental repertory was plundered with enthusiasm even for the benefit of areas of the liturgy with ostensibly little musical potential such as 'Responses to the Commandments'. For these, the church musician could choose from 'Beethoven in C; Gounod in D, G; Hummel in B flat; Mendelssohn in G, A; C. M. von Weber in E flat; F. Schubert in C, G, C, F, E flat, A flat', all in inexpensive Novello leaflets.[19]

Other London publishers were active in diverse fields. Boosey, for example, supplied much music for the brass and wind bands that flourished in the nineteenth century, particularly in northern England. No regional publisher for this medium apparently matched Boosey for scale of operation or duration of activity. Again, it is interesting that in a survey of music publishers established between 1844 and 1944 only one of the fourteen cited (Oxford University Press) possessed connections outside London.[20] But numerous smaller publishers continued to flourish. This is clear from the catalogue of the Music Publishers' Association, which appeared in *The Musical Times* in 1884 and listed (supposedly) all musical compositions published in Great Britain during each of the quarters (mathematically rather inexact) ending on 31 January, 31 March, 30 June and 30 September 1884. That neither this list, which proceeds by genre, nor the one in *The Catalogue of Printed Music in the British Library to 1980*, which proceeds by composer, is complete can be ascertained by detailed cross-checking; however, some interesting features quickly emerge.[21]

19. Judith Blezzard, *Borrowings in English Church Music 1550–1950*, London, Stainer & Bell, 1990, pp. 56, 71.
20. Scholes (1947), Vol. 2, p. 743.
21. 'The Music Publishers' Association Catalogue', *The Musical Times*, Vol. 25, 1884, pp. 113–19, 305–11, 488–95, 665–71; *The Catalogue of Printed Music in the British Library to 1980*, ed. Robert Balchin, 62 vols, Munich, K. G. Saur, 1984.

The most immediately striking one is the sheer volume of publications. Another is the overwhelming preponderance of London publishers. In addition to such well-known names as Ashdown, Augener, Boosey, Cocks, Enoch and of course Novello, I have found twenty-six previously unreported publishing firms which, on cross-checking, turn out to have been London-based. Only Forsyth, Hammond and Wood, apparently, were regional, despite *The Musical Times* list's claim to include all musical compositions published, and not merely those issued by members of the Music Publishers' Association. The vast majority of pieces were ephemeral, and almost all were by composers with plausibly English names (surname of composer, title of piece and name of publisher, without location, are the only details given). Some pieces were brought out by more than one publisher, not necessarily in different arrangements. Solo songs, piano music and dance music form the biggest categories. Novello cornered the choral music market in 1884, notching up more publications than Ashdown, Augener, Boosey, Cocks, Cramer, Curwen, Czerny, Davison, Donajowski, Forsyth, Hammond, Hays, Hutchings, Jeffreys, Lucas, Morley, Patey, Pitman, Ransford, Reid, Weekes and Wood combined. Not surprisingly for *The Musical Times*, the lists are rounded off with advertisements for yet more Novello publications.

No further lists like these were published. This is a pity, not least because information of this kind from other years might have shown whether 1884 was typical or extraordinary, or whether the output listed there followed any trends in the history of music publication. Many of these smaller firms simply went out of existence or were taken over by larger ones. It is time-consuming but not difficult to track down much of this music as individual items, since nearly everything appearing in *The British Library Catalogue of Printed Music to 1980* is accessible in single copies at the British Library. The few exceptions include stock lost in the Second World War but retained in the catalogue. What is more difficult is to gain any idea of how, when or by whom this music was used – for how long or with what response. This applies to almost all choral publications of the period except for the most significant and enduring: the accepted canon of nineteenth-century choral music, performances of which were advertised and commented upon in the media of the time but which may not have represented the choral singer's complete experience.

The Novello Influence

Although the hegemony of Novello in choral music publishing in nineteenth-century England was wide-ranging, profound and enduring, it seems not to have deterred other publishers from entering the market. However, the prominence of Novello has led not only to the establishment of, and emphasis upon, a particular repertory but also to a concentration upon the Novello output (sometimes to the exclusion of all else) in later investigations of nineteenth-century music-making. Perhaps this is justifiable to a degree, but an exclusively Novellocentric approach does not necessarily present a completely accurate picture. Sometimes, for the sake of brevity, Novello is the only publisher to receive mention in commentaries on English music of the period. But even in more detailed studies a similar situation tends to prevail. For example, in his recent paper on music publishers and the development of new music by British composers in the nineteenth century Lewis Foreman drew solely on Novello material, briefly citing just one item relating to another publisher (Curwen).[22] The section on music publishing in Brian Pritchard's thesis on music festivals and choral societies in England mentions only Novello, and little music in this context besides oratorio.[23] David Russell's study partly builds on Brian Pritchard's, dealing with the popular music societies (for example brass bands, choral societies) of West Yorkshire from 1850 to the start of the First World War. His chapter on music publishing acknowledges the possibility that the role of Novello has often been exaggerated, but no other publisher's work is explored, and the impression is conveyed that exclusive dependence on Novello for choral music was both the national and the local pattern.[24]

The problem of achieving a more balanced overview by finding out more about provincial music publishing seems to be a self-

22. Lewis Foreman, 'Music Publishers and the Development of the New Music by British Composers in the Later Nineteenth Century', paper presented at the Second Biennial Conference of Music in Nineteenth-century Britain, University of Durham, July 1999.

23. Brian Pritchard, *The Music Festival and the Choral Society in England*, unpublished PhD dissertation, University of Birmingham, 1968, especially pp. 594–600.

24. David Russell, *The Popular Music Societies of the West Yorkshire Textile District, 1850–1914*, unpublished PhD dissertation, University of York, 1980, especially pp. 133–38, 197–200.

perpetuating one. The concentration of a large proportion of England's music publishers in London has led to a concentration of potential research material, hence of research itself, on London. The acquisition by the British Library of the Novello Collection (largely material from Vincent Novello's lifetime) and the Novello and Company Business Archive, although entirely justified and laudable in that it makes these documents available for research, nevertheless serves to reinforce even more a Novellocentric outlook.[25] Even so, there can be few music-publishing enterprises whose historical documents end up in such a safe haven. If firms simply go out of business, their documents are unlikely to survive. The same often applies to concerns that merge with, or are taken over by, other organisations or undergo a change of proprietor. For example, Blackburn & Company of Leeds were eventually taken over by Music Exchange (Manchester) Ltd. Despite a personal contact and the best efforts of the proprietor of the second firm, I could find no trace whatsoever of any Blackburn choral catalogues, advertisements or similar material; but the firm had pleasure in forwarding a copy of its latest catalogue, which, it hoped, would be of interest. This included some piano and song albums that had previously been published by Blackburn & Company, but that was all. The present proprietor of Banks & Son, of York, reports the survival at the firm's recently acquired premises of a few work-books, old file copies, title listings and account-books from the nineteenth century. The present proprietor of J. Wood and Sons, of Bradford, can produce a handful of old minute-books from company meetings, a few press cuttings, and some account-books, together with miscellaneous letters.[26] But even items of these kinds, preserved more by chance than by design, are the exception. Because they are not catalogued, they have to be scrutinised in detail to see which of them, if any, will yield useful information on publishing activities. A further problem is lack of continuity: the materials tend to be fragmentary and haphazard rather than systematically organised, making it hard to build up any kind of picture or to identify trends. Very few items concerning the

25. London, British Library, Add. MSS 65382–65525 and 69516–69792.
26. I acknowledge with gratitude the help and interest of firms' proprietors as follows: Mr Tony Osborn of Music Exchange (Manchester) Ltd, Mrs Margaret Silver of Banks & Son, York, and Mr Richard Wood of J. Wood and Sons, Bradford.

music trade seem ever to have been placed on deposit in the local history sections of municipal or university libraries.

Survival of Musical Evidence

What about the music itself? Its chances of survival are often subject to commercial considerations or to the whim of fashion. If a publishing house needs space to accommodate new stock, if it is taken over by another firm or if it moves to different premises, decisions have to be taken about stock in hand. That which has the least money-making potential is the most vulnerable and may simply be destroyed. This means that much music is no longer available for purchase – which naturally limits accessibility to it for performance and study. Copies deposited in the British Library or similar institutions may be the only ones available, apart from those in enthusiasts' collections or fortuitously discovered in second-hand outlets. But the problem does not stop there. Cases have arisen in which a composer's autograph full score in the possession of a publisher – sometimes the only full score in existence, from which sets of performing parts were made – has disappeared without trace; this fate has even befallen works of such eminent composers as Sir Edward Elgar. If this can happen to Elgar, there may be even less hope for the works of composers whose music lacks an equally devoted following. The retention of manuscript and printed music in private hands does not always avert its eventual disposal or destruction by those who, in benign or sometimes malign ignorance, deal with 'deceased's effects'. The British Library, in common with similar institutions, has rescued many works, often in co-operation with music publishers. However, all this takes time, planning and effort.[27]

With choral music in particular, the necessity for multiple copies means that libraries cannot always continue to accommodate material that is no longer in demand. 'De-accessioning', a euphemism used in library circles to mean throwing out, is sometimes the only solution. I recollect being informed by telephone that a large municipal library nearby was getting rid of all the sets of choral music in its

---

27. *Lost and Only Sometimes Found: A Seminar on Music Publishing and Archives*, ed. Lewis Foreman, Upminster, British Music Society, 1992, *passim*; especially Foreman, 'A Practical Problem', pp. 9–13, and Hugh Cobbe, 'The British Library's Role', pp. 46–49.

stacks and that immediate attendance was required in order to save anything at all. Arriving by train with one helper and a hastily assembled assortment of carrier bags, I found trolleys already deployed to take piles of music to a skip outside the building. The only recourse was to keep ahead of the trolleys and grab whatever came to hand: the operation resembled looting. Similar incidents have more recently been observed in libraries elsewhere as well as on publishers' premises, invariably with hardly any notice given. There seems no other reason than negligence for this lack of notice, which means that the material cannot be surveyed and plans made for a more reasoned disposal of it.

Churches, too, face similar problems of storage. In these cases, there is an additional factor: an intact collection can preserve an overview of church-music practice and liturgical conduct in one institution at a particular time. Once a collection is dispersed, its corporate value is lost. Not only changes in liturgical text and practice but also changes in fashion, the availability of church musicians, the degree of these musicians' expertise, and the availability (or otherwise) of an organ may contribute to the use or disuse of particular music. If any of these factors renders music of a certain kind obsolete, it may well be dispersed or destroyed. Even so, some churches are marvellous repositories of music that goes back decades or even centuries; in other instances, a former incumbent, organist or church member may sometimes have rescued music that appealed to him or her – but it, too, remains vulnerable to loss. The result of all this is that much choral and church music published in the nineteenth century has simply physically disappeared: even some Novello publications are by now merely a name in an old catalogue or on a British Library list, to say nothing of the production of local publishers. Of the material relating to what many church or chapel choirs (or their associated local choral societies) sang, little or nothing remains, even from some fairly large establishments.[28]

Choral Music-making

In the light of the foregoing discussion, it is clear that the investigation of nineteenth-century choral activity in England is hampered by the non-availability of a full spread of material: not only of music but

28. Russell (1980), p. 351.

also of evidence about the total spectrum of music that was in circulation. For some types of investigation this is little hindrance. When seeking perspectives on this period, for example, it is natural for investigators to give particular attention to events or developments that, with hindsight, can be recognised as innovative, progressive or influential, either socially or musically. But in this kind of longitudinal overview the outlook of those who were participants in a particular movement, such as the rise of choral music, risks being submerged. A different approach is to study the choral music movement as an aspect of the conurbations in which it flourished: for example, Leeds, Bradford, Huddersfield and Halifax. The activities of the principal choral societies in such places as these are well documented from their inception to the present day, both by material relating primarily to these societies and in the wider context of local history of the towns themselves, or as a part of the social and economic history of the period.[29] The existence of numerous smaller choral societies is seldom taken into account: first, because many existed only briefly, so that documentation has largely disappeared; second, because they were not viewed as important from a musical, historical or social perspective. The same can be said of churches and similar institutions, where the Anglican tradition has been considerably emphasised, perhaps because it is relatively well documented and accessible and includes some music that has endured in the wider repertory. This emphasis has arguably been at the expense of other traditions, particularly those of Nonconformism, which employed mixed-voice rather than all-male choirs and whose institutions provided the basis of much choral activity and experience in the period under discussion. Russell (1980) addresses this imbalance throughout by presenting some statistics on small choral societies, but the lack of material prevents a meaningful assessment of much of what they sang.

Associated developments, such as the Tonic Sol-fa movement, the festival movement and what might be termed the oratorio industry, also contributed to the choral movement but did not define it. Music festivals were, by their nature, special events, and as such were often well documented. Even so, more attention was given (understandably)

---

29. See, for example, Robert A. Edwards, *And the Glory: The Huddersfield Choral Society, 1836–1986*, Leeds, W. S. Maney, 1986; *Victorian Bradford*, ed. David G. Wright and J. Anthony Jowitt, Bradford, Metropolitan Council Libraries Division, 1982.

to who did what in terms of patronage, performance reception and success than to the music that provided the vehicle for the event. The growth of the competitive or non-competitive choral festival, particularly in northern England in the 1880s, accelerated the demand for short choral pieces. There were many small festivals besides the well-documented ones held at Morecambe, in particular – the latter attracting national and international composers and adjudicators. The production of oratorios, intended for special occasions and capitalising on the overwhelming popularity of Handel's *Messiah*, Haydn's *The Creation* and Mendelssohn's *Elijah*, also accelerated during this period, giving rise to numerous Novello publications. Participation in the public performance of an oratorio required a special degree of commitment. To organise, direct or compose for a performance, even for a small local institution or festival, was a considerable undertaking – hardly what could be described as routine music-making and therefore something worthy of special note. Oratorios, and to a lesser extent cantatas, are by nature lengthy works usually requiring at least some degree of professional input. Yet because their performances are well documented in comparison with those of smaller, more routine works, it is all too easy to consider oratorios and cantatas as (besides hymns) the sum total of what the amateur Victorian choralist sang. In reality, there were many other types of music on offer that were just as likely to have been part of the singers' routine. A proportion of these appeared in the 'miscellaneous selections' (whose constituents were frequently not named in programmes) that sometimes formed the second half of a concert in which the first half consisted of a nineteenth-century cantata. This was a frequent pattern of concert planning, particularly among smaller choral societies. Even so, especially with regard to works that have fallen into obscurity, it is difficult to discover how these shorter items were received (even after reading between the lines of critics' reports of pieces programmed at special events) – and sometimes harder still to find out what they sounded like.

The perceived importance to music of the events collectively known as the nineteenth- and early-twentieth-century 'English Musical Renaissance' can perhaps partly be explained by reference to a similar sifting, with time, of an enormous amount of choral music and material concerning it. It was natural that the process eventually brought into prominence those works whose performances were well documented, that had remained in the repertory, and which (with hindsight) could be seen as having had some particular novel aspect or significance for posterity. However, the extent to which the music and ideas characterising this movement were adopted by contemporary performers, listeners or other composers throughout England was very limited. Undue emphasis has perhaps been placed on the 'English Musical Renaissance' as a historical current. For choral music, some measure of balance can be restored by examining what choirs sang as an alternative. This is by no means a plea for the reinstatement of neglected supposed masterpieces. For most of the time, people were not singing masterpieces, and it would be wrong to seek to elevate the bulk of their musical fare to that level. On the other hand, it is worth trying to establish what the late-nineteenth-century choral experience was in reality like rather than merely to concur with what later commentators think it should have been like. The attitudes of such influential early-twentieth-century figures as Martin Shaw, whose reaction against Victorian church music and hymns in particular was extreme in word and deed, prompted derision and then oblivion for much that had been the staple fare of many choral singers.[30] Any supposed divisions between music inspired by the 'English Musical Renaissance' and music not so inspired (perhaps in both senses of the word) cannot simply be attributed to a perceived fissure between popular music and art music. Both clear types may exist in choral and, indeed, in church music, but a firm boundary between them is difficult to find.[31]

A Provincial Publisher's Collection

Scrutinising the output of nineteenth-century music publishers can give some idea of usage and demand, possibly more accurately than surveys of concerts and special events often do. Moreover, some smaller-scale works that did not necessarily find their way into special events or were included perhaps only in 'miscellaneous selections' in concerts can be traced only by this means. This method may well result in a more faithful reflection of the day-to-day workings of choral singers. It is hardly surprising that many late-nineteenth-century music publishers in England prospered so conspicuously or

30. Blezzard (1990), pp. 87–88, 195–96.
31. Donald W. Krummel, in Temperley (1981), p. 53; Blezzard (1990), chapters 7 and 9.

that they produced vast amounts of music that they knew would sell: in this respect, later opinions of its quality are irrelevant. Much of the music demonstrably meant a great deal to performers and listeners. This is clear from the nature and frequency of dedications and from the mentions of particular institutions and events on the title-pages of many choral leaflets of the period, as well as from the existence of multiple editions and arrangements of some of the music.

Provincial publishers of choral music, sometimes (but not always) using material by composers not nationally known, may have sought to fill gaps left by the larger London firms. Contrary to what might be supposed, these smaller publishers, on the evidence of their music, were not trying to cater for choirs whose resources, in terms of musical expertise, numbers or finance, were inferior to those of the patrons of Novello or similar publishers. For the most part, the former seem to have been targeting the same markets. The extent of their output, where it can be estimated, suggests that their enterprise was rewarded.

One such firm was J. Wood and Sons, of which mention has already been made. Founded in 1850, from the 1880s to about 1914 it published a series of nearly two hundred choral items (the exact number is in doubt because possibly not quite all have been traced and examined); most are small-scale pieces for mixed voices. All trace of this publishing enterprise, including engraved printing plates as well as documentation, was believed lost when the company's Huddersfield premises were destroyed by fire in 1964. However, the collection, apparently intact or nearly so, survives in the British Library. It has been reassembled by the firm, offering a glimpse of what some of the music that choirs sang in the late nineteenth century was like. There is no implicit assumption here that any choirs sang exclusively from Wood editions: that would be as potentially erroneous as to suppose that all music worth singing in the late nineteenth century was published by Novello. It is not possible to ascertain the full extent to which music from the Wood collection was used either in the firm's immediate locality or further afield. The non-survival of documentation poses a limitation in this respect, since overviews of the period's choral activity do not supply the degree of detail that would be needed.[32]

32. For example, Russell (1987); *Music in England 1885–1920 as recounted in Hazell's Annual*, ed. Lewis Foreman, London, Thames, 1994; Reginald Nettel, *Music in the Five Towns 1840–1914*, London, Oxford University Press, 1944.

Several features of the Wood choral collection are other than might be expected on the basis of some conspicuous trends in provincial and London music publishing in the nineteenth century. The Wood enterprise did not use ornate covers; nor did it subsist on royalty ballads. It maintained a large and diverse list, survived for several decades and was not swamped by Novello. Nor did it cater only for Yorkshire tastes, although there were certainly choral arrangements of tunes with Yorkshire associations such as *On Ilkla' Moor baht 'At*, the tune *Old Foster* (as distinct from the most usual tune *Winchester Old*), commonly sung to 'While shepherds watched their flocks by night', and *Pratty Flowers*, the so-called 'Holmfirth Anthem' (which remains in print). Included were also pieces not specifically with Yorkshire associations but by composers with Yorkshire connections: for example, *Sweet and Low* by Joseph Barnby, whose musical career began in York, and 'God is a Spirit' from *The Woman of Samaria*, an oratorio by William Sterndale Bennett of Sheffield.

Several composers whose music was published by Wood are listed in Plate 1, which is a reproduction of the outside cover pages of the Wood edition, published in 1908, of John Liptrot Hatton's verse anthem *Out of the Deep*. Unlike Hatton, who was well known nationally for his glees, solo songs and church music, most of the composers in the Wood list were provincial composers, not all of whom seem to have been prominent in local musical life. Predictably, among those who were, some were connected with the Huddersfield Choral Society. They included Joseph Edgar Ibeson, who served as the Society's accompanist and deputy conductor from 1844 to 1915 as well as teaching music locally; John North, its conductor from 1885 to 1891 and briefly a partner in the Wood music business; and James Battye, conductor of the Huddersfield Choral Society from 1852 to 1858 and one of its founder-members. All these musicians concurrently held other appointments, chiefly with churches and other choral societies. Ibeson's and North's works were published exclusively by Wood. Other composers, including Battye, entrusted the majority of their works to Wood but were also published by London firms including Chappell, Curwen, Novello and Stainer & Bell, and even, sometimes, by such rival Yorkshire firms as Blackburn & Company of Leeds and Banks & Son of York. Not all the Wood composers moved in Huddersfield circles. For example, William Henry Ibberson, whose partsongs dating from about 1910 are among the chief delights of the Wood collection, had a degree in music and taught from his home address in Ilkley, West Yorkshire.

195. OUT OF THE DEEP .... *Anthem* .. .. .. J. L. HATTON 3¢

WOOD'S COLLECTION
OF
GLEES, ANTHEMS, TUNES, PART SONGS & C.

165.	MASSA IN DE COL' GROUND	*Glee A.T.T.B.*	MORLEY	4¢
166.	NOW THE DAY IS OVER	*Anthem*	H. STATHER	3¢
167.	COME UNTO ME	*Anthem*	H. STATHER	3¢
168.	SAVIOUR AGAIN	*Anthem*	H. STATHER	3¢
169.	THE SON OF GOD	*Anthem*	H. STATHER	4¢
170.	THE MERRY MOUNTAIN CHILD	*Song*	PERKINS	3¢
171.	THE MONKS VESPER	*Sacred Part Song*	W. H. CROSS	4¢
172.	COME HOME	*Glee S.A.T.B.*	DEAN	2¢
173.	AS SOME LONE SWALLOW	*Part Song A.T.T.B.*	E. A. LODGE	2¢
174.	AS SOME LONE SWALLOW	*Part Song T.A.T.B.*	E. A. LODGE	2¢
175.	LONDON CRIES'	*Comic Glee A.T.T.B.*	SELWOOD	3¢
176.	BE NOT AFRAID	*Chorus*	MENDELSSOHN	2¢
177.	NOW IN THE SACRED HOUSE OF GOD	*Anthem*	J. WILSON	3¢
178.	HARVEST GLADNESS	*Anthem*	ROBERTSHAW	2¢
179.	OLD MOTHER HUBBARD	*Humourous Glee S.A.T.B.*	H. STATHER	3¢
190.	MASSA IN DE COL' GROUND	*Glee S. A. T. B.*	MORLEY	4¢
151.	LONDON CRIES'	*Comic Glee S.A.T.B.*	SELWOOD	3¢
152.	THOU, LORD, IN THE BEGINNING	*Anthem*	BEAUMONT	3¢
183.	OLD KING COLE	*Humorous Part Song S.A.T.B.*	H. STATHER	2¢
184.	TO ARMS, TO ARMS, YE SOLDIERS	*Anthem*	W. H. RENSHAW	3¢
185.	I WILL GREATLY REJOICE	*Anthem*	H. KEETON Mus. Doc.	4¢
186.	O BE JOYFUL IN THE LORD	*Anthem*	C. STATHER	3¢
187.	HYMN TO THE NIGHT	*Part Song S. A. T. B.*	C. STATHER	3¢
188.	GOOD OLD JEFF	*A.T.T.B.& Bass Solo*	W. E. MORLEY	4¢
189.	ARM FOR THE BATTLE	*Anthem*	C. DARNTON	2¢
190.	QUEEN MAY	*Part Song S. C. T. B.*	C. DARNTON	2¢
191.	HARK TO THE BELLS	*Part Song S. C. T. B.*	C. DARNTON	2¢
192.	STAND FIRM FOR THE CAUSE OF TRUTH	*Anthem*	F. W. PEACE	2¢
193.	SING, O HEAVENS	*Anthem*	W. GRIFFITH	2¢
194.	O LOVE DIVINE	*Anthem*	ALEX LEE	2¢
195.	OUT OF THE DEEP	*Anthem*	J. L. HATTON	3¢
196.	LEAD, KINDLY LIGHT	*Anthem*	H. STATHER	3¢
197.	THE CHILDRENS HOUR	*Part Song S. A. T. B.*	J. W. ARMITAGE	3¢
198.	WHERE NATURE'S GRAND	*Glee S. A. T. B.*	J. BATTYE	3¢
199.	THERE'S GRANDEUR	*Glee A. T. T. B.*	J. BATTYE	3¢
200.	PACK CLOUDS AWAY	*Trio Ladies Voices*	W. H. IBBERSON	2¢
201.	SWEET AND LOW	*Part Song S. A. T. B.*	J. BARNBY	1¢
202.	THE HUNTING SONG	*with Pf. acc. Part Song S. A. T. B.*	MENDELSSOHN	2¢
203.	SWEET ALEEN	*Solo and Chorus S.A.T.B.* arr. by	J. E. IBESON	3¢
204.	GENEVIEVE	*Solo and Chorus S.A.T.B.* arr. by	J. E. IBESON	3¢
205.	MARCH TO THE PROMISED LAND	*Anthem*	FRED. W. PEACE	3¢
206.	TO DAFFODILS	*Trio for S.S.A.*	W. H. IBBERSON	2¢
207.	THE DEFEAT	*Part Song S. A. T. B.*	CHARLES CHAMBERS	3¢
208.	REJOICE IN THE LORD	*Anthem*	E. BANDEY	2¢
209.	THE SOWER WENT FORTH SOWING	*Anthem*	W. H. MAXFIELD	3¢
210.	ANNIE LAURIE	*Part Song S. A. T. B.*	arr. by H. STATHER	2¢
211.	THE WILDERNESS	*Anthem*	SIR JOHN GOSS	2¢
212.	BLOW YE THE TRUMPET IN ZION	*Anthem*	J. J. H. TAYLOR	6¢
213.	O PURE IN HEART	*Part Song S. A. T. B.*	HENRY KNIGHT	1¢
214.	OUR BLEST REDEEMER	*Anthem*	F. COOPE	2¢
215.	RISE MY SOUL. (*Elevation*)	*Hymn*	R. MELLOR	1¢
216.	THE SEA HATH ITS PEARLS	*Part Song S.A.T.B.*	CIRO PINSUTI	2¢
217.	THINKING OF THEE.	*Glee S.A.T.B.*	J. L. HATTON	2¢

67 New Street, HUDDERSFIELD | J. WOOD & SONS LIMITED. | 9 New Ivegate, BRADFORD.

Plate 1 Page from the catalogue of 'Wood's Collection', published in J. L. Hatton, *Out of the Deep* (1908). (Reproduced by kind permission of J. Wood and Sons.)

The choral composers published by Wood did not come only from northern England. Although many were, predictably, organists and choirmasters, none of the lesser-known among them (Barnby is the better-known exception) appears to have been associated with a cathedral. The geographical distribution of their origins and activities is diverse, at least in the case of those for whom such information can be traced. Few of the composers are known to later generations: those that are include Joseph Barnby, Dudley Buck the elder, John Liptrot Hatton, Felix Mendelssohn, Robert Lucas Pearsall (represented by his small-scale glees rather than by his larger, madrigal-style pieces) and Arthur Sullivan, although none of their works was published exclusively by Wood.[33]

Choral Music in the Wood Collection

The spare pages of the Wood choral leaflets, such as that shown as Plate 1, impart a considerable amount of information. They reveal, for example, that some of the printing work for Wood was contracted out to a London branch of C. G. Röder, the foremost Leipzig music-printing firm in the second half of the nineteenth century. The extensive publication lists categorise many of the pieces as glees, anthems and partsongs, but these categories conceal a rich variety of purpose,

---

33. Names of other companies that published works by composers in the Wood list can be found in Balchin (1984). Details of Ibeson's, North's and Battye's activities with the Huddersfield Choral Society are given in Edwards (1986); on Battye, see also Russell (1980), p. 202, and Roy Brook, *The Story of Huddersfield*, London, MacGibbon & Kee, 1968, pp. 274–76; some details concerning Battye and others were communicated in correspondence from Robert Edwards, Archivist to the Huddersfield Choral Society, to whom I am grateful. A small proportion of Wood composers, including William Patten, appears in James D. Brown and Stephen S. Stratton, *British Musical Biography*, Birmingham, 1897, reprinted New York, Da Capo Press, 1971. Various music-related classifications were consulted in trade directories as follows: *White's Clothing District Directory*, 15th edn, Sheffield, W. White, 1894; *Huddersfield and District Postal Directory*, Huddersfield, 1884; *Huddersfield and District Directory*, Huddersfield, 1876; *Huddersfield Directory and Year Book*, Huddersfield, 1867; *Huddersfield and District Postal Directory*, Huddersfield, 1900; *White's Directory of Leeds, Bradford, Huddersfield etc.*, Sheffield, W. White, 1866; *Kelly's Directory of the West Riding of Yorkshire, 1889, 1897, 1901, 1904, 1912*, London, Kelly's Directories Ltd, years preceding each title date. William Henry Ibberson's details come from the 1912 Directory.

style and size. The texts are generally conventional, with no special bias towards Yorkshire origins or purposes. The publications include vivid and complex secular festival display pieces and modest, foursquare partsongs; all appear in the same list, and only close examination of the music can reveal the scope of each piece. The music with sacred texts is diverse, too. It includes canticles, carols, hymns and anthems, the last category encompassing a large quantity and variety of music for churches, chapels and their Sunday schools, much of it intended for anniversary celebrations and festivals. Two titles, each of a piece for mixed choir with organ accompaniment and passages for solo singers, will testify to the esteem in which the named institutions (both Nonconformist chapels) and the music performed there was held:

> THIRD EDITION: *Bless the Lord, O my soul*
> Anthem composed and dedicated to the REV JOHN PEILL and the members of the choir, by FRANK ROEBUCK.
> Organist and Choirmaster of Moldgreen Congregational Church, Huddersfield

> *Prepare ye the way of the Lord*
> Anthem composed for the Centenary Celebration (January 1895) of LOCKWOOD BAPTIST CHAPEL. H[erbert] Stather.

In the first title the proclamation 'Third edition' suggests some degree of enduring popularity beyond the immediate area of the chapel for which the piece was composed, even though, as with almost all this material, no evidence apparently survives to corroborate this. In the second, linked to an establishment near the same town, Huddersfield, the composer introduces a colourful and dramatic piece that nevertheless would have offered little challenge either to the organist or to singers accustomed to a fairly foursquare, hymn-like style. Herbert Stather, an industrious and accomplished composer, though hardly an innovator, seems not to have belonged to the Huddersfield Choral Society circle of associates, nor to have taught music in, or resided in, Huddersfield or any of the other towns in the area. He wrote a considerable amount of music, including songs and a children's opera. His work, consisting chiefly of choral music, was published almost exclusively by Wood, the exceptions being published either by London firms or by J. A. Jones, Horsfall & Bailey and Stather & Kaye, three much smaller concerns in Huddersfield. The obscurity of the last name, combined with its inclusion of the surname Stather, suggests that there was an element of vanity publishing about the venture. Among the more picturesque examples of Stather's secular output in the Wood collection we find the following piece for mixed choir and piano, with passages for solo singers, dating from 1902:

THE BATTLE OF THE BALTIC. Words by Thomas Campbell.
Choral Ballad. Dedicated to the Members of the Huddersfield Co-operative Prize Choir and their esteemed conductor
D. W. Evans Esq.

This dedication suggests that the choir stood high in local esteem, and that this dramatic piece, almost resembling programme music in its colourful effects, was designed as a showpiece for a choir at the pinnacle of its ability. Although such music as this may nowadays be considered to add nothing to the choral repertory and its unfolding history, it was clearly no trifle to those who, in 1902, performed and listened to the piece or to the publishers who marketed it.

Concerning musical style, it is true that certain pieces in the Wood collection possess attributes considered repugnantly sentimental by post-Victorian generations – for example, poignant diminished seventh chords, dying-fall cadences and all the sentimentality implied by the direction 'religioso'. But these traits inform a far smaller proportion of the collection than might be expected, considering the era and the likely purpose of the music. Compositional styles in the collection are in fact much more varied than any stereotype could embrace. They include elements with dramatic, pictorial, ballad, gospel, romantic and ecclesiastical associations. These often run in parallel with various types of miniaturised pastiche, particularly of Handel, the influence of whose oratorios, especially in their use of counterpoint and recitative, is apparent but rarely overwhelming. Classical forms, too, are miniaturised: most frequently encountered in any kind of piece, irrespective of its size or purpose, are ternary form (ABA, with the second A section possibly modified) and rounded binary form (AB, concluding with some brief reference to the A section).

Some further features of the collection are other than might be expected, on the basis of received views of late-nineteenth-century English music, in which its more obvious features and directions are overemphasised. For example, Tonic Sol-fa notation makes its expected appearance – but only in a small minority of works. Composite works such as cantatas are rare. There is nothing in the collection either composed or arranged by Sir Walter Parratt, a native of Huddersfield active in music-making there until at least the 1870s and one of the chief upholders of the ideals of the 'English Musical Renaissance'. The influences of the Oxford Movement, the revival of plainsong and early music (unless Handel is reckoned 'early'), nationalism and folksong, all of which were conspicuous features of much late-nineteenth-century choral music in England, are completely absent. Although this absence is hardly surprising, considering the markets for which the Wood collection was apparently designed, the existence and apparently enduring success of this publishing enterprise (and possibly others like it elsewhere) shows that to divide English choral music of the period into innovative, worthwhile music on one side and ephemeral, trivial dross on the other is far too simplistic an approach.

Out of numerous possible examples from the Wood collection, two (one sacred, one secular) must serve briefly to illustrate particular features of the collection, even if they can give no more than a glimpse of it. Plates 2–4 are taken from an anthem for mixed choir and organ, *The Lord is my Strength*, by William Patten (1804-63), an organist from Fareham, Hampshire, some of whose sacred music was published also in London. *The Lord is my Strength* was published by Wood in 1899. It is in three sections, each cast in ternary form. An intriguing feature of the anthem is the way in which each section appears as an exercise in a particular style. The grandiose first section is clearly modelled on some of the more obvious features of Handel's choral writing. The more graceful second section seems to allude to Mendelssohn – in particular, to such passages as the opening of the trio 'Lift thine eyes' from that composer's most popular oratorio, *Elijah*. The exuberant third section recalls some of Haydn's more triumphant choruses. Despite the eclectic nature of this piece, it comes across as a coherent entity and is well written for all the forces employed. It is easy to see why it was popular.

One of the most engaging secular pieces in the collection is *The Arrow and the Song*, published by Wood in 1912, and illustrated here in Plate 5. This setting of Longfellow's popular text is by Francis William Sykes, whose only other publication, apparently, was a setting of the Nicene Creed published in London about 1882. Written for unaccompanied mixed choir, *The Arrow and the Song* bears favourable comparison with Elgar's early partsongs, while in no way being a mere reflection of their style. This piece would bear repeated hearing and

Plate 2 Page 3 of William Patten, *The Lord is my Strength* (1899), showing part of the first section. (Reproduced by kind permission of J. Wood and Sons.)

Plate 3 Page 7 of William Patten, *The Lord is my Strength* (1899), showing the opening of the second section. (Reproduced by kind permission of J. Wood and Sons.)

Plate 4 Page 9 of William Patten, *The Lord is my Strength* (1899), showing the opening of the third section. (Reproduced by kind permission of J. Wood and Sons.)

Plate 5 Page 4 of Francis William Sykes, *The Arrow and the Song* (1912). (Reproduced by kind permission of J. Wood and Sons.)

would be suitable for concert, festival or recreational use, although no clue is given to the original purpose of its composition. Despite its quality, the music and its composer have passed into oblivion.

The fate of this piece typifies that of the vast majority of those in the Wood collection, which is as diverse in quality as it is in style and purpose. Even though this music cannot and should not be classified among the masterpieces of its era, it would be a mistake to dismiss it as unworthy of recognition. It is arguable that much music of the kinds that feature in the Wood collection eventually dropped out of the repertory only because of changing fashions or social circumstances, rather than on account of a perceived lack of quality. Even if the best of this music is the tip of an iceberg of relative mediocrity, it is important to recognise that the whole iceberg, not just its tip, was the nineteenth-century choral singer's experience. This is a perspective too rarely taken into account, either in assessments of music of the period or in studies concerning the social, economic or cultural history of the most important locations for the development of choral music. Taking account of music-publishing enterprises in these and other provincial locations yields some insights that can produce a more rounded and detailed view. It leads towards a recognition of choral activity beyond that involved solely in the production of major concerts or services, large-scale competitive events or works that were identified later as landmarks in the choral repertory. All these are important factors in arriving at an accurate and balanced perception of nineteenth-century choral activity and of its significance to those who experienced it – as well as to those who look back, at some remove, on its history.

3

The Modernisation of London Concert Life around 1900

Simon McVeigh and Cyril Ehrlich

Historians have recently been much exercised with debate about changing patterns of consumption and the rise of consumerism. The pioneering work of J. H. Plumb, Neil McKendrick and John Brewer placed the focus firmly on Georgian Britain.[1] Subsequent research has explored the expansion and transformation of consumer culture in the later nineteenth century: the topics covered include shopping, the rise of a 'mass market' and the changing social role of goods and leisure, the relationship of the private and public spheres (as well as of suburbs and the centre) and the place of women in urban society.[2]

---

1. *The Birth of a Consumer Society: The Commercialization of Eighteenth-Century England*, ed. Neil McKendrick, John Brewer and J.H. Plumb, Bloomington, Indiana University Press, 1982. See also *Consumption and the World of Goods*, ed. John Brewer and Roy Porter, London, Routledge, 1993. On some implications for music, see Simon McVeigh, *Concert Life in London from Mozart to Haydn*, Cambridge, Cambridge University Press, 1993.

2. *Inter alia*, see: Peter Bailey, *Leisure and Class in Victorian England: Rational Recreation and the Contest for Control, 1830–1885*, London, Routledge and Kegan Paul, 1978; the same author's *Popular Culture and Performance in the Victorian City*, Cambridge, Cambridge University Press, 1998; *Leisure in Britain, 1780–1939*, ed. John K. Walton and James Walvin, Manchester, Manchester University Press, 1983; (on Bristol) Helen Meller, *Leisure and the Changing City, 1870–1914*, London, Routledge and Kegan Paul, 1976; Alison Adburgham, *Shops and Shopping, 1800–1914*, second edition, London, Barrie and Jenkins, 1989; Mary Douglas and Baron Isherwood, *The World of Goods*, New York, Basic Books, 1979; Karl Beckson, *London in the 1890s: A Cultural History*, New York, Norton, 1992; *The Victorian City: Images and Realities*, ed. H. J. Dyos and Michael Wolff, London, Routledge and Kegan Paul, 1973; H. J. Dyos, *Exploring the Urban Past: Essays in Urban History*, Cambridge, Cambridge University Press, 1982; the same author's *The Victorian City: A Reader in British Urban History, 1820–1914*, London, Longman, 1993; Erika Diane Rap-

Yet despite music's obvious role in the commercialisation of leisure (and of luxury goods for a widening market), it has barely figured in mainstream discussion.[3] The numerous cultural histories of London during the 1890s make hardly any mention of music or musical life, except in so far as Wagnerism inspired the decadent movement.[4] Even Erika Rappaport's *Shopping for Pleasure: Women in the Making of London's West End*, an exhaustive recent view of London's urban culture around 1900, makes only scant reference to concert life as opposed to the theatre.[5]

This omission is all the stranger, given the absolutely central role that music – live music, of course – played in the daily life of the city. This role is abundantly evident from the prominence and extent of its coverage throughout the contemporary literature, especially in newspapers and periodicals. For not only did the press expand prodigiously during the 1890s in terms of the number of titles: its attention to music also increased beyond recognition. The *Daily Telegraph*, for example, always included a dozen or more concert advertisements on its front page during the season (and many more for sheet music), while the *Standard* reviewed several concerts every day. Even suburban newspapers such as the *Brixton Free Press* reviewed concerts both central and local. Indeed it is scarcely possible to pick up a publication of the 1890s that does not comment on London's musical life: not mere gossip (though this exists, too) but serious and perceptive analysis of musical trends. The weekly periodicals – the *Athenaeum*, the *Spectator* and the *Saturday Review* – continued to give detailed coverage, but so, too, did family and women's magazines. To take one example, while *The Lady* naturally reported society events (including

---

paport, *Shopping for Pleasure: Women in the Making of London's West End*, Princeton, New Jersey, Princeton University Press, 2000; *Metropolis, 1890–1940*, ed. Anthony Sutcliffe, London, Mansell, 1984; and James Winter, *London's Teeming Streets, 1830–1914*, London, Routledge, 1993.

3. John Brewer's study of the eighteenth-century amateur musician John Marsh provides a notable exception (*The Pleasures of the Imagination: English Culture in the Eighteenth Century*, London, Harper Collins, 1997, Chapter 14).

4. For example, Beckson (1992). This situation contrasts markedly with the extensive literature on the theatre and on the music hall. On the latter see especially *Music Hall: The Business of Pleasure*, ed. Peter Bailey, Milton Keynes, Open University Press, 1986, and Dagmar Höher Kift, *The Victorian Music Hall: Culture, Class, and Conflict*, Cambridge, Cambridge University Press, 1996.

5. See footnote 2.

charitable concerts organised by philanthropic ladies) and recitals by
women teachers and 'debutantes', it also included serious coverage of
chamber concerts, early music or classical recitals, and major orchestral concerts (with detailed comparisons of pianists, of course, but
also with evaluation of the respective interpretations of Henry Wood
and Hans Richter, or of Artur Nikisch and Landon Ronald).

This extensive coverage reflects both the importance and the ubiq-
uity of music in London's daily life, something that the usual stand-by
of music historians – a cursory look at the *Musical Times*, itself limited
and partial – cannot hope to capture. Vicariously through the printed
word, knowledge of London's concerts reached vast numbers who
would seldom attend a concert hall in person. At the same time, the
populace shared in this culture through the piano music and ballads it
bought for home music-making, which formed a crucial link between
the public concert hall and the prevailing domestic piano culture.

Music's role in the frenetic social whirl, in addition to its commercial potential, is encapsulated in Arnold Bennett's fantastic novel *The
City of Pleasure* (1907), a fable in which 'the mass leisure industry had
remade urban life as an amusement park'.[6] Seventy thousand people
an hour are attracted to the mythical city by the one-shilling admission, extravagantly 'hyped' newspaper advertising and convenient
public transport in the form of tube and train (themes to which we
shall return). Attractions include 'the theatre, the variety theatre, the
concert hall, the circus, the panorama, the lecture hall, the menagerie,
the art-gallery, the story-tellers' hall, the dancing rooms, restaurants,
cafés and bars'. To inaugurate this 'new era of amusement enterprise',
a grandiose concert for fifty thousand people is directed by the impresario of the whole venture, Charles Carpentaria (a clear reference to
the name 'Wood'), a dashing and temperamental conductor whose
extravagant gestures and frenzied self-expression play directly upon
the emotions of the audience, as well as on their wallets: 'By turns he
whipped, tortured, encouraged, liberated, imprisoned, mopped up,
measured, governed, diverted, pushed over, pulled back, and turned
inside out his band [...] It was colossal.' Carpentaria conducts nothing but national hymns, his own compositions, and 'as a superlative
concession, Wagner and Beethoven'.[7]

6. Rappaport (2000), p. 147.
7. Arnold Bennett, *The City of Pleasure: A Fantasia on Modern Themes*, London,
   Chatto & Windus, 1907, pp. 8, 34–38.

Such widespread attention to music reflected the entertainment and cultural demands of an ever more populous capital city (whose inhabitants numbered some six and a half million in 1901). Londoners were enjoying more leisure time in the expansionist period of stability that followed the 1851 Great Exhibition, and middle-class recreation became ever more visible (already by the 1860s the younger generation had learned the 'habit of enjoyment', according to one journalist).[8] In addition, the metropolis increasingly became a magnet for provincial visitors coming up to town for a week of shopping and sightseeing as well as for foreign tourists: concerts were among the many attractions it offered.

Throughout retailing and entertainment, changes in style and business methods began to transform consumer culture. Economies of scale – chains of shops, theatres and, most notably, music halls – brought new efficiencies to businesses, their profitability enhanced by hard-sell techniques of advertising and visual display. Through an astute mix of opulence and economy, the new breed of entrepreneur brought luxury goods within the reach of a large and anonymous middle-class public. Nowhere is the change more clearly seen than in the development of the department store in London's West End, following the example of the Bon Marché in Paris. The original 'universal provider' Whiteley in Bayswater was succeeded by Harrods in Knightsbridge and by a cluster of stores around Oxford Circus, just along from the traditional 'carriage trade' of Bond Street. The most enticing and alluring of all, Selfridges, opened with American razzmatazz and marketing techniques in 1909.[9] These 'cathedrals of consumption' were highly proficient business enterprises, projecting a modern, exciting image through well-developed techniques of promotion and marketing; women, in particular, were lured to them by luxurious displays and by consumer comforts and attractions. Although centred on ladies' fashions and furnishings, these department

---

8. *Saturday Review* (1864), quoted in Bailey (1978), pp. 58–59. See also the related article reprinted as Chapter 1 of Bailey (1998).

9. On British department stores see *Cathedrals of Consumption: The European Department Store, 1850–1939*, ed. Geoffrey Crossick and Serge Jaumain, Aldershot, Ashgate, 1999, Bill Lancaster, *The Department Store: A Social History*, London, Leicester University Press, 1995, and Rappaport (2000). Histories of individual stores include those of Lewis of Liverpool (Asa Briggs), Harrods (Tim Dale) and Selfridges (Gordon Honeycombe).

stores sold goods across the entire range, with clearly marked prices and discreet service encouraging customers to linger and browse. They thus brought traditional luxuries and concepts of leisure to a new public, moulding tastes and preferences that were cumulatively reinforced by ladies' magazines.

The new consumerism was a highly public, urban culture that focused attention and prestige on central London, opening up the West End in a new social configuration: a 'free trade in pleasure'.[10] The store was conceived as a complete leisure centre, a place of recreation and amusement – a show in itself that was enhanced by restaurants and reading rooms. Newly independent suburban middle-class women were enabled by improved transport to visit the West End for shopping and lunch, perhaps taking in a visit to a ladies' club, an art gallery, a lecture or a theatre matinée or (although this has gone unnoticed by most historians) a concert.[11]

The years around 1900 saw the most energetic expansion of nearby theatreland, with newly luxurious theatres and wide roads across central London. A knowledge of the current season was an expected part of everyday experience and conversation. The area acquired 'a special aura as the center of fashionable and refined entertainment', theatre managers adding restaurants and matinées specifically in order to encourage middle-class perceptions of a 'respectable and fashionable social ritual'.[12] During the 1890s large and well-appointed music halls – the Alhambra and the Empire in Leicester Square – projected themselves as respectable places for the suburban bourgeois family. Prominent in the next decade, the Coliseum and Palladium were more opulent, even pretentious. With a capitalisation in 1900 of some £2 million, the Moss Empires aimed deliberately to satisfy 'a commercial instinct for the supply of wholesome amusement for the people. Its work, without any false veneer, is entirely commercial. Its first duty [...] is to conduct its business according to the rules of good citizenship; and its second duty [...] is to earn a satisfactory dividend for its shareholders.'[13] Classical music played its part in this transformation

10. See Rappaport (2000), p. 105.
11. Improvements in train, underground, tram and omnibus transport were particularly marked after the mid-1880s. Before this date transport links were by no means as convenient or comfortable as we might imagine.
12. Rappaport (2000), pp. 180–81.
13. Quoted in Bailey (1978), p. 168. See also Cyril Ehrlich and Brian Walker, 'Enterprise and Entertainment: The Economic and Social Background', in *Frank*

of the music hall, the pianist Mark Hambourg following Shake-spearean actors with 'no loss of prestige' to himself.[14]

While it would be a mistake to associate the efflorescence of London's concert life purely with women's lifestyles – audiences at the early Promenade concerts, for example, were predominantly male[15] – it should come as no surprise that music maintained a close relationship with West End shopping. The major concert halls and piano show-rooms were situated near the department stores in the heart of the West End. The stores themselves naturally sold pianos and all the latest player-pianos,[16] while their luxurious piano showrooms (most famously at Harrods) served occasionally as concert venues. All stores sold theatre and concert tickets as a matter of course. Increasingly, too, stores began to offer their own musical entertainments, not only to entice customers directly but also, more subtly, to ally consumerism with lifestyle, offering cultural education to those needing direction. (It was assumed without question that the 'middle-class public', or at least that part of it with money to spend, would – or should – emulate tra-ditional preferences for luxury goods and luxury leisure.) Selfridges put on music as part of the show, creating a classy atmosphere with string quartets playing Mendelssohn and Schubert hidden behind palms.[17]

Matcham: Theatre Architect, ed. Brian Walker, Belfast, Blackstaff, 1980, pp. 21–25.

14. Percy Scholes, *The Mirror of Music, 1844–1944*, London, Novello and Oxford University Press, 1947, p. 508.

15. Robert Elkin, *Queen's Hall, 1893–1941*, London, Rider, 1944, p. 28. For an example of an avid lady concertgoer, daughter of a prominent London surgeon see the references to the diary of Jeanette Marshall in Zuzanna Shonfield, *The Precariously Privileged: A Professional Family in Victorian London*, Oxford, Oxford University Press, 1987. In 1888–89 the number of concerts that Mar-shall attended each year shrank to twenty, testifying to a voracious appetite ear-lier. In 1885 she established a systematic record of critical assessments – of Berlioz, Brahms, Grieg, and so on – asserting after a concert of 1886: 'I am a Wagnerian to the backbone' (p. 161).

16. See for example Whiteley's magazine, and store catalogues published in facsim-ile by Alison Adburgham. On pianolas see Cyril Ehrlich, *The Piano: A History*, rev. edn, Oxford, Clarendon Press, 1990.

17. Gordon Honeycombe, *Selfridges: Seventy-five Years*, London, Park Lane Press, 1984. No British store matched the Bon Marché in Paris, where concerts by the store's own staff played an integral role that not only reflected a paternalistic attitude towards staff education and amusement but also attracted customers (Michael Miller, *The Bon Marché: Bourgeois Culture and the Department Store, 1869–1920*, Princeton, Princeton University Press, 1981).

The store's brash opening in March 1909 inspired the paranoid Harrods to retaliate by celebrating its Jubilee in the same week with daily concerts: the London Symphony Orchestra conducted by Landon Ronald accompanying Hambourg and other eminent soloists. Subsequently, Selfridges, too, put on more formal concerts in an attempt to match the cultured tone. By 1910 music was simply central to any kind of event. Commentators repeatedly noted that music was everywhere, that no restaurant could be without it.

How, then, did the more formal concert structures react to these consumer opportunities (and to the threats provided by competition)? Certainly, it was a crucial period of change and modernisation, revolving around the opening of Queen's Hall late in 1893.[18] At every level there were challenges to the existing order, affecting business organisation, audience structures and cultural expectations, labour practices and the music profession.

In broad terms, exclusive subscription systems of audience manipulation and management by direct personal arrangement were giving way to modern, impersonal business organisation. Budgeting was now based on filling larger halls with a heterosocial audience and on hard-nosed assessment of the drawing power of international stars. Impresarios sought not only to enlarge and widen their audiences but also to attract them ever more vigorously by means of assertive advertising and marketing ploys and through manipulation of the press. The facilities and, especially, the image of new halls played a crucial part in catering both for the audience's physical comfort and for its sense of cultural well-being. The growing market required and encouraged increasing specialisation, with a separation of venues for orchestral and chamber music and the identification of discrete audiences differing in both size and taste. Impresarios came to expect modern business dealings not only with hall managers and staff but also with musicians, who were now involved in an international network managed by powerful agents, including piano manufacturers. Agents with worldwide connections not only facilitated practical arrangements for their artists but (and this is the crucial point) also began to articulate the market by setting fees in a graduated scale reflecting drawing power, thereby establishing a worldwide hierarchy

18. This is at the heart of the authors' current project (with Leanne Langley): 'The Transformation of London Concert Life, 1880–1914'.

of solo artists. The new business tone was not compatible with the traditional, sometimes amateurish ways exemplified by personal letters to soloists a few weeks in advance. The Philharmonic Society, which in 1840 could invite Liszt only days before a concert, needed, half a century later, to begin negotiating with Vasily Safonoff's agent over two years before he eventually came to conduct in 1911.[19] At the same time, concerts became more closely intertwined with related business interests than ever before – notably with the sheet music market and with the still more powerful and pervasive world of piano manufacturing.

The most immediately striking aspect of London's concert life around 1900 is the proliferation of concerts: a sudden efflorescence on a scale previously unimagined (see Table 2). This continued without disruption until 1914. Opportunities for hearing music, and good-quality music at that, were expanding dramatically through extensions of the season, new timings during the week and the opening of new venues. The spring season, still restricted at the beginning of Victoria's reign to the few months running from February to June, had by the end of the century already expanded to encompass the period October–July; in 1895 the Queen's Hall Promenade Concerts, crucially, filled even the summer gap. Presumably, this phenomenon was linked to the growth of a democratic musical public resident in London all year round, which contrasted with the visiting gentry who had supported the traditional shorter season. The weekly diary began to fill up with ever more matinées, which were available, of course, only to men of leisure and to women. Meanwhile, Saturday afternoons became a popular time for major concerts, as London businesses and offices (though not shops) began to close at 1 or 2 p.m. on Saturdays.[20] Pioneered by the Crystal Palace, this concert schedule, unknown before the mid nineteenth century, was shared by the

19. Cyril Ehrlich, *First Philharmonic: A History of the Royal Philharmonic Society*, Oxford, Clarendon Press, 1995, p. 65; Royal Philharmonic Society Papers, British Library (henceforth abbreviated as RPSP), Loan 48.13/36.
20. Wilfred B. Whitaker, *Victorian and Edwardian Shopworkers: The Struggle to Obtain Better Conditions and a Half-holiday*, Totowa, New Jersey, Rowman and Littlefield, 1973, pp. 53–58. On British pioneering of shorter working hours see Gary Cross, *A Quest for Time: The Reduction of Work in Britain and France, 1840–1940*, Berkeley, University of California Press, 1989, and the same author's *Time and Money: The Making of Consumer Culture*, London, Routledge, 1993.

Saturday Popular Concerts at St James's Hall and eventually also by
the Queen's Hall symphony concert series.

Table 2: Three London seasons reported in *The Musical Directory*

---

(1) Series

QH = Queen's Hall
RAH = Royal Albert Hall
SJH = St James's Hall
dir = directed (i.e. promoted) by
cond = conducted by
The series have been reordered and their details lightly edited. The number
of concerts is given in parentheses.

1884–85 Season
Philharmonic Society, SJH (6: Feb to May)
Richter Concerts (Wagner etc.) (2: Oct to Nov; 9: Apr to Jun)
Crystal Palace Classical Orchestral Concerts (Sat: Oct to Apr)

Sacred Harmonic Society (6 oratorios: Nov to Mar)
Royal Albert Hall Choral Society (10 oratorios and *Parsifal*: Nov to Apr)
Bach Choir (2: including Bach's B Minor Mass)
Henry Leslie's Choir (2: madrigals, etc.)

Popular Concerts [SJH], dir Chappell [chamber music] (Mon, Sat: Oct to
Mar)
Hallé's Chamber Concerts (May to June)
Musical Artists' Society (4: new music)

London Ballad Concerts, SJH (9: Dec to Mar)
Covent Garden Promenade Concerts (Oct to Nov 1884; Aug to Sept 1885)
Bow and Bromley Institute (34 organ recitals, 4 oratorios)

Royal Academy of Music, Student Chamber and Orchestral Concerts (Oct
to Jul)

1894–95 Season
Philharmonic Society, QH (7: Mar to Jun)
Richter Concerts, SJH (4: May to Jun)
Crystal Palace Classical Concerts (Sat: Oct to Apr)
London Symphony Concerts, QH, dir Mayer, cond Henschel (9: Nov to
Mar)
Wagner Concerts, QH (3: Nov to Dec; 4: Apr to Jul)
Nikisch's Orchestral Concerts, QH (4: June)

Royal Choral Society, RAH (10 oratorios: Nov to May)
Bach Choir, QH (3 Bach concerts: Apr)
Queen's Hall Choral Society, QH, dir Newman (5 oratorios, etc.)

Popular Concerts [SJH], dir Chappell [chamber music] (Mon, Sat: Oct to Apr)
Wolff Musical Union, dir Vert (1: Nov)
Concerts of British Chamber Music, QH (4: Nov to Dec)
Nicholl, Webbe, Brousil's Subscription [Chamber] Concerts, QH (4: Nov to Feb)
Musical Artists' Society (5: Mar to Jul)
Sarasate Recitals, SJH (4: June)
Hann's Chamber Concerts, Brixton Hall (3)
Burmester's Violin Recitals, SJH (3 recitals, 1 orch: May)
London Ballad Concerts, QH, dir Boosey (11: Nov to Mar)
St James's Hall Ballad Concerts, dir Boosey (13: Nov to Mar)
Bow and Bromley Institute, organ recitals, oratorios (Oct to May)

Promenade Concerts, dir Newman, cond Wood (Aug to Oct)

1904–5 Season
Philharmonic Society (6: Mar to Jun)
Queen's Hall Symphony Concerts, cond Wood (11)
Queen's Hall Sunday Concerts, Queen's Hall Orchestra and LSO (Oct to Jun)
Saturday Orchestral Concerts, SJH (Oct to Feb)
Sunday Evening Orchestral Concerts, SJH (Oct to Feb)
Sunday Evening Orchestral Concerts, Exeter Hall (Feb to Sept)

Royal Choral Society, RAH (7 oratorios: Nov to Apr)
London Choral Society, QH (6 oratorios: Oct to May)
Handel Society, QH (1)
Bach Choir, QH (1)

South Place Ethical Society [Chamber Concerts] (Oct to Apr)
Richard Temple's Recitals, Steinway Hall (10: Oct to Jun)
Broadwood [Chamber] Concerts, Aeolian Hall (10)
Leighton House Chamber Concerts (5)
Monday Subscription [Chamber] Concerts, Aeolian Hall (Jan to Apr)
Joachim Quartet Concerts, Bechstein Hall (5: May)
Wessely String Quartet, Bechstein Hall (4: Oct to Mar)
London [Piano] Trio, Aeolian Hall (3)
Ingleton Trio Chamber Music Concerts, Broadwood's (3: Mar to May)
Charles Jacoby's Chamber Concerts, Hampstead (3)
Barns–Phillips Chamber Concerts, Bechstein Hall (4)
Mozart [Chamber Music] Society, Portman Rooms (9)

London Ballad Concerts, QH (8)

Royal Academy of Music, Chamber and Orchestral Concerts
Royal College of Music, Chamber and Orchestral Concerts
Guildhall School of Music, Chamber and Orchestral Concerts
Popular Concerts for Children and Young Students, Steinway Hall

Queen's Hall Promenade Concerts (Aug to Oct)

---

(2) Miscellaneous Concerts, Soirées, Matinées, Recitals (Oct to Aug)

	1884–85	*1894–95*	*1904–5*
St James's Hall	24	71	21
Steinway Hall	73	102	103
Princes Hall	51	30	–
Royal Albert Hall	8	3	5
Queen's Hall	–	153	72
Salle Erard	–	22	43
Bechstein Hall [Wigmore]	–	–	177
Aeolian Hall	–	–	107
St George's Hall	–	–	24
Other West End halls	31	37	39
Student	8	15	2
Crystal Palace, Westminster Abbey	5	1	4
Suburban	38	16	6
Total	238	450	603

---

(3) Concerts by amateur choral and orchestral societies (including suburbs)

1884–85	*1894–95*	*1904–5*
82	128	80

But the most potentially fertile area for expansion remained controversial. In England, unlike on the continent, Sunday observance
laws precluded public entertainment, and thus employment for the
concert musician, on the very day when a vast public was eager for
amusement. Sabbatarians were opposed not only to secular pleasures
but also to Sunday trading and travel, while social Sabbatarians

focused on labour issues relating to working on Sundays.[21] Ranged against these powerful forces were such organisations as the National Sunday League (1855), its 'Sunday evenings for the people' (1866) promoting 'intellectual and elevating recreation' with mixed popular concerts at suburban theatres and music halls ('The Council of the National Sunday League conscientiously and religiously believe in brightening the lives of the People on Sunday'). As the debate heated up – in 1896 national galleries and museums were allowed for the first time to open on Sunday afternoons – the issue of concerts came to the fore. No doubt mindful of Paris, where the popular concerts of Colonne and Lamoureux took place on Sunday afternoons, Robert Newman at Queen's Hall tackled the issue head on. He began with 'low-key' programmes (light orchestral concerts and oratorios) before elevating Sunday afternoon concerts to a central role in his calendar, where they became so much part of the norm as to include symphony concerts similar to those of the more prestigious Saturday series.[22] The large and comfortable London Palladium was likewise the setting for Sunday concerts in the 1910s (on the one free day of its normal music-hall programme). These were prestigious events at which Thomas Beecham was among the conductors and Fritz Kreisler played the Elgar Violin Concerto with the LSO.

The new concert halls added to the profusion, giving Londoners a choice between simultaneous concerts of the highest class. Thus on the afternoon of Saturday 25 February 1899 the Queen's Hall Orchestra performed Brahms's Third Symphony and Chopin's Second Piano Concerto with Vladimir de Pachmann; at the Crystal Palace Ernst von Dohnányi was the star attraction in Liszt's E flat Piano Concerto, while the partnering symphony was Beethoven's Eighth; Joseph Joachim led in Mozart's 'Dissonance' Quartet and Beethoven's E flat Piano Trio at the Popular Concert at St James's Hall; and a piano recital was given by A. Moscarella at Steinway Hall. Among other possible attractions were Albert Chevalier's daily afternoon show at the small Queen's Hall, the Moore and Burgess Minstrels at St James's lower hall and 'sacred and appropriate music' at Madame Tussaud's throughout Lent.[23] Such a confluence of events,

21. John Wigley, *The Rise and Fall of the Victorian Sunday*, Manchester, Manchester University Press, 1980.
22. There were similar developments in some provincial towns, notably Liverpool.
23. *Daily Telegraph* (25 February 1899), *Musical Directory*.

inconceivable fifty years earlier, was to increase still further in the first decade of the new century.

This rampant profusion was certainly not ideologically motivated, which contrasted, once again, with the situation in France, where the state actively encouraged, via financial subvention, concerts aimed at a broader public.[24] Essentially, the profusion was supply-driven: led by individual musicians, entrepreneurs or agents, music publishers and piano manufacturers. In terms of musicians alone, there was simply a flood: tuition and instruments were available and inexpensive as never before, and teachers no longer kept trade secrets to themselves (in contrast to the old guild system). The number of potential concert performers had increased beyond measure, unconstrained by any statutory regulations or need for qualifications. In the completely open British market anyone could promote any number of concerts – a situation that applied equally and in fact especially to foreigners (at least, until the outbreak of war, which brought a reaction against German musicians). There was indeed a 'free trade' in music. Moreover, many more women were involved than hitherto, even as violinists, since the concert platform had come to be regarded as almost respectable. The vast increase of available personnel led to a glut of impermanent symphony orchestras, the orchestral pool only partially being mopped up by music-hall orchestras and the like.[25] All this amounted to a colossal excess of supply over demand – in terms of the number of musicians and, as a direct consequence, of concerts.

This supply-driven profusion was soon perceived as absurd: for where were the audiences? True, there had been occasional complaints against excessive and poor concerts at least as early as the 1820s: talk of the papering of halls was commonplace in the 1830s and 1840s.[26] But with the explosion around 1900, this became of structural, continuous concern. By 1909 the concert reviewer for *The Lady* was

---

24. In Britain philanthropists (mainly women) adopted something of this role, but on a much smaller scale.
25. See Cyril Ehrlich, *The Music Profession in Britain since the Eighteenth Century: A Social History*, Oxford, Clarendon Press, 1985.
26. Simon McVeigh, 'The Benefit Concert in Nineteenth-century London: From "Tax on the Nobility" to "Monstrous Nuisance"', in *Nineteenth-century British Music Studies*, Vol. 1, ed. Bennett Zon, Aldershot, Ashgate, 1999, pp. 242–66, at p. 248. See also William Weber, *Music and the Middle Class: The Social Structure of Concert Life in London, Paris and Vienna*, London, Croom Helm, 1975, pp. 42–43.

complaining of the 'torrent of recitals', estimated (probably with exaggeration) to number one thousand in the previous year at the major recital halls alone, yet only ten per cent attracting a large enough paying audience to make the enterprise worthwhile.[27] The *Musical Times* even made a fanciful proposal for the central co-ordination of recitals at a single hall.[28] As for the size of the potential audience, Robert Newman is reported as saying that London concerts could never rely consistently on a public of more than 10,000 – and this was presumably distributed among numerous specialist tastes and factions.[29]

Why so many concerts? In many cases, making money directly from ticket sales was not the only, or even a primary, objective. Some musicians put on concerts in the 'benefit' tradition to secure their reputation as concert artists and to establish their credentials, while others sought to attract pupils or to display their achievements. By the late 1890s the exhaustive exploitation of a market by repeated celebrity appearances (in the manner of Paganini in the 1830s) was the exception, since in London only a few stars of the stature of Paderewski could be guaranteed to fill a large hall at practically any price. But a concert could sell other things. Concert life reflected the structure of the music industry as a whole, and in the prevailing piano and vocal culture many concerts existed primarily to sell sheet music or pianos. The relationship with publishing was most clearly articulated by the firm of Boosey, whose annual series of ballad concerts (inaugurated in 1867) served as explicit advertisements for its list of parlour songs. Originally, singers were paid royalties on the songs they introduced, but in later years the company maintained its own stable of artists, paying them to sing from the catalogue and advertising widely where each song was to be performed next.[30]

---

27. *The Lady*, 7 January 1909.
28. Scholes (1947), p. 204.
29. William Boosey, *Fifty Years of Music*, London, Ernest Benn, 1931, p. 66.
30. Ibid., pp. 26–27 (only the most prestigious singers retained the royalty privilege). See the daily deluge of advertisements on the front page of the *Daily Telegraph*. This is of course the opposite of the modern system, in which, instead of publishers paying performers in order to sell sheet music, performers now pay publishers royalties based on performing right for the privilege of using their intellectual property (Cyril Ehrlich, *Harmonious Alliance: A History of the Performing Right Society*, Oxford, Oxford University Press, 1989). William Boosey, who moved to Chappell in 1894, was at first a vociferous opponent of the change (see Chapter 6, note 21).

Towards the end of the nineteenth century the emphasis began to shift away from the sale of sheet music towards the marketing of pianos, a more thrusting and aggressive enterprise altogether: more international and more closely integrated into the worldwide concert structure. It is impossible to overestimate the scale and significance of the prevailing 'piano culture' before the era of recording. Increasingly strident 'American' methods of conducting these large international businesses impacted directly on concert life. Makers ever more forcefully demanded that their instruments be used and attempted to tie their 'own' pianists to the exclusive use of the firm's pianos (which were advertised prominently in concert announcements, in programmes and often on the side of the instrument itself). The central role of makers is epitomised by their decision to build their own halls next to their piano showrooms, as in the comparatively modest Steinway Hall (400 seats, 1878) followed by the much more significant Bechstein Hall (550 seats, 1901: renamed the Wigmore Hall in 1917) and the Aeolian Hall in 1904 (500 seats, promoting the up-to-the-minute technology of the Orchestrelle company's pianola). In these, of course, only the firm's own instruments could be used. The case of Chappell reflects interestingly on these varied connections. A publisher with an extensive light music catalogue, Chappell promoted ballad concerts at its own St James's Hall but (unlike Boosey) was also a prominent piano manufacturer. This branch of activity must surely have encouraged the firm to take over the Queen's Hall lease in 1902. Not only did Chappell thereby rid itself of the ailing St James's Hall, but it also acquired a means to place its English piano centre-stage at London's premier concert venue. The same firms of piano manufacturers played a leading role in the wider management of concert life, acting both as promoters in their own right and as agents for their own artists (often smoothing the way with impresarios by offering generous subventions for half or even the entire fee).

The example of the Philharmonic Society will serve to illuminate a number of these themes, for it illustrates the collision of an old-fashioned institution of the old order – reliant on appeals to tradition and goodwill – with many of the new imperatives. In the first place, the Society experienced the continuous and apparently intrinsic stress of making the books balance in the face of rising costs and limited, volatile income (see Table 3). With its irreducible labour costs, the very large orchestra that audiences came to expect (rising from sixty-six members in 1868 to ninety-eight by 1908) absorbed over half the income from subscriptions and tickets. Soloists, on the other hand, were pressed to appear for nothing or for nominal fees, out of respect for tradition or in the hope of future engagements: this applied not only to inexperienced debutants but even to a condescending Paderewski, who offered his services 'as is usually done by great artists on their first appearance'.[31] Andrew Black, a celebrated oratorio baritone, insisted on a typical ruse in order to preserve both his dignity and his fee-status: handed a cheque for twenty guineas, he immediately returned another for half that amount.[32] As mentioned above, piano-manufacturers often subsidised artists from their own stable. Steinway regularly supported the young English pianist Leonard Borwick and the Russian star Vasily Sapellnikov: in 1892 the firm contributed twenty guineas to the latter's fifty-guinea fee and by 1909 was offering to pay the whole fee.[33] The venerable firm of Broadwood was one of the Philharmonic Society's most loyal guarantors, making only the traditionally modest demands for publicity in newspapers and programmes. Some newcomers were more aggressive, the piano-manufacturer Ibach demanding not only more prominence for its own name but also gold medals for both Emil Sauer and Jan Kubelík.[34]

Yet certain features of Philharmonic policy remained unchanged. There was little attempt either to vary the seven-concert season (although in 1895 programmes were pruned back to a more manageable format) or to maximise the benefits of rehearsal by repeating programmes elsewhere.[35] Even under the progressive influence of Francesco Berger, the Society's secretary from 1884 to 1911, there were only muted approaches towards more modern marketing methods. Although the Philharmonic consented to sell single tickets – the cheapest a mere shilling, as in the case of Promenade tickets (see Table 4) – it rarely succeeded in filling a two-thousand-seat hall. The rare, but significant, exceptions were megastar appearances. During the 1890s and into the 1900s the balance-sheet was rescued by expensive

---

31. Letter from Mayer, 15 December 1890, in RPSP, Loan 48.13/23.
32. Letter from Vert, 23 November 1899, in RPSP, Loan 48.13/34.
33. Letters of 16 May 1892 and 11 June 1909, in RPSP, Loan 48.13/33. Further examples in Ehrlich (1995), pp. 172–73.
34. Ehrlich (1995), p. 172.
35. In 1897 a three-concert autumn series was attempted, an experiment resumed in 1908.

Table 3: Philharmonic Society. Selected Accounts
Sources: British Library, Loan 48.9/7 and 48.9/14

	1868	1888	1908
Income (£ in round figures)			
Members etc.	232	315	427
Subscribers	1,014	1,226	804
Single tickets/programmes	369	934	690
Investment	56	–	–
Sale of stocks	377	–	–
Advertising in programmes	–	–	153
Entrance fees	–	–	247
Guarantors	–	–	223
Total	2,048	2,475	2,544
Expenditure			
Orchestra	912	986	1192
Singers and chorus	213	35	22
Instrumental soloists	74	193	98
Conductors/composers	100	217	169
Extra concert	115	–	–
Other personnel	121	52	92
Rooms	130	277	270
Advertisements	115	344	288
Commissions	–	55	49
Printing and miscellaneous	212	299	333
Total	1,992	2,458	2,513
Profit	56*	17	31§

* Depended on sale of £377 capital.
§ Depended on £223 guarantees and £247 entrance fees (Fellows, etc.).

stars, their fees propelled into a different league by the earning power of international tours – Paderewski and Patti of course, and the violinist Kubelík; and, for the first time, a conductor in the shape of Artur Nikisch and a composer in that of Richard Strauss – developments that showed a new awareness of the market value of celebrities in these two areas. These single appearances could be highly profitable to the Society, fully justifying the high fees and cross-subsidising the entire season (see Table 5). Agents would often remind the Philharmonic of business realities, Hugo Görlitz gently insisting that Kubelík be billed as a star above the other musicians rather than take his place in alphabetical order (the Society, while assuring themselves that Kubelík was 'modest and a gentleman', found a compromise solution).[36] Agents' articulation of the market by fee-structures is often directly expressed in terms of financial drawing power: thus in 1903 Bechstein strenuously recommended Ferruccio Busoni and Vladimir de Pachmann, whose 'drawing power at the booking offices [is] in excess of their fees' (the firm sweetened the eighty-guinea joint fee with a contribution of its own).[37] Specific successes at home or abroad were called to testify. Thus Daniel Mayer argued in 1890 that Bernhard Stavenhagen was no mere unknown but an established favourite who 'drew so well' at the Popular Concerts the preceding season that he could not be expected to appear for under thirty guineas.[38] In 1905 Mayer pressed the claims of a pianist fresh from triumphs in South Africa: 'As the box-office at Queen's Hall will prove to you, after Paderewski, Mark Hambourg draws more money into the house than any other pianist.' This claim was followed by a tart throw-away line: 'Surely that ought to be a consideration to your directors at a time when concerts are not too well paying.'[39]

Care was taken to limit appearances, since no performer could sustain drawing power within London indefinitely. Exclusive clauses therefore often formed an important part of negotiations and contracts. One of the new violin stars, Mischa Elman, contracted to appear on 5 April 1906, bound himself not to play at any orchestral concert in London after 1 December 1905 nor to give a recital in the fortnight before the concert.[40] Such restrictive practices, similar to those that were more fully developed within the music-hall business, gave musicians power in their negotiation of contracts.[41] Thus in

---

36. Letter of 10 January 1903, in RPSP, Loan 48.13/13.
37. Ehrlich (1995), p. 172.
38. Letter of 11 November 1890, in RPSP, Loan 48.13/23.
39. Letter of 13 September 1905, in RPSP, Loan 48.13/23.
40. Letter from Mayer, 20 October 1905, in RPSP, Loan 48.13/23.
41. Bailey (1978), Chapter 4. The modernisation of the music hall – its thoroughgoing commercialisation and acceptance of market values, its efficient management dependent on economies of scale and mass audiences, its emphasis on opulent show and sensation, its national networks reliant on rail travel and the press, its professionalised labour force and hierarchies of fees and status, and its incipient trade unionism in response to exploitative management and agents – all have different resonances within contemporary concert life.

Table 4: Philharmonic Society. Individual tickets sold in 1878: a selection

Source: British Library, Loan 48.9/7

Date	Tickets							Programmes	
			Number sold at				Income £	Number	Income
	10/6	7/6	5/–	2/6	1/–	(rounded)	sold	£
14 Feb 1878	44	44	20	83	159	104	541	14
14 Mar 1878	138	10	4	65	154	38	450	11
28 Mar 1878	107	50	60	144	275	142	648	16

Table 5: Philharmonic Society. Proceeds from sale of individual tickets:
a selection

Source: British Library, Loan 48.2/11 and 48.2/12

Date	Income per concert, rounded (selected fees in parentheses)
1894	£123 (Borwick: free through Steinway; Tchaikovsky: Sixth Symphony, London première); £112 (Sauret: 10gn; Fanny Davies: 10gn; Tchaikovsky repeated); £110 (Sapellnikoff: £30); £336 (Paderewski: £100); £216 (Menter: £25); £106 (Saint-Saëns: 25gn); £136
1895	£171; £66; £373 (Patti: £100); £78; £150; £114; £105
1896	£98; £252 (Dvořák); £133; £110; £88; ?; £147
1902	£105; £85; £106; £197 (Kubelík: £50); £117; £75; £241 (matinée – Kubelík: £50)
1908	£129 (Wood debut); £138; £58 (Sibelius: £25); £75; £69; £170 (Nikisch: £50); £50

1899 Rachmaninov held out for an increase in fee from £25 to £35 if he were to be restricted from playing elsewhere first.[42] An agreement with Grieg's agent two years earlier had included an undertaking that 'he [Grieg] shall not appear in London, or nearer London than Brighton, before the date in question' – for which the agent negotiated a fee as high as 120 guineas.[43] All of this attests to a 'thirsty

42. Directors' Minutes, 29 September 1899, in RPSP, Loan 48.2/12.
43. Letter from Vert, 3 June 1897, in RPSP, Loan 48.13/34 (in the end Grieg did not appear because of illness).

market' eager for these high-level international figures. Yet at a lower level, too, William Boosey wrote into singers' contracts that they could not appear at charity concerts without his permission, so as not to dilute their drawing power.[44]

The Philharmonic Society usually succeeded through cajoling, flattery and subservience. Sometimes, however, it was forced to face market realities. Kreisler, who had quickly established his reputation in London, accepted twenty-five guineas on his Philharmonic debut in 1903 (his agent Narciso Vert already charged forty guineas elsewhere). But two years later the Philharmonic was assured that it 'would not do' for the violinist to play for less than seventy-five guineas; besides, it was argued, an appearance might adversely affect audience-sizes at projected recitals.[45] In other words, the Society was no longer needed – and, in fact, Kreisler did not play for it again until the première of Elgar's Violin Concerto in 1910.

The financing of serious orchestral concerts was balanced on a knife-edge because of high orchestral costs, star fees and limited audience sizes. According to George Henschel, who in 1886 founded the London Symphony Concerts, it was impossible for one individual to shoulder either the risk or the total financial burden of an orchestral series (his memoir lists guarantors exhaustively).[46] The Philharmonic Society likewise came to rely heavily on sponsorship, with a fellowship scheme and guarantors (see Table 3). Indeed, Steinway urged a bolder dependence on guarantors for 'new works and new artists of merit', since London already sustained plenty of self-supporting commercial concerts.[47] The New Symphony Orchestra is said to have received no subsidy, surviving by different means: large-scale Sunday afternoon concerts at the Royal Albert Hall and the London Palladium, international celebrity tours outside London (on the model of touring opera companies) and a pioneering involvement with recording and the cinema.[48]

In the last analysis, performing institutions, typically promoting fewer than ten concerts a year in London, were only a small cog in a

44. Boosey (1931), p. 96.
45. Letters from Vert, 21 August 1902 and 6 September 1905, in RPSP, Loan 48.13/34.
46. George Henschel, *Musings & Memories of a Musician*, London, Macmillan, 1918, pp. 319–22.
47. Letter of 30 November 1905, in RPSP, Loan 48.13/33.
48. Elkin (1944), pp. 45–46.

wider concert culture. Far more significant was the building of new halls, for in 1890 the infrastructure of London's concert life was notoriously deficient. The Crystal Palace at Sydenham was an uncomfortable train ride away and offered only temporary accommodation. Chappell's St James's Hall was marred by uncomfortable benches, cooking smells and the noise of minstrels' concerts below. Steinway Hall was small and never fashionable. So London was ready for something more fitting. The new venues, notably Queen's Hall (1893) and Bechstein Hall (1901), were in themselves symbols of modernity and of the new style of concert life. Purpose-built concert halls designed for round-the-year use, they rapidly achieved a dominant position in their respective spheres (orchestral concerts and recitals), both among artists seeking a venue and among concertgoers.

The primary intention of the original Victoria Concert Hall Company (1887) was to provide a more convenient and comfortable centre for orchestral music in the West End, its chosen site in Langham Place (north of Oxford Circus) being desirable and prestigious.[49] Queen's Hall, as the building was eventually named, followed in the wake of new halls in Leipzig (1884), Amsterdam (1888) and New York (Carnegie Hall, 1891), which it resembled not only in appearance but also as a statement on behalf of serious instrumental art located in an area of fashionable residences and shops. It represented a British attempt to match international musical standards, not so much out of a sense of civic pride (London's diversity and lack of a political centre or captive audience contrasted markedly with the situation in northern English cities) as out of embarrassment at the absence of a worthy modern concert hall. Yet, typically for London, this was a speculative venture without (initially, at least) a clearly articulated artistic vision – and a highly risky one, too, since it lacked both a secure audience base and the efficient economic foundation of contemporary music-hall ventures. If Queen's Hall outwardly resembled such flagships as the Coliseum or the Palladium, it lacked the national scope, the huge investment and the economies of scale that

49. Leanne Langley is currently working on the early history, and the present section draws on some of her research. The current literature includes: Elkin (1944); Arthur Jacobs, *Henry J. Wood, Maker of the Proms*, London, Methuen, 1994; David Cox, *The Henry Wood Proms*, London, BBC, 1980; and Barrie Hall, *The Proms and the Men Who Made Them*, London, George Allen & Unwin, 1981. See also Ehrlich (1995), pp. 159–62.

underpinned the music halls of Moss and Stoll, which represented 'big business' on a scale that no other form of entertainment before the cinema could match.

Constructed in the manner of a theatre or opera house – with separate entrances for socially distinct price levels – Queen's Hall had modern and luxurious decoration, seating and plush carpeting. In aspiring to this level of comfort, its ambience contrasted equally with the old drawing-room atmosphere of the defunct Hanover Square Rooms and the ecclesiastical austerity of the Exeter Hall and St James's Hall. It boasted all the latest personal amenities, including ladies' conveniences and an abundance of refreshment facilities (although the restaurant had to be abandoned after an official fire inspection). Acoustics were carefully tested, no doubt with the fiasco of the resonant Royal Albert Hall in mind. Robert Newman, salaried manager turned lessee, was solicitous in his attention to the audience, directing a new public towards higher norms of social etiquette and creating an atmosphere at once welcoming and attentive to the music (the audience was for the first time prevented from entering the hall until a break). Similarly, Newman won the trust of impresarios with his efficient management and disciplined staff, attending to tickets and admissions in an orderly and scrupulous way.

But what to put in the new hall? It appears, perhaps surprisingly, that neither the founding company nor Newman had a clear programme mapped out. Inevitably, the new hall made a slow start: any hall needs time to build a reputation with agents and artists, who would in any case have made their concert plans well in advance. As the manager of Bechstein Hall was later to document, the launch of a hall required an active and multi-faceted campaign that included advertising concert particulars in the *Daily Telegraph*, displaying large posters, hiring sandwich-board men and wooing major critics.[50] Newman was far from being a passive hall manager: he needed events, and fast. As he later remarked, the main initial objective was to get the hall known, by means of City dinners if necessary, in order to make inroads into the dominance of St James's Hall.[51] The Bach Choir was given three evenings free of charge in return for advice on

50. Cyril Ehrlich, 'The First Hundred Years', in *Wigmore Hall 1901–2001: A Celebration*, ed. Julia Macrae, London, The Wigmore Hall Trust, 2001, pp. 31–65.
51. Henry Wood, *My Life of Music*, London, Victor Gollancz, 1938, p. 92.

the hall's acoustics from Morton Latham, one of its committee members.[52] More significantly, the Philharmonic Society immediately transferred its base from St James's Hall, at some financial cost, as did Boosey's Ballad Concerts; the next season, Henschel's London Symphony Concerts followed suit.[53] Two high-profile series were given at Queen's Hall in 1894–95. Both were designed to emulate and outdo the Richter concerts at St James's Hall by focusing on his key repertoires of Wagner and Beethoven. A series of Wagner Concerts was conducted by Siegfried Wagner, Felix Mottl and Hermann Levi; another series was conducted by the charismatic Nikisch, whose interpretative style contrasted so markedly with that of the less demonstrative Richter.

But Newman was not content simply to accept outside bookings. Over the first few years he experimented with a wide variety of formats and concert patterns, many of which were new and imaginative. The Queen's Hall Choral Society was an early initiative, but more enterprising and eye-catching were the high-profile gala performances of *Cavalleria rusticana* and *I pagliacci* in the spring of 1894. Other resident ensembles followed, and eventually the Queen's Hall Orchestra, London's attempt to match the orchestral stability of continental orchestras, was formed. Newman approached his primary goal – dominance over other venues on the basis of high-quality orchestral concerts – obliquely and cautiously, showing an acute business sense in his careful assessment of each venture and quick jettisoning of any scheme that failed. Typically, he would start by putting on a short pilot series, extending or revisiting the formula in accordance with demand and meanwhile giving audiences a sense of involvement in the project. The autumn Promenade Concerts and Sunday afternoon concerts (both initiated in 1895) were joined in January 1897 by the flagship Saturday afternoon series, which dared to enter into direct competition with Crystal Palace only three years after the opening of the new hall. Newman also appropriated the model of the Handel choral festival for his spring orchestral festivals, introducing fine continental orchestras alongside his own. This kind of event was a clear assertion of the new cultural kudos attached to orchestral music.

52. We owe this information to Basil Keen, who is currently completing a doctoral dissertation on the history of the Bach Choir.
53. For the 1894–95 season only.

Within a few years Queen's Hall, together with its small hall upstairs, likewise became a standard venue for solo recitals (even if St James's Hall retained its reputation among established recitalists), quickly surpassing Steinway Hall and similar recital venues – at least until the building of the Bechstein and Aeolian Halls. Eventually, there emerged a reasonably clear division of function between the larger orchestral hall and the smaller recital hall: thus in 1904 the pianist Artur Schnabel, in typical fashion, placed his two London debuts a week apart, playing the Brahms Second Concerto at Queen's Hall and late Schubert at the Bechstein Hall. Yet even then the really big names could draw capacity audiences to the large Queen's Hall for solo recitals, as Schnabel himself was famously to do later.

Newman was the founding father of modern concert management and risk-taking entrepreneurship in London. He was the first, and for a time the most significant, full-time professional in the field, and some of his innovations became adopted as common practice in the course of the new century. Unprecedentedly, his energies were concentrated upon a single venue throughout the year – in contrast to the short-season, peripatetic and diffuse activities of his predecessors, who, in a more restricted market, had tended to be musicians or their agents. Newman purposefully cultivated a distinctive image for his hall, establishing a 'brand name' orchestra that was intended to cultivate at least a semblance of stability, employing a disciplined, permanent and businesslike house staff (in contrast to the often lackadaisical, temporary and not always scrupulous amateur assistants of the previous era), giving vigorous attention to ticket sales and employing unprecedented levels of advertising. The primary but elusive tasks of selecting repertoire, designing programme formats, marketing a newly articulated hierarchy of artists and building new and loyal audiences were thoroughly appraised and subjected to many kinds of original experimentation and systematic development. Some of the achievements of this remarkable innovator and of his closest colleague, Henry Wood – notably the Proms – have been acknowledged, though inadequately scrutinised. Others have been wholly ignored: in particular, the establishment of Sundays and Saturdays as prime times for concerts. The broader processes of fundamental change by which new networks and a substantial infrastructure were created now merit detailed research and historical analysis.

Ultimately, neither frenetic pace nor new venues and procedures were sufficient to establish a continuously healthy, sustainable concert life. Indeed, it is arguable that in the new century profusion went mad, lacking an audience sufficient for its sustenance. But the achievement of Newman and some of his contemporaries can hardly be gainsaid. Like the creators of modern shopping they began to teach a broad section of the public how to consume – this time music, not goods – with new discernment.

4

Debussy, Durand et Cie: A French Composer and His Publishers (1884–1917)

Robert Orledge

In the new era of Internet publishing and self-promotional Web sites it might seem that the comprehensive services that Durand et Cie provided for Debussy (and Ravel) in the first quarter of the last century no longer had any relevance. Like his father Auguste before him, Jacques Durand acted for his chosen composers as a benevolent factotum. This combination of legal and artistic adviser, impresario, public relations officer, moneylender and personal friend seems like a forgotten ideal in what is now a much more commercially orientated world. Thus, in a halcyon age when composers composed and publishers saw to everything else, Debussy could disdain the activities of the 'business-man' and pursue a path of financial incompetence in the knowledge that he was by no means unique and that Durand would always be there to put things right. Becoming something of a recluse after the scandals surrounding his marital life in 1904, Debussy might, in retrospect, have been attracted to the concept of managing all his affairs from a home computer: but as the only practical skills for which he showed any aptitude were *cordon bleu* cookery and gardening, I have severe doubts about this.

During the upheavals of the First World War the relationship between composer and publisher in France changed very little. Making light of the paper shortages and restricted concert life, Jacques Durand continued to bring out Debussy's new works within months of their completion, and he also embarked on a new and comprehensive French edition of the classics. With a far from scholarly brief, Debussy was put to work on Chopin, and Ravel on Mendelssohn, so that French pianists would never need German editions again. Debussy had earlier contributed *Les Fêtes de Polymnie* (1908) to Durand's equally well-meaning collected edition of Rameau, inaugurated under the general editorship of Saint-Saëns in

1894. After the Great War and Debussy's death the contractual advances paid to such composers as Ravel at last began to rise substantially. But it was the runaway success of Ravel's *Bolero* in the 1930s through technically improved recordings that assisted the breakdown of the old order and the move towards a more commercial postwar world, in which success would come to be measured as much in financial as in artistic terms. For, as Ravel freely admitted, *Bolero* was simply a superbly orchestrated crescendo with only minimal musical content. In the process, incidentally, *Bolero* also became a prime generator of the recurring rights income that has helped to subsidise Durand's portfolio of promising young composers up to the present day.[1]

Yet despite all our modern technological advances, it is still prestigious and desirable for a composer to hold an exclusive contract with a leading publisher. Debussy, in 1905, became one of the first composers to achieve this fortunate position. Similarly, there can be few people who would not vote for a return to the days of the salaried professional composer who needed no career other than music, or who would not welcome a publisher eager to bring out his/her latest work immediately and to take full responsibility for engraving, distributing and promoting it. And if we think that we could not exist without e-mail and the computerised financial transaction, we should remember that the prewar Parisian post was so frequent and efficient that Debussy's friend Satie could arrange his rendezvous by *carte-lettre* or *pneumatique* as he passed across Paris each day, and Debussy could remedy a financial crisis within hours, as we shall shortly see. Most composers had the telephone, too, except the impoverished Satie, who hated using it and took it off the hook when he visited friends, so as not to interrupt his conversations! And the main advantage for young composers was that there were many more small publishing houses operating in Paris in the late nineteenth and early twentieth centuries than there are today. Mergers and takeovers were just as common, but composers were far less often sacked in the process. The fact that Editions Durand (like Ricordi before it) were taken over in June 2000 by the German Bertelsmann Group (BMG) could well prove to be worse news for its

---

1. According to its director, Bernard Brossollet, in an interview with the author in Paris on 26 April 2000.

young composers than it would have been a century ago. Of course, the single-composer LP and CD would have been a considerable advantage to Debussy, and an even greater one to less well known composers such as Charles Koechlin, whose difficult and visionary orchestral music rarely achieved a second public performance. Against this, the 'contemporary classical' market of Debussy's and Koechlin's day was a far larger one in percentage terms, thanks to almost universal home music-making and the social desirability of regular concert and opera attendance. But first we should look at the establishment of the house of Durand.

Durand et Cie

The most remarkable thing about the Durand family was how quickly and decisively they could act when necessary. On the same day that Auguste Durand (1830–1909) and Louis Schoenewerk (born in 1814) set up the firm of Durand-Schoenewerk et Cie at the end of 1869, they also took over the extensive German and French catalogue of Gustave Flaxland, together with that publisher's centrally situated premises at 4, place de la Madeleine, Paris 8, where Durand et Cie remained until May 1980.[2] The Flaxland inheritance included Wagner's operas up to *Tannhäuser* and *Lohengrin*; early works by Brahms and Saint-Saëns; much piano music by Haydn, Mozart, Beethoven, Chopin and Schumann; a series of vocal anthologies entitled *Les Echos de …*; and much else besides. These became the basis of the everyday Durand repertoire, especially as regards the *Edition Classique Durand et Fils* begun by Jacques Durand in 1914.

After a legal action in 1885 Auguste Durand's six original associates were bought out. The firm was renamed Durand-Schoenewerk on 20 May 1886 in a five-year agreement, after which Louis Schoenewerk took the opportunity to quit on 18 November 1891. By 20 November the firm had been swiftly reorganised and was trading as A.

2. Marie-Auguste Massacrié-Durand was then organist at Saint-Vincent de Paul, and Léon-Louis Schoenewerk was a Parisian piano-maker. Six other associates were involved in setting up Durand-Schoenewerk et Cie on 30 December 1869. Fuller details can be found in Anik Devriès and François Lesure, *Dictionnaire des éditeurs de musique français*, Geneva, Minkoff, 1988, Vol. 2 (1820–1914), pp.151–53, 171–72.

Durand et Fils, Auguste having brought in his son Jacques as his partner.[3] This situation lasted until the death of Auguste on 31 May 1909, following which Jacques brought in his first cousin, Gaston Choisnel, renaming the family firm yet again, on 23 December 1909, as Durand et Cie. By this time the firm's composer list included Debussy, Dukas, Fauré, Franck, d'Indy, Lalo, Massenet, Pierné, Ravel, Roussel, Saint-Saëns and Widor, which made it the foremost publisher of contemporary music in France. Another cousin, René Dommange, became a partner in April 1921, shortly before the death of Choisnel, and the firm was kept in the Durand family by having Jacques's widow replace him in 1928. Jacques died at the home that Debussy knew well at Bel-Ebat, near Fontainebleau, exactly three months before the ballet première of Ravel's *Bolero*. From Auguste Durand Jacques learned to be an astute financial manager, with an eye on the main chance, as well as a tactful diplomat. He played a substantial part in upholding the terms of the Berne Convention in 1915–16 as regards authors' rights and pirate editions. In the early 1920s he donated all the Debussy manuscripts he possessed to what is now the Music Department of the Bibliothèque Nationale de France. Although very selective in the composers he took on, Jacques was an avid supporter of contemporary music, starting his own concert series shortly after Ravel's foundation of the Société Musicale Indépendante. He also instituted, shortly before his death, a biennial prize for the best French symphonic composition.

Debussy's Early Publications with Durand

Perhaps the most significant of Jacques Durand's accomplishments was that, like Debussy and Ravel (and his own father Auguste), he was a Conservatoire-trained composer. Jacques studied harmony in the class of Théodore Dubois (where he met Paul Dukas) and entered the composition class of Ernest Guiraud in autumn 1886, two years after Guiraud's favourite student, Claude Debussy, had won the Prix de Rome with his cantata *L'Enfant prodigue*. And it was in fact with this landmark achievement that Debussy's relationship with the house of

---

3. Marie-Jacques Massacrié-Durand (1865–1928). Auguste Durand, who was also a composer and music critic, had studied organ alongside Franck and Saint-Saëns at the Conservatoire in the class of François Benoist. The management change in 1891 cost Auguste Durand 225,000 francs (Devriès and Lesure (1988), p. 152).

Durand began. Jacques, who first met Debussy in 1884, describes in his memoirs how 'the painters carried the vote' in the final deliberations, and how his 'father, delighted by Debussy's success, let him know through Guiraud that he would willingly publish *The Prodigal Son*'.[4]

Returning from Rome in March 1887, Debussy persuaded Auguste Durand to publish several more of his works, notably the *Petite suite* for piano duet (February 1889) and the *Deux arabesques* (October 1891).[5] In a publicity event that foreshadowed the Concerts Durand of 1910–13 Auguste decided that his son and Debussy should perform the *Petite suite* together in an 'elite Parisian salon' on 1 March 1889. Perhaps because Debussy still had a reputation for subversiveness and modernism, the applause was little more than polite, for all that we now know it as one of Debussy's most charming early pieces. Jacques goes on to describe how:

> Debussy was very nervous before sitting down at the piano with me and had urged me not to go too fast. I promised. But hardly had we begun

4. Jacques Durand, *Quelques souvenirs d'un éditeur de musique*, Paris, Durand, 1924 [Vol. 1, up to 1909], p. 31: 'Les peintres avaient emporté le vote ... Mon père, enchanté du succès de Debussy, lui fit savoir, par Guiraud, qu'il éditerait volontiers *L'Enfant prodigue*.' This vocal score (subsequently replaced by Debussy's revised edition in January 1908) was his only work to appear under the Durand-Schoenewerk et Cie imprint. Ever cautious, Durand printed only one hundred copies in October 1884 (D. S. et Cie 3387). It did not sell especially well, as he needed to print only 180 more copies before the new 1908 version appeared. Debussy's only prior publication was the song *Nuit d'étoiles*, brought out by the Société Artistique d'Editions, d'Estampes et de Musique (E. Bulla) in 1882.

5. The *Petite suite* in an edition of four hundred (D.S. 4030), and the *Deux arabesques* (D.S. 4395–96) in editions of four hunded and five hundred (plus three hundred of them combined). At 5 and 6 francs respectively, the two separate *Arabesques* were expensive for their time, and by the time of their reprinting in September 1904 their prices had been reduced to 1 franc 75 centimes and 2 francs, respectively. All information about print runs and dates comes from the six handwritten *Livres de cotage* in the Durand Archives, now at 4–6, rue de la Bourse, Paris 2, and are cited by kind permission of Bernard Brossollet and Editions Durand. I should also like to thank Jacques Gondouin (their curator) and Dr Nigel Simeone (who studied them with me in May 2000) for all their help in the preparation of this chapter. Simeone's excellent article 'Mother Goose and Other Golden Eggs: Durand Editions of Ravel as Reflected in the Firm's Pinting Records', *Brio*, Vol. 35 (1998), pp. 58–79, is recommended as a parallel line of enquiry to my chapter.

when Debussy began to hurry; and despite all my efforts, I was unable to hold him back. He was in haste to put this public trial behind him. So I followed the somewhat hectic tempi as best I could, and the work finished with a *brio* that was, probably, an important factor in the public sympathy with which the work was finally greeted.[6]

To these Durand publications can be added the first version of Verlaine's *Mandoline* in late 1890,[7] and two settings of *Romances* by Paul Bourget (*L'Ame évaporée* and *Les Cloches*) in December 1891,[8] with their exquisite lithographed covers by P. Borie.

In 1890 there also appeared a de luxe limited edition of the *Cinq poèmes de Baudelaire,* which was sold by the Librairie de l'Art Indépendant without a publisher's imprint. According to Jacques Durand, it was his cousin Gaston Choisnel who prepared this beautiful edition, which was entered in the Durand catalogue only when it was reprinted in June 1902.[9]

Already, Claude and Jacques had become close friends who dined frequently together and sight-read the latest operatic scores at the piano. The other important early work of Debussy that Durand published was his lone String Quartet, which came out at the beginning of 1894: 150 copies of the separate parts (D. & F. 4738) plus sixty copies of the (for the time) customary large-format score (D. & F. 4778).

6. Durand (1924), p. 59, as translated in Roger Nichols, *The Life of Debussy*, Cambridge, Cambridge University Press, 1998, pp. 56–57: 'Debussy, très nerveux avant de se mettre avec moi au clavier, m'avait bien recommandé de ne pas presser le mouvement. Je le lui promis. Mais voilà qu'à peine étions-nous au début du morceau, Debussy se mit à presser; malgré tous mes efforts, je ne pus le retenir. Il avait hâte que cette épreuve en public fût passée. Je suivis donc le mouvement, un peu précipité, le mieux possible. Le morceau s'acheva dans le *brio* qui, probablement, fut pour beaucoup dans la sympathie honorable réservée à la *Petite Suite* en l'occurrence.'

7. Durand & Schoenewerk 4299. Like most of these early editions, it was printed by the Imprimerie E. Delanchy at Faubourg St-Denis, 51 and 53, with engraving carried out by L. Parent at rue Rodier 61. The evocative street scene on the cover was by Adolphe Willette, the designer of the famous Chat Noir cabaret.

8. D. S. 4436–37, each song in an edition of three hundred copies. The Durand & Schoenewerk number appears with the music on the inside pages, although the cover already reflects the firm's change of name to 'A. Durand & Fils'. Both songs enjoyed five re-editions before appearing with English translations in February 1906.

9. As D. & F. 6013, in an edition of four hundred copies. See Durand (1924), pp. 73–74.

This was the only Debussy score ever to possess an opus number (10) and was, again, something of an act of faith. But despite an acclaimed performance by the Belgian Quatuor Ysaÿe at the Société Nationale on 29 December 1893 and the distribution of complimentary copies to various Parisian ensembles, Jacques recalled: 'Our repeated efforts were in vain. No one wanted to trouble himself with this reputedly unplayable music.'[10] But just as Jacques becomes over-diplomatic in his second slim volume of memoirs,[11] side-stepping Debussy's real problems, so, too, his first volume can also be economical with the truth by stressing Debussy's lack of success before the watershed of *Pelléas et Mélisande*, despite all his (Durand's) efforts on the composer's behalf. Debussy, though often hypocritical and impulsive in his private letters, puts a new perspective on this situation when he complains to Ernest Chausson about the 'Barbarians of the place de la Madeleine',[12] who had just bought his quartet for what he considered the paltry sum of 250 francs. In fact, the parts and even the score sold fairly consistently, as Table 6 shows, although it seems that Durand promoted the work rather more vigorously after 1906, when Debussy had become contractually bound to the firm. Durand also brought out, in April 1905, an early miniature-score version of the quartet (Debussy's first publication in that format) that had reached the impressive sales figure of 23,800 by 1971. This suggests that far more people have studied the score than have actually played it.

In passing, we can also gain from Table 6 an idea of how much better Debussy's works sold than those of Jacques Durand himself. In all probability, Jacques copied the idea of composing an *Arabesque* from Debussy and then persuaded his father to publish it in larger quantities than his friend's *First Arabesque*. But whereas Debussy's sales (admittedly of two pieces rather than just one) had reached a total of 458,150 by 1930, poor Jacques's *Arabesque* (op. 13) had by then only just exhausted its original printing of five hundred! A complete reproduction from Durand's *Livre de cotage No. 2* (1879–97:

10. Durand (1924), pp. 93–94: 'Notre action répétée fut vaine. On ne voulut pas s'occuper de cette musique que l'on réputait injouable.'
11. Jacques Durand, *Quelques souvenirs d'un éditeur de musique, 2e série (1910–24)*, Paris, Durand, 1925.
12. From a letter of 23 October 1893, cited in Claude Debussy, *Correspondance 1884–1918*, ed. François Lesure, Paris, Hermann, 1993, p. 92 (where it is wrongly dated '24 octobre'): 'Barbares de la place de la Madeleine'.

Table 6: Print runs of Debussy's String Quartet (op. 10), as given in Durand's *Livres de cotage Nos 2–3*, followed by sales of Debussy's *Deux arabesques* (1891), compared with those of Jaques Durand's *Arabesque* (1893) and Auguste Durand's *6e valse* (1894)

4738: separate parts		4778: large-format score		6567: miniature score	
Jan 1894	150	Feb 1894	60		
Mar 1903	50	July 1898	50		
Apr 1904	50	Feb 1904	50		
Mar 1905	50			Apr 1905	100
1 Feb 1906	200	Jan 1907	50	Jan 1907	200
Feb 1908	300			Nov 1907	1,000
May 1910	300				
Aug 1912	300	Nov 1911	50	Dec 1911	500
Apr 1914	300				
July 1917	500				
May 1920	500	Mar 1921	100	Nov 1920	1,000
[7,700 by 1945]				[23,800 by 1971]	

4395: *Arabesque 1*		4396: *Arabesque 2*		4699: J. Durand: *Arabesque* (op. 13)		4868: A. Durand: *6e Valse* (op. 96)	
Oct 1891	400	Oct 1891	500	Oct 1893	500	Oct 1894	1,500
						Nov 1894	1,000
						Feb 1895	2,000
						Apr 1898	500
						Feb 1900	500
						Oct 1900	500
						Aug 1901	500
						Apr 1902	1,000
Jan 1903	100						
July 1903	500	May 1904	100			July 1903	1,000
Sept 1904	1,000	Sept 1904	500			Dec 1904	2,000
1 Apr 1905	1,000	12 Dec 1905	1,000				
June 1907	2,000	June 1907	2,000			Sept 1907	2,000
Sept 1908	2,000						
May 1909	2,000	Feb 1909	2,000				
Nov 1909	2,000	July 1909	2,000				
May 1910	2,000	1 Feb 1910	2,000				
Dec 1910	2,000	Nov 1910	2,000			Dec 1910	1,000
Feb 1911	6,000	Feb 1911	6,000			Feb 1911	2,000
'Editions sur clichés' [new printing]							
Apr 1912	10,000	July 1912	10,000			Dec 1912	1,000
Apr 1914	10,000	Apr 1916	10,000			Feb 1914	2,000

etc.	etc.			Jan 1930 [First reprint]	200	etc.	
Totals							
Apr 1930	142,000	Apr 1930	114,000	Jan 1930	700	Mar 1927	25,500

[Nos 1 and 2 combined: Nov 1930 202,150]

Total all Debussy sales: 458,150

Plate nos 2556–5223) shows that a new 'édition sur clichés' was introduced in 1912 after the annual demand for Debussy's *Arabesques* passed the ten thousand mark, but that the economic wisdom of buying both pieces together became more evident only in the later 1920s. Sold separately, the *First Arabesque* remained more popular than its companion. These salon pieces established the pattern that Debussy's piano works were his best sellers. By comparison, Auguste Durand's piano pieces sold much more strongly than his son's, as Table 6 also reveals, and his *6e valse* still turns up today in popular folios. Auguste awarded himself a higher initial print run, which dropped significantly after the initial novelty of his waltz had worn off. His sales did, however, pick up and maintain themselves consistently, but his overall sales of 25,500 by 1927 remained small in comparison with Debussy's *Arabesques*.

As further evidence of Debussy's popularity, re-editions of his *Petite suite* of 1889 topped the thousand mark after 1906, and its four movements were issued separately in January 1911. Sales of the complete suite had reached 12,950 by 1938, whereas Henri Büsser, who later orchestrated Debussy's suite and published his own *Petite suite* for piano duet in 1898 (D. & F. 5331), had sold only 1,200 copies of the latter by 1932.[13] So the public did indeed discriminate between composers, and it would seem that piano solos were more popular than duets. But there are some surprises: Debussy's later *Epigraphes antiques* sold much better in their original duet format of February 1915 than in Debussy's solo version of October 1915.[14] Then, if we make the assumption that two-piano arrangements are not popular, seeing that André Caplet's 1913 arrangement of Debussy's *Gigues* (D.

---

13. See *Livre de cotage No. 3* (1897–June 1910: Plate nos 5224–7799). None of these books is paginated.
14. D. & F. 9303–8 and 9370, respectively. The duet version sold 17,145 copies up to 1992, whereas the solo version sold only 5,444 over the same period (*Livre de cotage No. 4* (June 1910–1924: Plate nos 7800–10494)).

& F. 8936) has sold only 710 copies to date, it will come as a surprise to learn that Léon Roques's two-piano version of the *Golliwogg's* [*sic*] *Cake Walk* (D. & F. 8487) sold 12,500 copies between 1912 and 1984, as against only 5,600 of Jacques Charlot's piano duet arrangement over the same period.

By 1905 Debussy was finding himself outselling the popular Saint-Saëns in all genres, the largest overall increase in sales coming after the Second World War. Only Ravel, among living French composers of serious music, was to equal or exceed Debussy in popularity, especially with the piano solo version of his *Bolero* in the 1930s.[15] Most Debussy publications, however, started off with a print run of a thousand or less (even the first book of *Préludes* in 1910) and built up their sales gradually. These sales increased notably after the Great War (and Debussy's death). The exception was the patriotic *Noël des enfants qui n'ont plus de maisons* (D. & F. 9418), which was predictably popular during 1916–18 but then saw its sales gradually drop from a height of six thousand in 1917 to only five hundred in 1939. This composition returned to reissues of over a thousand copies only in 1990.

Debussy's Other Early Publishers

During the early years, when Durand publications were intermittent, Debussy naturally tried other channels. Always short of money to fund his love of collecting oriental *objets d'art*, he was not above the Beethovenian practice of selling the same composition to more than one publisher. Thus he sold a collection of seven pieces (including the 1890 version of the *Suite bergamasque*) to Paul de Choudens between January and March 1891 for the sum of 500 francs. This payment included 100 francs for his *Mazurka* and *Rêverie* for piano (14 March), which he then resold (together with four other songs) to Julien Hamelle for 150 francs on 30 August 1891.[16] Later on, the *Mazurka* and *Rêverie* resurfaced yet again among the other pieces sold to Choudens in a lot acquired by Eugène Fromont on 5 July 1902; *Rêverie* appeared also as the musical supplement to the journal *L'Il-lustration* (No. 2751) on 16 November 1895! So the story of

15. See the statistics in Simeone (1998), pp. 59–60.
16. See François Lesure, *Claude Debussy: Biographie critique*, Paris, Klincksieck, 1994, pp. 121, 227, and the same author, *Catalogue de l'oeuvre de Claude Debussy*, Geneva, Minkoff, 1977, pp. 68–69.

Debussy's editions can be something of a minefield, especially when there are two different versions of Verlaine songs such as *Mandoline*, or of the entire collection of *Ariettes oubliées,* published by Fromont in 1903. These songs had originally appeared in 1888, as six separate *Ariettes,* from 'the compassionate and philanthropic publisher' Veuve Etienne Girod, who was also to publish Debussy's early songs *Fleur des blés* and *Beau soir* in 1891 (E.G. 6256, 6259).[17]

Then comes the slightly mysterious but even more philanthropic figure of Georges Hartmann, whose own firm was declared bankrupt in 1891, but who somehow managed to act, until his death in 1900, as artistic director and adviser to Eugène Fromont.[18] As well as championing Bizet and Massenet, Hartmann arranged the publication by Fromont of Debussy's first orchestral masterpiece, the *Prélude à l'après-midi d'un faune*, and also of the first cycle for which the composer wrote his own Symbolist poems, the *Proses lyriques*, in October 1895 (E. 1085. and 1091.F.). Hartmann also acted as a benefactor to Debussy, paying him a monthly retainer of 500 francs (6,000 francs a year) from about 1894 onwards. Thus *Pelléas* (completed in short score in 1895) belonged as much to him as to anyone, and was naturally first published by Fromont.[19] Much of the two men's correspondence between December 1897 and February 1899 is taken up by false promises from Debussy about the advanced state of the three problematic *Nocturnes* for orchestra that were dedicated to Hartmann, but which the latter never heard in concert. Fromont went on to publish these pieces in 1900, continuing with the suite *Pour le piano* in 1901, the first set of *Fêtes galantes* in 1903 and the revised *Suite bergamasque* (now including *Clair de lune*) in June 1905. In a wicked moment Debussy described Fromont as 'the most determined busybody I know'![20] But the twentieth-century revolution in piano writing from the *Estampes* onwards was entrusted entirely to Durand.

---

17. Cited in Lesure (1994), p. 95: 'éditeur compatissant et philanthropique'.
18. Actually Romain-Jean-François Hartmann (1843–1900). For more details see Devriès and Lesure (1988), pp. 210–13. Hartmann was even more financially incompetent than Debussy or Satie, and had a penchant for gambling on horses.
19. The vocal score (E.1416.F.) in 1902 and the rare orchestral score (E.1418.F.) in 1904. Both lack the interludes that appear in the final Durand editions of 1907.
20. Lesure (1993), p. 185. Letter to André Messager of 12 September 1903: 'la plus déterminée "mouche de coche" que je connaisse'. Debussy was at that time having problems with Fromont over the printing of Act 5 of *Pelléas*.

The Durand Contracts of 1903–5 and *The Devil in the Belfry*

In effect, Auguste Durand became Debussy's main publisher from 1903 onwards, after the eventual success of *Pelléas* in 1902 led to Debussy's elevation to the rank of Chevalier de la Légion d'Honneur the following New Year. Durand could now be confident that Debussy had official recognition and international potential; his son Jacques was one of the very few personalities to remain a close friend of the composer after Debussy's marital scandals of 1904. Auguste also knew that Debussy's financial problems had worsened considerably since his allowance from Hartmann had ceased, and that Hartmann's nephew and heir was taking legal action to recover the money that Debussy had already received, claiming that this was only a loan! But if Debussy was no accountant, he was not above a little financial chicanery based on the correct perception that Durand needed him at least as much as he needed his publisher. For although the list of contracts in Table 7 shows that Durand obtained both the *Estampes* and the *Trois chansons de Charles d'Orléans* for a mere 600 francs on 17 August 1903, the earlier contract of 8 July (Plate 6) demonstrates that Debussy could obtain over twice as much for works that, so far as anyone knows, had not yet been committed to paper. The most remarkable thing about this contract is that all nine pieces **were** indeed completed by 1912, with very few changes made to their titles. In short, Debussy had a clear picture of his composing career well ahead of its realisation. The order of what were to become the first two orchestral *Images* was reversed, and the '2e Série I–III' materialised in 1907 for one rather than two pianos – but that is all. What the balancing three orchestral (?) *Images* might have been called remains an intriguing mystery. But if Debussy was here testing the water and only slightly exaggerating his intentions, he soon discovered that the key to the greatest financial success lay in theatrical projects.

Thus, by virtue of a contract of 14 October 1903 assigning Durand the rights to his Poe opera *Le Diable dans le beffroi*, Debussy had his monthly payments of 500 francs reinstated (up to a total of 12,000 francs) – on the strength of a brief scenario and a few musical sketches made on holiday the previous August.[21] In the contract these were

---

21. 3,000 francs apiece on delivery of the vocal and orchestral scores and 6,000 francs after the first performance at the Opéra-Comique in Paris.

Table 7: Debussy's contracts with Durand et Cie (1884–1916) (from the Archives of Editions Durand, Paris, and BN, Rés. Vm. Dos.13)

Given title of composition	Date	Fee in francs
L'Enfant prodigue (cantata)	7 Aug 1884	None stated
Petite suite (pf duet)	8 Dec 1888	None stated
Saint-Saëns: Introduction et Rondo capriccioso, (op. 28), arr. 2 pf, 4 hands	4 Mar 1889	100
Mandoline (Verlaine)	24 Sep 1890	100
Saint-Saëns: Caprice pour piano sur les airs de ballet d'Alceste de Gluck, arr. pf duet	2 Mar 1891	150
Deux arabesques (pf)	11 Apr 1891	200
Deux romances (Bourget)	17 Jun 1891	150
1er quatuor en sol (op. 10)	13 Oct 1893	250
Cinq poèmes de Baudelaire	16 May 1902	1,000
Rapsodie pour saxophone et orchestre	17 Apr 1903	100
Images (9: for pf, 2 pf or orch. See Plate 6)	8 Jul 1903	1,500
Estampes / Trois Chansons de Charles d'Orléans	17 Aug 1903	600
Le Diable dans le beffroi (Poe opera. Contracts 1 & 2)	14 Oct 1903	12,000*
Printemps (pf, orch, choir)	8 Mar 1904	250
Danses [sacrée et profane] (harp/ string orchestra)	7 May 1904	300
Les Fêtes galantes [sic] (Verlaine: 2e série)	4 Jul 1904	600
Masques; Isle joyeuse [sic] (pf)	29 Jul 1904	1,000
La Mer (orch)	22 Dec 1904	2,000
Le Diable dans le beffroi (Contract 3. See Plate 7)	31 Mar 1905	9,000
Images: 2e série pour orchestre (Ibéria; Ronde; Gigue)	15 Apr 1908	4,800
Trois chansons de Charles d'Orléans (choir; revised version)	23 Jun 1908	1,500
Children's Corner (suite for pf)	31 Jul 1908	3,000
Hommage à Haydn (pf)	31 Dec 1909	500
1ère rhapsodie (clar/pf or orch)	12 Jan 1910	1,500
12 préludes (pf; 1st book)	9 Feb 1910	7,000

Deux [sic] *poèmes [de Tristan]*		
L'Hermite ['Le Promenoir des		
deux amantes']	15 Apr 1910	1,000
Plus que lente [sic]. *Valse pour piano*	15 Apr 1910	1,000
3 ballades [de François] Villon	1 Jun 1910	3,000
Morceau à déchiffrer (clar/ pf)	18 Jul 1910	500
Le Martyre de Saint Sébastien		
(choir/orch; d'Annunzio)	9 Dec 1910	20,000
Livret de ballet de Masques et		
bergamasques	12 May 1911	500
2e Livre de 12 Préludes	31 Jan 1912	12,000
Khamma (ballet for Maud Allan)	29 Apr 1912	6,000
Crimen Amoris (theatre project		
with Charles Morice)	21 May 1912	20,000
Jeux. Ballet sur un argument de		
Monsieur Nijinsky (orch)	30 Aug 1912	6,000
Trois poèmes [de Stéphane] Mallarmé /		
La Boîte à joujoux (ballet pour enfants)	15 Jul 1913	8,000
Le Palais du silence (ballet for André		
Charlot, Alhambra Theatre, London.		
Libretto by Georges de Feure)	27 Nov 1913	25,000
Crimen Amoris, conversion to *Fêtes*		
galantes (Laloy)	27 Jan 1914	No fee
6 epigraphes antiques (pf duet)	15 Jul 1914	3,000
Berceuse héroïque (pf)	19 Nov 1914	500
Caprices en blanc et noir (2 pf)	9 Jul 1915	4,500
Sonate pour violoncelle et piano	9 Aug 1915	3,000
12 études: Nos 1–6 (pf)	3 Sep 1915	6,000
Nos 7–12 (pf)	3 Sep 1915	6,000
Sonate pour flûte, alto et harpe	19 Oct 1915	4,000
Noël des enfants qui n'ont plus de		
maisons	4 Dec 1915	1,500
Sonate pour violon et piano	5 Feb 1916	4,000
La Chute de la Maison Usher (one-		
act Poe opera)	26 Aug1916	15,000

*As monthly payments of 500 fr

Je soussigné Claude Debussy _____ *compositeur*
demeurant 58 Rue Cardinet Va Pari _____ *déclare*
avoir vendu et cédé à MM. A. DURAND et Fils, Éditeurs de Musique, à Paris,
4, Place de la Madeleine, avec garantie de tous troubles, revendications et évictions
quelconques, la propriété pleine et entière, sans aucune restriction ni réserve tant pour la
France et ses colonies que pour les pays étrangers, de ouvrage suivant dont je suis l'auteur:

Images

Douze pièces pour piano à 2 mains et à
2 pianos à 4 mains, ou orchestre.

1.ᵉ Série   2.ᵉ Série
I Reflets dans l'eau   I. Cloches à travers les feuilles
II Hommage à Rameau   II. Et la lune descend sur le temple qui fut
III Mouvements   III. Poissons d'or
II Ibéria   IV
I Gigues tristes   V
II Ronde   VI

En conséquence, MM. A. DURAND et Fils sont subrogés dans tous mes droits
et auront le pouvoir, à l'exclusion de tout autre, d'éditer, publier, graver, imprimer et
vendre à leur profit partout où bon leur semblera le dit ouvrage dans telle forme et
telle publication que ce soit, le faire exécuter dans les concerts ou établissements publics
sans que moi ni personne puissions jamais les en empêcher pendant toute la durée du
privilège accordé ou à accorder aux auteurs ou à leur famille par les lois présentes et
futures de tous pays. MM. A. DURAND et Fils auront également le droit de publier
tout arrangement de ce ouvrage pour quelque instrument que ce soit et pourront aussi
transmettre cette propriété en totalité ou en partie s'ils le jugent convenable à leurs intérêts.

Cette cession comprend le 1/3 des droits d'exécution publique, les parties contrac-
tantes se réservant leurs droits respectifs dans la Société des Auteurs, Compositeurs et
Éditeurs de Musique.

La présente vente et cession est faite moyennant la somme de :

quinze cent francs

dont quittance.

Paris, le huit Juillet *1903*

lu et approuvé
Claude Debussy

Plate 6 Contract between Debussy and Durand of 8 July 1903, showing how far in advance the composer planned his career. (Reproduced by kind permission of Editions Durand, Paris.)

Entre M. Claude DEBUSSY compositeur de
Musique demeurant à Paris 10 Avenue Alphand et
M.M. A. DURAND & FILS Editeurs de Musique demeurant à Paris, 4 Place de la Madeleine, il a
été décidé et convenu ce qui suit :

1° - Les primes concernant la cession du
"Diable dans le Beffroi" payées par M.M. A.

Nous disons :   DURAND & FILS sous forme de mensualité à M.
Neuf mille francs   DEBUSSY et s'élevant à la somme de : 9000 fr.

à ce jour sont affectées à l'acquisition par
M.M. A. DURAND & FILS des planches, titres,
etc. de la Partition Piano et chant et de la
Partition d'orchestre de "Pelleas et Mélisande"
appartenant à M. DEBUSSY ainsi que le solde
des Partitions Piano et chant et d'orchestre
restant encore en dépôt et le matériel copié
d'orchestre.

2° - Le paiement de la première mensualité pré-
vue au traité du "Diable dans le Beffroi"se
trouvera donc reportée au 15 Avril 1905. Le
1er Acte devra être remis à M.M. A. DURAND
& FILS le 15 Avril 1906 et la fin de l'ouvrage le 15 Avril 1907 au plus tard.

Fait Double à Paris, le 31 Mars 1905

Plate 7 Contract between Debussy and Durand of 31 March 1905, showing the takeover of *Pelléas et Mélisande*. (BN, Rés. Vm.Dos. 13 (3).)

expanded into a 'musical tale in two acts and three tableaux', of which Act I was to be delivered to Durand before 15 October 1904 and the rest by 15 May 1905.[22] When it became clear that Debussy was not going to deliver on time, a new contract (Plate 7) was drawn up on 31 March 1905; this postponed Act I until 15 April 1906, and the rest until 15 April 1907 'at the latest'.[23] In the process, Durand agreed to write off the 9,000-francs-worth of monthly payments that Debussy had so far received for his never-to-be-completed opera in return for assigning to Durand all the remaining copies of, and publishing materials for, *Pelléas et Mélisande*. Thereafter, the 12,000-francs-worth of monthly payments for *The Devil in the Belfry* were to start again from scratch on 15 April 1905, as we can see from Plate 7. This must have seemed like an advantageous deal to Debussy at the time, even if the long-term winner, as always, was the house of Durand. The problem was that Debussy's first wife, Lilly Texier, who had attempted suicide on 13 October 1904 after her husband's elopement with the singer Emma Bardac, was proving awkward about the impending divorce settlement. Before this was finalised on 2 August 1905, Debussy was forced to make provision for Lilly, which was where his exclusive contract with Durand of 17 July 1905 came in. Plate 8 shows how 80 per cent of Debussy's monthly payments on account for *The Devil in the Belfry* (his only regular income) was suddenly diverted from 16 August 1905 onwards into a 400-franc pension for Lilly. Since life with the extravagant and now pregnant Emma was proving even more expensive than he had anticipated, it can be seen that Durand – who had first appeared to be unusually generous – now held Debussy in a financial grip from which there was no escape and had secured *Pelléas* into the bargain. Debussy found himself obliged 'to present a minimum of four works a year' to Durand.[24] In the event that these did not generate the 4,800 francs needed for

22. From the Durand contract, of which another copy can be found in the Bibliothèque Nationale (BN), Rés. Vm. Dos. 13 (1): 'conte musical en 2 actes et 3 tableaux'.

23. BN, Rés. Vm. Dos. 13 (3). As far as we know, the opera never proceeded beyond its 1903 sketches; in effect, this project was also Durand's official way of replacing Hartmann as Debussy's benefactor, and on the same terms.

24. Contract of 17 July 1905 in the archives of Editions Durand, Paris, and cited by kind permission. 'M. Claude Debussy s'engage à présenter au minimum de quatre oeuvres par an.' This was, in fact, Debussy's permanent contract with Durand.

Lilly's pension in any future year, Durand would be entitled to reclaim the difference by other means, including from Debussy's author's rights as declared by the Société des Auteurs et Compositeurs Dramatiques (SACD) or by the Société des Auteurs, Compositeurs et Editeurs de Musique (SACEM).[25] This was a drastic clause that Durand finally removed in October 1913 after appeals from an impoverished (and often near-suicidal) Debussy.

Debussy's Worsening Financial Situation in 1912–13

The reality was that, despite his using Durand as his banker and accountant and also borrowing heavily from moneylenders, Debussy's debt to Durand grew incessantly and was nowhere near matched by income from his author's rights, even including those for the widely performed *Pelléas*.[26] By April 1912 his debt had risen to 42,866 francs 65 centimes; a year later, despite substantial payments for the ballet *Jeux*, it still amounted to 39,166 francs.[27] Jacques Durand calculated everything to the centime. To show how little he gave away, one need merely consider that he made Debussy pay 4 francs 50 centimes for three batons and buy his own score of *La Mer* (15 francs, both in cash) to send to Henry Wood in London; this occurred in January 1908 before the composer's first conducting trip to London![28] So it is perhaps understandable that Debussy should have occasionally tried to go behind Durand's back, such as when he signed a private contract with Maud Allan for *Khamma* in September

25. All rights to *The Devil in the Belfry* (which came to be symbolic of Debussy's contractual debt to Durand) were finally surrendered to Durand on 19 October 1910, even though Debussy's had also resold the first performance rights to it to Giulio Gatti-Casazza of the New York Metropolitan Opera for 2,000 francs on 5 July 1908.
26. Following standard French contractual procedure, Debussy shared these in the proportion of two-thirds to one-third with the librettist, Maurice Maeterlinck. For performances outside France, two-thirds went to the authors (split two-thirds/one-third between composer and librettist), while one-third came to Durand.
27. BN, Rés. Vm. Dos. 13 (15), which shows Debussy's accounts for 1912–13.
28. BN, Rés. Vm. Dos. 13 (19) – an account sent to Debussy on 11 April 1908. Durand did, however, give Debussy a ten per cent discount on all purchases. The prices in question help to give some idea of the contemporary value of the franc; in 1907 a cheap ticket to a Chevillard or Colonne concert cost six francs.

Plate 8 Monthly payments to Debussy of 17 July and 16 August 1905 show the conversion of 80 per cent of the receipts into a pension for his divorced first wife, Lilly Texier. (Reproduced by kind permission of Editions Durand, Paris.)

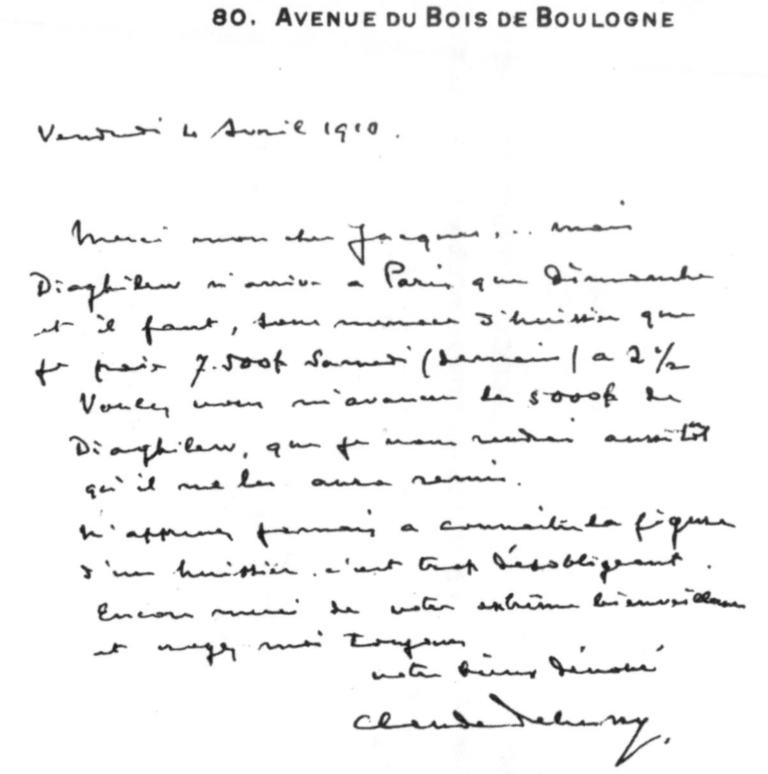

80, AVENUE DU BOIS DE BOULOGNE

Vendredi 4 Avril 1913.

Merci mon cher Jacques... mais Diaghilew n'arrive à Paris que Dimanche et il faut, sous menace d'huissier que je paie 7.500f Samedi (demain) à 2 h. Voulez vous m'avancer les 5000f de Diaghilew, que je vous rendrai aussitôt qu'il me les aura remis.
N'ayant jamais à connaître la figure d'un huissier. c'est trop désobligeant.
Encore merci de votre extrême bienveillance et croyez moi toujours
votre bien dévoué
Claude Debussy.

Plate 9 Letter from Debussy to Durand of 4 April 1913 requesting an advance of 5,000 francs. (Reproduced by kind permission of Editions Durand, Paris.)

1910, for a fee of 10,000 francs. Unfortunately, things soon went wrong, which meant that the long-suffering Durand and his lawyers had to be called in to sort matters out.[29]

We can see Jacques Durand at his patient best in what appears to be a typical episode that occurred while Debussy was finishing the orchestration of *Jeux* to meet Diaghilev's deadline. Plates 9 and 10 show how quickly Durand was able to respond to Debussy's problems. We begin with a letter written on the morning of Friday 4 April

29. For full details see Robert Orledge, *Debussy and the Theatre*, Cambridge, Cambridge University Press, 1982, pp. 128–41. In the end, Durand had to pay Charles Koechlin to complete the ballet's orchestration in 1912–13; as a 'thank-you' Debussy dedicated the score to Mme Jacques Durand.

Plate 10 A receipt signed by Debussy for the 5,000 francs that he received from Jacques Durand on the same day as his request (4 April 1913). (Reproduced by kind permission of Editions Durand, Paris.)

1913 in which Debussy tells Durand that 'under threat of a bailiff' he must repay 7,500 francs by the following afternoon. Diaghilev, who owes him money for the score of *Jeux*, is not returning to Paris until Sunday (6 April), so the composer asks Durand to advance him the 5,000 francs that Diaghilev owes.[30] The documents reproduced as Plates 9 and 10 show not only that Durand sent Debussy the money on the day of the request itself, but also that Debussy immediately signed and returned an official receipt for the advance. Presumably, Debussy added the other 2,500 francs himself.

There one might have expected the matter to end, but three further letters of 14 April 1913 (the only surviving exchange between Debussy and Durand) show that after Diaghilev handed over some money on 13 April, Debussy attempted to borrow an equivalent sum again in order to solve further domestic problems. Moreover, he wanted the money sent discreetly to an address in the rue Royale! Durand's reply that same day put the situation in a nutshell, pointing out firmly that Debussy 'is no doubt aware that the accounts of the place de la Madeleine and my personal account always end up becoming amalgamated and the solution that you suggest to me would not be a solution at all – for it is absolutely necessary to settle your debt in the interests of both of us'.[31] Despite his frankness, Durand managed to find a solution in the form of another advance on Debussy's forthcoming author's rights. With a polite thank you from Debussy and a plea that only part of these rights be appropriated, the episode was tactfully closed.

Debussy's Letters to Durand

The collection of Debussy's letters (1894–1917) that Jacques Durand published is equally tactful in that it omits many names and any

---

30. The relevant text of the previously unpublished letter in the Editions Durand archives is: 'Diaghilew n'arrive à Paris que Dimanche et il faut, sous menace d'huissier que je paie 7.500 f[rancs] Samedi (demain) à 2½ [heures]. / Voulez-vous m'avancer les 5000f[rancs] de Diaghilew, que je vous rendrai aussitôt qu'il me les aura remis.'

31. Letter of 14 April 1913 from Jacques Durand to Debussy in the Editions Durand archives, p. 1: 'Vous n'ignorez pas que les comptes de la place de la Madeleine et mon compte personnel finissent toujours par se rejoindre et la solution que vous me suggérez n'en serait pas une – car il est absolument nécessaire d'amortir votre compte, ceci dans notre intérêt réciproque.'

letters or passages that were even mildly controversial.[32] Debussy was a great letter writer, and, because he saw Durand almost daily (travelling to the publisher's office by chauffeured car), most of the letters come from periods when he was away from Paris. The complete correspondence falls into at least sixteen categories and deals with every aspect of their relationship. Many letters contain passages that relate to several categories, and many further examples for each category can be found for each of the sixteen listed below:

1 Proof corrections, as in Nichols (1987), letter 108, p. 137, concerning the missing bar in *Jardins sous la pluie* (August 1903).
2 Edition covers, their layout and their colour, as in Nichols, letter 109, p. 138, concerning the blue and pale gold cover to be used for the *Estampes* (1903).
3 His holidays, as in Nichols, letter 125, p. 153 (26 July 1905).
4 His compositional processes, as in Nichols, letter 155, p. 155, on the new version of *Reflets dans l'eau* written in Eastbourne (19 August 1905).
5 Durand's home at Bel-Ebat, as in Nichols, letter 129, p. 158 (11 September 1905). This is followed by a picture of Durand in 1905 looking typically dapper and reserved (Nichols, p. 159). He could easily have passed as a stiff-upper-lipped Englishman.
6 French artists with whom Debussy worked, as in Nichols, letter 132, pp. 162–63, on the conductor Camille Chevillard (11 October 1905). These letters were usually pretty scathing, hence the cuts in the 1927 edition.
7 Performances of his works abroad, as in Nichols, letter 142, pp. 174–75, on *Pelléas* in Brussels (7 January 1907). Again, these were invariably scathing.
8 What music can and should accomplish, as in Nichols, letter 154, p. 184, of 3 September 1907. Such letters are rare.
9 His other professional activities, as in Nichols, letter 178, p. 205, on judging woodwind competitions at the Conservatoire (13 July 1909).

32. Jacques Durand (ed.): *Lettres de Claude Debussy à son éditeur*, Paris, Durand, 1927. The complete correspondence is now in the Bibliothèque Gustav Mahler, 11 bis, rue Vézelay, Paris 8. Further letters appear in Lesure (1993) and in translation in François Lesure (ed.) and Roger Nichols (ed. and trans.), *Debussy Letters*, London, Faber, 1987.

10 Diaghilev and the Ballets Russes, as in Nichols, letter 179, pp. 205–6 (18 July 1909).

11 His true inner thoughts and character, as in Nichols, letter 194, p. 220 (8 July 1910). These are the rarest of all and reflect the fact that Durand became his main confidant after 1904.

12 His financial, domestic and medical problems, as in Plate 9 and Nichols, letter 215, pp. 243–44 (19 July 1911). In these letters Debussy often emerges as the self-pitying neurasthenic.

13 The dancer Maud Allan and her global problems with *Khamma*, as in Nichols, letter 227, p. 258 (2 July 1912). These were again very scathing and show that Debussy and Durand (like many of their contemporaries) were not averse to racist and sexist jokes.

14 The war and Debussy's inability to contribute usefully to it, as in Nichols, letter 264, p. 291 (8 August 1914). These are frequent and verge on the chauvinistic.

15 Editing, as in Nichols, letter 269, p. 296, on Chopin (24 February 1915).

16 His theatrical plans, as in his last letter of 1 November 1917, Nichols, letter 310, p. 334.

To these should be added the very rare letters of Debussy the 'business-man' – a term that he seems to have used only in the summer of 1915. Prior to this, Debussy refers to the same sort of very down-to-earth procedure setting out the facts by the phrase 'in legal fashion', as in a bullet-pointed letter of 30 July 1909, in which he explains to Louis Laloy why he went ahead and wrote the libretto for *Masques et bergamasques* himself.[33] 'Business-man' speak first occurs on 22 July 1915, when Debussy formally sends Durand the revised central tableau of *En blanc et noir* (Durand (1927), p. 138). But the composer quickly slips into his usual engaging style as he describes what he has achieved musically. 'Business-man' speak recurs at greater length in his unpublished letter to Durand of 9 August 1915, when Debussy is busy with the Cello Sonata and the *Douze études* during his last productive summer at Pourville. Debussy probably knew that this was around the time when Durand would be drawing up his contract for the Cello

---

33. Nichols (1987), p. 182. See also Orledge (1982), pp. 152–53, for a full account of this theatre project for Diaghilev, for which Laloy had intended to supply the scenario himself. Nothing came of the proposed ballet except Debussy's libretto, which Durand published in June 1910 (D. & F. 7821: one hundred copies only).

Sonata, so he carefully explained: 'A sonata for cello and piano will not sell like smaller pieces; however, virtuosi on this instrument have been asking me for one for a long time; and then, the cello repertoire is not rich!'[34] Passing on to his piano studies, Debussy reveals an intention to stock up his account with Durand in order to reduce his overdraft: 'Given the sum involved,' he continues, 'there is nothing I can do at this moment to redeem my account. When I send you the *Etudes*, which will inevitably represent a much greater sum, it is well within my intentions to make as much of a repayment as I possibly can.'[35] However much Debussy disliked being so direct, his letter seems to have had some effect, since the contract Durand issued for the *Etudes* on 3 September 1915 was for the then enormous sum of 12,000 francs (see Table 7).

But when there were general rather than immediately personal issues involved, Debussy showed far less concern than Durand. One of the best moments in Durand's rather businesslike memoirs is when he describes the dinner that his father Auguste arranged in order to bring Richard Strauss and Debussy together. Strauss, with the help of the Durands, had founded a German society to channel concert rights to composers, just as SACEM did in France. Strauss was full of his achievements, with which he bombarded a totally indifferent Debussy. The conversation was 'too commercial for his taste ... The dinner therefore passed with lively conversation on Richard Strauss's part and obstinate silence from Debussy.'[36] The ascendant star of Stravinsky, however, made a greater impact on Debussy, especially after *Petrushka* in 1911. Two days before the première of *Jeux* Debussy reminded Durand (as if he needed to) to declare his ballet to the Société des Auteurs. But the real reason for his postscript was to

---

34. Letter formerly in the Editions Durand archives: 'Une Sonate pour violoncelle et piano ne se vend pas comme des petits pièces; pourtant les virtuoses de cet instrument me l'on demandra [*sic*] depuis longtemps; puis, le répertoire de cet instrument n'est pas riche!' Debussy's contract, drawn up on the same day, included an advance of 3,000 francs.
35. Ibid.: 'Etant donné la somme, je ne peux cette fois rien affecter à l'amortissement de mon compte. Lorsque que je vous livrerai les 'Etudes', qui forcément représenteront une somme plus forte, il est bien dans mes intentions de ce faire dans le sens le plus large possible.'
36. Durand (1925), pp. 29–30: 'cette conversation, à son gré trop commerciale ... Le déjeuner se passa donc en conversation active de la part de Richard Strauss et en mutisme obstiné de la part de Debussy.'

make the observation: 'As it is not a question of a subsidised theatre, the division of rights can be arranged thus: 2/3 for the composer; 1/3 for the librettist; at least, that's how Stravinsky does it.'[37]

The 'Livres de Cotage' and Debussy's Compositional Preferences

Even though the theatre was the greatest potential source of income before the advent of the film score, *Jeux* was the only commissioned theatrical score that Debussy completely orchestrated himself. And such was Diaghilev's charisma that it was delivered only three weeks late! Few of Debussy's many projected theatre scores passed the drawing-board stage, and their number was undoubtedly stimulated by the financial success of the sketches for *Le Diable dans le beffroi*. Debussy's real interest, however, lay in his other Poe opera, *La Chute de la Maison Usher*, whose scenario he completed to his satisfaction only in 1917. It was perhaps because the theatre was such a potential money-spinner that Durand did not complain more about the unproductive hours Debussy spent on a one-act opera whose strange music he left more than half unfinished. A project such as *Le Palais du silence* or *No-ja-li*, for instance, showed that André Charlot of the Alhambra Theatre, Leicester Square, was prepared to pay 25,000 francs for a fifteen-minute oriental ballet in 1913 – an offer that Debussy would have been totally incapable of refusing. And before Durand was forced to send the Alhambra *Printemps* instead (recently re-scored by Henri Büsser), Debussy even approached Charles Koechlin with an offer to 'write a ballet for him that he [Debussy] would sign'![38] Even though Debussy jotted down a few ideas for the start of *No-ja-li* in January 1914, and despite the fact that the role of silence in music had always fascinated him, in this case a more conventional silence supervened, and the project, like so many others, fizzled out because it was not part of the career Debussy had mapped out **for himself**.

37. Letter of 13 May 1913: 'Comme il ne s'agit pas d'un théâtre subventionné, le partage des droits peut ainsi s'effectuer: 2/3 pour le compositeur; 1/3 pour le librettiste; du moins, est-ce ainsi que Stravinsky s'est arrangé.' The Ballets Russes première took place at the Théâtre des Champs-Elysées two weeks before *Le Sacre du printemps*. The librettist was named as Vaslav Nijinsky, even if the slight scenario from which Debussy worked was probably mostly by Diaghilev himself.
38. See Orledge (1982), pp. 186–205, for full details. Koechlin naturally refused the offer to compose *No-ja-li* for Debussy.

Next to the theatre, piano music was the biggest golden egg. Once Debussy was part of the Durand machine, this was what he was principally encouraged to produce. Since he was an excellent pianist, and piano pieces were on the whole shorter and required less effort to notate, this proved no great hardship. But given the compulsive non-completion and inclination to laziness that runs through Debussy's career, it is unlikely that we should possess as much piano music by him as we do, had he not been up to his ears in debt, or if Emma Bardac's financier uncle, Osiris, had not left his twenty-five million francs to the Pasteur Institute when he died in February 1907 in order to show his disapproval of her moral conduct.

Following on from this, a return to the Durand *Livres de cotage* can tell us more about why Debussy chose to write the piano music he did. First, in the case of the *Estampes*, the final toccata, *Jardins sous la pluie*, proved to be the bestseller by far.[39] Its frequent reprints had reached a thousand copies by 1905 (as opposed to the year 1909 for its companions); by 1929 it had sold 81,200 copies, as against eight thousand of *Pagodes* and 24,900 of *La Soirée dans Grenade*. Moreover, *Jardins* continued to be reprinted throughout both world wars. But it was the evocative title rather than its spectacular nature that promoted sales. Of the first series of *Images* in 1905, *Reflets dans l'eau* was reprinted far more often and in greater numbers than either *Hommage à Rameau* (for all its French associations) or *Mouvement* (another concluding toccata).[40] This fact would have been evident to Debussy by the time he began his first book of *Préludes,* with their evocative titles, in the winter of 1909–10, since *Reflets dans l'eau* had already enjoyed two reprints of one thousand copies each in April and October 1909. This fact may help to explain the presence of two 'watery' preludes in the first collection (Nos 2 and 10). The pattern persisted: by 1928 *Reflets* had sold 32,500 copies, as against 8,500 of the *Hommage* and 5,500 of *Mouvement*.

A similar pattern emerged (though not during Debussy's lifetime) with the second series of *Images*, where the most difficult piece, and the one with the most memorable title (*Poissons d'or*), proved the

---

39. Information from *Livre de cotage No.* 2. The three *Estampes* (D. & F. 6326 (1–3)) appeared in October 1903 in a print run of four hundred copies each.
40. Ibid., D. & F. 6615 (1–3), which appeared on 11 October 1905 in a print run of five hundred copies each.

most popular.[41] In fact, the only curious case arising from Debussy's first years with Durand was that of the companion pieces *Masques* and *L'Isle joyeuse* (D. & F. 6443 and 6446). Perhaps expecting it to be more popular than the difficult *L'Isle joyeuse*, Durand decided to bring out *Masques* in an edition of six hundred copies in September 1904, as against only five hundred copies of *L'Isle*. But again, the choice of title won out. As Table 8 shows, *Masques* fell in popularity as *L'Isle joyeuse* rose. Once more, a pattern that had established itself during Debussy's lifetime continued after his death. He would have been encouraged to write his *Etudes* in 1915 in the knowledge that technical difficulty did not harm sales.

Table 8: Print runs of *Masques* and *L'Isle joyeuse* from the Durand *Livre de cotage No. 3*

6443: *Masques*		6446: *L'Isle joyeuse*	
Sept 1904	600	Sept 1904	500
15 Nov 1905	500	15 Nov 1905	500
Apr 1908	500	Oct 1907	1,000
Jan 1910	500	Jan 1910	1,000
Apr 1912	500	Jun 1911	1,000
		Mar 1913	1,000
Feb 1917	200	Jun 1916	2,000
Feb 1918	200		
May 1919	300	May 1919	1,000
Jul 1920	1,000	Jun 1920	2,000
		Aug 1922	2,000
Jan 1924	1,000	Aug 1924	2,000
Jan 1926	1,000	Feb 1926	2,000
		May 1928	2,000
		May 1930	2,000
Feb 1931	500	Feb 1932	2,000
Total:	12,300	*Total:*	43,500
(by 1963)		(by 1966)	

41. Ibid., D. & F. 6994 (1–3), which appeared in December 1907 in a run of five hundred copies each, but with one thousand copies of all three as a set (as opposed to five hundred of the *Estampes* and five hundred of the first series of *Images*).

The proof that short, catchy titles were of paramount importance is brought home, of course, by *Golliwogg's Cake Walk* (D. & F. 7188 (5)), which outsold by far the other pieces in *Children's Corner* (despite a conservative initial printing of five hundred in September 1908), and whose sales passed the quarter-million mark in 1968. The damp squib at the other end of the scale was the academic-sounding *Hommage à Haydn* (D. & F. 7582), which hardly needed reprinting after its (perhaps snobbishly) optimistic run of one thousand copies in February 1910. Even so, with 1,700 copies sold in Debussy's lifetime, it achieved higher sales than any of the orchestral scores (full-size and miniature) – even those of such well-known works as *La Mer* and *Ibéria*. And that calculation takes into account duet or two-piano arrangements of the orchestral works, even in cases where Debussy made them himself (as applies to the duet version of *La Mer* (D. & F. 6606), with its famous Hokusai cover, which sold only one thousand copies up to 1921). In fact, sales of the first book of *Préludes* (D. & F. 7687), both separately and combined, easily outstripped the **total** sales of Debussy's orchestral works and their various reductions. The top three preludes proved to be *La Fille aux cheveux de lin*, *La Cathédrale engloutie* and *Minstrels*, which again shows the power of the imaginative title.

Sadly, this proved to be the height of Debussy's popularity in terms of commercial sales. If one considers the 335,061 copies of *The Girl with the Flaxen Hair* sold between April 1910 and 1992, sales of The Beatles' LPs or the Harry Potter paperbacks knock Debussy into a cocked hat – until one remembers that Debussy's piece is still maintaining its sales figures nearly a century after its composition despite all the vagaries of popular taste. His second book of *Préludes* (D. & F. 8697–8708) sold less well than the first, even though Durand optimistically increased the initial print run of the collected volume to two thousand in February 1913. The need to reprint the first book of *Préludes* after four months helps to explain why Debussy chose (or was encouraged) to repeat the experiment, even if he had some precedent in the twenty-four-prelude collections of Bach and Chopin. The second time round, there were no clear winners, although *Bruyères*, his cosy follow-up to *The Girl with the Flaxen Hair*, came out top, in the end nosing ahead of the spectacular *Feux d'artifice*.

After this, Debussy's greatest success came in November 1913 with the piano score of his children's ballet *La Boîte à joujoux* (D. & F. 8935), which contained attractive colour illustrations by André Hellé.

The fact that Debussy's 1908 *Children's Corner* suite kept reprinting in yearly issues of two thousand, coupled with his desire to write music for his little daughter Emma-Claude ('Chouchou'), lay behind the follow-up of *La Boîte*. But Debussy abandoned writing song cycles after the *Trois poèmes de Stéphane Mallarmé* of 1913, perhaps because these had always sold badly in comparison with piano music. Indeed, the Mallarmé songs did not pass the thousand mark in sales until well after Debussy's death in 1918.

In spite of the promotional work of the Concerts Durand after 1910, *La Boîte* was Debussy's last real success. Although Durand brought out a first edition of two thousand of each volume of the *Etudes* in memory of Chopin (D. & F. 9406–7), by which Debussy set so much store, this venture proved over-optimistic in the wartime atmosphere of 1916. Neither volume needed to reprint until 1923–24, and then only in much reduced numbers. Of the three final wartime sonatas, the Cello Sonata (D. & F. 9390) was initially the best seller, although sales remained steady rather than impressive until Debussy's overall popularity increased (in Japan, especially) in the 1970s.

Epilogue

I would maintain, contrary to a received opinion, that there was no decline in quality in Debussy's music after 1910: one has only to study such scores as *Jeux*, *En blanc et noir* or the *Etudes* to see this. Rather, his decline in popularity stemmed from the changing circumstances of the war years and the way in which Stravinsky came to dominate the Parisian musical scene by dint of his theatrical energy and Russian-inspired originality. If Jacques Durand ever thought he was fighting a losing battle with his ailing friend Debussy in 1916–17, he never let it show. Indeed, he continued to increase the initial print runs of Debussy's works, as we have seen, safe in the knowledge that such earlier successes as the *Deux arabesques* could compensate him for any deficit incurred. Since Debussy had come to trust his publisher's judgement, all his later works received their first private performances in front of Jacques, who was also the last person to receive a letter from the composer.

By mid-1917, when rectal cancer forced Debussy into silence, the friendship had lasted over thirty-three years, longer even than Debussy's stormier friendship with Satie, whose music Durand did not like, and the manuscript of whose *Véritables préludes flasques (pour un chien)* he had 'returned like a glove' in 1912.[42] In his memoirs, Durand expressed a belief that Satie had brought him these particular pieces mainly because he knew he loved dogs; he seems to have been genuinely sorry that Debussy's friend thought him 'a hardened traditionalist.'[43] But that quality, coupled with his unwavering judgements and economic astuteness, was what raised Jacques Durand to his position as the foremost French music publisher of his day. If Satie sneered at Durand behind his back, he none the less wanted to have his pieces published by him – like every other serious composer in the Paris of that time. And it has to be remembered that Jacques Durand unhesitatingly supported the quiet revolution that occurred as Debussy stripped music of its conventional form and gave it the rhythmic and timbral freedom that brought it into the twentieth century. As Debussy told Durand in 1907, 'Music consists of colours and barred rhythms'.[44] He might have added that his vision might never have become a worldwide reality without the meticulous editions, the faith and the business expertise of Durand et Cie.

---

42. As Satie told Roland-Manuel in a letter of 14 September 1912 (see the Drouot Richelieu Sale Catalogue, 24 Mars 2000, p. 62, lot 208): 'M. Durand m'a retourné – comme un gant – mon manuscrit.'
43. Durand (1927), p. 52: 'un traditionaliste endurci'. It was instead Eugène Demets who published Satie's *Real Flabby Preludes (for a Dog)*, in December 1912.
44. Durand (1927), p. 55, letter of 3 September 1907: 'Elle [la musique] est de couleurs et de temps rythmés.'

5

Nadia Boulanger (1887–1979): The Teacher in the Marketplace

Caroline Potter

Although Nadia Boulanger's reputation as one of the greatest music teachers of the twentieth century is secure, surprisingly little is known about her approach to teaching and the content of her classes. Nadia Boulanger herself is most to blame for this, as she rarely revealed anything of importance about her life or work to interviewers and always turned down offers to publish her teaching materials. She was always keen to emphasise that the musical work, rather than the performer or a commentator on the music, should be the centre of attention.[1] The aura of mystery that she created only enhanced her reputation, giving her students the impression that they belonged to an elite group.

Although one might presume that a teacher of her eminence would have taught only elite students, Boulanger taught a surprisingly varied student body that included those with little previous knowledge of harmony as well as successful students who were promising young composers. The three principal types of student she taught can, in general, be placed into separate categories by virtue of their financial status and their gender. Some of her students were young female amateurs who viewed music as an essential accomplishment for someone of their background; others were men who aimed for a professional career in music, usually as composers or performers. The third principal group – women who sought a career as music teachers – often considered Nadia Boulanger as a role model. My initial assumption was that there would be substantial differences between Boulanger's approaches as a teacher to these three groups of student, since the aims and objectives of the different types of pupil were clearly very varied.

---

1. For instance, in an interview with Irene Slade (recorded in 1960 on an LP preserved in the National Sound Archive, London).

While she was, of course, obliged to tailor the content of classes to the abilities of her students, there are several common threads running through her teaching career. In particular, the transmission of a central Western musical culture, based on great composers and the masterpieces they wrote, was fundamental to her outlook. Also, for many of her students, she represented the prestige, civilised qualities and socially desirable aspects of French culture. Boulanger handed down this cultural heritage to students from many different countries and backgrounds. Having studied the small archive of teaching material preserved in the Nadia Boulanger Collection at the Conservatoire National Supérieur de Musique de Lyon – one of the few sources to reveal information about her teaching of non-expert musicians – I can offer some insight into her teaching methods and the content of some of her classes.

Boulanger began teaching in autumn 1904, when she was a student at the Paris Conservatoire, in order to support herself and her family. She continued working almost until her death at the age of ninety-two in 1979, although in her last decade she was blind and extremely frail. Her father, Ernest Boulanger (1815–1900), was a composer (winner of the Prix de Rome in 1836) who ended his long musical career as a professor of singing at the Paris Conservatoire. One of his last pupils was the Russian-born Raïssa Myschetsky, whom he later married; she was around forty years his junior (there is some uncertainty over her year of birth) and always used the title 'Princesse', although there is no evidence to suggest that she was entitled to do so. Boulanger's family background was therefore musical (friends of the family included Charles Gounod and Gabriel Fauré) and, on her mother's side, supposedly aristocratic though not wealthy.

Nadia Boulanger's studies at the Conservatoire were crowned with first prizes in harmony, counterpoint, organ, fugue and piano accompaniment. She was often the youngest student in her class to obtain the prize. Her elderly father having died when she was twelve, she was obliged to support an ailing younger sister, Lili, and a mother whose claimed aristocratic background prevented her from working. Nadia Boulanger was therefore impatient to complete her studies and launch herself into a career. She reached the final round of the ultimate competition for composers at the Conservatoire, the Prix de Rome, in three consecutive years (1907–09), her best placing being the second prize that she won in 1908. These Conservatoire prizes were of crucial importance to her, being guarantees of her ability and status as a teacher.

Nadia Boulanger often said that her mother was the primary influence on her life and work; her mother taught her the importance of applying the highest possible standards to herself and, by extension, to others. Also, Boulanger's refusal to waste a minute of time – exemplified by her very busy teaching schedule – can be ascribed to her mother's influence. Her teaching day often began at 8 a.m. and continued until the early hours of the morning. For as long as she was able, she worked six days a week. She would often invite students to lunch or dinner and continue a class during the meal. Finally, her mother constantly stressed the importance of doing one's duty, and, as a teacher, Boulanger dedicated her life to her students.

At first, she taught solfège, harmony, counterpoint, fugue, piano and organ privately. Many of her students for these subjects came to her through word-of-mouth recommendation, often via family connections. The family's reputation as fine musicians must have provided her with many advantages when setting herself up as a music teacher. But at the same time, it was not considered desirable for a young lady of her social background to solicit work through advertisements.

She obtained her first official position in a music school in autumn 1907, probably thanks to her mentor Raoul Pugno, the pianist and composer with whom she jointly wrote some compositions. This music school was the private Conservatoire Femina-Musica, an establishment that, in the words of Boulanger's biographer Léonie Rosenstiel, 'catered primarily to well-to-do young Parisiennes' and was bankrolled by the periodicals *Femina* and *Musica*. Rosenstiel also notes that she would have been paid half the salary that a man would have earned for the same job.[2] This post entailed teaching elementary piano and the class known as *accompagnement au piano*. The latter was not simply a 'piano accompaniment' class but rather one in which students were taught auxiliary disciplines that included score reading, transposition and figured bass realisation.

Female pupils from financially comfortable families were, then as now, the most substantial and most lucrative market for a music teacher. Very few of Nadia Boulanger's female students became professional composers. One exception was Marcelle de Manziarly, a

2. Léonie Rosenstiel, *Nadia Boulanger: A Life in Music*, New York and London, Norton, 1998, p. 64.

pupil and friend from 1912 until the end of her life, although Manziarly, coming from a wealthy family background, never had to earn a living as a composer.

Although Nadia Boulanger studied composition at the Paris Conservatoire, which for a time provided an important creative outlet for her, she stopped composing around 1923. This abandonment of creative work was due to several factors: the death of Raoul Pugno in 1913; that of her younger sister, Lili, in 1918; the generally lukewarm critical response to her music; and, perhaps most importantly, her highly self-critical attitude towards her own music.[3] A journalist writing for *Samedi-Soir* noted that Nadia Boulanger could have become a composer, but she 'insists that she gave up writing because she had nothing new to say'.[4] Not only a perfectionist as a composer, Boulanger showed little interest in musical works besides those she considered to be masterpieces. Her teaching materials abound with references to 'works by the masters', and she firmly believed that the study of music was the study of musical masterpieces. As she once said: 'Just as I accept God, I accept beauty, I accept feeling, I also accept the masterpiece.'[5]

Boulanger's former pupil Georges Szipine, and others, believed that her failure to win first prize in the Prix de Rome could be ascribed to sexism.[6] Nadia Boulanger did not wish to discuss this possibility, refused to acknowledge that she could be seen as a role model for women composers and often said that women could not hope to combine an artistic career with family life. In an interview given in the year that she abandoned composition she was asked about the principal concerns of young women of the time. She replied: 'Artists think only of their art, and they consider it is totally incompatible with the joys of family life. From the day a woman wants to play her one true

---

3. For more details about her composing career see Caroline Potter, 'Nadia and Lili Boulanger: Sister Composers', *Musical Quarterly*, Vol. 83 (1999), pp. 536–56.
4. J. de Montalais, article dated 10 March 1951: 'Elle affirme pourtant qu'elle n'a plus écrit parce qu'elle n'avait rien de neuf à dire.' All articles without titles and/or page numbers were consulted in the archive of the CNSM de Lyon.
5. Bruno Monsaingeon, *Mademoiselle: Entretiens avec Nadia Boulanger*, Paris, Van de Velde, 1980, p. 30: 'Comme j'accepte Dieu, j'accepte la beauté, j'accepte l'émotion, j'accepte aussi bien le chef d'oeuvre.'
6. Interview with Bernard Keeffe for the BBC programme 'The Tender Tyrant' (first broadcast in September 1969), consulted at the National Sound Archive.

role – that of mother and wife – it is impossible for her to be an artist as well.'[7]

Her apparent lack of sympathy with the feminist movement is revealed by her oft-repeated belief that marriage and caring for children were the supreme female achievements. This view devalues Nadia Boulanger's own considerable professional success, since she never married and had no children.

Boulanger once described herself as 'a mere teacher',[8] again diminishing her own achievements. Whilst she was surely correct in implying that, in the musical sphere, teachers are rather less important than composers, it is also fair to say that teaching was the only branch of the musical profession in which she could have excelled. By the end of her long life, women composers had become less of a novelty than they were in the early years of the twentieth century. It is depressing to note that critics of Boulanger's music almost inevitably made reference to her gender, refusing to judge her music on its merits. Whatever obstacles Boulanger encountered in her teaching career, she was invariably taken seriously by her fellow professionals and gained a worldwide reputation that no other woman composer of her generation achieved.

D. F. Aitken, writing in the *Radio Times* in 1936, believed that Nadia Boulanger's pupils thought that she was the greatest teacher in Europe 'because she has no axe to grind. Years ago she gave up the idea of being herself a composer ... since she is not primarily a composer, she has no style of her own to impress on her pupils, no ready-made pattern by which to turn out so many little Boulangers with five years' struggle in front of them before they can recover any semblance of individuality.'[9] Although this is perhaps not an accurate assessment of the process of teaching composition, Aitken was right to emphasise that Boulanger was not a professional threat to her students, since she was not a competitor of theirs. In this sense, it could be said that Nadia Boulanger's conformity with the expectation that a woman

7. Interview in *Femina* (1913), p. 647: 'Les artistes ne rêvent qu'à leur art et le jugent absolument incompatible avec les joies de l'existence familiale. Du jour où la femme veut tenir son rôle véritable de mère et d'épouse, il lui est impossible de tenir son rôle d'artiste, écrivain ou musicienne.'
8. In an interview with the magazine *Minerva* (15 July 1928); cited in Rosenstiel (1998), p. 222.
9. D. F. Aitken, untitled article in the *Radio Times*, 13 November 1936, p. 19.

should not aim to become a professional composer worked, ironically, in her favour.

Nadia Boulanger's first pupils were young women from well-to-do families. She did not come into contact with different types of student until she obtained posts in music schools that offered entrance scholarships. One of these institutions was the Ecole Normale de Musique, founded in Paris in autumn 1919 as a more liberal competitor of the Conservatoire. The Ecole Normale lacked the qualifying examinations of that establishment and had no upper age limits for enrolment. In common with all institutions with that title, one of the principal functions of the Ecole Normale was to train teachers, although it also attracted students who were not aiming for a professional career. In Léonie Rosenstiel's words, 'Deserving poor students could find scholarships there; the Ecole Normale's society pupils subsidised the poor but gifted, their tuition money serving as the school's financial cushion, its insurance against bankruptcy.'[10]

Much to her disappointment, Boulanger was not appointed to a permanent teaching post at the Paris Conservatoire until 1946 (when she was named professor of *accompagnement au piano*), although she had applied for positions there since at least 1910. Even though three of her students (Marcelle Soulage, Pierre Menu and Renée de Marquein) entered the Prix de Rome competition in 1919, none of them listed Nadia Boulanger as his or her teacher. Perhaps this was not so surprising, since the Prix de Rome was a competition organised by the Conservatoire, whose students would not have wished to associate themselves too closely with a teacher from outside its walls.[11]

It is perhaps surprising that very few of Boulanger's best students were French (Jean Françaix being the best-known exception), although she was often described as the greatest living French music teacher of her time. However, she gained a particularly strong reputation in the USA as a teacher; her illustrious American composition pupils included Aaron Copland, George Antheil, Elliott Carter and Roy Harris, and she also taught many American amateur musicians. As Virgil Thomson, one of her first American pupils, wrote in 1962: 'Nadia Boulanger [...] has for more than forty years been, for musical Americans, a one-woman graduate school so powerful and so perme-

10. Rosenstiel (1998), p. 145.
11. Ibid., p. 147.

ating that legend credits every American town with two things – a five-and-dime and a Boulanger pupil'.[12] For her part, Boulanger believed that the training her American students received from her in Europe was particularly valuable to them because, according to her: 'they [Americans] do very well at school, they are very talented but, in many cases, they do not start from a solid base as their ear is not properly trained [...] Why is this the case? Because little children must not be tired!'[13] She considered that it was her job to rectify this lack of rigorous study and hard work that she detected in her American pupils.

Her first American students came to Paris to study with her in the early 1920s, either at the Ecole Normale or privately at her home in rue Ballu. Boulanger was also one of the founders, in 1921, of the Conservatoire Américain in Fontainebleau, which enhanced her association with students from the United States. She eventually learned to speak English well, although in the early 1920s she confessed to knowing only a few words of the language in which her American students were to be taught.[14]

The Conservatoire Américain was a singular institution. It was not, strictly speaking, a conservatory, since classes ran for only three months a year, during the summer (Nadia Boulanger once said: 'Summer is the best time to work').[15] Although catering for American students (and, later, those of other nationalities), it was based in Fontainebleau, to the south of Paris, and the musical education dispensed by Boulanger and others at this institution was quintessentially French. Moreover, many of Boulanger's colleagues in Fontainebleau were also professors at the Paris Conservatoire. Unsurprisingly, therefore, the pedagogic ideals of that establishment were also the focus of the Fontainebleau institution.

The Conservatoire Américain was founded by the American Walter Damrosch, a conductor and the president of the American Friends of

---

12. Virgil Thomson, article in *New York Times Magazine*, 4 February 1962.
13. Monsaingeon (1980), p. 26: 'Ils font des études brillantes, parce qu'ils ont des gens très doués, mais [...] les bases ne sont pas assurés dans beaucoup de cas, leur oreille n'étant pas développée [...] Pourquoi? ... parce qu'il ne faut pas fatiguer les enfants!'
14. Ibid., p. 25.
15. Charles F. Dupêchez (1981), 'Le Conservatoire Américain de Fontainebleau', unknown source: 'Les vacances, c'est le meilleur moment pour travailler'.

Musicians in France, an organisation founded during the First World War. During this war, both Nadia and Lili Boulanger had been involved with charities concerned with Franco-American relations, and Nadia played at several benefit concerts organised by Damrosch. Together with an American colleague, Damrosch founded a school for bandsmen in France after the war. This college, whose director was Francis Casadesus, was so successful that the idea for a permanent French-based music school for American students was mooted, and this idea resulted in the Conservatoire Américain.

In addition to providing music education of high quality, the purpose of the Conservatoire Américain was to give students a taste of French civilisation and culture, and, as a corollary, to perpetuate the notion that this was a necessary adornment for students from the New World. At the opening festivities for the Conservatoire Américain, Damrosch said to the students: 'Learn French and the French people, they have the civilisation of the ages [...] Their civilisation must be kept for the benefit of the world and it is a supreme privilege for you to share in its rich rewards.'[16] Aaron Copland, one of the institution's first students, said of Nadia Boulanger: 'Her intellectual interests and wide acquaintanceship among artists in all fields were an important stimulus to her American students: through these interests she whetted and broadened their cultural appetites'.[17] Some of the students received grants from American foundations; for instance, Virgil Thomson's studies in France were financed by a bursary from Harvard.

For Boulanger's amateur students, the social cachet of studying at the Conservatoire Américain was comparable to a year spent at a Swiss finishing school by a well-to-do young British lady. This 'civilising' function ensured also that the popular nineteenth-century view of music as a desirable social grace was sustained. Léonie Rosenstiel notes that the American students 'soon realized that Fontainebleau was a social as well as an artistic experience'.[18] Boulanger also kept a close eye on the social development of her students, inviting them to parties, where she ensured that their behaviour was proper and

16. Cited in Rosenstiel (1998), p. 153.
17. Aaron Copland, 'Nadia Boulanger: an affectionate portrait' (typescript at the Conservatoire National Supérieur de Musique, Lyon; later published in *Harper's*, October 1960).
18. Rosenstiel (1998), p. 156.

correct. From 1921 onwards, a select group of students was invited to spend part of the summer at Gargenville, which was regarded as a highly prized invitation. Since 1905 the Boulanger family had spent at least part of the summer in Gargenville, a village situated to the north of Paris, initially as guests at Raoul Pugno's summer home and later in their own property.

It is fair to say that Boulanger's value to her students was not confined to the classroom, and that her interest in their development as people, as well as musicians, exceeded the bounds of a healthy teacher–pupil relationship. Many accounts suggest that she expected her students to confide in her, and that she did not hesitate to express disapproval of the personal relationships of her students; in particular, she was jealous of those students who, having been close to her, chose to marry.

Paris has always been a magnet for artists from all over the world, and in the early decades of the twentieth century the city was a fashionable destination for American artists working in every genre. For instance, the writers Henry Miller, Gertrude Stein and Ernest Hemingway, among many others, left their mark on Parisian artistic life and directly or indirectly encouraged other Americans to make the pilgrimage to the city. The height of popularity of Paris amongst American expatriate artists coincided with the zenith of Nadia Boulanger's reputation as a teacher, in the 1930s. But as late as 1951 a journalist could write of the teacher: 'En Amérique, son nom est synonyme de tout ce que l'école française a de haut et d'excellent.'[19] From 1949, Nadia Boulanger was the director of the Conservatoire Américain.

This was not to say that she was uninterested in music outside the Western European classical tradition. Aaron Copland remembers that she was curious about everything, and that she was fascinated by the complexity of the jazz rhythms he was introducing into his music during the mid-1920s. Copland wrote: 'She had the teacher's consuming need to know how all music functions, and it was that kind of inquiring attitude that registered on the minds of her students.'[20] Moreover, the revised version of the opera she wrote in collaboration with Raoul Pugno, La Ville morte, features an extraordinary piano

19. Montalais (1951).
20. Copland (1960).

cluster. This revised version is dated September 1923 – before Henry Cowell's piano works including clusters were first heard in Paris.

Although the ability and experience of Boulanger's students differed widely, her approach was fundamentally identical, whatever the level of tuition: she believed that aural training should be the foundation of musical appreciation and instruction. She said: 'The great privilege of teaching consists in bringing one's pupils to examine their thoughts in depth, to say what they truly want and to hear exactly what they hear; this is why a thorough and lifelong training in the language of music is essential'.[21] All her students were expected to have the same basic training in the language of Western classical music, because, in her words, 'unless he [the student] knows grammar, he cannot talk'.[22]

The values that she had imbibed from her traditional Conservatoire music education, with its emphasis on solfège, were thus transmitted to her students; the basic training that she herself had received became the basic training undertaken by her students. Moreover, much of the rigid Conservatoire curriculum formed the nucleus of her teaching. On the first page of some material produced for her elementary harmony class, now housed in the Lyon Conservatoire, she noted, with reference to a four-part harmony exercise: 'The student should study the progressions every day, working part by part, and transposing them. One should be able to write and play them by heart, and to analyse them by ear.' Hers was a quasi-religious approach to music: the students were expected to take in, memorise and interiorise a text.

The concept of harmony is introduced in this first lesson via the harmonic series, for Boulanger subscribed to the theory that tonal chords could be derived from this series. More than once in her teaching material, Boulanger quotes Aristotle's dictum: 'Low notes contain high notes, but not vice versa'.[23] She stressed the importance of the fundamental note of any chord, and gave her students several basic

21. Monsaingeon (1980), p. 18: 'Le privilège très grand d'enseigner consiste à amener celui qu'on enseigne à regarder réellement ce qu'il pense, à dire réellement ce qu'il veut et à entendre nettement ce qu'il entend; d'où vient la nécessité d'un entraînement très grand dans la vie: la connaissance des mots.'
22. Interview with Robert Layton, broadcast by the BBC on 30 September 1969; consulted at the National Sound Archive.
23. In Boulanger's words: 'le grave contient l'aigu, l'aigu ne contient pas le grave'.

exercises focusing on the recognition of chord inversions. In a nutshell, she impressed on her students that Western harmony had its basis in Nature, thereby implying that harmony is a given, something with which one should not tamper. No doubt she resorted to this rationale to justify her distaste for serial music. Another expression she was fond of using – 'The history of music is the history of overtones' – likewise proceeded from the notion that music is an evolutionary art based on natural principles. Although the view that tonal chords can be derived from the harmonic series is not adhered to by all musicians who consider the question (it is particularly hard to explain the minor triad in this manner), its premise accords well with Nadia Boulanger's firm belief in the notion of hierarchy.

The harmony exercise book of an American, Kathleen Wolff, who studied with Boulanger in the mid-1920s, is available for study in the Boulanger archive at the Lyon Conservatoire. This material is dated 'Gargenville 1926'; Wolff was therefore one of a group of students invited to study with Boulanger over the summer vacation. In this exercise book, Wolff constructs triads and all types of seventh and ninth chords built on scales comprised of every interval, from a chromatic scale through to the whole-tone mode, and extending to scales consisting of perfect fifths. A beginner thus had to commence by writing down the basic building blocks of music. In Boulanger's harmony classes tonality could be stretched to its outer limits – but, equally importantly, these limits were never transgressed.

Boulanger's overview of her three-year-long harmony course as taught at the Ecole Normale de Musique reveals a similar approach. Students were provided with a handout detailing what they were expected to achieve by the end of each academic session, and all students were expected to recognise and use the full standard complement of figured bass symbols. The traditional French music education system requires students also to read and write in all clefs, four-part fugal exercises often being notated with a different clef for each voice (soprano, alto, tenor, bass). Lennox Berkeley recalled using these four clefs in the counterpoint exercises that he produced for Boulanger, although he also (privately) questioned whether this was a useful element of his training.[24]

Another prime concern of Boulanger's was that students should realise that a single chord can appear in several different tonal

24. Interview with Bernard Keeffe, broadcast by the BBC in September 1973.

contexts. She often required students to draw up a list of the possible functions of a single chord: a list that catalogued the different keys in which the chord could appear and specified, if necessary, the required resolution of the chord in a particular context. The harmonisation of Bach chorales was a favourite exercise that Boulanger gave to students of all standards, although elementary-level students were expected to use only the tonic, dominant and subdominant chords in root position.

The harmonisation of given melodies (known as 'chants donnés'), often in a prescribed style, was another task often undertaken by Boulanger students; not only did the student have to harmonise the given melody, but he or she also had to explain the reasons why a particular harmonisation was chosen. Some of these 'chants donnés' were clearly old favourites that had been used in many classes. Melodies by nineteenth-century composers such as Delibes and Dubois were frequently used, reflecting the French bias of the Paris Conservatoire curriculum. More interestingly, it seems that other melodies were composed especially for Boulanger's classes. The Lyon Conservatoire archive contains two fugue subjects composed in 1947 by Henri Dutilleux and a two-page melody in the style of Gabriel Fauré composed by Olivier Messiaen.

An overview of the history of early music in thirteen lessons in Boulanger's hand is also preserved at the Lyon Conservatoire. Dated 1932–33, an identical course exists in English translation; this material was used for classes that Boulanger took in Cambridge, Massachusetts, in 1941. As several dozen copies of most of these lessons survive in the Lyon archive, we may presume that they were used as lecture handouts. Most of Boulanger's French contemporaries ignored music composed before J. S. Bach, but her course starts from the Ancient Greek modal system (with a nod of acknowledgement to the Conservatoire professor of music history Maurice Emmanuel, a specialist in the field). Subsequent lessons cover such topics as the development of the Catholic liturgy, Gregorian chant, the troubadours and organum. Each class briefly surveys about a century, and the course illustrates the development of the musical language from monody to polyphony. It focuses on Boulanger's belief that 'the history of music is the history of overtones', since the teacher demonstrates that the earliest music was monodic and that composers gradually introduced the harmonisation of this monody first at the octave and then at the fifth, adding more intervals progressively as and when these were considered consonant.

This history course emphasises sacred music, partly because, as Boulanger stated, little was known about secular music of the period, but also doubtless because religious belief was assumed to be shared by the teacher and her students. In this history class outline, Boulanger also briefly mentions contemporary historical events and artistic achievements (emphasising contemporary cathedral construction) and suggests further reading. Music is therefore viewed within a historical context, and the teacher nods towards the notion of general culture. In her handouts Boulanger often praises symmetrical musical forms and shows a predilection for musical forms based on imitation and varied repetition rather than simple repetition.

I have already said that many of Nadia Boulanger's amateur students came from wealthy backgrounds. While the teacher appreciated the origins (and the money) of these students, the appreciation flowed in both directions. Many of her students were impressed by the supposedly aristocratic origins of Nadia Boulanger's domineering mother, who remained constantly at her side until her death in 1935. Boulanger came into closer contact with royalty when, in the late 1940s, Prince Pierre of Monaco appointed her *maître de chapelle* of his household. She remained in this post when his son, Prince Rainier, ascended to the throne. Boulanger's connection with the royal family of Monaco raised her public profile when she organised and prepared the music for the marriage of Prince Rainier and Grace Kelly in 1956. She later taught music to their daughters, Princesses Caroline and Stéphanie, as children. (Unlike her other students, however, the two girls were spared the rigours of a traditional French solfège course.) Boulanger often told her friend Topazia Markevitch, the second wife of the conductor, that aristocrats were 'good and modest and serene', and she strongly objected when someone of that background was criticised in her presence.[25]

It seems certain, therefore, that she herself refrained from criticising her royal or aristocratic students, not only because of this deferential attitude but also because she never attempted to push those of her students who were wealthy but not necessarily gifted, since they were not working towards a professional career. She aimed to develop their love of music, and it is true that these students also inadvertently cross-subsidised her would-be 'professional' students, most of who hailed from more modest backgrounds. The aspiring

25. Rosenstiel (1998), p. 368.

professionals were seeking a rigorous training from one of the most esteemed teachers of the time: a *curriculum vitae* bearing Boulanger's name and, even better, her seal of approval of the music composed by the student could open many doors for the serious student composer. A small number of future professional performers (including Dinu Lipatti and Jeremy Menuhin) studied in the same classes as these student composers.

The students invited to her home – group classes for these students took place on Wednesdays at 3 p.m. – formed a select group on whose music she commented, and whom she led in discussions centring on set musical works ranging from Josquin to twentieth-century composers. Most of the students at her Wednesday afternoon classes were men; most had ambitions to become professional composers; and all had proven musical talent. The music of J. S. Bach was the one constant feature of her history and analysis classes, and Boulanger significantly said of Bach: 'I believe that a musician should know the two books of "The Well-Tempered Clavier" and, if possible, some cantatas, in depth. I try to give this daily bread to my pupils at all cost. It would seem odd to me if someone had never read the Bible.'[26]

Teaching schedules drawn up in the last five years of her life show that in these sessions Boulanger led discussions that concerned works by living composers, who included Olivier Messiaen, Henri Dutilleux, Maurice Ohana and Iannis Xenakis.[27] The Wednesday classes, which had started in 1921, continued almost until the end of her life. The official end of the class – two hours later – coincided with a weekly 'at home' offered by Boulanger's mother Raïssa, for which selected students were invited to stay on. The other guests at these gatherings included such eminent artists as Stravinsky and Paul Valéry. It is clear that introductions to the celebrated artists and society figures who attended these tea parties could be highly beneficial to the students.

Once Boulanger was assured that her students had a sufficiently good ear and a strong grasp of traditional harmony and counterpoint, her primary aim was to discover their opinions about music and to

26. Monsaingeon (1980), p. 68: 'J'estime qu'un musicien doit connaître à fond les deux volumes du "Clavier Bien Tempéré" et si possible un bon nombre de cantates. J'essaie de les faire enfourner à mes élèves coûte que coûte. Il me paraîtrait un peu drôle que quelqu'un n'ait jamais lu la Bible.'
27. Document preserved in the Lyon Conservatoire.

encourage them to develop an individual voice. Lennox Berkeley wrote: 'She was an inspiring force, and her inspiration consisted in making us aware of the necessity of acquiring the technique which is indispensable for a composer [...] Apart from that, she helped us to form our own tastes by insisting that we had to know music by composers of the past in depth; on this foundation she could help us to develop our sense of form.'[28] Berkeley added that in his first year of study with Boulanger all he did was complete contrapuntal exercises, in which he was obliged to follow the rules of tonal harmony, however musical his alternative solutions may have been; Boulanger considered that he had a sufficiently sound grasp of harmony to be excused from her basic harmony course.

Those who merely parroted Boulanger's opinions did not win her approval; she once told a student who asked her if his harmonic language was what she required: 'Well, I have no idea, I don't know what you want. As long as I don't know what you want, you don't exist for me, musically speaking.'[29]

The music from different epochs studied during the Wednesday classes mirrored Boulanger's own concert programmes. Writing in the *Radio Times*, D. F. Aitken noted:

> Her method is summed up in the French word *rapprochement*. She will take several pieces of music from widely separate periods, in totally different styles. To the mere historian they will seem poles asunder. No one else would have thought of them in the same breath. Yet to her it is clear that each in its own way is saying the same kind of thing. And so she brings them suddenly together in one programme in the hope that her listeners may be able to appreciate for themselves the meaning that they have in common.[30]

This approach was seen as revolutionary at the time, although in a sense it was also an approach to programming that was very much of its time. Boulanger's belief that music from very different historical

---

28. Monsaingeon (1980), p. 124: 'Elle était une inspiratrice, et l'inspiration consistait à nous faire prendre conscience de la nécessité d'acquérir la technique indispensable au compositeur [...] A part cela, elle nous aidait à former notre propre goût en insistant sur la nécessaire et profonde connaissance des compositeurs du passé, sur la base de laquelle elle était en mesure de nous aider à bâtir notre sens de la forme.'

29. Ibid., p. 54: 'Mais je n'ai aucune idée, je ne sais pas ce que tu veux. Tant que je ne sais pas ce que tu veux, tu n'existes pas musicalement pour moi.'

30. Aitken (1936), loc. cit.

periods should be juxtaposed in concert programmes or classes fortuitously coincided with the neo-classical compositional movement that
she favoured. Aitken pertinently observes: 'The nineteenth century, in
Mademoiselle Boulanger's view, has been a dangerous influence. We
are only now getting back to the great tradition of the past – a tradition of order and restraint and discipline, in fact of classicism.'[31] I
believe that behind this generalised view of nineteenth-century music
lies, in part, a criticism by Nadia Boulanger of her own compositions,
which are quintessentially late-Romantic in their harmonic progressions, stretching the frontiers of tonality without ever quite breaking
through them.

Boulanger justified abandoning chronological order in many of her
history classes on pedagogical grounds. She remarked: 'I think that
styles differ only in appearance; people may be dressed differently,
but in their thoughts, their reactions and their beliefs, they are similar. You will find, across the centuries, there are some masterpieces
which are different on the surface, but whose thought processes are
similar, and which evoke similar thoughts in the listener's mind.'[32] As
an example of this, she cited Debussy's *Le Martyre de Saint Sébastien*
and a thirteenth-century motet.

This juxtaposing of musical works from different periods led to
stimulating discussions and discoveries, and it is likely that these connections were found particularly interesting by her composition students. Boulanger's central belief was that student composers should
be aware of their musical heritage, and should therefore understand
how their own music fitted into that tradition. While Boulanger's
amateur students were given a sound technical knowledge of the
workings of music and a general knowledge of the history of Western
music, her more advanced students were given extra challenges in the
form of these analysis classes.

Her skill as a composition teacher lay not in inspiring her students
through original creative work but in teaching them to understand a

31. Loc. cit.
32. Monsaingeon (1980), p. 67: 'Je crois qu'il n'y a différence que d'apparence entre
    un style et un autre; les gens sont habillés autrement mais dans leurs pensées,
    dans leurs réactions, leur foi, ils se ressemblent. Vous trouverez à travers les siè-
    cles quelques chefs d'oeuvre qui sont différents dans leur accoutrement mais qui
    sont semblables par la pensée qu'ils dégagent, par la pensée qu'ils font surgir
    chez l'auditeur.'

wide variety of musical styles, one or more of which might prove stimulating to them in their creative work. Nevertheless, from the 1930s onwards Nadia Boulanger became associated with the neo-classical style of composition. She was not free from musical prejudices; students interested in the techniques of serial composition, in *musique concrète* or in electronic music would have been well advised to look elsewhere for a sympathetic teacher. Boulanger said that she rarely discussed the music of the Second Viennese School 'because other people talk about it so much and it's played so much that I think one should throw a bit of light on music in shadow. I prefer to choose works which are in the shadow, or which are unjustly neglected.'[33] A laudable reason for choosing certain pieces; but Boulanger is, here, not being open about her distaste for pre-Stravinskian serial music, which was surely her fundamental reason for not discussing it much in classes.

Aaron Copland felt that Boulanger's critical and analytical skills, combined with her exceptionally broad knowledge of music, rendered her comments particularly valuable. He wrote: 'I am convinced that it is Mademoiselle Boulanger's perceptivity as a musician that is at the core of her teaching. She is able to grasp the still uncertain contours of an incomplete sketch, examine it, and foretell the probable and possible ways in which it may be developed. She is expert in picking flaws in any work in progress, and knowing why they are flaws'.[34] But, for a student composer, constant negative criticism could prove profoundly dispiriting, and it seems that praise from Boulanger was valued all the more because it was dispensed so rarely.

Boulanger said that all that a composition teacher can do is 'to develop in a pupil the faculties which will allow him to manipulate the tools of his trade. The teacher has no control over what he will do with this tool. I can't give someone the capacity to invent, no more than I can take that capacity from them; I can, however, give him the freedom – that's the right word – to read, to listen, to see, and to understand'. Composers need their own language and, according to

33. Ibid., p. 68: 'parce qu'on en parle tellement par ailleurs et qu'on la joue tellement que je crois qu'il faut projeter un peu d'éclat sur l'ombre. Je sélectionne plus volontiers des oeuvres qui sont dans l'ombre, ou mal connues.'
34. Copland (1960).

her, 'within this established language, the freedom to be themselves [...] The ability to be yourself is already a sign of genius.'[35]

Her approaches to harmony and the history of music were systematic and thorough, and her teaching materials for these disciplines could easily have been published. Many publishers suggested to her that she should collate her material and make it available to a wider public. Although Boulanger toyed with this idea, she never followed it up. Léonie Rosenstiel believes that this was because she struggled with the written word and was a perfectionist who was reluctant to sanction the appearance of her writings in a permanent form. It is true that Boulanger disliked reviewing concerts, no doubt because the short lapse of time between writing and publication was anathema to her perfectionist temperament. But the harmony and history course materials now housed in the Lyon Conservatoire were clearly developed over a number of years, and are models of lucidity. Moreover, her teaching material did not change over the years; her belief that her system of training was the only one suitable for students of Western music was unshakeable.

I am sure that the real reason for Boulanger's refusal to publish her courses was her feeling that personal contact between teacher and student was just as essential as the transmission of cultural information and values; we have seen that her concern for her students went far beyond musical matters. If her material had been published, it is possible that some students would have regarded a book purchase as a cheaper and more practical option than coming to Paris to study with Boulanger. However, her elite students undoubtedly valued her personal presence and criticism more than the rigorous aural training, harmony and counterpoint lessons, which could, arguably, have been disseminated as successfully via publication. Also, her amateur students would surely not have been dissuaded from the exciting prospect of studying in France with her by the easy availability of a book.

35. Monsaingeon (1980), p. 52: 'Tout ce qu'un professeur peut faire consiste à développer chez l'élève les facultés qui lui permettent de manipuler des outils. Sur ce qu'il fera de l'outil, le professeur n'a pas d'action possible. Je ne peux pas donner d'invention à quelqu'un, je ne peux pas non plus la lui enlever; je peux lui donner la liberté, je dis bien, de lire, d'entendre, de voir, de comprendre [...] Il faut un langage établi et puis, dans ce langage établi, la liberté d'être soi-même [...] Etre soi-même, c'est déjà être génial.'

Virgil Thomson wrote in 1962: 'America does not greatly need her now, though she remains our Alma Mater [...] She loves us for old times' sake, as we love her; and she adores revisiting us. But her real work today is with students from the just now developing musical regions.'[36] He thereby implied that Nadia Boulanger's principal value was as a teacher of the fundamentals of Western musical culture to those who lack this foundation. Thomson's view supports Boulanger's own opinion that one can effectively teach only the basics of the musical language, and that only those students who have mastered these basics are capable of realising their musical talent.

Aaron Copland certainly believed that her magnetic personal presence played a significant role in her success as a teacher. He wrote: 'By a process of osmosis, one soaks up attitudes, principles, knowledge, reflections [...] Nadia Boulanger knew everything there was to know about music.'[37]

36. Thomson (1962).
37. Copland (1960).

6

Copyright as a Component of the Music Industry

Dave Laing

Introduction

The music business can be defined as the ensemble or complex of practices and institutions that make possible and regulate the production, distribution and consumption of music.

Since music is generally situated in the sphere of the communicative, this definition has the merit of being structurally homologous with the tripartite and venerable model of communication that posits a linear relay between sender, message and receiver. For the purpose of this chapter, it also provides the boundary that 'contains' its primary object of analysis: the role of intellectual property rights in relation to the music business.

Any sustained attempt to unpack the components of 'production', 'distribution' or 'consumption' would immediately and inevitably begin to complicate and problematise this neat triad. For instance, should 'production' include performance and recording as well as composition, and, if so, in what dimension? And how far can a model of musical production (or any form of semiotic or symbolic production) be based on the political economy categories of relations, forces and means of production? Here is one of the – no doubt several – junctures where such an analysis would be confronted by Adorno, who, it will be recalled, deployed certain categories drawn from the discourse of production in his *Philosophy of Modern Music* and elsewhere.[1]

---

1. See for example, the references to the 'productive forces' of Wagner in Theodor W. Adorno, *In Search of Wagner*, London, New Left Books, 1981, p. 47; to 'technical forces of production' in Berg in the same author's *Alban Berg*, Cambridge, Cambridge University Press, 1994, p. 300; and the various references to 'musical material' in Stravinsky and Schoenberg in Adorno's *Philosophy of Modern Music*, New York, Seabury Press, 1980.

The sphere of 'distribution' could in turn be subject to examination. If the 'work' of the composer – while recognising the complexities of this category evident in the papers from the previous Liverpool Music Symposium[2] – is taken as axiomatic of a certain type of 'production', then its performance or its recording might be identified as 'distribution'. But in those modes of musical practice where the creation of recordings can plausibly be regarded as belonging to the sphere of 'production' the more mundane industrial processes of manufacturing, marketing and retailing would occupy the space of 'distribution'. Here, too, would probably be the place of the 'cultural intermediaries' of music, such as broadcasters and journalists.

In turn, the space of 'consumption' must be orientated to that most Janus-faced of signifiers, 'the market', with its twin denotations as a simple geographical space of exchange and as the most ideologically charged category of classical economics. And should this 'consumption' include the modes of apprehension of music by its consumers: not only in their role as purchasers of tickets and records but also as the 'listening subjects' identified by David Schwarz or the seven types of listener enumerated by Adorno (again)?[3]

More generally, the question will arise as to whether the 'music business' is a singular object, or whether there are separate, if parallel, music businesses. At least two dimensions are at stake here. First: how far can the musical production and consumption in pre-market or non-market social contexts (those of religious observance or work songs, for instance) be considered in the same manner as those of contexts where music is routinely commodified? Second: in those commodified contexts, are the dissimilarities between the business of 'serious' music and that of 'popular' music so great that they should be subject to different analytic processes?[4]

2. *The Musical Work: Reality or Invention?*, ed. Michael Talbot, Liverpool, Liverpool University Press, 2000.
3. See David Schwarz, *Listening Subjects: Music, Psychoanalysis, Culture*, Durham and London, Duke University Press, 1997.
4. For a statistics-based approach that treats the serious and popular sectors as part of a unitary United Kingdom music industry see Cliff Dane, Andy Feist and Dave Laing, *The Value of Music: A National Music Council Report into the Value of the UK Music Industry*, London, University of Westminster, 1996, and Cliff Dane *et al.*, *A Sound Performance: The Economic Value of Music to the United Kingdom*, London, National Music Council, 1999. For a coruscating, if at times incoherent, account of the mismanagement of the contemporary classical music

For present purposes, those will remain roads not taken. Instead, this chapter has a more modest goal: to consider one aspect of the Western music business beneath the horizon set by 'production, distribution and consumption' and at the level of the other part of my initial proposition, that of the 'ensemble or complex of practices and institutions'. This 'ensemble or complex' in turn activates or inhabits the three axes of the music business by simultaneously enabling and regulating the production, distribution and consumption of music.

The 'practices and institutions' can be further specified as comprising heterogeneous elements drawn from a range of sources. These sources include (but are not necessarily limited to) economic, technological, aesthetic, cultural, legal and governmental practices and institutions. Richard Johnson suggests the forms of combination of such source elements in this comment:

> Just as cultural production has its own 'material' conditions, so economic production and consumption depend on cultural conditions: knowledges, social values, and priorities, specific ideologies, distinct discursive conditions and forms of identity and subjectivity.[5]

What is proposed here, then, is that the 'music business' is profoundly heterogeneous: it is never 'itself'.

Further, at any particular moment and in any particular space the 'ensemble or complex' of which the music business is composed will be configured in a manner specific to that conjuncture. The configuration can be described in terms of specific **articulations** of the various elements. The theory and methodology of articulation have been elaborated within cultural studies by Stuart Hall, who has used the analogy of an articulated lorry or truck where

> The front (cab) and back (trailer) can, but need not necessarily, be connected to one another. The two parts are connected to each other, but through a specific linkage, that can be broken. An articulation is thus the form of the connection that can make a unity of two different elements under certain conditions. It is a linkage that is not necessary, absolute, determined and essential for all time.[6]

business see Norman Lebrecht, *When The Music Stops: Managers, Maestros and the Corporate Murder of Classical Music*, London, Simon & Schuster, 1996.

5. Richard Johnson, 'Sexual Emergenc(i)es: Cultural Theories and Contemporary Sexual Politics', *Key Words*, Vol. 1 (1998), pp. 74–94, at p. 80.
6. Stuart Hall and Lawrence Grossberg, 'On Postmodernism and Articulation: An Interview with Stuart Hall', *Journal of Communication Inquiry*, Vol. 10 (1986), p. 54.

From such a perspective no particular element is always already situated as a primary determinant of the shape or trajectory of the music business. An element may be regarded as necessary for the functioning of the business, but no single element is sufficient for that functioning. To come closer to the topic of this chapter, it may make sense in particular contexts to call the music business a 'copyright industry', but this is not necessarily more or less relevant than a definition of music as a 'cultural', 'creative', 'service' or 'manufacturing' industry.

The Music IPR System

The purpose of this chapter is to examine a significant component of the music business and to specify its shifting position within the overall schema of the business. The shorthand term for this element is 'copyright' and there is a long history of ideological and rhetorical debate about the efficacy and ethics of music copyright. This history deserves more attention than it has had, and some of the pro- and anti- copyright meta-discourse is briefly mentioned below. Primarily, though, the chapter is concerned with an exposition of 'copyright' as it impacts on the music business: in particular, the differential effects produced through its articulation with other elements at specific historical moments or conjunctures of the music business.

In terms of the sources of practices and institutions introduced above, copyright is a typically hybrid element of the music business. Focusing on the figure of the 'author' (a pivotal trope of 'copyright'), the post-structuralist legal scholar Anne Barron states: 'Authorship, in Western culture, designates a legal status, a mode of aesthetic production, a form of moral subjectivity, a figure of political citizenship/sovereignty, and a representation of paternity.'[7]

Barron's list shows that 'authorship' is an institution that is based on, and inflects, elements drawn from law, aesthetics, psychology and psychoanalysis, ethics, politics and gender cultures. It is, however, significant that her list begins with the 'legal status' of authorship, and it is pertinent to conclude that the most consistently active component

---

7. Anne Barron, 'No Other Law? Author-ity, Property and Aboriginal Art', in *Intellectual Property and Ethics* (*Perspectives on Intellectual Property*, 4), ed. Lionel Bently and Spyros Maniatis, London, Sweet & Maxwell, 1998.

of the shifting copyright and authorship system is that which derives from law.[8]

Within the discourse of the law and of legal-juridical practices and institutions, copyright itself is now only one segment of a broader system of Intellectual Property Rights (IPR) that includes also patents, designs and computer software. This section of the chapter starts by introducing the components of the IPR system as it affects music. Next, the impact and effects of IPRs in four spheres of the music business are described. These four examples are taken from different phases of the development of the business, and they cover different aspects of the IPRs involved in the music business.

The IPR system in relation to music is composed of three sectors or dimensions that are here called, respectively, the Text of the Law, the Copyright Market, and Policing and Punishment.

The Text of the Law

This term refers to the legal discourse within which IPRs are established. IPRs are institutionalised in specific intellectual property legislation adopted by national legislatures. These Laws invest various legal-economic categories of persons and companies with specific rights and powers.

The growing internationalisation of intellectual property transactions in the twentieth century was the catalyst for a process of homogenisation of national legislations. This process culminated in the World Trade Organisation treaty of 1993. This ruled that any nation state wishing to become a member of WTO must, *inter alia*, have in place an IPR system containing minimum standards derived from the Berne Convention for the Protection of Literary and Artistic Works.[9]

The Text of the Law provides three principal elements for the IPR system as a whole. First, it assigns positions and powers to the various categories of legal entity associated with the production of ideas, artworks or inventions. In the case of music, these entities include the authors of musical works and of sound recordings (the 'copyright

8. As Samuel Weber has pointed out, music's association with the Law has a fundamental status in Western thought, deriving from Plato's Laws. See Samuel Weber, 'Nomos and the Magic Flute', *Angelaki*, Vol. 3 (1998), pp. 61–68.
9. See Dave Laing, 'Copyright and the International Music Industry', in *Music and Copyright*, ed. Simon Frith, Edinburgh, Edinburgh University Press, 1993.

owners') and the performers of musical events. Copyright laws also determine the status of the 'non-author' – often, as in the United States law, by denying employees (of newspapers, film studios or record companies, for instance) the rights accorded to authors, even if the employee is the creator of a work.

Second, the Text defines limits to the exercise of the powers assigned to the owners of copyright. These limits will include the time frame within which a work remains in copyright (and after which it becomes part of the 'public domain') and the various types of 'fair use' of a work (i.e. those uses that are not subject to the control of the owner of copyright).

Third, the Text defines the illegal acts that transgress the law of intellectual property and will prescribe penalties for the commission of illegal acts. The range of such acts may be quite considerable and include plagiarism, piracy, bootlegging, parallel importation and passing off.[10]

A further characteristic of the Text of the Law concerns its interpretation. Although juridicial-legal discourse is as vulnerable as any other discourse to the caprices of the signifier (and any consequent ambiguity or flexibility of 'meaning'), the burden of interpretation or exegesis of the Text is invested, because of the weight of power attached to the Law, in a specialist group: the judges. Like religious leaders in certain faiths, the judges have the duty to impose their interpretation of the Text.

The Copyright Market

For the economic exploitation of the powers of copyright ownership to take place, a set of market mechanisms are needed. These are generally not provided in the Text of the Law, but they are to varying

10. On plagiarism see Robert C. Osterberg, 'Striking Similarity and the Attempt to Prove Access and Copying in Music Plagiarism Cases', *Copyright, Entertainment and Sports Law*, Vol. 2 (1983), pp. 62–103. On piracy see Gillian Davies, *Piracy of Phonograms*, London, ESC Publishing, 1986. On bootlegging see Clinton Heylin, *The Great White Wonders: A History of Bootlegs*, London and New York, Viking, 1994. On parallel imports see Gerald Dworkin and Richard Taylor, *Blackstone's Guide to the Copyright Designs and Patents Act 1988*, London, Blackstone, 1989, pp. 68–69. For a discussion of an example of 'passing off' see Jane M. Gaines, 'These Boots were Made for Walkin': Nancy Sinatra and the Goodyear Tire Sound-alike', in *Contested Culture: The Image The Voice and the Law*, London, BFI Publishing, 1992, pp.105–42.

degrees articulated with the Text since their efficacy depends in part on their legally enforceable conditions of existence. Three important examples of these mechanisms are briefly discussed in the following paragraphs.

The first market mechanism is the institution of the authors' collection society that undertakes the 'collective management' of copyright on behalf of a large number of individual owners of copyright. These societies operate on a national basis; some, notably those in continental Europe, have become massively powerful bodies that cast a long shadow over the national musical life. In addition to performing their principal function of licensing music, collecting royalties and distributing them, such societies as SACEM in France, GEMA in Germany and SIAE in Italy play a major role in the patronage of music and in lobbying governments for increases in the level of protection for 'authors'. To date, the only scholarly account of a collection society is Cyril Ehrlich's history of the Performing Right Society.[11] A dispassionate account of other European societies is long overdue.[12]

The second example concerns the mechanisms by which prices are set in the copyright market. While most national IPR systems emphasise the need for a negotiated agreement to be made between owners of copyright and those who wish to use the copyright, there is also a 'back-up' mechanism for arbitration in the event of failed negotiations. Such a mechanism is often provided in the Text of the Law and has legal or quasi-legal powers. It may be an existing higher court or a specialist copyright board or tribunal.

The third market mechanism is the 'compulsory licence', which provides a certain countervailing power for the copyright users. Under this mechanism, the owner of copyright is not permitted to prevent a user from broadcasting or recording a musical work. However, in doing so, the user is committed to paying 'equitable remuneration' to the owners of copyright. The level of that payment is likewise intended to be set by negotiation but is frequently referred to the arbitration body.

11. Cyril Ehrlich, *Harmonious Alliance: A History of the Performing Right Society*, Oxford, Oxford University Press, 1989.
12. For the principles of collective management see Mihály Ficsor *et al.*, *Collective Administration of Copyright and Neighboring Rights: Study On, and Advice For, the Establishment and Operation of Collective Administration Organisations*, Geneva, World Intellectual Property Organisation, 1990.

It should be noted that the copyright market constitutes only one aspect of the overall market for musical goods and services. In particular, it should be emphasised that these copyright mechanisms have only an indirect effect on the supply and demand marketplace where the exchange between consumers and suppliers of music occurs. In many of its manifestations, the copyright market is a subset of the 'internal' market, whereby different segments of the music industry buy and sell among themselves. For the ultimate supplier of music to the audience (the concert promoter, broadcaster or record retailer, for instance) copyright is a cost to be borne, either as a direct payment to the collecting society or a fixed component of the price of a musical commodity.

Policing and Punishment

This third dimension of the IPR system is linked closely to the other dimensions of the system but also has its own efficacy. In order to maintain the integrity of the Law and to ensure the smooth operation of the copyright market, the boundaries of each need to be patrolled and any incursions should be identified and punished.

The modes of surveillance and of intervention are again articulated according to the Text of the Law, but to varying degrees in varying contexts. For example, the division of labour between state agencies and privately organised industry teams in the investigation process is largely dependent on the Law's definition of 'criminal' and 'civil' offences. But while the Text may provide the authority for certain types of intervention (civil actions by one author against another for plagiarism, seizure of suspect goods by customs officials, modes of pre-censorship by government officials, etc.), the forms taken by the practices of intervention and surveillance are determined by a range of pressures deriving not only from the authority bestowed by copyright ownership but also from public policy, cultural mores, the availability of relevant technologies and other factors.[13]

Copyright discourses

The academic and theoretical discussions of copyright tend towards a polarisation between the apologists for copyright or intellectual

13. For a review of national systems of policing copyright see *Enforcement of Copyright and Related Rights Affecting the Music Industry*, ed. Paul Supnick and Sarah Faulder, Apeldoorn and Antwerp, Maklu, 1993.

property and those who subject it to a critique. Most apologies for copyright rely on justifications drawn from legal or economic discourse, while copyright's critics tend to use arguments taken from economics, aesthetics and politics.

From the viewpoint of conventional legal theory, intellectual property rights are a particular variant of the law of property – but one that is underpinned by an alleged social utility: that giving creators property rights will stimulate the production of scientific knowledge and aesthetic and cultural artefacts.

The preamble to the United States Copyright Act of 1909 is still used as a touchstone in IPR matters – for example in the highly influential 1995 report from the US government on Intellectual Property and the National Information Infrastructure (NII). Quoting from the 1909 Act, the report states: 'The enactment of copyright legislation [is based upon] the ground that the welfare of the public will be served and the progress of science and useful arts will be promoted by securing to authors for limited periods the exclusive rights to their writings.'[14]

This brief statement contains four key elements of the pro-copyright orthodoxy. First, it makes a claim a claim that copyright monopoly is beneficial to 'the welfare of the public'. Second, it maintains that copyright monopolies stimulate the 'progress of science and useful arts'. In most encomia to copyright this justification includes a reference to the financial incentives supplied by the monopoly to authors and inventors. Third, it asserts that the basic form of copyright needed to achieve these aims is 'for authors to have [...] exclusive rights to their writings'. This introduces the central legal 'person' of the author: that figure celebrated by conventional legal scholars in such terms as the following: 'Copyright is about sustaining the conditions of creativity that enable an individual to craft out of thin air an Appalachian Spring, a Sun Also Rises, a Citizen Kane.'[15]

In this proposition the necessary conditions for creativity are those whereby an ample supply of 'thin air' is guaranteed to individual authors. This unreconstructed notion of the Romantic idea of an

14. Bruce A. Lehman *et al.*, *Intellectual Property and the National Information Infrastructure: The Report of the Working Group on Intellectual Property Rights*, Washington, DC, US Department of Commerce, 1995.

15. Paul A. Goldstein, 'Copyright', *Journal of the Copyright Society of the USA*, Vol. 38 (1991), pp. 109–10.

'individual' author subject to almost mystical fits of inspiration has been subjected to a range of critiques in the past few decades, but even here we can point out (1) that Copland's 'musical materials' in *Appalachian Spring* consisted of traditional Shaker melodies as well as of thin air, (2) that Hemingway's prose was drawn from the general inheritance of English-language writing and (3) that the creation of the Hollywood film *Citizen Kane* owed much to the skills of cinematographer Gregg Toland and to various scriptwriters and actors, as well as to the undoubted genius of Orson Welles. In fact, the copyright law governing film production invests the copyright of the film not in the director (Orson Welles) but in the studio that commissioned and financed the film.

The fourth key element of the statement is that the rights of authors are to subsist for 'limited periods'. This is the only element found in the NII report rubric that envisages a brake on the powers granted to authors. In pro-copyright philosophy this limitation on the duration of copyright is often described as providing a 'balance' between the interests of authors and of those of the wider polity. In doing this, the fourth element acts as a guarantor of the first: 'the welfare of the public'.

The following comment is typical of a certain line of critique of copyright:

> Copyright ownership has become a means of establishing and maintaining the monopolisation of the production, distribution and communication of cultural expression [...] Filmed entertainment is produced within the capitalist social structure of accumulation in order to make a profit. Copyright serves as the mechanism by which this creativity is financed, produced and privately appropriated.[16]

This statement comes from Ronald V. Bettig's book *Copyrighting Culture*, whose basic argument is that copyright is a form of what the author calls 'possessive individualism', which arose in tandem with the capitalist form of market economy and therefore is (or, as he says here, 'has become') a legal and socio-cultural form that unequivocally sustains capitalist economic and political formations.

It is relatively easy to point either to internal contradictions in these positions or to aspects of copyright that do not conform to them. For

16. Ronald V. Bettig, *Copyrighting Culture: The Political Economy of Intellectual Property*, Boulder, Westview, 1996, pp. 240 and 109.

example, as various authors have pointed out, the dependence of the future of intellectual production on guarantees of economic success has seldom, if ever, been empirically demonstrated rather than simply asserted. Indeed, the fact that intellectual production has occurred in societies that lack a copyright system suggests that copyright protection is not an essential support for such production but only a contingent one.

On the other hand, after asserting that copyright is an accessory of capitalist exploitation, Bettig himself quotes with approval the fact that 'a number of musicians have donated [...] royalties from particular musical works to activist groups', while others 'have used their copyright control to prohibit the use of their work in promoting products or causes of which they disapprove'.[17] In other words, from Bettig's political economy perspective, there can be disharmony within copyright systems between the interests of different groups of those holding IPRs under the Law.

The second primary discourse claiming to be able to 'place' copyright is that of economic theory, whether grounded in classical economics or in political economy. From the viewpoint of this orthodox economics, intellectual property rights represent something troubling: a monopoly. Nicholas Garnham has succinctly summarised the position in the context of an attempted solution to the 'free rider' problem, as exemplified by copyright piracy: 'Against a background of a general belief in the desirability of free competitive markets, and of the general political and cultural desirability of a marketplace in ideas, the state underwrites a monopoly and the producers' right to a monopoly rent.'[18] As Garnham emphasises, the prevailing economic ideologies of the current era, whether called liberalism, neo-liberalism, Reagonomics or whatever, are deeply hostile to what they perceive as monopolies. Indeed, the Treaty of Rome (the ultimate legal guarantor of the single market of the European Union) is founded on a commitment to competition in 'free markets', and its frequently quoted articles 85 and 86 (dealing with the 'abuse of a dominant position') are brandished against alleged cartels and monopolistic practices. Additionally, some national

17. Ibid., p. 236.
18. Nicholas Garnham, *Emancipation, the Media and Modernity*, Oxford, Oxford University Press, 2000, p. 57.

intellectual property legislation makes collection societies subject to scrutiny by government-appointed agencies. To this extent, elements of the copyright system itself are subject to surveillance and policing.

The operation of copyright monopolies within the music industry means that, for example, only Virgin Records is permitted to manufacture and issue to the public copies of albums by the Spice Girls. There is no possibility of Sony or Universal providing price competition by issuing a rival Spice Girls product. Competition does exist, of course – but further downstream in the value chain: in distribution at the retail site, where the interface with consumption occurs. There are Internet sites that will inform the Spice Girls fan where she can purchase the album at the lowest price.

In Law, as we have seen, the 'natural' monopoly conferred on music rights owners is limited in its operation. This is a reflection of the anti-monopoly pressures exerted by the economic interests of music users (broadcasters and others) on the legislature. For example, this property right has a time limit. After fifty years copyright in a sound recording comes to an end, and anyone may issue copies of it to the public. Where a musical composition is concerned – be it a song or a symphony – the copyright expires seventy years after the death of the author.

This is, of course, a considerable period of time. To take a well-known example: if Sir Paul McCartney lives until 2030, not only his own compositions but also those he composed with the late John Lennon will remain in copyright until at least the end of the twenty-first century. In contrast, the earliest recording by the Beatles, issued in 1962, is due to enter the public domain as soon as 2012. The contrast between these two periods of property rights discloses something about the influence of cultural factors on the process of law-making: the residual aura of authorship guarantees that this will be more highly rewarded than the 'industrial' connotations of recording.

The economic and cultural roles of 'public domain' compositions and recordings – those no longer attracting copyright protection – are of some significance. In economic terms, concert promoters, broadcasters and recording companies find it cheaper to programme public domain works, even though the price of tickets or CDs does not necessarily reflect this. Similarly, the lack of any legal compulsion to pay artist royalties had by the beginning of the twenty-first century encouraged the growth of a 'reissue' market for recordings made before 1950, particularly in such genres as jazz, blues and classical music. In the classical sphere, the continuing popularity among audiences of music from the eighteenth and nineteenth centuries may possibly be connected with the public domain status of such works.

Compulsory licences represent a second limitation on the monopolistic exercise of copyright. Such licences, permitted under the rules of the Berne Convention, are frequently granted by governments. The licences are intended to empower broadcasters to use copyright music, subject not to the explicit permission of right owners but only to the broadcasters' intention to pay 'equitable remuneration'.

Case Studies

The final section of this chapter presents four case studies in the articulation of copyright in the music business. They are, in chronological order:

1 the establishing, in the 1850s, of the performing right for composers;
2 the granting to record companies, in the early twentieth century, of the status of 'copyright owner';
3 the role, since the 1970s, of patent owners in the marketing of five generations of audio and audio-visual home entertainment systems;
4 the uncertain status of music copyright owners in the cyberspace market.

The Performing Right for Composers

My first case concerns a new market precipitated by the creation of a legal right.

In this market the buyers are firms and institutions using music in the conduct of their business while the sellers are the composers of that music and their representatives (music publishers or collection societies). The origin of this market can be traced precisely to Paris in 1848, when three composers attended a cabaret show at the Café Concert des Ambassadeurs. There they heard performances of a song written by one of them and a sketch written by the other two. After the performance, the three refused to pay their bill, telling the proprietor of the café: 'You use the products of our labour without paying us for it. So there's no reason why we should pay for your service.'[19]

The case went to court, and the composers won on appeal. The decision extended an existing law on theatrical performances to all musical works and all public performance of those works. This decision created a new category of legal right – the performing right – and with it a new economic relationship between music user and copyright owner.

As a result of the decision, these composers and others including music publishers founded a society to enforce and administer their performing rights.

In doing so, they established the principle and practice of the collective administration of rights, based on the fact that – with the possible exception of opera performances – it was impossible for a single composer or publisher to monitor every use of his or her work by singers, bands, promoters or, in the twentieth century, broadcasters. Accordingly, the new society was entrusted with the task of monitoring music use, issuing licences to music users, negotiating fees, collecting fees and finally distributing the money raised to the composers and songwriters whose works were adding value to other people's businesses.

This French body, SACEM, was the forerunner of the dozens of national societies and agencies that today exist in order to collect payment for the use of musical works. In the subsequent 150-plus years the global market based on the performing right has grown in size and is now worth over $3 billion annually.[20]

Although the French court had established a new form of copyright, it did not easily or automatically translate into either a position of economic power for the collection societies or one of affluence for authors.

The performing right was a threat to established business practices, including some within the music business itself. Music publishers and concert promoters used public concerts as a means of promoting sales of sheet music. In Britain many opposed the proposal to charge

19. Jacques Attali, *Noise: The Political Economy of Music*, trans. Brian Massumi, Manchester, Manchester University Press, 1985, pp. 77–78.
20. *World Music Publishing Revenues*, New York, National Music Publishers Association, 1999.

performance royalties, which was regarded as an extra expense that would drive up the cost of concert tickets (this despite the fact that the publishers themselves would benefit from the royalties). The leading publisher William Boosey later recalled: 'I considered the payment of a fee for the performance of new music, and even established music, was calculated to injure seriously the sales of established favourites, and was very detrimental to the popularising of new work.'[21]

A further effect of the 1848 legal judgement was to establish a parity between composers of popular songs and those of 'serious' music. The parity was resented by the serious music business and, in Attali's words, 'was perceived by the bourgeoisie as an attack on its privileges: formerly the bourgeoisie alone had had the right to have financial dealings in music. Money was its kingdom. The common people were not supposed to have anything but street music, music that was "valueless".'[22]

Record Companies as 'Copyright Owners'
The second case study shows how differential levels of IPRs have inflected the power relationship between important categories of participants in the music industry.

The case concerns the 'neighbouring rights' granted to record companies and performers, with particular reference to the dominant position assumed by the record industry in the second half of the twentieth century. A key factor in this dominance has been ownership of copyright in sound recordings by record companies rather than by musicians.

That grant of ownership was one of two important innovations created in the United States copyright legislation of 1909. This law was drawn up, in part, to take account of new technologies that had changed the configuration of cultural production in the previous one or two decades. Probably the most important of these were the cinematograph and the various means of mechanical reproduction of musical works, notably the phonograph and the pianola and pianoroll. These technologies did not 'fit' the Law's existing definition of the 'copy' of a musical work, whose prevailing form was the printed

21. William Boosey, *Fifty Years of Music*, London, Ernest Benn, 1931, p. 58.
22. Attali (1985), p. 78.

version of the score. Piano-rolls and phonograph cylinders or discs embodied copies not of works but of performances.

The mood of the legislators and of the United States president, Theodore Roosevelt, was strongly influenced by a perception that music publishers had created a dangerous monopoly.

During the hearings that preceded the 1909 act it emerged that the president of the Music Publishers Association had encouraged eighty-seven publishers to give exclusive rights to the Aeolian pianola firm for piano-rolls of works controlled by them, in return for a 10 per cent royalty. The legislators undertook to curb this perceived monopoly, and the resulting legislation provided the early record labels with a legal status comparable to that of the (then) all-powerful music publishers. Although authors of musical works were also granted a 'mechanical right' in those works, this right was severely curtailed by two other provisions of the 1909 act. First, the law imposed a low royalty rate to be paid by piano-roll, cylinder and disc companies; second, it was made illegal for publishers to grant an exclusive mechanical right in a song to a single record or piano-roll company. In the words of Russell Sanjek: 'For the first time in US history, the peacetime bargaining process between supplier and user was to be regulated by the government. The fixed two-cent royalty and a compulsory-licensing provision were to guard against any future music-copyright monopoly.'[23]

The United Kingdom copyright law of 1911 adopted a similar approach to that of the 1909 United States law, so that the price to be paid by British record companies to publishers for the use of a song (the mechanical royalty) was set by statute rather than by free market negotiations.

The judicial impetus for this legislation was twofold. In 1899, a British court ruled that the reproduction of music by such mechanical devices as pianolas, barrel-organs and phonographs did not infringe the copyright in the musical works that were reproduced. Peacock and Weir comment: 'Thus protected by the law, a sizeable industry developed in Britain for the manufacture of mechanical instruments.'[24] In 1908, however, an inter-governmental meeting called to

23. Russell Sanjek, *American Popular Music and Its Business: The First Four Hundred Years*, Vol. 3 (*From 1900 to 1984*), New York, Oxford University Press, 1988, pp. 22–23.
24. Alan Peacock and Ronald Weir, *The Composer in the Marketplace*, London, Faber, 1973, p. 49.

revise the Berne Convention decided that the success of the mechanical music business – and particularly the spread of sound recording – justified the introduction of a mechanical right for composers. As a signatory to the Berne Convention, the United Kingdom government was obliged to amend its domestic legislation accordingly. After much debate, the legislators introduced a restricted mechanical right that included a compulsory licence intended to prevent 'the largest and wealthiest firms in the gramophone industry' from obtaining 'a monopoly in the most popular works'.[25]

British record companies also gained control of sound recordings through the Law's definition of the 'author' of a sound recording. That definition was carried forward into successive national copyright laws, including those of nation states that had been British colonies. The definition is now to be found Section 9, sub-section 2, of the 1988 Copyright, Designs and Patents Act of the United Kingdom which reads: 'The author of a sound recording or film is the person by whom the arrangements necessary for the making of the recording or film are undertaken.'

This designation of the status of 'author' of a recording excludes the musician or producer who makes the sounds that materially constitute the recording in favour of the person (or company) that organises the recording process by financing and inciting it. In almost all cases, this is the record company that signs an artist to its label.

There is a crucial difference between this concept of authorship and the authorship of what the British law calls a 'work' (e.g., a book, painting or song). The law defines the author of a work simply as 'the person who creates it'. Here, 'author' includes songwriter or composer of music.

Musical performers are invisible in both the US and the UK laws of 1909 and 1911, respectively. This perhaps reflected the almost complete invisibility of performers in the very early years of sound recording. A 1895 'broadside' announcing new recordings from the United States Gramophone Co of Washington DC lists many musical selections by the type of voice or instrument ('barytone', basso', 'clarinet', etc.) but does not name the soloist.[26] And though, by 1909, a putative

25. Ibid., p.50.
26. Jerrold Northrop Moore, *Sound Revolutions: A Biography of Fred Gaisberg, Founding Father of Commercial Sound Recording*, London, Sanctuary, 1999, p. 23.

star system was emerging through the best-selling recordings of
Caruso, Melba and others, there was no lobby to persuade legislators
to recognise in law the contribution to the nascent recording business
of all performers. The contribution of recording artists did not
receive international legal recognition until 1961, the year that the
Rome Convention for the Protection of Performers, Producers of
Phonograms and Broadcasting Organisations was adopted.

The economic legacy of the asymmetry between the legally established status of the songwriter and the legal invisibility of the recording artist are that (in Europe and North America, at least) the former
is better paid than the latter. Elsewhere, I have analysed the operation
of a typical recording contract to show that the amount of royalties
eventually received by an artist is less than half that to be expected
from simply observing the 'headline' royalty rate.[27] This is because of
a series of deductions enforced by record companies, through which
the musician pays for promotion, for packaging, for television advertising and other elements.

Patent Owners and the Marketing of Home Entertainment Systems

The third case study shifts the focus to a different type of intellectual
property right: the patent. While copyright is the form of property
right granted to creators in the broadly aesthetic or semiotic sphere,
patents refer to the area of 'invention' of technological or scientific
processes or machines.

The specific patents to be discussed are those involved in new forms
of recording technologies and consumer electronics products. One
way of understanding the dynamics of the recorded music business is
to regard it as a series of shifts in the technologies of recording and
playback. As Gronow and Saunio point out:

> Ever since the invention of sound recording the industry has always
> brought onto the market, every second decade or so, some technical
> innovation with the announcement that it signifies the perfection of
> sound reproduction. Electrical recording was followed by the LP disc in
> 1948; in 1958 was the turn of stereo. Manufacturers of both recordings

27. Dave Laing, 'George Michael's Contract, or Copyright and Power in the
    Contemporary Recording Industry', in *Changing Sounds: New Directions and
    Configurations in Popular Music. Papers from the 10th International Conference
    of the International Association for the Study of Popular Music*, ed. Tony
    Mitchell, Sydney, UTS, 2000, pp. 256–9.

and equipment had received quite a fillip to their sales from the new technology. Their basic repertoire has had to be recorded anew three times.[28]

Since the 1970s five principal forms of new home entertainment technologies of this type have been marketed. These are:

- quadraphonic audio
- videotape cassette
- digital audio disc
- a digital successor to analogue audio tape
- a digital successor to the video tape cassette

Of these five patented technologies, two were failures – quadraphonic and digital audiotape. This was in part because two or more incompatible technologies were put into the marketplace by rival firms. Competition at this level caused confusion among consumers, who were discouraged from buying any of the competing products.

In the case of quadraphonic audio (a system that tried to improve the listening experience by providing four channels of sound and four speakers), the Anglo-American firms CBS and EMI created a system called SQ, while Sansui of Japan had its QS system. 'Of course, the systems were not compatible, so that the SQ equipment could not play QS records. The result was that quadraphonic sound lasted only a couple of years and was given a quiet burial.'[29]

The rival versions of a digital successor to the highly successful tape cassette were launched in the late 1980s by Sony of Japan and Philips of Europe. Sony had its Minidisc, a smaller version of the (by then) highly popular Compact Disc (CD). Philips mimicked the cassette with its Digital Compact Cassette (DCC). Initially, both formats were marketed as pre-recorded music carriers – and neither found a market. It was only several years later that Sony relaunched the Minidisc as a recordable medium and achieved small but growing sales, first in Japan and then elsewhere.

In these two examples, the competition between owners of intellectual property rights in incompatible new technologies played a significant role in market failure, articulated with other factors such as lack of consumer demand or faulty marketing strategies.

28. Pekka Gronow and Ilpo Saunio, *An International History of the Recording Industry*, London, Cassell, 1998, p. 185.
29. Loc. cit.

The early history of the videotape cassette shared with these failures the fact of a competition between owners of intellectual property rights in incompatible new technologies. In this case, the competitors were Matsushita's VHS system and Sony's Betamax; but the outcome was different. The expensive format war resulted not in the failure of the technology itself but in the victory of VHS, a technology that was licensed to numerous manufacturers by Matsushita. The expert view of this outcome was that the Sony technology was superior but that the company had committed an error in failing to make agreements with film studios to issue video cassette copies of movies in the Betamax format. Consumers wishing to view well-known films were thus obliged to buy VHS machines.

Finally, two of the five patented technologies became commercially successful in a relatively short time. These were digital audio (i.e. Compact Disc) and digital video (i.e. DVD).

In both cases, there was an agreement within the consumer electronics industry to offer a single standard across all hardware and software products. In the case of the Compact Disc, the patents were controlled by Philips, Sony and others. As established transnational manufacturers, the patent holders might well have kept a monopoly of production in their own plants. Instead, their strategy of granting the use of patents to competing firms played a significant role in the widespread take-up of CD by consumers.

Their reward was a considerable income from the licensing of the patents. By 1995 patent owners were being paid $500 million a year in royalties by CD hardware and software manufacturers. Over the twenty-year duration of the patents, it is probable that as much as $10 billion has been paid in patent royalties.

This articulation of the ownership of IPRs with a specific industrial strategy played a major role in the commercial success of CD. A key aspect of that strategy was the involvement of the owners of significant quantities of recorded music copyrights. The need for the availability of a range of 'software' titles for consumers to play on the new hardware had been impressed on Sony by the Betamax debacle. In the case of CD, Philips was the owner of the PolyGram catalogue of classical and popular recordings. PolyGram became the 'product champion' for CD and set about persuading other major record companies to manufacture pre-recorded CDs of the repertoire in their catalogues.

The history of the development of what is now DVD (Digital Versatile Disk) began in a similar manner to that of the VHS–Betamax story but ended as a reprise of the CD story.

At the early research and development stage, there were two competing digital video systems. One was under development by Sony and Philips, partly to make possible a further patenting of their CD technology. A larger consortium of Matsushita, Time Warner and others developed the second. In 1995 all the protagonists agreed to pool their patents in a single DVD format. This agreement has allowed DVD to follow the path of CD and be launched as a single compatible format, albeit with incompatible regional variants in an attempt to deal with piracy, with different theatrical release dates and with differing censorship regimes.[30]

Music Copyright Owners in the Cyberspace Market

The final case study involves IPRs and the on-line environment, with specific reference to music right owners.

Given the continuing evolution of Internet activities, any discussion of the fate of music in the World Wide Web must be provisional in its conclusions. This account begins by determining to what extent the new on-line music business represents a break with the established 'off-line' business.

From this perspective, it is clear that much Internet activity is a continuation of 'off-line' industry practices in a new environment. For instance, many music-based Web sites act as marketing devices and information sources concerning particular musicians, genres or music organisations. Further, there are an increasing number of sites that play a role similar to that of ticket agencies and record shops. At these sites the consumer can purchase tickets and CDs that are then sent by the site-owner via the mail. Such transactions are sophisticated versions of pre-existing 'off-line' methods of the mail order sales of recorded music conducted by record clubs and others. Finally, numerous radio stations 'stream' their existing programmes on the Internet, permitting listeners from anywhere in the world to hear their transmissions.

However, since about 1998 improved digital technologies have made possible some important on-line innovations in the distribution of music, notably in what is termed 'digital downloading'. Through this technology digital recordings can be transferred from a Web site to the hard disk of a computer without being packaged in an optical disc such as a CD. The *de facto* technical standard for this process at

30. 'DVD Format Rivals Agree to Talk', *Music & Copyright*, Vol. 75 (13 September 1995), p. 5.

the time of writing is known as mp3, a term that is also the name of a leading firm involved in digital downloading.

The response of music rights owners to the arrival of digital distribution technologies such as mp3 was confused. Record companies and collection societies were initially hostile to this first generation of music hardware technology not controlled by the music industry or its allies in consumer electronics. The hostility took the form of legal action as copyright was articulated with technology and some owners of Internet music sites were sued for promoting copyright infringement in the services that they provided to consumers of recorded music. The courts found in favour of the music rights owners, and the site owners were ordered to make payments to the transnational music companies. Crucially, however, these in turn have sanctioned the business practices of such sites, on the understanding that copyright royalties will be paid on a regular basis.

The most significant of these legal actions concerned the Napster company, which had introduced a more radical version of the mp3 system, one that facilitates 'swapping' or 'file-sharing' recordings among individual consumers without permission from, or payment to, copyright owners. During 2000 and early 2001, an estimated sixty million consumers used Napster and downloaded billions of files each containing one recorded music track. The successful legal action against Napster left untouched other similar Internet sites, and technical experts believed that it would be impossible for copyright owners and their lawyers wholly to eradicate file-sharing of this type. In addition, there was evidence of a legal counter-attack designed to persuade US legislators to extend the definition of 'private copying', one of the exceptions or limits to copyright, to include file-sharing.

Although the future development of the file-sharing phenomenon cannot be predicted at the time of writing (early 2001), its popularity is such that it can be understood as a mutation in the forms of consumption of music that has impacted on the economics of music distribution.[31]

31. It may be significant that a report by music industry experts for the UK government on the prospects for music on-line is called *Consumers Call the Tune: The Impact of New Technologies on the Music Industry. A Report by the New Technology Group of the Music Industry Forum* (London, DCMS, 2000). On a similar topic see Paul Brindley, *New Music Entrepreneurs*, London, Institute for Public Policy Research, 1999.

The current 'fall-out' from this highly volatile combination of technological innovation, copyright conservatism and new modes of consumption includes the tentative introduction of new 'business models' for recorded music distribution that would involve subscription payments in place of single payments for individual recordings or even a system of free access to recordings analogous to the current modes of finance for commercial broadcasting.

One effect of this momentum of the on-line music business is to decentre the vertical integration evident in the off-line business of the late twentieth century, when a small number of transnational corporations were able to control all phases of the business, from 'upstream' production to downstream distribution and consumption.

In some cases, this integration involved not only the production of musical goods and services but also the hardware used by consumer to listen to the music software. Thus the CD and DVD instances discussed above involved a high degree of synergy between hardware and software interests. Sony and Philips owned both the patents for delivering the music and, through their record and music publishing companies, a large proportion of the copyrights to be delivered.

In the on-line world, music business corporations have, at present, no ownership or control of important new technologies of distribution and consumption. Instead, the on-line power structure now favours a new kind of distributor from the worlds of telecommunications and of personal computing. Just as recording artists had been unequally matched against the record companies, so, too, the record companies and collection societies now find themselves in an unequal relationship vis-à-vis the Internet Service Providers. There are also signs that copyright owners are no longer regarded by governments as sacrosanct. While recent US, European Union and World Intellectual Property Organisation Treaties have extended off-line copyright protection to the on-line dimension, the treaties pointedly declined to make ISPs responsible for acts of copyright infringement that take place on Web sites serviced by an ISP.

New forms of vertical integration will affect the unstable position of copyright owners in on-line markets. In 1999 a merger was announced between the ISP America Online (AOL) and Time Warner, owner of one of the five transnational music companies. This will undoubtedly be followed by similar developments as Internet companies seek to take control of music, film and other copyright material. Such mergers will tend to institutionalise the subordinate position of copyright owners such as the large record companies.

Conclusion

The four case studies outlined above illustrate the shifting relations between the legal, economic, cultural and other forces at work in the music industry.

In the case of the introduction of the performing right, a legal innovation produced the conditions for the development of a new market for music. Although 'copyright' played a crucially influential part, a second stage of innovation was needed: at the economic level. It took the introduction of institutions dedicated to the collective management of performing rights to actualise this new copyright market for the benefit of composers and music publishers.

In the case of the record company's ownership of copyright, an asymmetrical economic relationship was produced by further legal innovations. But the forms taken by these innovations – the invention of the 'mechanical right' for composers and the recognition of record companies as IPR owners – were themselves the result of the application of political-economic forces concerned with issues of monopoly power.

The third and fourth case studies present examples of market situations overdetermined not by the introduction or the deployment of IPRs as such but by commercial strategies within which IPRs played a necessary but secondary role. Thus the failure of quadraphonic audio or of Sony's Betamax was nothing to do with the facts of patent ownership. These failures were, rather, the result of ruinous competition between technologically incompatible products in a field where consumer confidence has been shown to depend on the operation of a patent cartel whose monopoly position ensured compatibility between all software and hardware products in the marketplace.

Finally, the current phase of development of the on-line music business (the subject of the fourth case study), is characterised by evolutionary developments in the spheres of distribution and consumption. At the level of distribution, there is an emerging hierarchy in which the author as property owner is now structurally subordinate to the owner of the means of distribution. In the sphere of consumption, new forms of what the copyright system defines as either piracy or private copying seem to be acting as catalysts for innovations in the way recorded music is traded.

7

Illegality and the Music Industry

Simon Frith

Music and the Law

The starting point of this chapter is straightforward: the music industry is dependent on the law. All business in capitalist societies is dependent, of course, on the law: on enforceable contracts and on markets whose 'freedom' is a matter of regulation. But the music industry is especially dependent on the law. Some of the implications of this have already been described by Dave Laing in his sophisticated account of 'The Text of the Law' that defines the copyright system.[1] But copyright is only one of the legal issues with which contemporary music-makers have to be concerned, and I can best illustrate the peculiar importance of the law for everyday musical life journalistically. While I was writing the first draft of this chapter in autumn 2000, I noted the following:

- The issue for 30 August of *Music and Copyright* (a high-priced fortnightly subscription newsletter for music industry executives and investors) carried a press release from the Mechanical Copyright Protection Society detailing its anti-piracy actions in the UK in the first six months of 2000. These began with a raid on a house in Caerphilly in which five hundred CDs were taken and finished with a seizure of 2,500 mp3 files at a computer fair in Hull. In total, during this period, sixty people were arrested and goods worth £2.7 million confiscated.
- The September 2000 issue of *Business Affairs Report* (a quarterly supplement of the British trade paper *Music Week*) carried five stories:

---

1. See Chapter 6.

Massive Attack talk to lawyers over Tories' conference tune. 'Massive Attack have not and will never support the Conservative Party or their policies,' the statement says. 'Their music has been used by the Tories without their knowledge or permission.' Conservative central office has made light of the usage, but the law states that permission must be obtained from the copyright owner before compositions can be appropriated for specific use – for instance, in connection with a political campaign.

IFPI litigation expert to lead piracy team. This is a story about personnel changes in the International Federation of Phonographic Industries, the music business's international trade body. 'This appointment reflects the growing importance of plant litigation in IFPI's work, and the increasing effectiveness of our strategy to make the CD pirates pay for their infringements.'

Auditors face up to Internet nightmare. This is a story about the difficulties facing musicians who want full information about their on-line sales. 'Whatever contract is signed between the artist and the internet company, the artist's lawyers have to make sure there is a sufficient audit clause to enable us to go wherever we want in order to find information.'

Stop me if you've heard this one before ... 'Sampling is now an everyday part of the music-making process but getting clearance can take a long time and the legal framework can be a minefield. Matt Pennell examines the penalties for misappropriating someone else's work.'

My word is my bond. How can musicians signing their first recording deals 'ensure they are not signing away their fundamental rights in the process'? A guide to contract law.

- On 3 October, under the headline 'Copycat singer loses fight over song', *The Guardian* reported that the High Court in London had ruled that Ludlow Music was entitled to substantial 'and possibly even exemplary' damages from Robbie Williams, his co-writer Guy Chambers and their publishers, EMI Music and BMG Music, for the 'substantial' copying of Loudon Wainwright's *I Am the Way (New York Town)* (itself a licensed parody of Woody Guthrie's *I Am the Way*) evident in Williams's *Jesus in a Camper Van*. 'Ludlow Music had initially given the go-ahead for the Williams and Chambers song but a dispute had arisen over their demand for a half share of the copyright. They were not satisfied with an offer of 25%.'

- On 4 October, in common with every other British broadsheet newspaper, *The Guardian* reported the latest Napster news: 'Online music company Napster received a stay of execution yesterday as a US appeal court allowed it to continue business until a final verdict on its future is reached. Napster, which allows its 32m users to download music without charge, is being sued for copyright infringement by the entertainment industry.'
- On 7 October *New Musical Express* noted: 'Badly Drawn Boy aka Damon Gough has been forced to release a new pressing of his debut album, *The Hour of The Bewilderbeast*, after major publishing company BMG objected to the use of a lyric from Taja Sevelle's 1987 hit 'Love is Contagious' [...] The Mercury Prize winner has also had to change the artwork on [...] *Bewilderbeast* for its American release. The cover – a collage by Gough himself, including a picture of Woody Allen – used images without the copyright owners' prior consent.'

I want to draw two immediate conclusions from this not unusual sample of news stories. First, for music industry executives most business problems are legal problems. Arguments about investment and technology, management and markets, are addressed through law; and, while other creative industries have their own interests in the ownership, management and exploitation of intellectual property rights, in the case of the challenge of digital piracy – to video and computer software sales, for example – they seem not to share the record company belief that all their problems can be solved via the right legislation. Seventeen of the twenty pages of the November 2000 issue of *IFPI Network*, the glossy 'Newsletter of the International Recording Industry', are devoted to legal matters, and even the two-page special report on the 3rd Platinum Europe Awards Ceremony lays emphasis on EU Vice-President Neil Kinnock's call for 'sensible laws to deter copyright abuse and combat piracy', and the Corrs' comment that 'many people would not dream of stealing a CD from their local record shop. In the same way we don't think it's cool to go cyber shoplifting.'[2] In general, we could say that every

---

2. Consider, too, Chris Smith's various pronouncements as UK Minister of Culture. The present Labour government's policy on music (in contrast to its policy on film, television and sport) is concerned almost exclusively with musical rights and global legislation.

technological development since the printing press has been, for the industry, a threat demanding legislation.

My second observation is that music court cases – whether musicians against their managers, one songwriter against another, session players against their employers or stars against accountants – are a familiar item of news entertainment. There are obviously disputes in other cultural industries. Actresses fall out with their agents; journalists sue publishers for wrongful dismissal; game show inventors claim that they have been ripped off. But no other sphere of entertainment has such a steady stream of public disputes as the music industry; in no other industry is the law used so routinely in the pursuit or defence of earnings.[3] Only music industry cases feature stars of such interest to the tabloids as Elton John, George Michael, the Smiths and Charlotte Church. Contractual and copyright disputes in the television or publishing industries are confined (if reported at all) to the business pages.

Why? Why is the law so important for music industry policies and disputes?

To begin with, music is particularly vulnerable to theft by its nature: it is easy to carry off, as it were, whether in an unlicensed performance or an mp3 file, as a photocopied score or a pirated CD. Music crosses boundaries with ease; its transmission cannot be centrally controlled. It is routinely consumed in ways in which technical qualities count for little; its market is both big and disorganised enough to make its illicit production and distribution financially viable on both a large and a small scale. One consequence is that much of the creative energy that has shaped the history of mass mediated music has been generated at the margins of the legal music world by musicmakers and hustlers, whose only means of access to audiences and markets has been illicit. (Think, for example, of the role of payola in getting small-label rock 'n' roll and R & B on to US radio in the 1950s.)

This is the context in which one could say that in the West, at least, the law has overdetermined music industry practice. Copyright law depends on an idealised account of the individual creator and offers

---

3. Anthony Seeger made the same point about the USA ten years ago: 'US musical practice is filled with conflict and adjudication, as anyone who has spent much time with professional musicians or reads Billboard can attest.' 'Ethnomusicology and the Law', *Ethnomusicology*, Vol. 36 (1992), pp. 345–59, at p. 353.

protection to an author's work (which becomes vulnerable to theft in the very act of publication). The music industry is based on contracts between artists and publishers or record companies that spell out a series of mutual obligations, and lawyers are at the heart of the industry's everyday practices. The contracts that they write determine what music is published, how and when. The implication here is that even if artists need publishers to get their works to market and publishers need artists to provide goods for sale, artists and publishers also have opposed interests (in the distribution details of copyright fee income, for example), and musician/publisher contracts take their place in a world of parallel contracts: between artist and manager, artist and agent, artist and promoter, and so on. If the relationship between musician and manager, for example, is (as the International Managers Forum suggests) like a marriage, then this is a business in which everyone needs a pre-nuptial agreement. The ambiguities of the relationships here are encapsulated in the use of the word 'exploitation', and I doubt whether there is a single successful rock or pop star who has not at some stage threatened, or been threatened by, legal action (see any star biography).

We can add to this that music consumers themselves are likewise subject to legal regulation. Public gatherings of people in order to make or listen to music require various forms of licence, with the result that the history of live popular music from pub room and music hall to night clubs and raves has itself been shaped by the law, while the most significant media use of records – by radio – has in Europe, if not in the USA, been a matter of state policy: to be able to broadcast music at all means being licensed to do so, and stations are routinely licensed to play only particular kinds of music.

The paradoxical effect of the sheer weight of legal argument on music practice is that the law has less authority in the music industry than in any other business. This is apparent from a number of perspectives. Few music consumers, for example, believe that home-taping or file downloading is theft (and for those who do, this probably adds to the attraction). The very terms used to describe illegal or unlicensed recordings and broadcasts – piracy, bootlegging – have positive as well as negative connotations; they imply that goods are seized from corporations in order to become more accessible to the people. Much of the recent argument about Napster has been conducted in these terms: what is theft for musicians such as Metallica is, ironically, liberation for their more political fans. Consumer rhetoric here draws on the belief that musical communities of any passion are formed in resistance to state or corporate control. In this kind of rock ideology the illegal is the political, and one can discern an equally contrary attitude to the law among artists, for whom copyright is often seen more as a constraint on creativity than as a protection for it, and for whom the emphasis on individual invention on which the industry rests can also provide a justification for defying contractual obligations.

If, then, the music industry been shaped by the Text of the Law, as Dave Laing argues, it has also been marked by graffiti, by a diffuse pleasure in the illegal (which is one reason why the industry has to invest so much in the pursuit of legislative change and enforcement). And there is a final point to make here. In its various campaigns for copyright protection and the harmonisation of global laws, the music industry has suggested that without such protection there would be no music. Composers and performers would down tools; recording studios would close. The threat of illegal music-making to this position is not just financial but also ideological: it suggests that the copyright regime for the circulation of music goods may not be necessary at all. Dave Laing himself has shown how the development of an international music industry meant imposing a Western legal framework on countries in which musical production and consumption had previously worked perfectly well.[4] Even within Western countries, there are musical worlds (such as independent dance music in 1990s Britain) that sustain themselves commercially perfectly well without recourse to copyright.

Music and Copyright

The purpose of a copyright regime is to protect works and their authors from unlicensed copying. These days, this is thought of primarily in terms of technological reproduction: copying in the photocopying sense, an original work being illicitly taped or pressed or filed in such a way that it can be marketed as the property of the copier rather than of its original owner. The work's original author is

---

4. Dave Laing,'Copyright and the International Music Industry', in *Music and Copyright*, ed. Simon Frith, Edinburgh, Edinburgh University Press, 1993, pp. 22–39. See also Roger Wallis and Krister Malm, *Big Sounds From Small Peoples: The Music Industry in Small Countries*, London, Constable, 1984, Chapter 6.

acknowledged (if not paid): a bootlegged Radiohead CD or a down-loaded Madonna track is valuable only if it is a genuine copy of the original work. The ethical issue is not passing off someone else's work as one's own, but theft – the selling of something one has no title to. To download an mp3 file via Napster or to buy a pirated CD at a record fair is to be a receiver of stolen goods.

But this is not the only way of copying a musical work. Copyright law is designed also to protect writers from plagiarism, i.e. from having their work passed off as an original composition by someone else. Plagiarism, as all academics know, is a difficult crime to prove. It is not enough to show similarity between two works: one has also to establish the intent to deceive and prove that the copier did indeed know – have access to – the original. It is always easier for more successful writers to claim that they were plagiarised by less successful ones – as in most sampling cases – than vice versa. Most unknown writers who emerge to claim they wrote the original of a big hit or theme tune fail to convince courts that their own song was actually ever heard by anyone.

Plagiarism cases – and their settlement – are common enough (as I was editing the final version of this chapter, *Music Week* was reporting that 'former Spandau Ballet guitarist and songwriter Gary Kemp is preparing legal action against Rui Da Silva, his label and music publishers after claiming a version of his recent number 1 uses a sample from Chant No.1'.[5] The rise of sampling, as this story suggests, has given new impetus to publishers to trawl through every new hit, hoping to come up with something to which they can claim a right. But what may be a clear principle for lawyers is less clear for musicians. Plagiarism law rests on the concept of an original work, the source of the copy that is claiming falsely to be original. Original in this context means something originated – created at a particular moment by an identifiable author or authors – and something distinct, distinguishable from any other work. The musical problem, as Robert Osterberg notes, is that 'in contrast to literature, painting and other fine arts, the possibilities for originality in music are not boundless'. He quotes a key US court ruling:

> Musical signs available for combination are about 13 in number. They are tones produced by striking in succession the white and black keys

5. *Music Week*, 27 January 2001, p. 1.

as they are found on the keyboard of a piano. It is called the chromatic scale. In a popular song, the composer must write a composition arranging combinations of these tones limited by the range of the ordinary voice and by the skill of the ordinary player. To be successful, it must be a combination of tones that can be played as well as sung by almost anyone. Necessarily, within these limits, there will be found some similarity of tone succession.[6]

There is a whiff of snobbery in this judgement – the reference to ordinary voices and players – and on the whole, courts have assumed that evidence of copying is harder to establish in low than high music. As another American judge put it: of the various possible permutations of musical notes, 'only a few are pleasing; and much fewer still suit the infantile demands of the popular ear'.[7] One consequence of such assumptions, as Osterberg notes, is that a common defence in plagiarism cases is to show that the melodic phrases in dispute can be widely found in other works as well. Such evidence dispels 'any possible inference of copying because it precludes any logical basis for an inference that the similarities in the accused song had to result from copying the claimant's song'. Thus in the *Chariots of Fire* case, heard in London in 1987, in which Vangelis and his publishers were sued for plagiarising the work of another Greek composer, Evangelous Papathanassiou, the court was persuaded 'that the similarities in the pieces were commonplace in music and not copied'.[8]

The implication of such rulings is not that popular songwriters are by their nature serial plagiarists but, rather, that given pop composers' shared objective of appealing to audiences with conventional musical expectations and common cultural grounding in previous pop hits, it is hardly surprising that they routinely write similar songs quite independently.[9] What is involved, one could say, is the necessary use of

6. Robert C. Osterberg, 'Striking Similarity and the Attempt to Prove Access and Copying in Music Plagiarism Cases', *Copyright, Entertainment and Sports Law*, Vol. 2 (1983), p. 87. The quotation comes from a 1923 US Federal Case, Marks *v*. Leo Feist Inc.
7. Loc. cit. Quotation from a 1951 US Federal Case, Jones *v*. Supreme Music Corp.
8. Cited from Peter Carey and Richard Verow, *Media and Entertainment Law*, Bristol, Jordans, 1998, p. 45. See also Osterberg (1983), p. 91.
9. In 1976 Judge Richard Owen ruled in a New York court that, although George Harrison did not deliberately plagiarise Ronnie Mack, 'Nevertheless it is clear that *My Sweet Lord* is the same song as *He's So Fine*. Under the law this is infringement of copyright, and is no less so even though it may have been sub-

clichés, and in this respect there are comparisons to make with other art forms. People would probably agree that if passage A in a book by novelist A were identical to passage B in a book by novelist B, copying must necessarily be involved. But what if the two books were Mills and Boon romances? Here, we would be much more likely to accept that different authors, working to the same narrow formula, had come up independently with identical plots, characters or love scenes.

This leads to a second kind of argument: originality is a problem for the music business, a matter of recurring legal dispute, not simply because of the limited combinations of notes available but also because commercial music-making is not really a matter of individual creativity at all. This is the logic of Adorno's analysis of jazz and popular song in terms of standardisation, for example. His point was that in musicological (and literary) terms all pop songs are much the same, because that is their point: repetitively to give audiences what they already know they want. And in day-to-day music business terms this is a perfectly reasonable point. Most pop music is formulaic: there may be clear distinctions between different musical genres but genre rules themselves are quite precise. They are spelt out clearly in the how-to-write-a-hit-song books that have been on sale for a hundred years or more. In 1918 Chappell, Britain's largest music publishers, were still not paying pop lyricists royalties as required by the 1911 Copyright Act, 'on the [Adornoesque] grounds that lyrics are merely a repetition of the same words in a different order and almost always with the same ideas'.[10]

The Chappell position was that it was inappropriate to use a law based on the protection of individual authors' original ideas in a business in which 'creativity' actually meant the efficient application of compositional rules. In the context of commercial pop, then, the distinction of one number from another lies in marginal rather than

consciously accomplished.' Harrison himself conceded: 'I wasn't consciously aware of the similarity between *He's So Fine* and *My Sweet Lord* when I wrote the song as it was more improvised and not so fixed.' As he reflected ruefully later: 'I still don't understand how the courts aren't filled with similar cases – as 99 percent of the popular music that can be heard is reminiscent of something or other.' Quoted in Fred Bronson, *The Billboard Book of Number One Hits*, New York, Billboard Publications, 1985, p. 286.

10. See Simon Frith, 'Copyright and the Music Business', *Popular Music*, Vol. 7 (1987), pp. 64–65.

essential musical differences: in titles, in the briefest of hooks, in sound gimmicks – above all, in the details of a particular performance (which cannot in any case be copyrighted). One reason why sampling became a legal minefield so quickly was that it entailed the copying of precisely these differences. In the first sampling case to be reported widely in Britain (it was settled out of court), Pete Waterman's 1987 action against the M/A/R/R/S hit *Pump up the Volume*, the disputed material was the brief sound of a woman's cry.[11] What was at stake here (as in most sampling cases) was not originality but recognisability. The assumption was that records succeed because of some feature that has immediate appeal. To copy this is to steal not so much a musical idea as a hit quality. Court cases in such disputes refer not to the expert evidence of a musicologist, explaining how two numbers have the same structure, but to the common sense of a judge who can recognise, like any other lay listener, that a sound on this record was appropriated from that one. The problem, then, is that sounds (as opposed to notes) are as much the responsibility of record producers and sound engineers as of composers and instrumentalists. Who is the author here?

My concern, though, is not to explore the complexities of plagiarism or sampling law (fascinating though these are) but to suggest that, far from being an anathema, 'copying' is normal in pop music-making. (The reason why copying cases come to court is financial, not ethical; plagiarism cases are only ever brought against records that are successful.) The same argument can be made from a different perspective: originality is a problem for popular music not just because of standardisation and the constraints of serial musical production but also because of improvisation, the impulse of folk and vernacular music. As John Collier Lincoln notes:

> Few songs that went on to become jazz standards in the early days were original compositions in the sense that later popular tunes, like 'Star Dust' of 'Body and Soul' were. Most were pieced together out of musical material that was floating loose around bandstands – fragments of hymns, blues, work songs, operatic arias, or traditional themes with ancient histories.[12]

11. See Simon Frith, 'Music and Morality', in Frith (1993), pp. 1–21, at pp. 6–7.
12. Cited in Frith (1993), pp. 63–64.

In subjecting this world to copyright law, in 'fixing' such malleable music as a score or record, authorship is less a matter of originality than of staking a claim. As Lincoln adds, at a time when 'many of the musicians could not read music, much less write it down, they perforce had to get someone like [Clarence] Williams to set the music down for them. In many cases, the amanuensis would supply harmonies, add verses, or change the tune in other ways and felt entitled to credit.'[13] In the organic development of folk music, in other words, copyright describes a kind of random pause in which an assigned author (in collusion with a publisher) lays claim to something that as a matter of 'originality' is essentially collective.

Much the same argument can be made about the use of beats and samples in rap music. The sampler might be a new tool, but its use involves old principles of musical composition; there is an obvious continuity between jazz improvisation, Jamaican dub and scratch mix deejaying. Existing tunes or phrases are the basis of new compositions; 'copying' (or 'versioning') are themselves creative activities. When Grandmaster Flash turned the turntable into a musical instrument, confusing the distinction between music consumption and music production, he was continuing a Black musical tradition, not transforming it.[14]

The problem of sampling, in short, is not that the technology has made possible a new form of theft but that the music industry has a new way of claiming musical ownership. Digital sampling, as Paul Théberge puts it, has allowed for 'new forms of compositional activity' but also 'created the conditions for a new form of value in musical sounds'.[15] In this context, illegality is a misleading concept. What is at stake is not an orderly world invaded by larcenists with machines but a creative world invaded by lawyers, as corporate copyright owners seek to regulate everyday musical practice. Indeed, it could be argued that the reality of music-making has never borne much resemblance to the legal fantasy of the lone individual creating an entirely original work. (There is obviously an echo here of the liberal economic construct of the rational individual buyer or seller in the marketplace.)

13. Loc. cit.
14. See Steve Jones, 'Music and Copyright in the USA', in Frith (1993), pp. 67–85, at pp. 80–81.
15. Paul Théberge, 'Copyright Reform in Canada', in Frith (1993), pp. 40–66, at p. 62.

Quotation, for example, is a commonplace of musical composition, whether as a matter of artistic irony and self-consciousness or in the casual use of a shared musical language and reference to the everyday soundscape.[16] The use of the law to regulate these practices seems to mean less the defence of creativity than its suppression – the prevention of musical activity either by directly refusing permission to quote or, indirectly, by demanding an unreasonable fee.[17] (One of the most striking aspects of quotation cases – as in the Robbie Williams and Badly Drawn Boy disputes already mentioned – is the disparity between the length of a disputed quotation and the percentage of a work's royalty earnings demanded.)

There are other aspects of popular music culture that I could discuss here: the importance of cover versions and cover bands for everyday music-making, for example. Copying has always been a perfectly acceptable practice commercially, whatever we might think of it aesthetically (from white covers of Black tracks in the 1950s to the strange phenomenon of cover bands such as the Bootleg Beatles in the 1990s). There are many performing musicians who make their living sounding like someone else, and rock musicians, in particular, have always learnt to play by copying, picking out a guitar line on a record over and over again. As Steve Jones suggests, copying (and sampling) can, in fact, be a way of establishing credibility, displaying one's understanding of the form in which one is working.[18]

But the example that I want to give of the gap between legal rhetoric and musical practice is different. Since they own the copyrights, record companies have had a free hand to remix digitally material from their back catalogue. This is not just a technical matter. Such remixing involves aesthetic decisions about sound, balance, texture

16. For discussion of quotation in the high musical world, see David Schwarz, 'Listening Subjects: Semiotics, Psychoanalysis and the Music of John Adams and Steve Reich', in *Keeping Score: Music, Disciplinarity, Culture*, ed. David Schwarz, Anahid Kassabian and Lawrence Siegel, Charlottesville and London, University Press of Virginia, 1997, pp. 275–98, at pp. 280–83.

17. For an excellent discussion of such effective censorship focusing on the case of Double Dee and Steinski's *Lesson 3* see Robert Christgau, 'Down By Law', *Village Voice*, 25 March 1986. In some such cases – as with the US band Culturcide or the UK producer V/VM – the illegal use of other people's music is a deliberate political act.

18. Steve Jones, 'Critical Legal Studies and Popular Music Studies', *Stanford Humanities Review*, Vol. 3 (1993), pp. 77–89, at p. 88.

and volume, and the results can be gross distortions of the original. Sometimes, the artists involved can be powerful enough to protest (George Martin took over the digital remixing of the Beatles back cat-alogue; Jimmy Page insisted on supervising Led Zeppelin on CD), but they often have no enforceable rights in their music at all.[19] There are many records out there that appal the named artists aesthetically, and from which they hardly benefit financially, but which are, none the less, perfectly legitimate, the result of remixing practices and licens-ing deals over which they have had no control at all, and against which the copyright system offers little defence.

The Industry's Response

The music industry has always accounted for itself ideologically in its campaign against piracy. By and large, as a matter of legislation, the campaign has been successful. Regulation of the use of music has been extended as technological possibilities have changed. Governments have been persuaded that live performance, phonograph records, radio, analogue taping and digital storage, and now the Internet, are threats to profits and therefore musical creativity; laws have been passed nationally (and harmonised internationally) to protect music rights owners accordingly (see Chapter 6). National differences remain. The USA offers less extensive protection of performer and composer rights than most European countries, for example, and in many non-Western countries copyright laws may change, but there is little concern to enforce them. But I am less interested here in the material effects of anti-piracy campaigns than in their ideological force. Music consumers have, on the whole, been more ambiguous about the problem of piracy than music law-makers.

The ambiguity is reflected in the use of the term 'piracy'. Pirates are obviously criminals, thieves, parasites on other people's creative work without concern for the consequences (in many countries, for exam-ple, piracy has a much more destructive effect on nascent local music businesses than on the global leisure corporations). On the other hand, the historical image of the pirate – buccaneering, free-spirited,

19. This has been a particularly obvious problem in jazz. See Peter Pullman, 'Digital Doldrums: Do CD Reissues Honor Jazz History or Mangle It?', *Voice Rock & Roll Quarterly*, March 1991, pp. 3–4.

bold – has a continuing positive resonance. There exists a vague feeling that pirates steal from the rich, sometimes (like highwaymen or Robin Hood's outlaws) for the benefit of the poor.[20] Consumers do not generally weep over EMI's or Sony's reduced profit margins.

One problem for the industry is that it has applied the term 'piracy' to a wide range of activities that seem rather different morally and economically, whatever their shared illegal status. **Home taping,** for example, is treated by the industry as domestic piracy: people are acquiring and illicitly copying a record (from a friend, the library or music radio) instead of buying it; there is an assumed correlation between home taping activity and the loss of rights income. But this is to reduce musical activity to buying, selling and stealing records. In reality, people tape tracks for a variety or reasons, few of them simply economic. They transfer tracks from CD to tape for convenience – to play in the car, on a Walkman or while doing the chores. They compile their own anthologies. They exchange tapes in order to build up libraries beyond what they can afford. They sample other people's records before deciding what to buy for themselves. Indeed, such tape exchange is a key aspect of musical sociability – what music lover has not said: 'Oh, I'll tape this for you', or 'Can you make me a copy of that?' Home taping, in short, has become an essential part of the networking process in which markets for particular musical genres emerge. Far from being a threat to the industry, home taping contributes crucially to the ways in which people learn about both new and old acts and nurture the musical enthusiasm on which the industry depends.

Arguments of the 1980s about home taping are now being rerun with reference to mp3 technology and Napster. For example, the EU's Directive on Copyright and Related Rights in the Information Society, an attempt to update copyright law for the digital age, called forth an aggressive lobbying effort by IFPI for the introduction of a clause forbidding copying for private use (which the Directive allows) and counter-lobbying by hardware manufacturers, digital companies and consumer groups to protect the rights of domestic copiers.[21] In the

---

20. For a recent historical celebration of this aspect of piracy see Peter Linebaugh and Marcus Rediker, *The Many-headed Hydra, The Hidden History of the Revolutionary Atlantic*, London, Verso, 2000.

21. See, for example, 'Tom Jones Joins European Parliament Debate on Music Copyright', *Business Am*, 29 January 2001.

USA the debate about the legality of Napster (essentially a software that allows the exchange of home tapes on a global scale) is still making its way through the courts and being argued out on a myriad of Web sites. What is already obvious, though, is that Napster use, like home taping, must be treated as a social activity – one from which the industry has potentially as much to gain as to lose.[22]

Bootlegging (another term that romanticises theft) is different from home taping in that it is a form of organised crime: someone has to organise bootlegs' production and distribution. But, again, the term 'bootleg record' is used mostly to describe the provision of musical material that has not been made available by its rights owners – studio out-takes, recordings of live concerts, sessions taken off air or, as in the dance scene, white-label advance copies of tracks that may never be released. Bootlegs are sold to fans who wish to add to their record collections (bootlegs are rarely bought in preference to a major label release), and the cannier rock acts with a dedicated fan base (such as the Grateful Dead) release their own bootlegs, as it were. This is par-ticularly true for musicians in genres in the nature of jazz, folk and new country that are rarely heard on radio and arouse little industry interest. Live concerts become the venue for selling instant tapes of previous live shows, and, just as it is hard to imagine a self-proclaimed music fan who does no home taping, so it is hard to imagine one who owns no bootlegs. There is certainly a marked gap between the dra-conian powers the record industry has here ('It is illegal to make, sell, buy, distribute or advertise bootleg music') and their enforcement. Bootleg CDs are readily available at record fairs and in specialist shops; there is even an ongoing bootleg consumer guide, *Hot Wacks*.[23]

Whatever the industry's rhetorical position, then, bootlegging is viewed as less of a threat than **straight piracy**: copied records (and

22. For Napster activism see Jon Cooper and David M. Harrison, 'The Social Organisation of Audio Piracy on the Internet', *Media, Culture and Society*, Vol. 23 (2001), pp. 71–89. For the music industry's continuing confusion over how best to exploit and protect its rights on-line see Charlotte Goddard's excellent report 'OnLine Music for Revolution', *The Magazine of the Digital Economy*, 17 January 2001.

23. See Samuel Cameron, 'Should Bootleggers Face the Music? The Economics of Illegally Recorded Music', *Briefing Notes in Economics*, Vol. 23, July 1996, pp. 1–4; and Clinton Heylin, *Bootleg: The Secret History of the Other Recording Industry*, New York, St Martin's Press, 1996.

record packaging) passed off as the real thing. (IFPI's anti-piracy
activities are now focused on illegal manufacturing plants.) But while
it is indisputable that such piracy is organised crime, organised often
on a large scale by criminals with no interest in music whatever, this
activity does also reflect a genuine problem of supply. IFPI's geographical figures on pirated record sales show that these are highest
in countries in which legitimate records are likely to be in short
supply and/or relatively expensive. In the long term, then, even
straight piracy could be to the industry's benefit, establishing Western
record-buying habits and changing local musical tastes in advance of
a properly regulated legal market.

The music industry's concern with supply – Where did this record
come from? Who owns the musical rights? Who licensed it? – has
meant a neglect of questions of demand: why do people tape records,
download mp3 files or buy bootlegged and pirated CDs? And there
has always been an anomalous retail sector in copyright terms: the
second-hand record shop. None of the money paid for second-hand
records is returned to rights holders, and I do not know of any study
that examines the size or shape of this economy, although it is obviously important for fans and collectors and sustains an extensive network of shops and fairs and magazines such as *Record Collector*.[24]
One part of the appeal of used record shops is precisely that their
stock is not controlled by corporate marketing strategies and does not
entail 'the exploitation of back catalogue'. Second-hand shops offer
an alternative, serendipitous history of pop that has been, among
other things, a source of inspiration for club DJs and remix engineers
(as in the case of Norman Cook/Fatboy Slim).

The suggestion that the dynamic of the music market comes from illegal (or extralegal) consumer activities is most often made, though, with
reference to **pirate radio**, which has been seen as a necessary challenge
to over-regulated broadcasting even within the music industry itself,
despite the breaches of copyright involved. In the case of such pop

---

24. The music industry overlaps directly with the used record sector in its provision
    of 'cut outs', records that (like remaindered books) are the left-over stock of
    titles no longer published and sold cheaply without payment of any royalties to
    their authors. The potential profits of the cut-out market have certainly been
    exploited by criminal elements within the music industry: see William
    Knoedelseder, *Stiffed: A True Story of MCA, the Music Business and the Mafia*,
    New York, Harper Collins, 1993.

pirates as Radio Caroline in the 1960s and such dance music pirates as Kiss in the 1980s, record companies clearly believed that the promotional gains of getting their music on the airwaves outweighed the loss of broadcast fees. Certainly, the pirate broadcasters who flourish these days do so within particular musical communities. Records are produced, distributed and illegally broadcast by the same group of people.

At the heart of all the arguments about piracy are two kinds of legal issue, two kinds of ideological conflict. The first problem concerns music as property and the clash between the owners of musical rights and the owners of musical commodities. For most commodities, the ownership of something means that one can do with it what one likes; the suggestion that a record's creator can prevent certain uses thus seems bizarre. In this context, arguments about illegality defy common sense. The second problem is that the law suggests a distinction between public and private musical activities that is, in practice, difficult to sustain. There is a recurring suggestion, for example (as in the EU Copyright Directive presently being debated), that breaches of copyright should be allowable if carried out in private, and the industry has long sought technological means of ensuring that CDs or DVDs can be copied once (for domestic purposes) but no more. The difficulty – obvious in uses of the Internet – is that music is essentially sociable. Private musical pleasures cannot be disentangled from music's social use.

The Roots of Illegality

As a live and/or public activity, commercial popular music has always been associated with illegal activities. It has accompanied, and has provided the setting for, 'night life' and all the threats of hedonism and indiscipline thus implied. Music hall was associated with drunkenness and prostitution as well as the sale of alcohol and sex; jazz with brothels and speakeasies. Throughout the twentieth century dance clubs were taken to be the setting for drug abuse: opium, cocaine, heroin, cannabis, amphetamines, ecstasy, etc.; dance halls were the setting for violence; rock festivals meant hallucinogens and public sexual promiscuity. Music has long been the pretext for the clandestine gathering of sexual and/or political dissidents; moralists have blamed music for social problems from the white slave trade in late-nineteenth-century New York to the rise of neo-Nazi youth groups in late-twentieth-century Europe.

This is all familiar enough, and I have no space here to disentangle history from myth. Suffice it to say that, if the vast majority of people enjoy music without doing anything much illegal at all, it is equally true to say that, some illegal activities – drug dealing, most obviously – have been dependent on the public music business, and that music clubs were the most important setting for the transformation of sexual morality (and thereby legislation) in the twentieth century. The immediate consequences of the perceived threat of public music were, however, different: commercial music promoters constituted, from the start, a problem for the state; their activities became subject to an ever-increasing complex of regulation, licensing, law and policing.[25]

In very general terms, five kinds of issue seem to have been involved.

First, music has been seen as an **excuse** for bad behaviour spilling over from the loosely immoral to the positively illicit. The sexual charge of dancing to music thus encourages behaviour – underage sex, perverse sex, commercial sex – that in itself breaks laws. The hedonistic charge of collective music listening encourages the use of stimulants (drink or drugs) that, in turn, reinforce the loss of inhibition, the irresponsible pursuit of pleasure, spontaneous violence and vandalism. The state's concern is to regulate musical gatherings so that they **stay within acceptable limits**.

Second, music has been seen as a problem **in itself**: as noise, sound pollution or a public nuisance. The state's concern here is to regulate musical events so that they do not impinge on people who have no wish to be involved with them (this was one of the parliamentary arguments for regulating raves, for example).

Third, music is seen as the articulation of a **subversive politics**. I am using politics in a broad sense here. What is at issue is the state's fear of what might be going on in that music room at the back of the proletarian pub or ethnic community centre. The everyday life of political groups of all sorts is organised around musical activities. I grew up going to CND and Trotskyist pub-folk nights; I was later involved in

---

25. See, for example: *Music Hall: The Business of Pleasure*, ed. Peter Bailey, Milton Keynes, Open University Press, 1986; Ronald Morris, *Wait Until Dark: Jazz and the Underworld, 1880–1940*, Bowling Green, Bowling Green University Press, 1980; Michael Clarke, *The Politics of Pop Festivals*, London, Junction Books, 1982; Matthew Collin, *Altered State: The Story of Ecstasy Culture and Acid House*, London, Serpent's Tail, 1997.

Communist Party arguments about the politics of discos and in the promotion of punk and reggae acts for anti-racist groups. Music has been as important a recruiting tool for political as for religious sects.[26]

Fourth, there is a legal issue that is of more direct interest to the music industry (although the latter looks to the state for support): public music use must be licensed; fees must be paid to rights holders for their material. In Britain the Performing Rights Society has its own police force: agents whose job is to track down the **unlicensed use of music** and to prosecute rogue club and pub owners and concert promoters accordingly. The problems here have partly been technical – the PRS routinely needs magistrates and judges to clarify what constitutes a 'public performance' – and partly logistical: it is not always so easy to track down the public use of music in private places (in the 'blues' party tradition of the British-Caribbean community, for example).

Finally, the state has also been concerned to protect the customer from the **dangers** of public gatherings. Again, such health and safety concerns have a long history – from protecting music hall patrons from the risk of fire to protecting dance club patrons from the risk of dehydration.

To list the issues with which music promoters have to be concerned is to suggest that, as in the record industry, musical activity is overdetermined by the law. Promoters of contemporary rock festivals, for example, spend as much time dealing with local regulatory agencies – on the details and costs of sewage disposal, catering, transport, security, shelter, noise level, the environment and back-up medical and fire services – as they do negotiating the details of artist contracts with agents, managers and record companies. But the point I want to stress here is that while the state lays down the regulatory framework within which music promoters and club owners have to operate (planning laws, laws on the sale of alcohol, etc.), many of the public concerns about public music are met by the industry's self-regulation.[27]

26. For discussion of music and political mobilisation, see Ron Eyerman and Andrew Jamison, *Music and Social Movements*, Cambridge, Cambridge University Press, 1998, and Simon Frith, 'Politics and the Experience of Music', *Sosiologisk Årbok/Yearbook of Sociology*, Vol. 4 (1999), pp. 217–31.

27. There are obvious parallels here with the history of the cinema industry, although in Britain the state has also been directly involved in the provision of musical venues. On the problems of state youth clubs and rock 'n' roll in the 1950s see Ray Gosling's classic insider account *Sum Total*, London, Faber and Faber, 1962.

On one hand, this has meant more or less effective self-policing (door and gate policy, the use of bouncers); on the other hand, it has meant what we might call formal self-regulation, as potentially disruptive musical activity is turned into something more disciplined, more respectable. The originally chaotic music hall thus became family entertainment, the variety show; music hall artists became dependent for work on their acceptability to a small number of agents and owners of music-hall chains. In dance halls, similarly, the initially disruptive joy of ragtime and early jazz became the routinised pleasure of organised mass dancing, strict-tempo.[28] In the 1950s the early threat of rock 'n' roll was absorbed by the package show; in the 1990s the ecstasy of acid house was absorbed by the corporate rationality of the Ministry of Sound. Orderly musical consumption is, after all, as important for the music market as for the state.

But while in commercial terms self-regulation has been largely effective – music while you play is as orderly as music while you work or shop – it has been less successful in ideological terms. Disorder, one could say, is built into the system. In capitalist countries leisure is understood as the site of excess, irresponsibility and 'licence'; one feature of popular music, since the mid nineteenth century, at least, has been to map out this excessive space: the urban space-of-the-night as celebrated in any number of disco tracks. What are involved here, in other words, are not simply commercial interests touting leisure goods to the quiescent masses but also active pleasure-seekers occupying these commercial sites for their own purposes as part of a strategic assault on boredom.

I am deliberately romanticising night life here in order to make the point that, in the continuing tension between order and disorder in the popular music industry, the disorderly have always had the best tunes. The critical consensus is that dangerous music – music that engages with excess and disorder – is more valuable than safe music, i.e. music that goes along with the authorities (this is the pop version of modernism). This argument has recurred in musical history; it has been applied to jazz, to rock, to dance music, even to country. The music that is most highly valued is that which, however symbolically,

28. See Susan C. Cook, 'Passionless Dancing and Passionate Reform: Respectability, Modernism and the Social Dancing of Irene and Vernon Castle', in *The Passion of Music and Dance*, ed. WilliamWashabaugh, Oxford and New York, Berg, 1998, pp. 133–50.

challenges the text of the law: sex and drugs and rock 'n' roll! The music that is most despised (except in its occasional return as kitsch) is 'easy listening', the white bread version of musical excitement, from Paul Whiteman to Simply Red. The point here is not that such acts are not highly successful commercially but that they are unconvincing aesthetically; so we have the odd situation where respectable musicians have to present themselves as unrespectable, rather than vice versa.

And there is a further point here. One aspect of the political changes of the second half of the twentieth century was the decline of class-based political groupings rooted in the experience of work and the rise of political activity based on identities (gender, sexuality, age, ethnicity, race) articulated in the home, away from work. This was the context in which music became politically important, a way of articulating identity and difference. The music that matters most in such politics is the kind that appeals to people most intensely, or which can be used most effectively to keep other people out (this is obvious in the numerous local forms of rap): that which is implicitly and explicitly a threat.

Here to Stay

Put together these experiences of live and public music with my earlier arguments about rights and recorded music, and it is no longer surprising that, even in a highly commercial music world, there is strong ideological support for illegal musical activity. One assumption here is that the industry excludes certain social groups from its money-making activities; these therefore have every right to use illegal means of access to the music market (whether via payola, pirate radio or digital technology). There are equally strong strands of artistic and/or avant-garde anarchism that maintain that 'the Man' has no right to 'our music', that bureaucracy stifles creativity. In this context the music industry's continuing recourse to law is just one more indication that it is laying claim to something, music, that it cannot really own.

At the beginning of this chapter I asked why the music industry was so litigious. I have suggested that the answer has two components. First, the industry's legal structure has been laid over musical activities – activities of music-making, music-using, everyday musical life – that do not, in fact, match the description of music assumed by the law. Second, for cultural-historical reasons, the underlying ideology of popular music, its particular relationship to public leisure and pleasure, has tended to pitch music against the law, to see it as a practice defined against rather than by regulation, whether this regulation is commercial or legislative. Such an argument (most obviously in the history of rock) becomes a further basis for defying or ignoring the industry's rights regime. The result is a continual conflict, since the industry's profits depend on enforcing the rules of the commercial music game on participants who think they are playing something different.

'The basic issue in commercial recordings', writes Anthony Seeger, 'is trust', and the problem is that there is a negative correlation between trust and the law.[29] It is not just that the law is necessary to the industry because of the degree of existing mistrust but also that the law adds to the mistrust through its very attempt to fix the unfixable. In sociological terms, what is peculiar about the music industry is the gap between its informal and formal organisation. Music is by its nature sociable; musicians and their audiences are linked by ties of trust and friendship. To make money of music the industry has to rationalise these ties: to bring in the law. And that is when the trouble starts.

---

29. Seeger (1992), p. 351. For contrasting accounts of trust, the law and mistrust in the music business see Steve Feld, 'A Sweet Lullaby for World Music', *Public Culture*, Vol 12 (2000), pp. 145–71, and Mike Jones, *Organising Pop: Why So Few Pop Acts Make Pop Music*, unpublished PhD Thesis, Institute of Popular Music, Liverpool University, 1997.

8

The Tarnished Image? Folk 'Industry' and Media

Mike Brocken

> One aspect of the traditional music scene that has long been recognised is that it lacks a professionally managed infrastructure. Some of the informal amateur structures within the folk scene are at times one of its greatest strengths but at other times one of its gravest weaknesses.[1]

Some years ago I conducted a selective review of the contemporary folk industry and media from a popular music perspective as part of my doctoral thesis.[2] I concluded that historiographical pressures concerning what folk music actually was and how (or, indeed, whether) it should be marketed had acted in such a way as to minimise economic and cultural progress and positively encourage an inefficient, albeit dedicated, distribution network of information and music. I further suggested that this happened to such an extent that some folk music lovers who entered the 'industry' and attempted to market the music were subject to over-sensitivity and socio-political (and thus generic) pressures and judgements. They had allowed themselves to be deflected from the pursuit of profit by continuing to perceive an opposition between heritage (the natural) and enterprise (the mass-produced); this dichotomy remained central to a continual struggle for meaning.

Although I concluded my discussion of this problem by suggesting that certain sections of the folk music industry and media were beginning to face the challenge of commerce, my monitoring of both areas in the intervening years has revealed no substantial progress

---

1. Pete Heywood, 'Editorial', *The Living Tradition*, Vol. 13 (January–February 1996), p. 4.
2. Michael Brocken, *The British Folk Revival: An Analysis of Folk/Popular Dichotomies from a Popular Music Studies Perspective*, PhD dissertation, University of Liverpool, 1997.

away from the margins of popular music production. My conviction is that the music of the folk 'movement' (if it may still be described as such) remains largely hidden from, and consequently unheard by, the vast majority of the general public. Moreover, despite the efforts of such singers as Billy Bragg, and certain progressive elements within the folk music industry (the Internet-based magazine *Musical Traditions*, for example) to raise the profile of the genre in the United Kingdom, it seems to me that what little is revealed of folk music participation remains tarnished by the revival's own countenance. After an interval of over four years I cannot but ask whether the folk revival has moved into an irretrievable period of decay – or whether it is merely going through the transitional pains of adjustment to the vagaries of postmodernity in popular music production and reception.

The following account, in short, submits that the relationship between what can be conceived as folk music and its presentation remains a significant and persistent problem for the commercial sector of the folk revival. This relationship dictates that the methods and forms of presentation be accompanied by an ever-present sanction of the unacceptable. In circumstances where the range of any music that reaches the public ear is determined at least partly by the nature of the establishment that produces and disseminates it, any such sanction inevitably influences the course of mercantile development.

For example, one of the few advances in profile-raising that the folk 'commercial' sector appears to have made in recent times is in receiving more grant aid from regional and government arts development directorates. Alan Bell, organiser of the Fylde Folk Festival, in spring 2000 became chairman of a new organisation named Folkus (the Folk Arts Network of the North West) because he was 'frustrated by the lack of recognition for the folk arts on his home patch'.[3] Bell is regarded highly in the North West of England for his tireless campaigning for folk music and dance, and it is expected that he will succeed in attracting sponsorship from a variety of funding bodies. Similarly, the relative success of the Folkworks organisation in the North East is a credit to the hard work of fund- and profile-raising on behalf of folk music. However, activity of this kind hardly signals economic growth. In fact,

3. Pete Heywood, 'Heard it on the Grapevine', *The Living Tradition*, Vol. 37 (March–April 2000), pp. 12–15, at p. 12.

one could view this tendency to seek external sponsorship as a desperate measure aimed at underwriting the accumulated debt incurred by various folk-related projects. Folkworks rely on funding from Northern Arts, Durham City Arts, Durham County Council and the Arts Council of England. The organisation is also a registered charity. These networking bodies have not elicited any notable creative successes in the folk music sector, nor have they expanded investment or production. In fact, they appear to exist for the purpose of rescuing festival societies from non-profit situations while maintaining, on the musical front, a 'them versus us' stance. One has to ask whether they unwittingly encourage a commercial backwardness.[4]

Despite its conspicuously more trendy incarnation as 'Shoots and Roots', the 2000 Edinburgh Folk Festival was forced to fold prior to its customary Easter event, the November 1999 'Shoots and Roots' having fallen well short of its budgeted income targets. The basic problem was that not enough people were attracted by the presentation of the programme, even though, according to its artistic director Dave Francis, the festival sported 'a balanced commercial and artistic blend and [was] supported by a good publicity campaign on a limited budget'.[5] Perhaps some justifiable suspicion emanates from funding bodies when they observe that what they perceive to have once been a moderately thriving media and production sector of the popular music industry is now failing so spectacularly to sell itself that it has to resort to funding applications to prop up unstable financial proposals. Not surprisingly, the Scottish Arts Council and Edinburgh City Council both decided not to throw good money after bad after considering the size of the EFF Society's overdraft. The same commentator who recorded the words of Dave Francis quoted above relayed the following 'off the cuff' comments of an unidentified EFF organiser:

> We really set ourselves up as suckers, don't we, when we believe something is worth doing because of its intrinsic worth. Better to be

4. The use of the expression 'folk arts' is not without significance here, since the term 'folk music' has frequently been replaced by 'folk arts' (or 'roots') for grant portfolio purposes during the late 1990s. Marion Leonard of the Institute of Popular Music (University of Liverpool) found fundraising for her Coventry/Liverpool Irish Music and Dance Exhibition 'Talking Traditions' (June 2000) difficult, because it was considered to fall within the purview of folk 'music' rather than folk 'arts'.
5. Heywood (2000), p. 14.

thoroughly crassly commercial – the folks with the purse strings
seem to understand that so well; they know the price of everything
and the value of nowt! Thatcher's legacy.[6]

Thatcher's legacy, perhaps; but the decline in the revival's ability to
market itself has recently been reflected widely in similar falling figures and failing projects. The closure of the Edinburgh Folk Festival
followed closely on the heels of the failure of the 'Continental
Ceilidh' in Lanark, which left a trail of debts to artists. In June 2000,
when these lines were originally written, the HTD Records Summer
Folk Day had just been cancelled on account of 'very bad advance
ticket sales'.[7] My own experience of co-promoting the folk duo Show
of Hands at Liverpool's Neptune theatre in May 2000 bears similar
witness not only to apathy and declining public interest but also to
misdirected, irrelevant and consequently unsuccessful marketing.
Despite the relative success of the venture, the nature of the promotional material foredoomed it to unprofitability. Indeed, the 'traditional' associations suggested by the advertising material probably
bewildered many. The number of people willing, under these terms,
to invest culturally or financially in folk music reception in Liverpool
is undoubtedly decreasing. So far as one can see, this process looks
like continuing.

   There are a number of interconnected reasons for this sorry state of
affairs. The first is the decline in folk and acoustic music as an everyday musical tool or form of expression: a narrative with recognised,
prefabricated musical and social articulations. One can no longer
assume that an audience exists for any music project that stands for
apparent unity and totality of meaning. Every signifier (in this case,
the sound of folk music) eventually 'empties' itself of meaning when
it becomes historically disengaged from a particular foundational,
synchronic signified (i.e. the thing that it purports to represent: in this
case the 'folk revival'). The signified cannot remain umbilically tied to
that which it initially symbolised.

   Therefore, although young people in the Britain of the 1990s were
ready to embrace music of 'past' eras, they did so in contexts in which
it was possible to rearticulate the signifier. The psychedelia, easy and

---

6. Ibid., p.15.
7. Unsigned editorial, *Hit The Dust* (HTD Records newsletter), Vol. 27 (June–September 2000), p. 1.

loungecore 'revivals' of the mid-1990s are good examples of this. Others are the continuing fascination with the Swedish pop group ABBA and with 1970s disco, as well as the seemingly ever-present 'revival' of Mod. Whereas the folk revival has adopted a somewhat dogmatic rhetoric that relates current practice directly to a historical, identity-giving foundation, other genres are able to present empty signifiers to which one can attach meaningful but essentially disconnected signifieds.[8] All music is a symbolic representation and inevitably experiences the vagaries of indefinite extension to which all symbols are subject: an open-ended horizon rather than a determined relation.

Unlike other genres, however, folk music is not readily presented as one that embraces this empty horizon – it is not presumed to enfold a groundlessness. Rather, folk (or 'traditional') music is presented to its audience and to its practitioners as an embodiment of apparently concrete argumentative practices and historical solutions (even though this cannot be so for a symbolic signifying practice). This presentation continues to cultivate a conflict perspective rather than openly to acclaim rearticulation. As the anonymous quotation above implies, we are bequeathed an image in which the values 'inherent' in the music are those of ideology, conflict and difference. Our resulting perceptions are those of a music 'scene' that represents a challenge to the domination and exploitation of the masses by popular culture and also a struggle for control of the means of production.

At the same time, there has been a steady decline throughout the whole United Kingdom in the importance of manually based music-making and a concomitant steady growth of home studios and computer-based music software. This is part of the great social revolution of our age, and it is a phenomenon by no means confined to Britain. I am not suggesting that folk music production and dissemination will ever cease as a consequence of this change, but technology is helping to challenge the conventional wisdom of taste cultures in complex industrial societies such as our own. The inherited categories

---

8. The popularity of the 1992 motion picture soundtrack *Reservoir Dogs* (MCA MCD10541) is a good example in this connection. The new presentation of such hit songs as *Little Green Bag* by the George Baker Selection and *Stuck in the Middle With You* by Stealer's Wheel clearly displays significant recontextualisations. *A priori* notions of these songs are overturned by the movie and its reception processes.

of high culture, folk culture and popular culture, together with the host of associated aesthetic gatekeepers (who include critics, reviewers and opinion-makers), are being subverted by the heterogeneous, mass-mediated cultures of the computer age.

Our increasing prosperity has created a bigger demand for services to cater for our leisure, and this has also had its effects on folk music commerce. Despite the failure of the Edinburgh Folk Festival, a modicum of growth has occurred in recent times in the folk festival sector (it is estimated by the English Folk Dance & Song Society that three million people now attend folk festivals each summer). However, it could be argued that under these circumstances folk festival culture is a mere reflection of this wealth and leisure. Cheryl Hunt, a spokesperson for the Chester Folk Festival, has expressed to me her concern that festival presentations as a whole are failing to expound folk music as a participatory practice and instead (to paraphrase her words) are 'exhibiting the music inside an event culture where the music merely accompanied the happening'. In May 2000 she stated in a newspaper interview: 'The extra events we plan to put on will be very much aimed at audience participation in the form of workshops, sessions, singarounds, dances, etc.'[9]

But these depictions also have their problems. While such folk performance and reception processes are viewed by many as reflecting a respect for heritage and tradition, these images no longer represent the informal rules and expectations that guide our everyday behaviour (our 'folkways', so to speak). In fact, they can (and do) reek of musical virtuosity and elitism. Sessions and singarounds do not belong to the common musical parlance of young people of the twenty-first century and do not relate to their social mores or everyday social interactions. The social/musical language of the revival, therefore, is not only constrained by its most visible expositions but in addition comes across as antiquated and esoteric – not the greatest incentive to trade! The culture of the folk music revival remains stuck in an 'ideal' form incapable of adjusting to the 'real' and ever-changing patterns of society.

For any popular music genre to survive in the twenty-first century, its commercial arm needs to understand how to market that music.

9. 'Folk Festival's Extra Events', *Chester and District Standard*, 18 May 2000, interview with Cheryl Hunt, p. 19.

Perhaps the one basic axiom valid for all popular music presentation is that the music is obliged to speak on at least two levels at once: first, to other musicians and to the concerned minority that cares about specific meanings; second, to the public at large, which cares about other issues pertaining to its chosen way of life. However, the revivalists tend to demarcate themselves strictly in the marketplace: either as increasingly dated but charming 'ancients' (note the William Jackson album entitled *Celtic Tranquility*), or else as partisans endorsing the solemn 'historical' burden of the coal mine and the pawn shop. It is this second association, perhaps more than anything else, that alienates the youth of 2000, with its middle-class aspirations.

To be involved in folk music commerce, therefore, is to align oneself with one or other version of an apparently fixed musical-cum-social policy at a time when the predominant drive in British society and trade is to move away from integrated packages of this kind. In an explosive age of social pluralism and new forms of stratification that is witnessing a rebirth of social snobbery via hedonism and liberal elitism as well as via multicultural tolerance (and its obverse, racial hatred), the activities and language of the folk revival look increasingly anachronistic. Conversely, the modern world of commerce appears to many folk revivalists as increasingly degenerate in relation to a mythical past.

The Fear of Affluence: An 'Industry' as Such?

Certainly, the pop industry's concern for market share continues to be viewed by many within the folk scene as being at odds with folk ideas about authenticity and credibility and, especially in the context of the pop industry's marginal status *qua* industry, remains an object of suspicion for 'folkies', who suspect something amiss and untrustworthy. Chris Sugden writes of 'reducing [music] to the lowest common denominator in order to suit the mass market'.[10] The popular music industry is seen as drawing attention shamelessly to ephemerality – as concentrating on the materiality of people's lives. This conflicts with what survives of the idealistic optimism of the folk revival. Significant numbers of active folkies react negatively towards anything

---

10. Chris Sugden, 'There Are Three Ways of Being "Folk"', *The Living Tradition*, Vol. 20 (March–April 1997), p. 37.

resembling popular music 'business'. At times, they seem to prefer an inefficient marketing network that remains true to its traditions to an efficient one modelled on the practices of capitalist industry. Moving forward via individual initiative, a basic tenet of the popular music industry, often appears less acceptable than advancing via group activity. As a result, there is a very deep-rooted hostility to any attempts at increasing sales via outright commercialism; ambitious projects such as the English Folk Dance & Song Society's 'Root and Branch' (of which more later) have first to justify themselves by being 'thoroughly stimulating [...] extremely important and worthwhile'.[11]

Yet despite an ideological reluctance to admit that the capitalist system and present-day reality can have anything to commend them, coupled with a general feeling that once the folk revival 'ceases to be able to appeal to idealists and starts to attract careerists it will lose the moral force which is its greatest traditional asset',[12] the folk music industry in Britain stubbornly endures through a network of relatively small, independent businesses (many of them part-time) and the devotion of enthusiastic amateurs. This network includes record companies, distributors, instrument makers and repairers, retailers, festival organisers, promoters, artist agencies, folk clubs and a periodical-dominated media system. All of these business and media strands compete with each other for musicians, articles and, indeed, consumers; but they also attempt, as if in recognition of a common heritage, to co-ordinate their activities informally through the folk-music-related social networks that have survived into the twenty-first century. These networks are bound together in a kind of ideological commonwealth. From a pragmatic business perspective, however, this network often turns out to be something of a chaotic labyrinth. Jeremy Horrall, proprietor of the Telford's Warehouse venue, has complained:

> It can be a bit of a nightmare, to be honest. We've had to cancel many times after having a folkie on our [advertising] board for ages. Alexander's [another venue in Chester] have had the same trouble – even with Martin Carthy. He was due there last autumn but failed to show [...] didn't know anything about it, apparently. It's no good, really. I'm not

11. Eddie Upton, review of *Root & Branch*, 'What's Afoot?', quoted in *Root & Branch* publicity material, EFDSS, summer 2000.
12. Interview by the author with Geoff Speed, BBC Radio Merseyside folk music presenter, May 2000.

suggesting that Martin is unprofessional – far from it – but the (I think) Farndon folk club who 'booked' him into Alexander's certainly are![13]

Perhaps the British folk music 'industry' is not (and would not necessarily claim to be) an industry as such, but is instead a rather dispersed community made up of business associates, friends and like-minded enthusiasts. Some parts of this community do admittedly attempt to make a living out of the genre (the Adastra agency, for example), but many others, among whom one may mention Alan Surtees, organiser of the Bridgenorth Folk Festival, and the promoter and writer Chris Hockenhull, do not. All of them appear to desire a wider recognition for the music – but not under 'any' terms. For example, recent advertisements in Volume 37 of the folk magazine *The Living Tradition* entice prospective purchasers with such descriptions as 'folksinger, storyteller and community musician' (Pete Castle, p. 24), 'a cerebral musician' (Cormac Breatnach, p. 26), 'spirited sets and honest songs [...] and love of the tradition' (Firebrand, p. 48). In this way, the folk music trading sector and media see as their joint task to confirm the existence not only of a musical style but also of a valuable historical-cultural entity. There is a general consensus in favour of non-concession – a fear, even, that the music or the artist as a visible attestation of an authentic aesthetic could in some way be compromised.

While such anxieties are perhaps understandable, given the apparent historical nature of the music, they shade into another fear that is far more pernicious (and financially damaging): that once a folk music artist acquires the trappings of popular music, he or she will begin to adopt popular music attitudes and habits of mind, becoming totally commercial and corrupt or, at best, losing touch and sympathy with the folk revival. Although there is a history of folk artists leaving the revival for the sake of commercial success (the names include Isla St Clair, Billy Connolly, Mike Harding, Gerry Rafferty and Barbara Dickson), it is easy to show how inconsistent this negative attitude is, since all of the above-named artists, along with many others, have been proud to draw attention to their folk origins. It also appears ill-considered to take it as axiomatic that authenticity and commercial success are antithetical, since both can logically be components of the same accomplishment. The problem with the rank categorisation of

13. Interview by the author with Jeremy Horrall, proprietor of Telford's Warehouse, June 2000.

musical parameters is that there is, quite literally, no area in music (not excluding Gregorian chant) that has not at some time or other been visited and uplifted by musicans of a commercial persuasion.

If this seems a rather dismal portrayal of the way in which cultur-ally inhibitive generic barriers continue to block the path of expan-sion for certain kinds of music in Britain today, it illustrates accurately the articles of faith to which many folk adherents continue to cleave. In actual fact, the *ad hoc* anti-commercial formulations discussed above are not peculiar to the folk revival but are in fact replicated in one form or another in probably every other 'scene' within present-day popular music. Sara Cohen, Ruth Finnegan and Barry Shank, amongst others, have described comparable invocations of authentic-ity in different locations and scenes.[14] This evidence suggests that small sectors within all musical communities strive for authenticity by bucking trends. In any case, as folksinger Bob Buckle testifies, 'pop star' egos and antics are not confined to pop music: 'Although I enjoyed playing at the Robert Shelton workshop in Liverpool this year [2000], I thought that the egocentric attitude of a certain folk performer was well out of order. It's not only the "Atomic Kittens" of this world who suffer from egomania, let me tell you!'[15] However, an assertion that the 'fundamental honesty of most British folk music business people is a facet which signifies a "difference" from other popular music production practices' remains vehement within the ranks of the folk revival.[16] It is claimed in addition that the integrity of the average British 'folk businessperson' is exceptionally high (one might cite Tony Engle of Topic in this connection). Major problems exist, however, for any enlightened folk revival entrepreneur. These stem not only from his or her attempt to reconcile the conflict between respect for 'tradition' (whatever **that** is) and the imperatives of successful marketing, but also from the ambiguity of the assump-tions that gave rise to folk's brand of musical and social egalitarian-ism in the first place. These tenets came into being in non-repeatable

14. Sara Cohen, *Rock Culture in Liverpool: Popular Music in the Making*, Oxford, Clarendon Press, 1991; Ruth Finnegan, *The Hidden Musicians: Music-making in an English Town*, Cambridge, Cambridge University Press, 1989; Barry Shank, *Dissonant Identities: The Rock 'n' Roll Scene in Austin, Texas*, Hanover, Wes-leyan University Press, 1994.
15. Interview by the author with Bob Buckle, folksinger, June 2000.
16. Geoff Speed, May 2000.

historical circumstances (in the brief heyday of Guild Socialism, actually) and through the mediation of what one can only term scholarly elitism, as represented by such early collectors as Cecil Sharp. Both factors make the proclamation of folk's 'authenticity' and the sanctification of its 'difference' highly problematic. An artistic manifesto along these dogmatic lines is workable only in the context of a fixed world view – in this instance, a view that finds a musical language tolerable only if it can be explained as a primordial function, a 'natural' form of expression in the Roussellian sense.

It is also true that the language and marketing of the folk revival carry a residue of that social climate just after the Second World War, when workers and bosses seemed to stand unalterably opposed to each other and integrity was often equated with hard Left political ideology, low commercial aspirations and chronic inefficiency. Indeed, the previously mentioned Topic Record Company grew, via the Topic Record Club (founded in 1939), directly out of the Workers' Music Association, which was founded in 1936 by the London Labour Choral Union and the Co-operative Musical Association. In reality, the WMA was little more than a nebulous offshoot of the Communist Party of Great Britain. The Workers' Music Association commissioned A. L. Lloyd to write *The Singing Englishman* in 1944 and *Folk Song in England* in 1967 and, within the milieu of postwar utopianism, the executive of the WMA fashioned 'tradition' in its own image, thinly disguising itself in the process as the vanguard of a peace movement.

The folk revival took wing in an age of apparent certainty – that of the onward march of the 'progressive' movement (with whatever more precise political inflection its individual adherents chose to add to it) – but was in time overtaken by a different era symbolised by the fall of the Berlin Wall, to which it reacted by becoming embattled, uncertain and protectionist.

During my four years of doctoral research (1993–97) it became evident to me that at some point in the recent past the folk revivalists squandered a golden opportunity to broaden the appeal of their music. Having once missed the bus, the revival as a whole had got itself trapped in a vicious circle from which it has since become ever more difficult to escape. Thrown back for support on a hard core of older adherents in the 1980s and 1990s, it found its appeal increasingly narrowed to the horizons of this declining group, trapped among the slogans and banners of the past (as witness, the 'Raise Your

Banners' event in Sheffield).[17] For this reason, its ability to attract the young steadily declined. Today, much of the folk media finds itself continuing to express the ideas and ideals of a conservative (with a small C) minority group resistant to change.[18]

At a time when class structures at least appear more fluid than ever before, the folk music 'industry' continues to champion, and attempts to merchandise, a way of life that is in several respects whole decades out of date. If one is to talk sensibly of growth within folk music's commercial sector, the primary objective must perhaps be to deflate its pretensions and empty it of outdated ideological baggage. This may appear an over-harsh indictment since, after all, there are many enlightened musicians active in the revival. But the folk 'industry' and media taken as a whole remain overly cautious and preservationist. These actions reflect not only its origins in the aftermath of the Second World War, but also the deceleration that took place in the early 1980s.

Record Labels – Plausible Inefficiency?

By the late 1970s popular music reception had visibly fragmented, as many young people turned to cheap forms of technology in order to create music. As punk rock and new wave came to incorporate cheap synthesisers and drum machines, and as technologically enhanced dance music began to evolve alongside rap and hip-hop, the folk scene failed – perhaps for the first time since the war – to recruit *en masse* a new generation of followers. In addition, by the early 1980s the major industrial players in the popular music marketplace, having temporarily lost ground to a host of independent labels, were forced to re-invent themselves with leaner, younger, more dynamic appendages that were similarly bent on using technology rather than tradition to its fullest capacity. In addition, many major record companies began also to employ teams of young accountants who saw little future in uncommercial acoustic music and systematically removed from their rosters many leading British folk artists, among whom were Ashley Hutchings, John Martyn and Al Stewart.

---

17. It is hardly necessary to draw the parallels with classical music and jazz, both of which have experienced comparable 'greying' for reasons (primarily those of non-commercialism) that are partly the same.
18. See the Letters pages ('Opinion') of *The Living Tradition*, Vol. 36 (January-February 2000), pp. 4–6, and the subsequent replies.

In consequence of the growth–contraction economic cycle that started to overtake many small business people and entrepreneurs by the mid-1970s, such independent record companies as Transatlantic, Island, Topic, Leader, Trailer, Ash, Kicking Mule, Village Thing, Peg and Mooncrest (B&C), and Criminal – all previously very sympathetic to folk and folk/rock – began to mutate, to sell out to a major with little interest in their back catalogues or to disappear altogether. This caused a huge depression in the folk 'industry' (which places music before economics, as we have observed). The highest-profile casualty was Nat Joseph's Transatlantic label, but Topic (by that time Britain's longest-running independent record label) also found the going very tough.

Topic survived thanks to the managerial acumen of Tony Engle, who set up a wholesale distribution network similar to the once defunct but now re-emergent independent Rough Trade cartel. Direct Distribution (as it was named) came to handle at least fifty per cent of all United Kingdom folk distribution and was also a clearing house for independent American labels, among them Bearcat, Blacktop, Philo and Rounder. With the assistance of their wholesale markets, in alliance with Engle's proactive reissue campaigns, Topic reached its golden anniversary in 1999. Yet, like most record labels centred on folk, this company, though reputedly obdurate, has a vacillating approach to business and periodically lurches into crisis, displaying an inability to keep financial order. At the time of the Symposium (in 2000), several Direct Distribution staff had been lured away from Topic by Proper Distribution, and Topic appeared to have been plunged into financial jeopardy yet again. There were even reports (thankfully spurious) of a visit from the Official Receiver. At least two perspectives on this unhappy event spring to mind. One could argue with some force that poaching of this kind reflects the unacceptable face of the record industry – the sort of activity that Topic disavows by its very existence. Conversely, however, one can hardly blame staff for wishing (as this writer was anonymously but reliably informed at the time) 'to escape the incessant amplification of compliant inefficiency'.

In fact, a disturbingly large proportion of folk music record labels are, like Topic, in deficit even at their present rate of expenditure, which in most cases is well below the requirements of even moderate efficiency. Yet this weak business sense in the folk music industry ironically confers plausibility on it among its leaders and consumers (often the same individuals) by appearing to validate the mystifications of the 'them versus us' ideology embedded in the revival. So it comes as no surprise to learn that many folk music labels continue to exist uncomplainingly as hand-to-mouth organisations that scorn forward planning. While there remains almost a dread of competition, sales and marketing cannot but remain sluggish and inefficient. The happenings at Topic just mentioned suggest that one cannot even begin to discuss the specific problems of sectarian seclusion and outworn convention in the folk music community – not to speak of the question mark over the possibility of an efficient and dynamic folk-music-based economy – without appreciating how prominent a part ideology, rules and canons play in the equation.

Nevertheless, a handful of folk music labels have shown an ability to become 'materialist' organisations *malgré eux*, attracting both idealists and the vilified careerists mentioned earlier in their bid to establish viable businesses. I quote from my dissertation the opinion of David Longly, of the Whole Wide World Record Retailer based in Yeovil (he is also a former employee of Projection, a casualty of the years around 1990). In October 1996 Longly stated:

> I cannot agree that involvement in the folk industry (cottage or otherwise) implies that the heart must rule the head. This attitude has led to the downfall of too many independent labels, festivals, promoters and indeed festival merchandisers, whose enthusiasm for their business activity led them to undervalue administrative and financial considerations. For the public to get the best choice, the best value and the best service, folk businesses must become more professional. Professionalism means being on top of your job, controlling costs, good presentation and most importantly establishing long term trust relationships with suppliers and customers. It does not mean a ruthless drive to dominate the market by monopolising product and driving all competition to the wall. Happily, the tendency in the folk world is weighted towards co-operation and I detect a community of shared interest and understanding developing which can only be of benefit to the customer.[19]

Whether or not Longly's 'tendency in the folk world [...] towards co-operation' is actually a sound business platform in the arena of popular music remains to be seen, but such survivors as Cooking Vinyl, Fellside and Park have found themselves needing to engage with those

---

19. David Longly, 'Come Write Me Down', *Folk Roots*, Vol. 160 (October 1996), pp. 80–82, at pp. 81–82.

very market forces that were redefining traditional ideas about music-making and recording. Cooking Vinyl, for instance, is a fiercely independent label from London launched in 1986. Of all the independents, it has come closest to attaining a 'folk' hit single with Ancient Beatbox (1989) and Billy Bragg (various releases). Arguably the 'biggest' folk/rock band of the 1990s, The Oysterband, is still signed to Cooking Vinyl. The same label also markets a few rock groups that have little or no connection with the folk scene but are at least in possession of an indie or punk kudos (Poison Girls, Père Ubu, the Wedding Present, etc.). This suggests that Cooking Vinyl is fully aware of the capacity of differing genres to follow their individual paths and refuses to accept the conventional, quiescent concept of an archetypically 'traditional' (i.e. 'folk') music.

For many years Fellside was a typically folk part-time operation, but in order to present folk music professionally to a wider public its proprietor, Paul Adams, went full-time. It now has an active jazz subsidiary (Lake), a URL (www.fellside.com) and a catalogue of new releases by such luminaries as Sandra Kerr and the experimentalists Trykster. It has also reissued former Topic releases, including Frankie Armstrong's *Lovely on the Water* (FECD 151). In the autumn of 1999 Fellside issued a CD of the original music for the 1970s children's TV series 'Bagpuss' (mainly the work of Sandra Kerr and John Faulkner, with Oliver Postgate). Perhaps not surprisingly, this release has become its best seller to date.

Park Records recently celebrated its tenth anniversary – no mean achievement for a folk-related record company – but it was able to do so only by widening the base of its market. Omnipresent since the label's launch has been Maddy Prior; Maddy's penchant for musical innovation has manifested itself in Park's policies. Northumbrian piper Kathryn Tickell is likewise signed to Park. Tickell has taken Northumbrian instrumentation to a global audience, as well as guesting with such celebrities as the Penguin Cafe Orchestra and Sting. Jacquie McShee, the Carnival Band and Lindisfarne are also on Park's roster.

The survival and modest growth of Cooking Vinyl, Fellside and Park suggest that at least some folk-based labels have responded to the need to broaden the genre (and thus its appeal), taking their products successfully to purchasers outside the forty to fifty-five age-range, where folk's most loyal public is now concentrated. This is an important step since it is still young people, irrespective of social group and disposition, who set trends. Any record company has eventually to come to the realisation that it cannot avoid engaging with the youth market, irrespective of the musical genre purveyed. Not only is British society obsessed with the idea, the image, of youth: it is also a fact that consumers between the ages of ten and twenty-four are the most avid purchasers of discs. There is some evidence that a handful of folk music independents are at last recognising a need to 'follow the money' and to market themselves in a more dynamic, less staid, way in order to reach out to the legions of youth. These companies have remained steadfastly independent. Yet they have managed to upgrade their media relations via press releases, kits and advertising material aimed at stimulating first-time interest in folk music. Other small-time operators, such as instrument makers, have made similar attempts to combine economic development with a salutary relativism. Perhaps the reservoir of pure idealism is indeed starting to run dry.

Small-time Operators – Instrumental Entrepreneurs

The folk 'industry' continues to harbour a number of specialist instrument manufacturers. Guitars, melodians, bodhrans, mandolins, pipes, citterns, bouzoukis, flutes, harps, whistles and fiddles are often hand-crafted, their makers relishing the chance to produce an instrument for a connoisseur. There are many craftsmen-manufacturers who produce high-quality instruments in small production runs. They include Andy Perkins (banjos), Dave Shaw and Julian Goodacre (pipes), P. G. Bleazey (flutes, recorders and drums), Tim Phillips and Andy Holliman (violins), Kevin O'Connell (bodhrans), Colin Keefe and John Marlow (various plucked stringed instruments including mandolas, citterns and guitars) and Hugh Forbes (harps). Pen pictures of three of these dedicated makers can shed light on developments in a different area of the folk revival.

Fylde Guitars (which supplied me with my first fingerpicking guitar in 1978) was set up by Roger Bucknall in the early 1970s. He later experienced financial problems, going out of business in 1980. Having re-established himself, he expanded into snooker cue manufacturing during the booming 1980s, but then 'positively contracted' in order to meet the more specialist needs of the 1990s, making a practice of selling direct from the works rather than via agencies. We can see from this that, however satisfying in its own right, the making of high-quality instruments is financially precarious. In the first instance, Roger was attracted by the idea that hand-building guitars was gradually disappearing as a craft:

> From the start I approached things differently from other makers. This country has a long history of failed manufacturing attempts in guitars, mostly because the makers had an 'arty' approach to the business, and didn't consider that it was necessary to make a profit. Apart from the thing about making musical instruments, I have always been fascinated by the way things are done, and spend a lot of time inventing production methods, so I was able to set up ways of making the guitars that were more accurate and productive than was usual at the time [1973]. Nowadays all of the bigger makers employ all sorts of clever jigs and tools, but at the time I think Fylde could have shown most of them a few tricks.[20]

Hugh Forbes has built harps, many of which are modelled on medieval or Pictish designs, for fourteen years. He is a Canadian who began by building guitars but was captivated by the romance of Celtic Britain and now sells harps to continental Europe, Japan, North America and South Africa. He freely admits, however, that whether many of the instruments actually get played is another matter! Forbes has identified an interest in the mythologised history of Scotland and Ireland and exploited it. None the less, and perhaps in contrast with Roger Bucknall, Forbes also sees himself as belonging to a local community:

> Yes, I do all sorts of things [...] I run 'build a harp in a day' courses for youngsters, and two-week courses, too. I dearly want more harps in schools. Cost has been against it previously, but now I'm offering a basic kit instrument at around £150, easily affordable [...] I'm establishing a trust, also: the Historic Harp and Clarsarch Trust for educational and research work. I'm handing over designs for my cheaper instruments, so they can control the royalties.[21]

On the other hand, Colin Keefe (who has been building a new finger-picking guitar for me) constructed his first guitar – an electric – on a Black & Decker 'workmate' bench in his bedroom and between 1985 and 1991 went to college to study instrument-making. After a short time with Patrick Eggle Guitars he took a certificate in adult education

---

20. Interview by the author with Roger Bucknall, April 1994.
21. Steve McGrail, 'The Harpmakers', *The Living Tradition*, Vol. 37 (March–April 2000), p. 47, quoting Hugh Forbes.

teaching and initiated the manufacture of his own instruments. For Colin, education, craftsmanship and a heavy dose of musical broad-mindedness have been part of the essential rite of passage:

> I'm now teaching just the one evening class at a local Community College. Business is busy enough for me. I currently have fourteen instruments on order [...] from a thirty-four-string Celtic harp to an eight-string electric! Along with this, I have a large workload of restoration and repair jobs.[22]

The future direction for these small manufacturers is difficult to predict, but noteworthy changes in attitudes and values are occurring. Many ingrained music stereotypes are being challenged by their existence, and all three men mentioned above seem to be generating kinds of business that were not open to them only a few years ago. The experiences of these entrepreneurially minded craftsmen suggest that, in reality, outright socialism or capitalism are only ideal types that are rarely, if ever, encountered in pure form. Consideration of any economic situation must include context and contingency: rhetoric about purity, class struggle and sell-outs is unproductive. Forbes and Keefe, for example, belong to a new breed of craftsman that manages to combine central elements of both capitalism and altruism, refusing to elevate one musical genre over another or trade in rhetorical platitudes about the specialisation of musical traditions. What, however, of the media?

The Media (1): Broadcasting – Specialisation or Marginalisation?

Throughout the 1950s the exposure of folk music on the radio gradually increased to a point where, by the 1960s, folk artists could be heard at various times on the BBC. Following the advent of Radio 1 in 1967, however, folk music became perceived as too specialised for pop listeners. Radio 2 producers likewise viewed folk as a specialised genre and effectively ceased to broadcast it during the day. This specialisation (and thus marginalisation) was highly contextual since, by the late 1960s, all popular music was undergoing pigeonholing of one form or another on the part of the so-called experts. Thematic specialisation and the social codes and conventions that went with it overtook folk music, thereby producing a specialised context within

---

22. Interview by the author with Colin Keefe, Luthier Guitars, June 2000.

which it subsequently came to be confined. Indeed, Frances Line, a great supporter of folk music, described her station's main objective during her period as head of BBC Radio 2 in the 1980s, as 'ratings by day, reputation by night'. Retrospectively, it can be seen that a process of cultural prioritisation and categorisation developed, and then compacted; as a consequence of massive digital communication/recreation competition during the 1980s, night-time radio specialisation resulted only in further marginalisation (preaching to the converted).

But there are other, more strictly pecuniary reasons for the dearth of folk music on the radio. During the late 1990s BBC local radio stations became increasingly orientated around sport-and-talk. Although this worked to the financial advantage of local radio, it tended to erode radio's long-standing support for folk music. Inherited needle-time and performance fees are a perennial source of conflict between Phonographic Performance Limited (PPL) and the BBC local stations in a situation where PPL and Performing Right Society (PRS) fees can amount to as much as ten per cent of the annual turnover. In these circumstances it pays to minimise the broadcasting of music of any kind. Special deals are struck, however, for the repeated use of certain popular music tracks. In 1999 a new contract to that effect was signed between BBC local radio stations and the PPL. As a result, a new batch of in-house CDs was produced by the BBC for continual play by the stations, the fees having already been agreed. With the possible exception of a few numbers by such artists as John Denver, Cat Stevens and The Seekers, songs that could accurately be described as 'folk' scarcely figured in this new batch of 'core radioplay' CDs.

Folk music programmes today invariably occupy evening slots on BBC local or regional radio. This means that they too have suffered from the ever-rising interest in Premier League football. Practically all folk and jazz programmes are required to be pre-recorded for local radio. This enables them to be rescheduled (or 'dumped', as I was informed by a BBC Radio Merseyside personality), should a footballing occasion prove too enticing.

It would be fair to claim that folk music has been condemned to a degree of radio exile. After much media speculation Andy Kershaw was finally removed from the DJ roster at Radio 1 in May 2000. Mike Harding's Pebble-Mill-based hour of folk music each Wednesday on Radio 2 is now the sole nationally broadcast folk programme in the United Kingdom. Very few commercial radio stations display anything more than a fleeting interest in folk music, and their DJs seldom have even a basic knowledge of the genre. Most of the regional folk programmes broadcast on radio have been entrusted to enthusiastic amateurs. My own experience of broadcasting at BBC Radio Merseyside confirms that local radio has come to rely entirely on these enthusiasts, without whom there would probably be no folk music programmes left on air at all. But the neglect has arisen not simply because the institutions have treated folk music unfairly. It is quite clear that the traditional authority of folk music, grounded in custom and habit, no longer reflects the roots of many visible aspects of British society.

For instance, while the BBC continues to promote the Radio 2 Young Tradition Awards, one wonders whether these awards have an unintentionally negative effect on interest in folk music amongst younger listeners. The most obvious point remains true: that although Radio 2 is currently the most popular BBC national radio station, the vast majority of its listeners are white and aged over forty. The editor of *Folk Roots* (more recently transmuted into *F-Roots*), Ian A. Anderson, comments:

> As far as I know the entry rules have never specified what tradition the competitors should come from, but the finalists are always white anglo/celts. There has never been any sign of young musicians from the multiplicity of other cultural traditions in the UK today, and no clue apparently given that they would qualify, be welcome or be fairly judged. Of course I don't know what efforts the BBC makes to remedy this, but they aren't working.[23]

In this instance, 'tradition' is allowed to be defined by the myth of its origins – those that appear to predate the contaminating expansion of the culture industry of multinational capitalism. This view, both essentialist and metaphysical, of what constitutes folk identity continues to be mythologised and turned into folklore in a number of disturbing ways: indigenist, nationalist and 'thirdworldist'.

The Media (2): Journals and F-Roots – A Hidebound Media?

There are today a number of folk publications available in Britain. It would be misleading, however, to declare that they were all accessible on the 'open'market. They range from fanzine-like publications, processed on computers and/or photocopiers (e.g. *North West Buzz*,

---

23. Ian A. Anderson, 'The Editor's Box', *Folk Roots*, Vol. 160 (October 1996), p. 17.

Shire Folk), to the long-established EFDSS publications (*English Dance & Song and Folk Music Journal*), not forgetting such top-of-the-range product as *F-Roots* itself, which is very glossy and highly professional, even giving away to its readers a couple of free CDs every year. *F-Roots* can occasionally be purchased at W. H. Smith, but many of the others are hard to find.

Between *North West Buzz* and *F-Roots* there exists a pyramidal structure of magazines with regional perspectives. Examples of these are *Taplas*, *The Living Tradition*, *Irish Music*, *Set and Turn Single*, *North West Folk* and *Folkwrite*. Magazines remain important points of contact for local musicians and mouthpieces for the local folk organisations, such as the North West Folk Federation. Despite the proliferation in the UK of media conglomerates (e.g. Emap), none of the British folk journals has fallen under their sway.

For instance, the EFDSS has always published writings for its members. The *Journal of the Folk Song Society* was founded in 1899 for the purpose of publishing collected songs. Since 1936 the society has also published a quarterly entitled *English Dance & Song* that enjoys runs of about 4,500–5,000. Both publications have an academic slant and for many years represented the rather cloistered opinions of the EFDSS hierarchy. More recently (2000), however, the Society has attempted to address the changing nature of folk music definitions with projects such as the CD-magazine *Root and Branch*. This is perhaps the most 'radical' venture in policy and marketing that has ever emerged from this organisation, a bulwark of folk music preservation: the creation of a linked CD and magazine that aim to explore the diversity of music traditions.

Each issue of *Root and Branch* contains a full-length CD, articles and essays, facsimiles and photographs. Its content embraces song, music, collectors, performers and historiography. Every issue has a theme that links the text, graphics and music. For example, the second issue ('Everybody Swing') deals with the era following the Second World War in which the folk revival gathered momentum, delivering an interesting historical account of those years. The selection of tracks on the CD, however, is even more absorbing, since it includes music from such diverse sources as Big Bill Broonzy, Lord Kitchener, Ken Colyer and George Webb's Dixielanders (full recognition, perhaps for the first time by those at Cecil Sharp House since the memorable 'Folk Blues Happening' of 1965, that popular music can forge its own traditions). In June 2000 Phil Wilson stated on behalf of the society:

Times have changed and we need to look to the future. We need to think about the role of the EFDSS in a world that is progressively becoming globalised. Cultural differences are breaking down [...] so what is our role? As a first question who do we represent? [...] We need to ask more questions. How many people in Britain are involved in folk culture? [...] Are there as many people involved as some people say? Three million go to festivals but how many of these are the same people? Are we really reaching new audiences?[24]

Wilson's point about 'new audiences' is a genuine concern. The magazine with the highest profile and the biggest sales in the folk world is *F-Roots*. This magazine delves into what it describes as 'roots' music; the name of the journal was in fact changed from *Southern Rag* in the 1980s in order to encompass the growing market in this country for world music. In 1998 the word 'Folk' itself became abbreviated to 'F' in its title (in imitation of, say, the pop group M-People). This must be seen as a highly symbolic shift in the magazine's ethos – an attempt to capture the attention of a younger readership.

Sadly, despite this transformation, *F-Roots* continues to present folk music as an anodyne substance soaked in the values and mores of its largely middle-class clientèle. Folk music soundtracks are mediated in terms of what the journal perceives its audience demographics to be. This approach takes account of age, class, ethnic and gender locations and (not least) financial stability; but it fails to subject to debate either its own global perception taken from that demographic standpoint or its own sense of good taste. Describing this form of literature as 'cultural capital', Roy Shuker cites an apt aphorism of Bourdieu to the effect that 'nothing more clearly affirms one's class, nothing more infallibly classifies, than tastes in music'.[25] Certainly, if *F-Roots* is anything to go by, it would appear that nothing more clearly affirms class than the **media's** interpretation of one's taste in music!

F-Roots presupposes, true to the EFDSS tradition, a core of natural, unspoilt musical truth: a distinction between 'real' music and the 'artificial' products of the manipulator. Interestingly, the very use of the word 'roots' in the context of a British folk magazine clearly conveys the idea that 'folk' is of the First World, whereas 'roots' are proper to the Second and Third Worlds. British musical isolationism

---

24. Phil Wilson, 'Who Are We? The EFDSS and the Future', *English Dance & Song*, Vol. 62/2 (summer 2000), p. 9.
25. Roy Shuker, *Understanding Popular Music*, London, Routledge, 1994, p. 16.

may have been successfully challenged by *F-Roots'* warm embrace of 'roots' music, but the implication remains that foreign musical forms are to be sampled as exotic novelties. 'Roots' music is written about as if it were the creation of 'unspoilt' (for which read: backward) natives, who, as much for our benefit as for their own, continue to interpret reality in a way forgotten by time. The term carries strong hints of an imperialistic past and a neo-imperialistic present.

Even in the most recent copies of *F-Roots*, the demand that attention be paid to, say, African or Latin American art is still framed within a dichotomy that ascribes essences to categories. This opposition is articulated in various ways: as that between the local (pure) and the international (corrupted); between the past (rootedness) and the present (dissolution); or between popular culture (participation) and mass culture (alienation). In this Manichaean scheme of things, modern life is found guilty of having destroyed the characteristics of true identity through a conglomeration of external influences that are invariably deemed baneful and threatening and which lead to falsifications or travesties of original, authentic culture. *F-Roots* is, perhaps, a good example of a cultural product that finds itself obliged to authenticate its own judgemental relevance. Even though it is itself a product, it cultivates the self-image of an arbiter of aesthetic pleasure and a cheerleader of collective nostalgia without ever acknowledging the limits of its own discourse.

Analysis: The New Frontiers?

The presentation of folk music assumes something more than just a musical style. It is a point of identification, an expression of something 'authentic' and a source of affective alliances between fans, business partners and professional musicians (indeed, many professionals could earn far more money in non-musical careers). However, the needless polarisation that opposes the authentic to the commercial has stultified growth in all but the most progressive areas of the folk commercial sector. The folk media still largely feel that folk music portrayal cannot encompass both polarities. In Volume 157 of *Folk Roots* Ian Croft asked how the folk revival was expected to succeed when growth led – apparently – to the destabilisation of the reasons for being involved in the first place. Pete Heywood, editor of *The Living Tradition*, continues to question whether a traditional music agency (such as exists in the United States) would strive to serve the folk scene or to control it. It appears that, for these writers at least, folk music has become rationalised as an 'artistic' and specifically traditional music that needs vigilance and networking on the part of its adherents to prevent it from 'selling out'.

This sell-out, however, remains problematic so long as the folk media deliver up a Pygmalion-style judgement over tradition in such an idealised, obsessive manner. Folk music rationale continues to be encased within a self-fulfilling prophecy of dissociation and isolation from pop traditions. This is clearly illogical. Economic and political circumstances have changed so much that many folk music perspectives created and nurtured within the era of utopianism after the Second World War have been obsolete for some time.[26] It is now possible to speak of (and market successfully!) a hip-hop tradition or a surf tradition quite easily. Yet the folk media's theoretical development since the glory days of quasi-Marxism has been modest, and a simplistic hate–love attitude towards popular music and urban society still saturates most folk writing, leaving the reader with a composite image of the twisted dialectics of inextricable contradictions about the apparent overabundance of cultural product.

With a few notable exceptions, the folk 'industry' and media continue to define themselves negatively: by what they perceive themselves not to be. For some, the apparent incompatibility of folk art and mediated commerce remains at the nexus of the folk revival's existence. Folk music is still seen as having heroically evaded commercial structures, whereas mass art has been captured by them and watered down as a consequence. I quote the words of folk writer Chris Sugden on this point: 'I have a vision. I think that we could work towards a folk equivalent of real ale. Real ale aims to be an honest, natural product, not altered to suit some idea of modern tastes [...] promoted for its own intrinsic qualities [...] The Campaign for Real Folk – I'll drink to that.'[27] Folkies who share Sugden's outlook always assume that technology and trade have historically been **external** influences upon music: that music has somehow struggled **against** these authorities. Yet to divorce musical communication from technology, production and finance, even in a pre-industrial society, is

---

26. See Colin Harper, 'Light and Shade: Davy Graham and Bert Jansch', *Mojo*, Vol. 80 (July 2000), pp. 62–76, at p. 74.
27. Sugden (1997).

as fraudulent as separating 'real' from 'manufactured' ale. As Keith Negus writes:

> Musical composition and performance have always depended on the instrument technologies available; whether European classical music, orally transmitted folk music, music of different regions of the African continent or contemporary popular music with its complex industrial networks of production and distribution. The character, conventions and reception of a particular music have been shaped by the machines of sound creation.[28]

No genre of music can ever achieve full independence from the economic pressures of a market economy. Sugden's view leads to an impasse: the folk industry and media attempt to function as relatively non-commercial businesses, marketing and discussing a potentially commercial music, while at the same time protecting that same music from the influence of a commercial structure that would bring its message to an infinitely greater number of people. So long as this relationship with an 'outside world' of popular music continues to be a problem, folk music will forever be hard to find on the radio, on stage and in the record shops. Only the already converted, willing to expend effort on searching out product, will be served with any degree of satisfaction.

The defects of the ideologies and strategies thus far intrinsic to the folk music commercial sector are obvious and glaring. It is not difficult to see what is needed to put them right. One has to remember, however, that folk music lovers regard themselves as existing within an egalitarian movement. This means that the real changes must occur in the minds of large numbers of those involved if any commercial and organisational progress is to be made. Reforms must, in other words, be approved by the folkies themselves. There must accordingly be a 'root and branch' change of attitude towards presentation, historiography and commerce. Folk music lovers themselves are not only the ones ultimately responsible for folk music's failing visage: in a very real sense, they are also its main victims.

Of course, it takes great courage to persist in presenting and marketing the values of one's choice as absolutely binding – a voice crying out in the wilderness – but a little pragmatic modesty on the part of

---

28. Keith Negus, *Producing Pop: Culture and Conflict in the Popular Music Industry*, London, Edward Arnold, 1992, p. 28.

folk music discourse is surely also needed in order to present the music to a public that wishes to absorb it into its existing lifestyles. Without that modesty, the folk music industry's attempts simultaneously to sell product and to confirm the historical validity of its flawed thesis creates merely a symbolic phantom: an ideal that represents a frozen vision from the past. A pressing alternative surely lies in the use of folk commerce and media as a means of continuous confrontation with ideas about the authentic and unique, an engagement with the presentation of the hitherto unpresentable. Such a confrontation is not a cynical rejection but a positive act of faith in the multifarious valid uses to which folk music can be put.

For some years, there has been a folk magazine on the Internet that goes by the name of *Musical Traditions*. Its editor, Rod Stradling, actually published my doctoral dissertation there in its entirety, despite its popular music perspective. *Musical Traditions* also helped me to finish compiling the discography of the Topic label that I began as part of my study. This journal has recently been joined by a new Internet magazine called *freefolk.com*, the editor of which is Mike Raven. So perhaps the e-mail and the World Wide Web, where all others have failed, can reconfigure and recontextualise avowedly 'authentic' folk art in the most modern of all contexts. Advanced technology is now providing a home base for conflicts and debates over precisely what constitutes 'real' folk music. This is surely a clear indicator that folk music can indeed move forward without suddenly abandoning its cherished dialectic about the anterior. The folk revival, which traditionally has looked towards the past, must now widen its focus to include the future if it is to be commercially viable.

Any reconfiguration must also include a reformation of the structure of the folk business world, purging it of its stagnant, conservative elements and harnessing the winds of change instead of resisting them. The folk industry has to make itself more purposeful, more cohesive, more effective and (that dread word!) more popular. It would assist those in the folk music industry if folk music were to be regarded as merely one genre among many rather than as a superior and non-mercantile musical soundtrack. The present splendid isolation of folk, which finds itself dissociated even from other popular music genres, is largely antediluvian, reflecting the issues and events of yesterday, not of today. The revival has to discover a new dynamic to replace the old, fading appeal to working-class solidarity and opposition to capitalism in any form. The commercial sector has to break down the rigid generic barriers and remove the paralysing sense of 'superiority' (and, conversely, of insecurity) that underlies the presentation of the music.

But in order to do this the folk media have somehow to question the attitudes of those whose aspirations they exist to express. These several encounters must go hand in hand if the folk revival, its 'industry' and its networking are to get anywhere. For let us be clear about the alternatives: the choice certainly lies between growth and stagnation, but it will rarely be posed directly. There will always be extraneous issues that intrude – special complications or mitigating factors. If the folk 'industry' and media refuse to jump the hurdle, the consequences will not be immediately catastrophic. It may well be some time before the consequences become noticeable at all. All that will happen is that the slow slide towards impotence and failure will accelerate until it is finally too late to do anything about it.

9

Collective Responsibilities: The Arts Council, Community Arts and the Music Industry in Ireland

Rob Strachan and Marion Leonard

This chapter is concerned with how various forms and practices of popular music are addressed and represented within agendas for the arts and in the development of cultural policy. Discussion will centre on the funding policies of the Arts Council of Ireland,[1] the largest funding body for the arts within the Republic. Using the Arts Council as an example, the chapter will discuss how popular music is valued and supported by funding bodies and how views of the music industry are built into institutional understandings of popular music practice. The intention is to question the way in which the music industry is popularly defined as a self-sustaining economy. Specific reference will be made to grassroots initiatives aimed at supporting popular music in Ireland and to the relationship that community-based groups have with policy-makers, the Arts Council and the music industry. We argue that the questions thrown up by the issue of grant funding for popular music highlight broader debates between different arts organisations over what the 'use value' of the arts can or should be. Popular music will be used to examine the tensions between the 'fine arts', 'cultural industries' and 'community arts' models that were central to the debates around cultural policy in the second half of the twentieth century.

The research for the chapter was conducted in Dublin as part of a European-funded project that mapped and assessed support for small businesses working within the music industry in the city.[2] What became apparent during this research was that any satisfactory

---

1. Hereafter referred to simply as the 'Arts Council' when the Irish context is clear.
2. See Marion Leonard and Robert Strachan, *Information for Cultural Industries Support Services: Dublin Case Study*, published at http://www.mmu.ac.uk/h-ss/mipc/isiss/cas_dub.htm (1999).

understanding of 'support' required the examination of the activities of a complex patchwork of organisations and institutions. These latter included national government, education and training institutions, general business support agencies, the unemployment agency and arts funding bodies. In fact, many of the major sources of support originated in non-sector-specific institutions that were seemingly unrelated to 'the music industry'. Moreover, we encountered a wide range of practitioners who were deeply involved with popular music in their everyday working lives but did not necessarily conform to commonsense notions of 'music industry workers'. The sheer variety of individuals and organisations that we came across raised the inevitable question of how the 'music industry' should be defined: whom does it include and whom does it exclude?

Typically, the music industry has been conceived as a narrow range of multinational companies and commercially successful entrepreneurs. Following this logic, a definition of the music industry in Dublin should include the offices of major multinational and independent record companies, the Irish Musical Rights Organisation (IMRO) and a range of managers and promoters working in the city. However, this would be too exclusive a definition of the industry. We argue that a working definition of a local music industry needs to include the activities of practitioners working at different levels of music practice and production and therefore should not be tied solely to high-profile, economically buoyant companies. Thus a broader categorisation of the music industry is needed: one that takes account of those providing and following education and training programmes, community music initiatives and studios, and popular music performers working at any level from amateur to professional. Such a categorisation can offer a clearer picture of the range of individuals and organisations working within the popular music sector and moves away from a model in which popular music is necessarily tied to the economic imperatives of the recording industry and its ancillary businesses. In this context, arguments of definition are far from purely academic, since cultural policy strategies, priorities and decision-making within arts funding often rest upon unproblematised and familiar notions of the music industry. Our chapter argues that a more representative model of the 'music industry' is required in order to address the needs of popular music practitioners within the context of the arts and cultural policy.

Context

Before examining specific examples relating to popular music and its relationship to the Irish Arts Council, it is necessary to sketch a broader picture of what has informed institutional logic within arts bodies. One can trace ideological traits within historical moments that have a bearing on how the arts are perceived and, consequently, how they are funded. The Arts Council of Ireland was formed in 1951, six years after the Council for the Encouragement of Music and the Arts (CEMA) became the Arts Council of Great Britain.[3] This latter step marked a change in direction, since a large part of CEMA's work had been concerned with participation in, and access to, the arts in the provinces. Under the leadership of John Maynard Keynes, the transition into the British Arts Council was marked by a shift of emphasis: from participation to excellence; from amateur to professional; and from the funding of local amateur orchestras to that of professional opera companies and orchestras. The British and Irish Arts Councils were formed in a similar cultural climate in which notions of what support for the arts should and should not entail became manifest in national policy. The primary aim of both institutions was the stimulation of interest in the arts, along with the maintenance of a national tradition within them.

Grounded within a traditional 'fine arts' model, the main work for both bodies consisted of subsidy for individual artists and for collective bodies such as theatres, opera companies and orchestras. Subsidy was here founded upon a high/low polarisation between art forms: thus certain forms belonging to the Western art tradition enjoyed prioritised funding because of their perceived aesthetic superiority and implied intrinsic value. The Royal Charter issued upon the establishment of the British Arts Council stated that this body's role was to 'increase accessibility [...] and improve the standard of execution of the fine arts'.[4] Geoff Mulgan and Ken Worpole have outlined what they see as the four main ideological tenets that underpin the British

3. For a full account of this transition see Robert Hewison, *Culture and Consensus: England, Art and Politics since 1940*, London, Methuen, 1995. On the influence of the British experience on the formation of the Irish Arts Council see Bernadette M. Quinn, *Musical Landscapes in the Representation of Place: The Case of Irish Tourism*, Working Paper No. 19, Service Industries Research Centre, University College Dublin, January 1998.
4. Quoted in Hewison (1995), p. 43.

Arts Council's thinking. They point, first, to the nineteenth-century version of the 'trickle down theory', in which the encouragement of excellence within the 'high' arts would 'by unexplained osmosis, enhance the standards of all forms of cultural activity'. Second, they note that the establishment of the British Arts Council constituted a move away from the encouragement of amateur activities and towards a more professional view of the arts. Third, that the funding of high arts was necessary for the 'moral and spiritual treasury of the nation'. Finally, that protection against commerce and commercialism was central to the new body's thinking.[5] Ultimately, as Robert Hewison suggests, the concentration on high arts, professionalism and 'excellence' led to 'a narrow definition of culture that excluded both the amateur and the popular'.[6]

Such concepts as 'excellence' and 'professionalism' are similarly prominent in Irish Arts Council literature, and there is also evidence to suggest that the ideological subtext of political positions pertaining to the arts remains to some extent grounded in this 'fine arts' model. Jane Tynan, for example, sees Fianna Fáil's arts policy documents as indicative of this political party's concept of the artist as an autonomous individual standing at a remove from political, social and economic issues. Tynan quotes Sile de Valera, Minister for Arts, Culture and the Gaeltacht, as stating, in relation to the role of art in society: 'Art is an expression of individuality. If not that, it is nothing.' [7] Veering away firmly from the political content of collective action, De Valera asserts: 'The artist must never be a creature of any political party.' [8] However, Tynan queries this statement, asking: 'Why not? Surely the artist lives in society like everybody else and as such has the same responsibilities and rights to participate as other citizens.'[9]

It is clear that the continuation of institutional support for a model of 'fine arts' could bring about a marginalisation of popular music within funding policies. However, popular music has managed to

---

5. Geoff Mulgan and Ken Worpole, *Saturday Night or Sunday Morning: From Arts to Cultural Industry: New Forms of Cultural Policy*, London, Comedia, 1986, p. 21.
6. Hewison (1995), p. 43.
7. Jane Tynan, 'Temple Barred: Community Arts beyond Dublin's Southside', in *Vision in Division: Community: Arts in Divided Societies*, supplement to *Fortnight*, Vol. 364 (1997), pp. 12–14, at p. 12.
8. Loc. cit.
9. Loc. cit.

secure a presence within the international arts agenda, since wider developments have allowed alternatives to the 'fine arts' position to be assimilated within policy. From the 1980s onwards policy-makers and academics have successfully argued that popular music has a role to play in employment and urban regeneration initiatives. This argument proposes that popular music be eligible for support and funding from public bodies in order to stimulate growth and to turn the music industry into a sustainable and valuable economic sector within a given region. These developments are in tune with general shifts in arts policy in Western Europe over the past twenty years towards a cultural industries model. The term 'cultural industries' was used first in the 1980s by the Greater London Council to signify a shift in thinking about cultural production and consumption.[10] Central to this repositioning was a broadening of the definition of the arts within policy to include such components of popular culture as film, sport, advertising and popular music, together with an acknowledgement of the place of popular cultural forms within the economy. As Justin O'Connor argues, the issue of the cultural industries 'has forced itself on the European agenda, signalled by the growing interest of DGV (Employment) in "cultural" issues'.[11] For instance, a 1999 European conference in Berlin was convened to discuss the subject under the premise that 'culture should no longer be considered just a social ornament. Rather, culture in general and the arts in particular, ought to be seen as a laboratory of new ideas in every respect.'[12] The integration of cultural industries issues into the arts and cultural policy agenda has manifested itself similarly in numerous local initiatives instigated by local councils and lobby groups in Britain.[13] At a

10. For in-depth analysis of this process see Mulgan and Worpole (1986), Ruth-Blandina M. Quinn, *Public Policy and the Arts: A Comparative Study of Great Britain and Ireland*, Aldershot, Ashgate, 1998, and Justin O'Connor, *The Definition of 'Cultural Industries'*, published at http://www.mmu.ac.uk/h-ss/mipc/isiss/policy.htm (August 2000).

11. Loc. cit. DGV is the European Union's discussion group on 'Employment, Industrial Relations, Social Affairs' that informs European policy on these matters and administers funding for specific projects and regions.

12. *A Working Culture. II: Cultural Change and the World of Work*, conference pack, Berlin, 1999, p. 3.

13 http://www.mmu.ac.uk/h-ss/mipc/isiss/cas_dub.htm. Specific examples and general issues surrounding local support of popular music industries include studies of London (Mulgan and Worpole, 1986), Merseyside (Sara Cohen, *Rock Culture*

national level, it is seen in the UK Department for Culture, Media and Sport's concentration on the creative industries as a facilitator for economic growth,[14] or in the 1999 launch of the New Deal for Musicians.

This shift in thinking has its counterpart in developments affecting cultural policy in Ireland, where the music industry has actively lobbied the national government. For instance, in a speech to the Fianna Fáil Annual Conference Sile de Valera hailed the economic success of Irish musicians as a template for the arts in general. After outlining the music industry's contribution to the national economy, she commented: 'It's still surprising to some people when they hear the phrase "The Economy of the Arts". I suppose it goes back to the romantic notion of the artist starving in a garret, working away for pure art's sake [...] But some still tend to think of art as a stand-alone thing. Music is arguably the best illustration of how outdated that thinking is.'[15] The contrast between this positioning of popular music and the earlier comments made by De Valera highlights an issue central to the current climate in arts funding. There is an apparent dualism according to which both the 'cultural industries' and the 'fine arts' conceptions of the arts are woven into contemporary policy: a situation having major implications for the way that popular music is viewed and funded by the Arts Council.

Even though popular music has worked its way on to the cultural policy agenda, government, arts institutions and critics have all generally viewed popular music chiefly as a facilitator for economic growth. There has been little discussion of how popular music can be used as a tool for opening up access to the arts, facilitating capacity-building, encouraging social integration or aiding multiculturalism – not to speak of offering a general educational value. These uses of music are central to the philosophy of community arts organisations.

in Liverpool: Popular Music in the Making, Oxford, Oxford University Press, 1991), Manchester (*Culture Industry: Arts in Urban Regeneration*, ed. Derek Wynne, Aldershot, Ashgate, 1992) and Norwich (John Street, 'Local Differences? Popular Music and the Local State', *Popular Music*, Vol. 12 (1993), pp. 43–55).

14. See Department for Culture, Media and Sport, *Creative Industries: The Regional Dimension: The Report of the Regional Issues Working Group*, DCMS, London, 2000.

15. Sile de Valera, *Speech at Fianna Fáil Árd Fheis*, published (4 March 2000) at http://www.irlgov.ie/ealga/speeches.htm.

Emerging all over Europe in the late 1960s and early 1970s, the community arts movement sought to take the arts out of their traditional gallery or concert hall setting into the wider community and to foster relationships between 'professional' artists and the population at large. The development of community arts marked a move away from an aesthetic agenda contained within the European high art tradition. Instead, the arts were valued for such extrinsic reasons as their ability to encourage social empowerment in disadvantaged areas or among social groups restricted by factors of ethnicity, disability or social deprivation. These aims were facilitated through practical strategies that included 'artists in residence' programmes, workshops and festivals. Much popular music activity has been facilitated in recent decades by individual community arts groups or music collectives, and by such co-ordinating organisations as Kontaktnätet in Sweden and Sound Sense, the UK development agency for community music.

The major exponent of community arts work related to popular music in Ireland is the music collective movement. The work of music collectives in Ireland is diverse. It includes a multitude of community music initiatives that give young people free access to rehearsal space, recording studios and instrumental tuition, together with educational programmes of the kind run by the Markettown Music Collective, which works with underprivileged schools in the north side of Dublin. Further, a non-profit DIY Festival of community and independent music is held annually in Dublin. The collective movement's umbrella organisation, the Federation of Music Collectives (FMC), is a major facilitator of access to the arts, offering fundamental support to musicians in Ireland. Based in Dublin, the FMC works at grassroots level as a contact point for music collectives throughout the Republic, assisting the establishment of new collectives and facilitating the work currently undertaken by these groups. One of the aims of the FMC is to offer training for members of collectives. For example, in 1998, in partnership with the Portadown Music Collective and the Re:Sound Music Collective, the FMC ran a twenty-week music industry course aimed at improving the skills of its members. Regional workshops and master classes reflecting the educational and training programmes offered by collectives in different areas are likewise co-ordinated by the FMC. However, training towards careers in the music industry is only one small facet of the collective movement in Ireland, since many more groups within the organisation focus on access to the arts, general educational issues and routes to social inclusion. Angela Dorgan, central co-ordinator of the FMC, regards the main work of the collective movement as being to facilitate access and participation rather than primarily to serve an economic role. She summarises the remit of the collective movement as 'developing education, developing access, developing participation amongst working-class people [...] Our organisation would argue that popular music is the most used, the most listened to. It's higher as far as participation is concerned. It's higher as far as audiences are concerned. It's higher as far as relevance to everyday life is concerned, which is kind of an upward battle with someone like the Arts Council.'[16] Thus the FMC capitalises on the accessibility of popular music in order to facilitate programmes that widen participation in the arts.

The Arts Council of Ireland

As the Irish government's primary arts funding and advisory body, the Arts Council acts as the major support agency for the arts in the Republic. Its core functions are defined as 'supporting the creation and dissemination of the work of Irish artists in all creative and interpretative disciplines, and promoting the maximum possible public access to, and participation in, the contemporary arts'.[17] In 1998 the revenue funds available to the Arts Council were 23.5 million Irish punts. Music activities typically offered grant assistance by the Arts Council are described as 'music resource organisations; commission of new works; performance; recording and publication of contemporary music; professional ensembles; specialist publications and festivals; events aimed at transfer of skills and understanding of music performance, such as workshops and master-classes'.[18] In addition to its support of institutions, the Arts Council provides a number of bursaries to individuals such as composers, instrumentalists and conductors, and operates the Skidmore Jazz Award for performers. In contrast, popular music barely registers in the aims and objectives of the organisation. Although popular music is included in the list of 'areas covered', a 1997 policy document of the Arts Council defined

16. Interview with Angela Dorgan by the authors, dated 2 July 1998.
17. The Arts Council/An Chomlairle Ealaion, *The Arts Council of Ireland: Awards and Opportunities*, Dublin, 1999, p. 2.
18. Ibid., *About the Arts Council: The Development Agency for the Arts in Ireland*, Dublin, 1998, p. 10.

its role in support of music as primarily to fund resource organisations and to provide bursaries to individual performers and composers in the fields of 'jazz, contemporary, choral and traditional music'.[19]

Consequently, these named musical genres receive a preponderance of funds. Classical and traditional music and jazz are supported through grants to such organisations as the Contemporary Music Centre, Music Network, Irish Traditional Music Archive, Na Piobairi Uilleann, Baile Átha Cliath and the Improvised Music Company. These institutions act as facilitating agents articulating their members' needs to funding bodies, tour managers and local arts organisations. Music Network, for instance, provides a support and networking service for musicians and arts enterprises working within classical music, jazz, Irish traditional music and world music, while the Contemporary Music Centre provides a similar service for the promotion and nurture of contemporary Irish classical composers. Alongside Ireland's three major opera companies, these support organisations constituted the major beneficiaries of the Arts Council's music budget in 1998. The Contemporary Music Centre received I£213,683; the Irish Traditional Music Archive, I£194,943; Music Network, I£250,000; Opera Ireland, the Opera Theatre Company and Wexford Festival Opera were granted a total of I£1,236,000. In contrast, the Federation of Music Collectives, the major support organisation for popular musicians in the country, received in 1997 a mere I£16,000, a sum that increased to I£30,000 in 1998. When its share of funding is calculated (even if opera is left out of the discussion), popular music accounts for under 3.3 per cent of institutional support for music grants to organisations (as compared with 63.7 per cent for classical music and jazz and 33 per cent for traditional music). Leaving aside this institutional support, the vast majority of awards to individuals and to smaller organisations and ensembles went to kinds of music other than popular music.

The Arts Council and Popular Music

At present, popular music in Ireland does not have a representational agency such as exists for other types of music. Approaches to the Arts Council for popular music projects have to be made, perforce, on an

---

19. Ibid., *The Arts Council Annual Report*, Dublin, 1997, p. 9.

individual basis. This situation possibly has a hidden knock-on effect in that there may be a shortfall of direct applications to the Arts Council from popular music projects precisely because individuals are not being channelled towards it by a sector-specific support agency that can give advice and assistance with applications. However, popular music has not always lacked a representational body. Indeed, Ireland has in many ways been a pioneer in its support for popular music. From 1988 the Arts Council employed a popular music officer, and in 1992 support was increased to allow for the opening of Music Base, an information and support service for the music industry. Grant-aided by the Arts Council, Music Base provided an information, advice and advocacy service for musicians and music businesses in addition to acting as a consultant to various arts bodies. Musicians and small (or 'micro') enterprises in the sector were able to obtain advice on copyright and publishing. Business advice was similarly offered free of charge to small record labels and promoters through the organisation's drop-in information centre. The centre also maintained an open-access music industry database and information library. Operating from the same offices, the Federation of Music Collectives and Music Base worked in partnership to provide a range of support for popular music practitioners at all levels. However, despite their close relationship, the objectives of the two organisations remained discrete. Music Base was concerned chiefly with providing information and facilitating growth for popular music practitioners, whereas the FMC provided advice for, and communication between, grassroots, community-led initiatives.

In 1997 the Arts Council ceased to fund the Music Base facility, which consequently had to close its operations. In the wake of this withdrawal of funding there appears to have been some confusion concerning the distinct roles of the two organisations. The Arts Council suggested that much of Music Base's activity had subsequently been 'assumed by the Federation of Music Collectives'.[20] However, Angela Dorgan of the FMC commented that, while much of the work of Music Base had been channelled towards the Federation, this had resulted in an increased workload that was not matched by a commensurate increase in grant support. She argued:

20. Indecon International Economic Consultants, in association with Pricewaterhouse Coopers, *Succeeding Better: Report of the Strategic Review of the Arts Plan 1995–1998*, Dublin, The Stationery Office, 1998, p. 62.

Music Base provided an essential service. The amount of people in and out [of] the doors there was just unfathomable. I never realised just how much until now [that] they are coming to me we keep getting the queries. Music Network keep sending the queries to us; the Arts Council send the queries to us; Arts Officers send the queries here; but unfortunately […] we just don't have the staff. I'm doing a whole other job that I already wear seven hats for. Since Music Base, I have had to make myself available to bands and musicians to do four other jobs.[21]

It is clear that there is a strong demand for support of the kind provided by Music Base. As Dorgan continues: 'It makes me mad when we are asked to justify our means […] we did an audit and we had 113,000 people in a six-month period use the service of the Federation and its members.'[22] However, by arguing that the role of Music Base has been taken over by the FMC, the Arts Council has failed to recognise that Music Base and the collective movement were established to fulfil quite different needs. The Arts Council is overlooking the central community arts focus of the FMC organisation and suggesting by implication that the only way to view popular music is by reference to business and employment.

Popular Music: A Self-sustaining Economy?

The pressure on the FMC to fulfil roles lying outside its general ambit can be related to wider problems arising from traditional perceptions of popular music within the arts establishment. First, and perhaps most important, there is an obvious problem in that the 'popular music industry', and by implication popular music itself, tends to be perceived as self-sustaining. In short, this 'commonsense' positioning of popular music within the cash nexus works either to inhibit funding of the genre by arts bodies or, at best, to marginalise popular music initiatives at the grass roots. By viewing popular music purely in terms of its industrial context, the Arts Council effectively sidesteps any questions relating to its cultural significance or inherent worth as a cultural form. Maura Eaton, Music Officer of the Arts Council, makes this distinction clear:

21. Interview with Angela Dorgan by the authors, dated 11 February 1999.
22. Loc. cit.

The other thing to remember is that there is a whole music industry side of things which gives support as well [...] I always point this out to people because people think: 'Why aren't you doing more?'. But the IBEC, Irish Business Employers Confederation, [has] a music industry group which the music industry itself worked towards getting [...], and they have published various reports. They are lobbying government directly for support for popular music.[23]

It is interesting that Eaton chooses to point to the Irish Business and Employers Confederation as an example of support provided for popular music. This is not a body that acts on behalf of popular musicians, educators or, indeed, those involved in community projects. Rather, the organisation works solely in the interests of industry within the country, which includes music business interests. While it is true that business quangos and trade federations have provided a lobby within Ireland that has sought to influence government policy on behalf of the indigenous music industry, it must be noted that an organisation such as IBEC has a particular agenda that likewise categorises popular music in unambiguously industrial terms. IBEC and similar bodies made up of industry representatives, such as the FORTÉ steering group, quite naturally pursue strategies that further their own business opportunities.[24] Policy objectives put forward by these groups generally encourage a strategy of outward

23. Interview with Maura Eaton by the authors, dated 22 February 1999.
24. Indeed, throughout the 1990s there were a number of reports commissioned by industry groups that attempted to influence government policy in Ireland. These include: International Federation of the Phonographic Industries (IFPC), *The Music Industry in Ireland*, [Dublin], 1993; Simpson Xavier Horwarth, *A Strategic Vision for the Irish Music Industry*, Dublin, 1994; Irish Business and Employers Confederation, *Striking the Right Note*, [Dublin], 1995; IBEC Music Industry Group, *Raising the Volume: Policies to Expand the Irish Music Industry*, [Dublin],1998; Coopers and Lybrand, *The Employment and Economic Significance of the Cultural Industries in Ireland*, [Dublin], 1994; Stokes Kennedy Crowley, *A Report on the Irish Popular Music Industry*, [Dublin],1994; Paula Clancy and Mary Twomey, *The Irish Popular Music Industry: An Application of Porter's Cluster Analysis*, Dublin, NESC, 1997. For a fuller discussion of these reports see Marion Leonard and Rob Strachan,'The State, Cultural Policy and the Politicisation of Music Industry Concerns: The Case of the Republic of Ireland', in *Changing Sounds: New Directions and Configurations of Popular Music*, ed. Tony Mitchell and Peter Doyle with Bruce Johnson, Sydney, University of Technology, 2000, pp. 279–83.

investment in existing companies and support for the promotion of Irish companies and artists in export markets. Significantly, national policy initiatives have generally had a heavy reliance on a top-down approach in which advantages given to large multinational companies are represented as having a knock-on effect for smaller and grassroots businesses.[25]

However, by focusing on the industrial context of popular music, policy-makers have often failed to acknowledge the complexity of popular music production, consumption and use in everyday life. For instance, the Irish Arts Council's strategic proposals for 1999–2001 within *The Arts Plan* argue that although 'outside RTÉ [the Irish national broadcasting corporation] there is little full-time or long-term employment in music and the working conditions of artists in traditional and classical genres tend to be uncertain [...], a large number of composers and writers in popular, rock and other commercial areas in music can earn a regular income from their work'.[26] The second part of this statement suggests that popular music can provide stable employment and a long-term career. However, the figures used to back up this claim represent only the number of estimated FTEs (full-time equivalents), which do not give an accurate picture of employment within the sector. Employment related to popular music is actually fluid – often part-time and part of the black economy, since many practitioners simultaneously draw unemployment benefits in order to survive.[27]

Moreover, the notion that popular music is a self-sustaining entity rests on a narrow and selective conceptualisation of the form. While it is clear that the history of popular music's dissemination through mass media channels has caused it usually to be situated within the context of its status as a commercial product, this perspective provides only a partial picture of popular music activity. Much work within popular music studies has pointed to the fact that the vast majority of popular music practitioners never make a living out of

25. See Leonard and Strachan (2000).
26. The Arts Council (1999), p. 41.
27. See, for example, Dave Laing, 'The Economic Importance of Music in the European Union', in *Music in Europe: A Study Carried out by the European Music Office with Support of the European Commission (DGX)*, Brussels, European Music Office, 1995, pp. 4–60.

playing or producing popular music.[28] Angela Dorgan points out that of the thousands of musicians who come through the Irish collective network: '5 per cent of those musicians will make it commercially; 0.5 per cent of them will make a living out of it; 95 per cent won't. So, what we are involved in is channelling: trying to encourage this other 95 per cent to keep on this art form and to channel it into different directions, whether that is through workshops, through just giving them access to each other [or through] just playing live.' Dorgan argues that 'it is the 95 per cent that the Arts Council has to take responsibility for'.[29]

The funding policies of many arts institutions still appear to be informed by a thinking that maintains the dualisms of high/low and commercial/uncommercial in their conception of 'the Arts'. Maura Eaton explains: 'Of course, we [the Arts Council] do worry about it [funding for popular music], because there is a side of popular music that is art. You know: that is non-commercial, even though it is in the commercial world. That is something that I want to see: where it can fit in or where we can cater for it'.[30] Underpinning this statement are two unspoken premises that inform the way in which arts funding is allocated to music. First, such an argument rests upon a belief that jazz, classical music, Irish traditional music and folk do not exist in the 'commercial world'; second, it assumes that popular music is to be deemed worthy only if judged so by the aesthetics of high art. Both premises are clearly problematic.

The most commercially successful Irish-based and Irish-owned record companies, in both the domestic and international markets, are those whose output is centred on traditional music or on music that has a basis in this genre. Irish independent labels Enigma, Dolphin, Grapevine, Lunar and Dara have had global success with such artists as Christie Moore, Davy Spillaine, Delores Keane and The Dubliners. Indeed, all top ten labels cited by IBEC in *Raising the Volume* (1998) as successful models of Irish record companies (with

---

28. On this subject, see, for example: Cohen (1991); Ruth Finnegan, *The Hidden Musicans: Music-making in an English Town*, Cambridge, Cambridge University Press, 1989; Mike Jones, *Organising Pop: Why So Few Pop Acts Make Pop Music*, unpublished PhD thesis, Institute of Popular Music, Liverpool University, 1997.
29. Interview with Angela Dorgan by the authors, dated 11 February 1999.
30. Eaton, loc. cit.

the exception of Ritz, which specialises in middle-of-the-road artists such as Daniel O'Donnel and Charlie Landsborough) release music with a basis in traditional music.[31] Thus the success of indigenous record companies producing and marketing traditional music far exceeds that of those involved in rock, pop, R & B and dance musics.[32] Further, Irish traditional music has had an undoubted effect on the nation's economy via tourism. For example, Bernadette Quinn's research among tourists visiting Ireland showed high levels of awareness of, and connection with, Irish traditional music, since almost sixty per cent of them experienced live traditional music during their stay.[33] Traditional music has been utilised by the tourism industry, both in economic and symbolic terms, through its appearance in international advertising and its association with Irish regions specifically targeted at the tourist market. This is borne out by Quinn's assertion that 'the deep rooted nature of Irish musical landscapes is being increasingly recognised by the Irish tourism industry as a symbolic landscape which can be used to construct representations of Irish tourist space'.[34]

Clearly, Irish traditional music not only operates in the 'commercial world' but does so with significant economic success. Yet the Arts Council sees no contradiction (as it does with popular music) in funding various projects for the promotion and preservation of the genre. A further contradiction of this 'art versus commerce' polarisation is that many of the Arts-Council-funded support bodies and initiatives aimed at contemporary classical music, Irish traditional music and jazz are actually concerned with attempting to make those forms more commercially viable. Implicit within audience development initiatives, for instance, is a desire to widen audience attendance not just in terms of demographics but also with a view to increasing attendance figures at live events. The driving factor here is a commercial one, in that the greater the number of people who attend concerts and

31. See note 24.
32. A distinction must be drawn here between indigenous Irish record companies (i.e. those which are based in and operate from Ireland) and Irish artists signed to multinational record companies. Most Irish rock and pop artists who have achieved international success record for the latter, which means that most of the financial return for their effort accrues to companies based outside Ireland.
33. Bernadette Quinn (1998), p. 21.
34. Ibid., p. 28.

recitals, the more self-sustaining orchestras, jazz ensembles and promoters will become. The Arts Council's mission statement explains
that one of the organisation's primary aims is give individuals support
not in terms of subsidy for subsidy's sake but, rather, 'to improve the
viability of the arts as a career, in Ireland and abroad'.[35] There is also
evidence suggesting that the concentration on the professionalisation
of the arts within these support bodies has served to alienate grassroots and community initiatives. For example, in a case study of
Music Network, Breathnach and Doyle found that a strict interpretation of 'professionalisation' meant that there was dissatisfaction
among 'a large and growing number of voluntary music and arts
organisations', which felt that they had remained unserved by the
body.[36]

Decisions about funding allocations by the Arts Council are not
based simply on a distinction between the self-sustaining 'industry' of
popular music (which can therefore take care of itself) and other,
'uncommercial' musics that need support and subsidy.[37] Rather, a
series of value judgements underpin the dominant thinking of the Arts
Council. Whereas Irish traditional music is valued for its central place
in the country's national heritage, and classical music and jazz are
valued as art musics, popular music fits into neither category.[38] The
underlying assumption of the Arts Council's strategies seems to be
that Irish traditional music, classical music and jazz are inherently

35. Currently consultable at http://www.artscouncil.ie/english.html.
36. Catherine Breathnach and Niall Doyle, 'Music Network: A Case Study in the
    Management of Organisational Change', in *From Maestro to Manager: Critical
    Issues in Arts and Culture Management*, ed. Marian Fitzgibbon and Anne Kelly,
    Dublin, Oak Tree Press, 1997, pp. 111–35, at p. 116.
37. Added to this, it is difficult to isolate musical forms that have not been subject to
    the structures and dynamics of the marketplace. For example, many commenta-
    tors have pointed out that the production and consumption of classical music
    has in recent centuries been situatd within an industrial and economic context.
    For instance, Tyler Cowan (*In Praise of Commercial Culture*, London, Harvard
    University Press, 1998) points to the influence on eighteenth-century and nine-
    teenth-century composers of the sheet music publishing industry and shows how
    major career decisions were made in the light of economic factors. Chapters 1–5
    of the present volume provide many other examples.
38. In the European context jazz has gone through a process of enculturation in
    terms of its relationship with critical canonisation and the academy. As a result,
    it is today often divorced from its Afro-American roots and instead viewed,
    taught and studied entirely as an adjunct to Western art music.

superior to, and under threat from, popular forms. Hence there is a high spend on areas such as audience development, archival work, networking between musicians and tour support for the former kinds of music, whereas there is only minimal investment in the latter.

Conclusion

It appears that Arts Council funding for popular music is restricted because of the assumption that the production and consumption of the form takes place within a self-sufficient industry. Such a position seems to be consonant with the 'fine arts' model that makes the aims of the Arts Council antagonistic to those of commerce. However, the fact remains that many music agencies supported by the Arts Council are involved in programmes that aim to make certain types of music (Irish traditional music, classical music and jazz) more viable in the marketplace. Moreover, on occasions when funding has been given to individual musicians performing popular music, the purpose has been to strengthen their position within commercial networks. One example is the 'Arts Flights' scheme, which has enabled musicians and record companies to attend music industry conferences such as MIDEM. These contradictions suggest that much of the Arts Council's thinking on music is value-laden in being based on traditional high/low distinctions between art forms. Such a position is central to the maintenance of 'glass walls' between musical genres in situations where funding allocations are informed by aesthetic distinctions and value judgements.

The classification of popular music in its entirety within the commercial arena ignores the important role that it plays in social development, in empowering disadvantaged communities and in opening up possibilities for creativity and expression across a wide social spectrum. As Sandy Fitzgerald, from the City Arts Centre, Dublin, comments: 'Most good community arts work is about liberating creativity within people themselves, and that really boils down to providing mechanisms to listen a lot of the time, and to encourage and develop, and it's not about creating access to the artist in the traditional sense.'[39] Both the FMC and individual music collectives base their work on the premise that popular music has an important role to play

---

39. Interview with Sandy Fitzgerald by the authors, dated 2 July 1998.

in aiding social development. Many music collectives in Ireland are located in areas of high unemployment that have experienced a variety of social problems. In these conditions, popular music provides an outlet for creativity and a conduit for self expression and empowerment in areas of high social exclusion. As Angela Dorgan comments: 'Most bands just want to play! A lot of bands don't want to get signed, don't want to be famous, don't want to get a record deal. [They] just love playing and love meeting other people that they can learn a new riff from or meet another DJ who they can do a tour with and just play and play and play.'[40] Indeed, the very accessibility of popular music means that it can be a key facilitator in enabling young people to become involved in arts programmes and projects. As Fitzgerald also points out: 'If you're talking about young people, they have very little or no interest in what you might call the traditional arts; their culture is really wound around where they live, where they're based, what their life is like, what their environment is like.'[41]

The evidence suggests that there is a disharmony between traditional notions underpinning arts funding and the move towards a cultural industries model. The Arts Council is attempting to absorb ideas and policies taken from the latter while at the same time maintaining much of the rhetoric (and monetary subsidy) inherited from the former. Although there is undoubtedly room for a healthy pluralism in the thinking of arts funding bodies, the current strategy of the Arts Council of Ireland is problematic for many popular music practitioners. They are caught in a dualism where music is valued either as inherently worthy or as a mechanism facilitating economic growth. The evidence suggests, further, that the ideals and motives of community arts (in relation to popular music) have been left behind in the wake of a paradigm shift towards a cultural industries model. Because popular music has been situated within a purely industrial context, popular music initiatives based in community arts tend to fall between the two positions. They are neither 'high art' nor potential economic miracles. Any future arts funding should take into account all the possible benefits that popular music can offer. As UK community music worker Martin Dempsey puts it: 'With the integration of technology, vision and reasonable levels of funding, music making and dissemina-

40. Interview with Angela Dorgan by the authors, dated 11 February 1998.
41. Fitzgerald, loc. cit.

tion not only provide valuable social interaction but can also provide beneficial economic and cultural activity.'[43] Popular music initiatives should be approached in a holistic manner in which community initiatives work alongside and complement strategies that promote the economic growth and employment potential of music.

43. Martin Dempsey, 'Communities, Music and Technology – Liverpool "99"', in *Community, Music and New Technology*, ed. Lee Higgins, Liverpool, MIMIC, 2000, pp. 43–47, at p. 47.

10

Paying One's Dues: The Music Business, the City and Urban Regeneration

Sara Cohen

This chapter focuses on the music business in order to explore connections between music and the city. More specifically, it examines
policy initiatives of the 1980s and 1990s aimed at developing city-
based music industries and thereby improving music's contribution to
urban economies.[1] Using the English city of Liverpool as a case study,
the first part of the chapter describes several such initiatives, while the
second part highlights key features of the discourse that they generated and outlines the main occupational groups involved with formu-
lating and implementing them.[2] These groups are shown to have
often conflicting interests in, and perspectives on, the music business
and its connection with or value for the city and to promote a
'rhetoric of the local' that serves to further their own interests. So
although Liverpool's music-industry policy initiatives have tended to
be strictly concerned with economics and with music's economic
impact on the city, they have also been very much about culture and
politics, representing a political battlefield in which different groups
have struggled to control connections between the music industry and

1. Following Roger Wallis and Krister Malm, *Big Sounds from Small Peoples: The
   Music Industry in Small Countries*, London, Constable, 1984, music policy is
   defined as direct or indirect intervention in and support for music practice by
   local, national and international governing bodies, based on conceptions of
   music's social, cultural or economic significance.
2. The chapter draws upon ethnographic research conducted in Liverpool during
   the 1980s and 1990s. The research involved participating in and observing
   policy-related events and practices and interviewing at length many of those
   involved. Some of this research was conducted for a comparative project on
   music industry policy-making in Liverpool, Manchester and Sheffield, and I
   would like to thank my co-researchers on this project and the Economic and
   Social Research Council in Britain for supporting and funding it.

the city, and promoting a contested discourse that connects the music industry with city identity. The chapter ends by considering some of the implications of this for how we think about and value the music business and its connections with the city.

Developing City-based Music Industries

Most major British cities house a variety of music businesses. In Liverpool during the 1980s and 1990s, for example, there were businesses concerned with the staging of live music performance (such as venues, festival organisations, PA and lighting companies); others concerned with music as a recorded medium (examples are recording studios, studio equipment manufacturers and repairers, record retailers and DJs) or with both live and recorded fields of musical activity; one or two associated businesses (such as law firms specialising in the music and entertainment business and companies producing and distributing music-related merchandise); and bodies engaged in both commercial and publicly funded activity (including community music activity and further or higher music education and training). Many of these organisations dealt with a range of music genres, while some were associated with specific genres (local classical, dance, folk and country music 'scenes', for example, had their own particular network of businesses that included specialist retailers and live performance venues).

Most of these businesses were small, some being run by a single person on a freelance or self-employed basis, but there were a few organisations that had over one hundred employees (such as the dance 'superclub' Cream and the Royal Liverpool Philharmonic Society). Similarly, record retailers ranged from tiny specialist local shops to large branches of nationwide retail chains such as HMV and Virgin. The existence of many businesses was perennially threatened by the unpredictable nature of the commercial music market and by local economic decline, which resulted in a lack of investment in local music-making. Work within local music businesses tended to be part-time, voluntary and sporadic, but this type of employment was characteristic of the arts and cultural industries in general – as was its flexibility, with people frequently moving between different skills and jobs, and continually trying to devise alternative strategies for financial survival and innovative means of keeping ahead of fast-changing trends in music and the music business.

From the late 1980s Liverpool's music businesses began collectively to be referred to as a local music 'industry'. This was largely due to initiatives that emerged in London during the early 1980s, when Britain suffered from a general economic depression and Margaret Thatcher's Conservative government cut arts funding substantially. In response to this, the Left-wing Greater London Council (GLC) broadened its definition of the arts to include popular culture and the cultural industries, which it defined as 'those social practices which have as their primary purpose the transmission of meaning'.[3] These industries included ones based around film, the performing arts, broadcasting, advertising, sport, publishing and music. The GLC identified them as 'new growth' industries with long-term wealth-generating potential, arguing that they generated employment and income, and made a positive contribution to a city's image and quality of life, thereby helping to revitalise urban areas. In order to counter widespread economic recession and changes in patterns of employment, the arts and cultural industries should therefore be invested in and developed strategically rather than merely subsidised and preserved.

The GLC thus pioneered an arts and cultural industries strategy that, for the first time in Britain, linked culture firmly with economic development and economic policy. Britain had traditionally been more uneasy than continental Europe with the terms 'culture' and 'cultural policy' and had tended to use the narrower terms 'arts' and 'arts policy'. Government subsidy and support had formerly been reserved either for the so-called 'high' arts cultivated by a social elite, which were seen to have educational, aesthetic and moral value, or for community arts, which emerged during the 1970s and emphasised training, access and social value.[4] The more commercial forms of popular music and the music industry had traditionally been regarded as the domain of the market rather than of the state and had tended to be ignored, left alone or supported through indirect measures. The GLC was abolished in 1986, and it was in northern cities controlled by Left-wing Labour councils that arts and cultural industries strategies became a visible response to the decline of manufacturing industries and rising unemployment. These strategies were supported by

3. Nicholas Garnham, *The Cultural Industries and Cultural Policy in London*, London, Greater London Council, 1987, AR 1116 and IEC 940.
4. See Chapter 9, p. 250, for a fuller account of the rise of community arts.

research that emphasised the economic importance of the arts,[5] taking a lead from the culture-led regeneration initiatives of various North American and Western European cities.[6]

As part of these strategies, some city governments began to finance and support popular music activities and facilities for economic reasons rather than just for their social or entertainment value.[7] Increasing attention was paid to music's 'impact' on local economies, although the extent of this impact is notoriously difficult to measure.[8] In 1989 I conducted for Liverpool City Council a survey of Merseyside music businesses and their local economic impact. This survey revealed major gaps in the provision of facilities and services, including ones in financial, legal and business advice, in information services and technological support, and in manufacturers, publishers and distributors. Almost twenty-five per cent of the businesses surveyed spent nothing on local goods and services, and over twenty-seven per cent had no full-time employees. The survey contributed to a report which concluded that there was a general failure to develop and promote music talent in the region, largely because of a lack of relevant skills, information and physical resources.[9] Thus, while Liverpool was

5. Such as John Meyerscough, *The Economic Importance of the Arts in Britain*, London, Policy Studies Institute, 1989.
6. From the waterfront development of Baltimore to the music festivals of Rennes. On the latter see *Cultural Policy and Urban Regeneration: The West European Experience*, ed. Franco Bianchini and Michael Parkinson, Manchester, Manchester University Press, 1993.
7. See, for example, Simon Frith, 'Popular Music and the Local State', in *Rock and Popular Music: Politics, Policies and Institutions*, ed. Tony Bennett *et al.*, London, Routledge, 1993, pp. 14–24, on Sheffield; John Street, 'Local Differences: Popular Music and the Local State', *Popular Music*, Vol. 12 (1993), pp. 43–55, on Norwich; and Mark Boyle and George Hughes, 'The Politics of the Representation of "The Real": Discourses from the Left on Glasgow's Role as European City of Culture, 1990', *Area*, Vol. 23 (1991), pp. 217–28, on Glasgow.
8. Sara Cohen, Adam Brown and Justin O' Connor, 'Measuring the Value of the Local Music Industry', unpublished paper presented at the British Phonographic Institute at a workshop organised as part of the ESRC's 'Media Industries' programme (1997). During the late 1990s Britain's new Labour government, too, began to emphasise cultural policy and the arts and cultural industries. By that time, the music industry had gained increased recognition for its contribution to the British economy. The *British Invisibles Report* (1993, p. 28), for example, stated that music had a net surplus on overseas trade of £571 million, which was comparable with that of Britain's steel industry.
9. *Music City*, Liverpool, Ark Consultants (for Liverpool City Council), March 1991.

renowned as a 'music city', it did not have a music-business infrastructure capable of generating much financial benefit for the city
from this status. Other regional UK cities were in a similar position.
The 'global' music industry dominated by large multinational multi-
media conglomerates tended to be concentrated in a few of the
world's capital cities, including London. Hence those involved with
regional music production tended to have, or to aspire towards, business dealings with London-based companies. It was assumed, for
example, that of the few Liverpool rock bands that would eventually
get signed up by major record companies, most would in consequence
move to London where so many of their key business contacts were
based.[10]

Culture-led urban regeneration strategies seemed an obvious focus
for Liverpool in view of the city's severe economic decline and the
fact that its image and identity had in the recent past been so strongly
linked with culture. Yet cultural policy was not a priority for Liverpool city council until 1987. Between 1983 and 1987 the Labour
Party had majority control of the council. The party was dominated
by an extreme Trotskyist faction, the Militant Tendency, which was
rooted in trade unions and in traditional working-class areas of the
city. The Militants emphasised production and manual work and
lacked networks with the city's business sector. They prioritised local
taxation and housing policies, treating art, culture and the city centre
as peripheral concerns. Popular culture was regarded generally as
leisure and entertainment – a commercial rather than a public-sector
concern – while the cultural industries were widely perceived as 'soft'
and thus both a poor replacement for 'proper' industries and jobs and
a distraction from urgent housing and welfare needs. Liverpool City
Council thus had a Department of Arts and Libraries but no specific
cultural or arts policy and no distinct arts committee. Support for
local arts, community arts and other cultural activity was channelled
through Merseyside Arts, a body that was disbanded in 1989, when
North West Arts took over responsibility for the region.

By 1987, however, various factors had combined to push the arts
and cultural industries to the centre of Liverpool's political and economic agenda. Liverpool City Council had consistently been at the
forefront of opposition to aspects of Conservative government policy.

10. See Sara Cohen, *Rock Culture in Liverpool*, Oxford, Oxford University Press,
    1991.

In 1986 it threatened to bankrupt the city unless the government gave it more money and borrowed from foreign banks to support the city's extensive public housing programme. The Council was consequently disqualified from holding office by the House of Lords and its leaders expelled from the Labour Party. This paved the way for the rise of the New Left and a new realism in Liverpool. The city's newly elected Council recognised the limits to its resources and the need to involve a wide range of organisations in policy-making. Consequently, partnerships began to emerge between the Council and city-based central government agencies, and between public and private-sector agencies. The Council also followed the line that money spent on housing would never be recovered but that investing in the city as a cultural attraction would bring economic returns.

In 1987 the Council published its Arts and Cultural Industries Strategy, the key objective of which was 'to maximize the contribution which the arts and cultural industries make to the economic and social well-being of the city'.[11] The arts and cultural industries were defined very broadly and the strategy emphasised business and employment development as well as community provision and improvement of general quality of life. In order to implement the strategy, the Council established an Arts and Cultural Industries Unit within its Department of Arts and Libraries. All these developments were initiated by a few young council and arts officers who had a professional interest in the arts and promoted the ideas initiated by the Greater London Council. During the late 1980s and the 1990s the Council did not implement a specific music policy as such, but it did at least instigate, or become involved with, several music-industry policy initiatives, the most significant of which are summarised below.

Music City

Liverpool City Council's Arts and Cultural Industries strategy was promoted through some high-profile initiatives, which included bold, innovative schemes to develop local film production and exploit local rock music talent. A 1988 report entitled 'City Beat' proposed that the Council should establish a Liverpool-based and council-run music

11. An *Arts and Cultural Industries Strategy for Liverpool*, Liverpool City Council, November 1987.

production and management company that would develop and commercially exploit local musical talent in order to generate revenue for the city.[12] The company would be non-profit-making and of limited liability, with profits re-invested in the company and in related cultural industries initiatives. The proposal was criticised by local music practitioners, who expressed doubts about the Council's ability to run such a company, were concerned that the company's existence would be threatened when a new Council was elected, suggested that the proposal lacked knowledge and understanding of the music industry, and criticised the Council for proposing a scheme that duplicated or competed with existing private-sector businesses – and for not consulting them about the initiative.[13]

Consequently, the Council commissioned one of these critics, a local music manager, to conduct a study entitled 'Music City' that would assess the current state of Merseyside's music industries, identify their training needs and establish key areas for effective public and private investment. The *Music City* report (1991) emphasised the importance of an integrated cultural industries development strategy linked to the development of physical infrastructure, suggested ways of maximising the contribution of the music industry to Merseyside's economy, and advocated partially developed proposals to establish a Liverpool Institute of Performing Arts, a Music Information Centre and a major international music festival.[14] The report received little response from Liverpool City Council, which had by that time become involved with the staging of the 1991 John Lennon Memorial Concert, a major international music event that was intended to raise the city's profile, lay the foundation for future events and place Liverpool 'on the map' in terms of such events. The concert was, however, surrounded by controversy and resulted in substantial debts. Few contemporary Liverpool rock musicians were involved, a fact that prompted the organisation of an alternative and simultaneous event named Liverpool Now! The latter became an annual showcase of local musical talent aimed at London-based record companies and was partly funded by Liverpool City Council.

12. Geoff White, *City Beat: Report for Liverpool City Council*, August 1987.
13. The term 'practitioners' is used in a broad sense to refer not only to musicians but also to those involved with music businesses, music education and training or other types of music practice.
14. *Music City* (1991).

The Liverpool Institute of Performing Arts and the Local Music Industries

The creation of the Liverpool Institute of Performing Arts (LIPA) was spearheaded by Paul McCartney, who was keen that it should be based in his old city-centre school, which had become disused and derelict. LIPA was to be an international 'centre of excellence' offering vocational higher education and training and first degrees in the Performing Arts validated by Liverpool John Moores University, but it also had to suit the political and educational priorities of Liverpool City Council. The initial model for the Institute was music-focused, with an emphasis on world and community music, distance learning, open resources and collaboration with the city's existing music organisations. Later on, however, less emphasis was placed on music and collaboration and more on the development of purpose-built in-house facilities and resources of high quality. LIPA received funding from local, national and European public-sector agencies as a major city 'flagship' that would attract outside investment and international students to Liverpool, help to regenerate part of Liverpool city centre and improve the city's image, create full-time jobs and new businesses in the local arts and cultural industries, and help to develop existing businesses within those industries.[15]

Such a high-profile initiative inevitably attracted controversy. Concerns about LIPA were raised by various local groups, including policy-makers and music practitioners.[16] At a 1993 music-business seminar aimed at local music practitioners, many of the one hundred or so participants expressed concern that the local music industry had not been properly consulted or represented with regard to LIPA (and other policy initiatives), and collectively decided that an association should be established in order to promote the industry. The Merseyside Music Industry Association (MMIA) was duly set up as a democratic body with statutes, an elected Working Committee and regular open meetings. Its committee consisted of music practitioners from

15. Bergen Peck, Case Study on The Liverpool Institute for Performing Arts presented at an international seminar entitled 'Arts and the Development of the Local Economy' organised by Brouhaha International and held at St George's Hall, Liverpool, in 1993.
16. See, for example, *Music City* (1991) and Sara Cohen, 'Popular Music and Urban Regeneration: The Music Industries on Merseyside', *Cultural Studies*, Vol. 5 (1991), pp. 332–46.

the public and private sectors, and the association was run on a voluntary basis with around one hundred members drawn from all areas of the industry. One of its first leaflets stated:

> Why **you** should join the Merseyside Music Industry Association. What's happening to music on Merseyside? Liverpool is famed throughout the world as a centre for popular and orchestral music. So why does the local picture so often seem fragmented and stagnant? We have the talent, facilities and contacts to build a thriving music industry here … With your help we can **all** put Merseyside back on the map!

MMIA organised a series of music-business seminars that provided a public forum for discussion and debate on the local music industry. It produced a video (which was never actually released) to inform policy-makers about the industry; this included interviews with various local rock and pop stars. In 1994 its Development Plan for the industry was completed. The plan outlined collective strategies for improving the status and effectiveness of the industry, primarily through centralisation of information and training and via investment in businesses and services. The plan took into account the needs of different music genres and a broad range of music activity stretching from community music to business enterprise. It advocated the establishment of a staffed Music Industry Resource Unit as well as the creation of a post of Music Officer within Liverpool City Council (the council already employed a Film Officer). It further recommended that the Council should support a Liverpool bid for Britain's annual Sound City competition.[17] However, the committee had little time or money with which to publicise and promote MMIA and attract new members – a situation that hampered its aim to represent the local music industry.

European Funding and a Local Music Development Agency

By this time, it had been announced that Merseyside had been awarded Objective One Status, which is the European Union's highest funding category reserved for its poorest regions. This was the first time that an area of Britain had been categorised as such; it meant that £1.25 billion EU and UK central government funding was to be spent

---

17. This is a national competition sponsored by BBC Radio 1 that rewards the winning city with a week of high-profile media coverage of its popular music.

on Merseyside between 1994 and 1999 in order to encourage sustained growth and job creation and enhance the region's competi-
tiveness in the global marketplace.[18] Specified within the region's
Objective One plan was the role that culture, media and leisure industries could play in economic development. Objective One thus presented Merseyside with a unique opportunity to develop cultural
policy, and it illustrated the growing influence of EU funding on
British arts and cultural industries development.

Merseyside's Objective One status was launched with much publicity and hype on the part of the local media and gave rise to much
rumour, gossip and debate. This was an entirely new fund with its
own peculiar objectives, rules and regulations and a complicated bidding process.[19] To a large extent, the region was unprepared for it and
lacked appropriate structures and expertise to deal with it. The first
year of Objective One was characterised by confusion and criticism,
cynicism and disenchantment being expressed by those in competition for funds, administering funds or advising on the whole process.
Local music businesses, for example, complained of difficulties in
gaining information and advice on application procedures and in
finding time to complete the relevant documentation. Most could not
afford the consultants or administrative back-up employed by larger
organisations and despaired over the maze of procedures and paperwork involved. MMIA tried to assist its members by summarising in
lay terms the Objective One planning document, and its Development
Plan highlighted a compatibility between the aims and objectives of
MMIA and those outlined in the Objective One programme.

Local arts and cultural businesses appeared to face particular problems submitting Objective One bids.[20] Two arts consultants were consequently commissioned to investigate the region's arts and cultural
industries sector and to prepare a report and strategy relating it to

18. The funding was directed at developing new rather than existing structures, and
it was to be distributed via a partnership involving the EU, central government,
the five local authorities responsible for the Merseyside region, and various
training or development agencies and community or voluntary groups.
19. Private businesses, for example, were not allowed to apply for funds directly but
could apply through 'eligible bodies', although there was much confusion over
how such bodies should be defined.
20. In the first round of the Objective One bidding process all of its five drivers were
greatly oversubscribed to, except for the one specifically relating to the culture,
media and leisure industries.

Objective One principles, objectives and criteria. This would help Government Offices for Merseyside to make informed decisions about the sector and to assist those within the sector to gain access to Objective One funding. The consultants divided the sector up into separate subsectors (moving image, radio, design, music, visual arts, theatre, events and festivals) and organised a series of meetings to discuss subsector strengths and weaknesses. Twelve music practitioners attended the music subsector meeting, which was held at Liverpool City Council in February 1995. Four ran their own commercial music businesses, six were involved with subsidised music organisations and two came from higher education. The meeting was disturbed by various tensions. The business people felt patronised by the consultants' flip-chart pyramid model of a typical industry; those involved with MMIA objected to what they regarded as a duplication of work that MMIA had already done; and a couple of businessmen questioned the representativity of the meeting, suggesting that people working in the industry were being excluded from the policy-making process. These objections angered the consultants, who resented the way in which the meeting had been 'hijacked' by some of those present.

The consultants' report was subsequently written and accepted as a policy document but was criticised by MMIA for misrepresenting and misunderstanding the music industry.[21] The Chair of the Association documented his personal criticisms of the report in a letter to the Government Offices for Merseyside, in which he also called into question the consultants' competence. The letter caused consternation among local policy-makers, who became concerned about its potentially damaging effect on the funding process. Members of MMIA's Working Committee were not invited to further meetings concerning Objective One and cultural policy, although some of them tried to demonstrate to consultants and policy-makers their willingness to collaborate with others in order to help to co-ordinate a package of complementary Objective One music bids. Eventually, consultants were commissioned by a partnership of public sector organisations to design a series of arts and cultural industries bids around a template model based on the existing Merseyside Moving Image Development Agency. The emphasis was now on establishing

21. Pete Booth and Geoff White, *Objective 1: Arts and Cultural Industries Study. Final Report*, March 1995. This unpublished document is referred to hereafter as the Booth/White Report.

'enabling agencies', which would co-ordinate the development of
each arts and cultural industries subsector and distribute grants to
related businesses. A group of music practitioners were persuaded to
discuss music's subsector bid, and a long series of meetings took place.
These gave rise to much confusion and friction as well as demanding
considerable effort and energy on the part of all those concerned. A
great deal of time was spent on submitting funding bids and generating and juggling with statistics, including those indicating the
turnover of the local music industry and its potential growth and out-
puts. Eventually, however, a successful bid was submitted to establish
a Merseyside Music Development Agency (MMDA), which was
awarded a total of £1,120,000 during its first year.

MMDA was launched in July 1998 at the House of Commons in
London. Its main aims were to attract inward investment to Merseyside from the music industry in order to lever down public funding
from Europe and other sources and to create a network of music initiatives that would develop and support the local music industry and
thereby attract further investment. Particular emphasis was placed on
offering the music industry financial incentives to spend within the
region. Local managers were targetted initially, largely because of their
control over financial advances from record companies for the development of local music product. Working on a voluntary basis,
MMDA's Board of Directors met weekly but also held regular meetings with other relevant individuals and organisations. The Directors
represented a wide range of perspectives and experiences drawn from
public, private and voluntary sectors (two were women and two were
black – which was considered highly unusual in view of the fact that
the music industry was notoriously white and male-dominated). They
spent a great deal of time debating not only how to interpret and operate within the specific rules and regulations of Objective One but also
the moral and ethical issues raised. The issue of accountability, for
example, was discussed at length in order to explore ways of establishing an agency that was led by the music industry but would at the
same time avoid conflicts of interest and allegations of corruption.[22]

22. Despite the care taken to address such issues, they later became a means by
    which the agency could be attacked through leading articles in a local newspa-
    per. A legal case was in consequence brought against the paper, which agreed to
    settle out of court, but the articles generated criticism of the agency and tensions
    among its directors, showing the existence of broader factions and conflicts of
    interest among local music practitioners.

Cultural Quarters

At the same time, there also existed a long-running and often problematic attempt to establish a 'cultural quarter' in a specific area of
Liverpool city centre. During the 1980s and 1990s many cities in the
UK, Western Europe and North America developed so-called cultural
quarters, which were areas containing a concentration of art and cultural activity. Such quarters were often a focus for city-wide urban
regeneration initiatives, and their aims included attracting more
people into city centres in order to revitalise their night life and
evening economy; to improve the appearance and image of city centres, and to foster a community of interrelated cultural businesses that
would generate employment and revenue. Much of the area in Liverpool city centre had become run-down and deserted, yet it also
housed a variety of restaurants, cafés, retailers and resident groups,
including Europe's oldest Chinese community, in addition to some
modern developments. Moreover, parts of the area were home to
many music businesses and had a contemporary cultural vibrancy and
a vibrant night-time economy based around bars and dance clubs,
which included, from the early 1990s, the dance 'superclub' Cream.
In 1989 Liverpool City Council sold off much of this area for just £8
million to a London-based property development firm that had stated
its willingness to work with the council in order to develop the area
as a cultural quarter. However, the company went bankrupt before
any development work could begin. Property in the area was subsequently bought up by other private developers but was left to decline.

In 1994 the council backed another regeneration scheme for the
area. A consultancy report was produced which advocated, among
other things, establishing a National Centre for Contemporary Popular Music, with the Liverpool Institute of Performing Arts as its key
partner; but the initiative was eventually taken over by a public/pri-
vate partnership that launched a long and complex consultancy and
planning process involving a wide variety of interest groups. Music
practitioners were not specifically targeted in this process, but the
Action Plan eventually produced for the quarter identified a 'Cream
Zone' and announced plans for the expansion of Cream's activities
(including even the establishment of a Cream Hotel). Reports were
also written on the management of the night-time economy and
on the potential for digital networks in the quarter, but no specific
cultural industries strategy was drawn up, despite the flagging up of

creative and cultural industries in planning documents. The initiative was eventually named 'The Ropewalks' and received £71 million of public and private-sector funding, although distribution of this funding was beset by various difficulties, delays and controversies. By this time, two other cultural quarters had emerged in Liverpool city centre: the Cavern Quarter, which was a private-sector initiative based around an area with strong Beatles connections, and the Hope Street 'Arts Quarter', which attracted strong support from public sector agencies. The latter was steered by a group connected with the Royal Liverpool Philharmonic Society (located in Hope Street itself) and promoted classical, traditional and popular music and events, some of which were specifically aimed at children. Each 'quarter' had its own committee, newsletter and festival.

The Practice and Discourse of Music Industry Policy-Making

The policy initiatives briefly described above (City Beat, Music City, LIPA, MMIA, MMDA, Ropewalks) were formulated and implemented by a small group of policy-makers, consultants and music practitioners representing different and often competing interests in the music industry and its connections with the city. Having described some of Liverpool's music industry policy initiatives, I now focus in more detail on the interest groups and discourses involved.

The policy-makers were located in various public-sector organisations, including Liverpool City Council, the regional arts board and locally based central government agencies. Few of them had specialist knowledge of, or much interest in, the music industry; in general, the policy-makers tended to be wary of the industry's associations with illicit or disreputable activity – from 'rip-offs' and underhand dealings to drug-taking – and of its rebellious and anti-establishment image.[23] To some extent the industry itself promoted such associations: 'Rock's ritual representation of itself as an oppositional, resistant form may not have entirely obscured its close articulation to capital but it has certainly established rock music as a "dirty" category of social practice – from which governments have customarily kept their distance.'[24] Many policy-makers, noting the glamour of the

23. See Chapter 7 for a fuller discussion of popular music's 'illegal' and disreputable associations.
24. Bennett *et al.* (1993), p. 9.

music industry and the high media profile of its stars, tended to regard it as highly commercial and successful and thus best left to its own devices, although some were keen to capitalise upon such character-istics. The City Beat initiative, for example, was aimed partly at attracting maximum publicity for Liverpool City Council's new Arts and Cultural Industries Strategy.

Certain policy-makers, however, were increasingly interested in the wealth-generating aspects of the music industry and in developing a local music industry for the benefit of the local economy. They employed consultants to inform and advise them on music and other arts and cultural industries and to develop particular initiatives. A striking feature of Liverpool arts and cultural industries policy-making throughout the late 1980s and the 1990s was the central involvement of a small, close-knit group of professional arts consul-tants. Unlike the music practitioners who were occasionally employed by public, private or community organisations to research and develop particular projects, these were consultants who specialised in the broad area of arts and cultural industries and enjoyed close con-nections with public-sector agencies. It was they who had lobbied for the introduction of cultural policy in Liverpool, breaking down divi-sions between high art and popular culture and arguing for the eco-nomic impact of the arts and cultural industries. Several of them had pursued similar career paths, moving from an involvement with com-munity arts to positions with local authorities and local arts boards before becoming freelance consultants and professional funding bid-ders employed for their knowledge of the intricacies of public and EU funding. Some of them socialised together and were collectively referred to by several local arts practitioners as the local 'Arts Mafia', the 'Garden Party Network' or 'the Sainsbury Group'– descriptions that betrayed a shared perception of them as a middle-class clique.

Meanwhile, the music practitioners involved with music industry policy-making in Liverpool tended to have a background in rock and pop music and, like the policy-makers and consultants, were over-whelmingly white and male. Most had some experience of the public sector and its funding mechanisms (for example, through their involvement with subsidised arts activity). Their interest in policy-making generally stemmed from a long-standing involvement in the local music industry and a concern that it should receive appropriate investment for the benefit of those working in it and of the city as a whole. They believed that the right kind of policies, strategically targeted and properly implemented, could have an enabling potential, helping to create an appropriate environment in which the local industry could flourish. Most other local music practitioners, however, were uninterested in local policy-making, felt alienated from it, were suspicious of the intentions of Liverpool City Council and sceptical about its abilities – or were opposed in principle to the idea of government involvement in the music industry, believing that the industry should generally be left to its own devices and that any kind of government involvement would do more harm than good.

Tensions often arose between and among the policy-makers, consultants and music practitioners involved with Liverpool's music-industry policy initiatives. Discussed below are some of the conflicts and debates that the initiatives raised over how the city's music industry should be defined, categorised and represented for policy-making purposes, over the value of the industry for the city and its compatibility with city policy-making, and over how the industry was perceived and understood within the policy-making process.

In general, there was little professional contact between policy-makers and music practitioners, although this was starting to change with the launch of the Merseyside Music Development Agency (MMDA) in 1998. The Merseyside Music Industry Association (MMIA), in contrast, attracted little support from policy-makers and arts consultants, who did not attend its meetings and seminars, despite regular invitations, and did not respond to its Development Plan despite having been presented with it. Music practitioners struggled to make the music industry conform to policy-making conditions and criteria. They often had difficulty following the language and complex procedures and paperwork of policy-making (some MMIA Board members referred to policy-makers as 'The Suits' and continually had to translate policy terms into 'music speak'), and continual changes in the language of cultural policy during the 1980s and 1990s, as well as in the structures through which such policy was made, created additional confusion. In addition, the involvement of some music practitioners with policy-making left them feeling rather detached from the local music industry and its practices and processes.[25] The consultants, meanwhile, described their role as that of providing a 'bridge' between

25. According to a personal communication to the author and co-researchers from the directors of MMDA in 1997.

policy-makers and music practitioners (although some music practitioners regarded it as more resembling a barrier).[26]

Under the Militants, Liverpool City Council had generally regarded the arts and cultural industries as a poor or 'soft' replacement for 'proper' local industries such as car manufacturing. Many policy-makers remained reluctant to acknowledge the existence of a local music 'industry' since they associated music with culture, or with entertainment and consumption, rather than with production and economics. Most music practitioners, on the other hand, seemed happy to talk of a local music industry. The term 'industry' sounded respectable and businesslike, helping to emphasise music's value to the local economy. MMIA was keen to emphasise to policy-makers and potential sponsors that music was an industry just like any other and should be recognised and invested in as such, promoting the Association under the slogan 'Music: The New Industry for Merseyside'.

Nevertheless, some of the music practitioners involved with the MMIA, and with the subsequent MMDA, had reservations about using the term 'industry'. Several of those involved with community music, or who received arts subsidies, were concerned about the commercial and institutional connotations of the term. They preferred to emphasise instead the informality and nonconformism of local music-making and its social, cultural or artistic value, arguing that music was more than business. This irritated those running commercial music businesses, who were anxious to emphasise music's business and economic aspects but were annoyed by any suggestion that they were therefore unconcerned about the music itself. The emphasis of Liverpool's music-industry policy initiatives on music's economic value thus concerned or alienated those who believed that music should also be valued as art or culture. The Working Committee of MMIA argued that the economic emphasis of Objective One accommodated an integrated approach that could combine music's cultural, educational, community and business aspects, but that it was important first to link music strategically with local economic development in order to get hold of public funding before it was spent on another sector.

Liverpool's music industry policy initiatives raised debates not only about connecting music with industry but also about connecting regional music with industry. One lecturer at LIPA insisted that the

26. According to a personal communication to the author and co-researchers from Geoff White in 1997.

notion of a city-based music industry was unrealistic in view of the structure and organisation of the industry nationally and internationally and the absence within regional cities of such key elements of the industry as publishing and manufacturing. These views were echoed by several employees of London-based music companies. When the local music industry was recognised, further problems arose over how it should be defined, particularly in view of the variety and diversity of activity within it and its interaction with other, related industries such as film and television. Some music practitioners talked of 'the music industry' when they were actually referring only to activities and organisations concerned with recording rather than with live performance and clubs, while others preferred to talk, in the plural, of local music 'industries' or adopted a much broader definition of the industry. There were also music practitioners (including the ones running Cream) who recognised the existence of a local music industry but did not regard themselves as part of it because their business dealings were normally with companies based outside the city and its surrounding region.[27]

Tensions emerged not only over the use of the term 'industry' and over how a city-based music industry should be defined but also over the way in which such an industry was categorised and represented. Members of the Working Committee of MMIA objected to the description of music in consultancy and policy documents as a 'subsector' of the local 'arts and cultural industries' rather than as an industry in its own right, and also to the inclusion of the music business within the broad category of 'arts and cultural industries', because of the way in which this 'lumped together individual bead makers with large music corporations', and commercial organisations with those based upon subsidies. Meanwhile, one of the authors of the Booth/White report described music as the most 'difficult' of local arts and cultural industries to deal with.[28] The report itself pointed to an absence of 'leadership' in the local music sector and suggested that this absence presented problems for local economic development. It also described music as the most fragmented and divided of all Merseyside's arts and cultural industries subsectors, pointing to 'hostility

27. According to a personal communication to the author and co-researchers from Darren Hughes in 1996.
28. Personal communication from Geoff White to the author and co-researchers in 1997.

between people and organisations who should naturally be partners' and stating that this antagonism was a barrier to development.

It could be suggested, rather cynically perhaps, that in order for the consultants to maintain their central position as a channel of information, knowledge and influence between policy-makers and music practitioners, it was sometimes in their interest to emphasise a lack of knowledge and understanding of the arts and cultural industries on the part of policy-makers and a lack of representation and co-ordination within those industries. A relatively new 'player' such as MMIA, originating from outside the usual cultural policy-making networks, might thus appear as a rather unwelcome intruder, complicating the arts and cultural industries sector and challenging the consultants' control over it.

The Working Committee of MMIA responded to the Booth/White report by pointing to normal and healthy differences of opinion (rather than hostility) within the industry and to increasing collaboration and co-operation partly resulting from the work of the association itself. However, the music industry's overtly commercial image meant that it was generally perceived as strongly competitive, and many music practitioners described the local industry as highly factionalised (during the late 1990s a comparison with the Bosnian conflict, which was regularly in the news headlines, was drawn on several occasions). While policy-makers and consultants perceived this divisiveness to be a weakness, many music practitioners regarded it, rather, as a strength, arguing that it indicated a high degree of individual creativity, independence and ambition; some even believed that it made the industry incompatible with civic policy-making and therefore doubted the chances of success for an initiative such as the MMIA.

Policy-makers and consultants were thus criticised for the way that they defined, categorised and represented the music industry. They were also accused of misunderstanding it. The City Beat initiative, for example, was regarded as too bureaucratic for an industry in which spontaneity and quick decision-making were paramount. The estimated success rate for the artists involved was thought naive, considering that on average under one per cent of local bands secured a record deal – and few of those that did achieved success thereafter. The Booth/White report was criticised for, among other things, ignoring the specificities of the music industry and relying on an industry model that excluded the exploitation of music ownership rights, perhaps the industry's most profitable aspect. Policy initiatives and documents such as these encouraged music practitioners to establish organisations that would enable those working within the music industry to define, describe and assess it themselves for policy-making purposes, bypassing the consultants and making more direct contact with policy-makers. One consultant criticised MMIA, however, for trying to create a large democratic body in imitation of policy-makers in order to gain the latter's support, suggesting that policy-makers 'would see through this straight away'.[29] Ironically, when music practitioners tried to convince policy-makers that they represented a respectable, well-organised industry, they were perceived as being too bureaucratic and businesslike – not creative, entrepreneurial or dynamic as the music industry was supposed to be.

Music Industry Ideology and its Connections with the City

The above debates suggest that music-industry policy-making in Liverpool involved a power struggle between those with different interests in, and perspectives on, the music industry and its connections with the city, and that it was a political arena to which some gained access and acquired positions of control and a voice, while others were excluded and silent. One notable feature of the discourse surrounding such policy-making was the way in which it promoted a 'rhetoric of the local' that all of the interest groups involved could draw on and use to their own advantage. This rhetoric was characterised by ideological constructs that are commonly associated with the music industry but situated them within a geographical frame connecting them with the city.

Within music-industry ideology the notion of 'making it' usually refers to a conventional model of success within the industry typified by the career paths of the Beatles and other well-known rock and pop musicians. Elsewhere, I have described in detail the desire of many Liverpool rock musicians to 'make it': their obsession with success and their struggle to sign a contract with a record company that could help them to release the records and attract the audiences that would make them successful.[30] Yet only a small percentage of such musicians

29. Personal communication from Geoff White to the author and co-researchers in 1996.
30. Discussed in Cohen, *Rock Culture in Liverpool*.

managed to get 'signed up', and only a few of those musicians went on to achieve the success that they desired. Some commentators have therefore described the music industry as being based on the production of failure.[31] In the discourse surrounding Liverpool's music-industry policy initiatives 'making it' tended to be presented as a geographical route to a success that entailed leaving Liverpool for London, where the major music companies were situated, and consequently achieving national, then global, fame. This journey has become an established part of rock mythology, and it is one that many rock musicians from British regional cities have aspired to follow. Popular music-making has thus been presented as a conventional 'way out of' the city. The departure from Liverpool for London of successful local musicians (and their earnings!), such as that of the rock band Frankie Goes to Hollywood, was a starting point for Liverpool's early music-industry policy documents and a concern raised by all the above-mentioned policy initiatives. It was also discussed at length by music practitioners attending local music business meetings and seminars, provoking such comments as: 'Liverpool is good at producing good artists and product which we then send to London'; 'We've got to stop the haemorrhage'; 'keep success local'; and 'a lot of people who are still here (in Liverpool) have not been very successful [...] success leaves'. Those who remained in the city were consequently associated with the idea of failure.

The rhetoric surrounding Liverpool's early music-industry policy initiatives was pervaded by a feeling of loss and by a sense that Liverpool was a city that had been socially and economically betrayed and left behind. Those who stayed were perceived as dependent on or tied to the city (one musician said that Liverpool sometimes seemed like a 'prison'.[32] An article in a national newspaper stated rather harshly: 'No one in Liverpool has any respect for anyone who actually stays here out of choice. Indeed, they think there must be something intrinsically wrong with him.'[33] In other British cities a similar rhetoric of loss was provoked by musicians departing for London, but the rhetoric seemed to have a particular resonance in Liverpool, largely

---

31. Mike Jones, *Organising Pop: Why So Few Pop Acts Make Pop Music*, unpublished PhD thesis, Institute of Popular Music, Liverpool University, 1997, is a prime example.
32. Personal communication to the author in 1997.
33. Stanley Reynolds in *The Guardian*, 18 December 1997.

perhaps because of the city's dramatic population decline of the 1970s and 1980s, when many left the city to seek employment elsewhere, but perhaps also because of the city's port culture, in which migrant groups, such as the Liverpool Irish, sang songs that conveyed strong sentiments of home and away, departure and return (the folk song 'The Leaving of Liverpool' is a particularly well known example).

Some of those involved with discussions about Liverpool's music-industry policy initiatives suggested that the lack of a music-industry infrastructure in the city, and the pursuit of activities and lifestyles necessitated by success, excused the departure of musicians from Liverpool, but others censured musicians for being greedy and 'deserting' or 'selling out on' the city. The notion of 'selling out' is usually an accusation aimed at musicians or music businesses perceived to have compromised their artistic integrity for commercial gain by, for example, engaging in financial dealings with major rather than independent music companies. Here, however, the notion of 'selling out' is perceived in geographical terms. References were frequently made to the Beatles' betrayal of their local roots. (Such comments were hardly new, however, since the leading article in the first newsletter of Liverpool's new Beatles fan club was entitled 'Did The Beatles turn their backs on Liverpool?'[34] In the early 1980s the manager of the well-known Liverpool 'Indie' rock band Echo and the Bunnymen was questioned in the music press about his forthcoming move to London offices and about the accusation that by moving he was 'selling out and deserting Liverpool'.)[35]

Successful music practitioners such as these were often accused of leaving Liverpool without having 'paid their dues' to it. Exactly what this payment of dues should involve was rarely clearly stated, but it was a notion that carried much weight, as illustrated by one young rock musician planning a move to London, who felt obliged to state that he refused to feel guilty about leaving, adding: 'I think I've paid my dues here.'[36] Within the music industry the notion of 'paying one's dues' tends to be used frequently with reference to conventional stages in the achievement of rock music success, according to which

34. *Across the Universe: Liverpool Beatlescene's Own Newsletter*, Liverpool, Liverpool Beatlescene, Autumn 1993.
35. *Melody Maker*, 4 April 1981.
36. Personal communication to the author in 1991.

musicians begin their careers with regular live performances, through which they will learn the tricks of the trade, build up a following and gain the attention of record companies and the national media. If, however, musicians are regarded as having skipped a stage in this process, they may be accused of having failed to 'pay their dues'.

In the discourse surrounding Liverpool's music-industry policy initiatives the idea of debt was strongly expressed in geographical terms. Once again, the Beatles have been made a familiar target of this kind of rhetoric. One Liverpool councillor said of them: 'I agree, as quite a number of the committee have said, that once they left Liverpool that was it. They haven't put a penny back into this city that they've taken their living out of.' Another said: 'In my long life of public work I come across people who I think statues should be erected to far more than The Beatles – people who have really contributed to the city.'[37] A 1994 report on Beatles tourism referred to 'a question that locals and journalists always ask: "What have The Beatles ever done for Liverpool? [...] Still the Scousers say: "So what? They left Liverpool in 1964. The Beatles themselves have never done anything positive to help this area".'[38]

The Director of LIPA responded to such comments by telling an audience of music practitioners: 'A lot of people wouldn't be here without McCartney.'[39] A businessman involved with Beatles tourism warned the same audience: 'If anyone asks what the Beatles have done for Liverpool [...]' – and he proceeded to point out what the Beatles had 'put back' into the city, singling out LIPA as 'Paul McCartney's personal contribution to the city'.[40] The above-mentioned report on Beatles tourism insisted that LIPA helped to prove that the Beatles had never forgotten their roots, while an organiser of the Liverpool Beatlescene fanclub suggested that LIPA represented 'perhaps the best indication of Paul's true feelings for Liverpool'.[41] The *Music City* report stated in 1991 that 'Liverpool, unlike its neighbour Manchester, seems to have established a trend for its successful bands **not** investing in major projects in their city', but then suggested that Paul McCartney's plan to

---

37. Both comments were made during the programme 'Dancing in the Rubble' (Radio 4, 29 October 1982).
38. *Marketing Plan*, Liverpool Cavern City Tours Ltd, 1994.
39. Addressing an MMIA event in 1994.
40. Dave Jones, speaking at the same event.
41. As communicated to the author in 1997.

establish an Institute of Performing Arts in his old school building 'set a valuable precedent'.[42] Meanwhile, a well-known Manchester music practitioner repeatedly drew contrasts between Liverpool and Manchester musicians regarding their commitment to their city, arguing: 'If The Beatles had done to Manchester what they did to Liverpool, the people there would have been furious. No one has put anything back into [Liverpool, which has] a history of leaving and not reinvesting'; Paul McCartney's recent LIPA initiative had come, he suggested, 'too late'.[43]

Such discussions about 'debts' between musicians and cities indicate a reified notion of debt that includes ideas about exchange and reciprocity, hence the familiar use of a kinship metaphor to describe the relationship between people and places, as in the description of the Beatles as 'Liverpool's favourite sons'. People are seen to 'put something into' such relationships or to 'take something out' of them; one party is usually perceived as contributing, needing or deserving more than the other, or as being more exploitative than the other. If any musicians achieved success, their relationship with Liverpool was intensely scrutinised, and lines of debt and accountability more tightly drawn. One local musician said of the Beatles: 'I don't think they owe anything back to the city, but they owe everything to the city. LIPA shows that McCartney knows full well that he owes everything to the city [...] They don't owe it back, but they owe it to the community. Like parents with kids, you can't turn around and say: "You owe me".'[44] Again, this notion of debt may have been particularly strong in Liverpool, not only because of the city's severe economic decline but also on account of its poor media image and political emasculation within the UK, which had encouraged a rather defensive stance towards London, where central government was based and the mass media concentrated. In some of the rhetoric surrounding the policy initiatives Liverpool and its music industry were portrayed as being implicated in a kind of colonial relationship with London. Liverpool was frequently described (punningly) as a 'pool'[45]

---

42. *Music City*, p. 5.
43. Anthony H. Wilson, speaking at the University of Liverpool in 1990.
44. Personal communication from the songwriter Gerry Murphy to the author and co-researchers in 1997.
45. In 1995 the Merseyside Development Corporation launched an expensive image campaign under the slogan 'Merseyside: A Pool of Talent'.

or 'stream'[46] of musical talent and creativity; local talent was perceived as being seduced and lured away, poached and commercially exploited by the London-based music industry, which was described by one local musician as 'the glittering bright lights at the end of the motorway'.[47]

Here, again, the ideological opposition between creativity and commerce familiar to music and to other arts and cultural industries, as well as the music industry's ideology of independence, was cast in geographical terms. Rock musicians in Liverpool commonly discussed commercial concerns and pressures, which they perceived to be a constraint upon their creative music-making, exchanging familiar tales of creative musicians exploited by commercial music organisations. Some musicians thus opposed 'major' to 'independent' record companies, associating the latter with the 'do it yourself' ethos of the 1980s punk scene, with creativity and with particular ideals such as honesty, whereas the former connoted co-option, commerce and a lack of integrity.[48] The discourse surrounding Liverpool's music-industry policy initiatives often gave rise to debates about the dominance of London and the commercial exploitation of local creativity on the part of London-based music companies, and about the possibility of achieving relative autonomy for local music industries.[49]

Some commentators argued that Liverpool musicians could not be dissuaded from moving to London because such a move was too integral to their career development and to the ideology of success. Others, however, suggested various strategies for 'putting Liverpool **back** on the map' and encouraging local musicians to return to, or stay and invest in, the city. MMIA was featured in a Liverpool newspaper urging Liverpool musicians who had 'made it' and moved away to 'return home';[50] at music business seminars the Association's secretary cited examples of successful musicians who had not only chosen to stay in Liverpool but had also attracted other stars up to the

46. Music was thus portrayed as a natural local resource (similar metaphors were adopted in New Orleans during the 1980s, when music was promoted as something that could be 'tapped into' to replace the city's collapsed oil industry).
47. A Liverpool rock musician speaking in 1994 at an MMIA business seminar.
48. Discussed in Cohen, *Rock Culture in Liverpool*.
49. Similar debates were provoked by music-industry policy initiatives in other regional cities, among them Manchester and Sheffield.
50. *Merseymart*, 7 April 1994.

city to record in local studios.[51] Arguments were produced in favour of greater investment into community music activities and facilities in order to prevent the city from 'losing all our kids',[52] and into higher education to ensure 'that product stays in the region rather than traipses off to London. Why have to go to London? Why not Liverpool again?'[53] However, claims that LIPA would help to improve the situation met with some scepticism: 'There's talent going to be coming to Liverpool in the guise of the LIPA studio, the LIPA thing, but what's the use in training them in Liverpool for them to then get off and take their talents to London when there's people up here who could nurture that talent and [...] sell that talent.'[54] Many were agreed that Liverpool needed to develop a music-industry infrastructure that would help to retain music practitioners and their earnings within the city and to attract investment from London-based music companies.

In March 1997 English Partnerships organised a workshop to discuss the 'Ropewalks' cultural quarter initiative in Liverpool city centre. The event was aimed at those involved with, or affected by, the initiative, including businesses, residents and community groups. Cream had been prioritised in the development plan for the quarter, and the Head of External Affairs at Cream, who was attending the workshop, responded angrily to a question about what Cream had done for the community. In a long and impassioned speech she pointed out how many local people Cream employed and how the company had improved the physical environment around the club; she attacked the implication that Cream was somehow separate from 'the community', complaining that anyone in Liverpool who achieved any sort of success was consequently not considered to be part of the city. She also mentioned local pop stars who had left the city, while she had chosen to stay in and contribute to it, engaging, for example, in voluntary work with local schools and community festivals. Cream, she argued, had shown how you could both stay and be successful.

Liverpool's music-industry policy initiatives of the 1980s and 1990s thus promoted a rhetoric of the local that featured ideological

---

51. Speaking at MBTC and MMIA events held in 1993 and 1994, respectively.
52. Martin Dempsey, an MMIA Working Committee member, speaking at a MMIA event in 1994.
53. Martin Lloyd, Head of City Technology College, speaking at the same MMIA event in 1994.
54. Phil Beddard of 3Beat Records. Personal communication to the author and co-researchers in 1997.

constructs commonly associated with the music industry and situated them within a geographical frame that connected them with the city. The rhetoric conjured up images of a bounded city so weakened and under threat that, like a faulty container, it leaked talent or, like a wounded body, bled and haemorrhaged. Yet many of those involved with the initiatives could undoubtedly recognise the romantic and insular nature of this sort of rhetoric (one festival organiser received a round of applause at a 1994 MMIA event when he described parochialism as 'a sin of Liverpool' and warned that the city would be 'doomed' if that attitude continued), and many did also engage in much more practical discussions concerning the development of Liverpool's music industry, recognising the futility of calls to challenge the London-based industry or bring it to Liverpool and advocating instead more realistic ways of capitalising on and promoting local talent and success in the light of their knowledge of the structure and organisation of the music industry and of the flow of income within it.

What all this suggests is how public rhetoric can be strategically deployed for political purposes and in order to further the interests of the groups involved. The rhetoric in question served the interests of the city state, for example, because it helped to promote local integration and to harness local identity for the purpose of gaining support for city policy initiatives; it served the interests of arts consultants because it helped to convince policy-makers of the need for policies aimed at developing the local arts and cultural industries and thus drawing on their particular expertise; it served the interests of the local media, which were concerned to encourage a sense of city allegiance and to be seen to represent the city's interests and act as its main voice; it served the interests of those self-selected music practitioners who were concerned to lobby policy-makers for greater recognition and support for the local music industry and to mobilise other music practitioners to join them in such efforts; finally, it served the interests of ordinary music practitioners, who simply wanted the opportunity publicly to voice their complaints about various injustices that they believed hindered them and their music-making.

Conclusion

This chapter has explored connections between the music business and the city by examining how they are created through the practice and discourse of policy-making. The first part of the chapter outlined the specific context in which the notion of city-based music industries emerged, and described particular policy initiatives aimed at developing and promoting connections between the music industry and the city, while the second part examined how such connections were debated and contested by the interest groups involved. Music-industry policy-making was shown to be overtly concerned with music's economic connections with the city, but it also acted to connect music with local culture and politics. It raised, for example, conflict and debate over what popular music and the music industry are, and over their respective connections with the city and with local identity. It was also implicated in power relations between different places (particularly the British centre and its margins),[55] as well as between groups with different interests in the music industry and in its connections with the city.

Music-industry policy initiatives similar to those of Liverpool have emerged in other cities – from Sheffield and Manchester in Britain to Austin and New Orleans in North America. However, the way in which these initiatives have been formulated and implemented, as well as their effects, have inevitably been shaped by the particular social, cultural, economic and political characteristics of the cities concerned. Bianchini and Parkinson have described cultural policy in Liverpool as a 'tale of missed opportunities'.[56] Certainly, music-industry policy-making in the city has been hampered by the city's notorious economic and political problems and also by the continual involvement of the same few consultants and practitioners – a situation that has contributed to an entrenchment of positions, intensifying divisions between the groups concerned. In addition, while the discourse promoted by Liverpool's music-industry initiatives is similar to that of other cities (the same rhetoric of the local, for example, has surrounded initiatives in Sheffield, Norwich[57] and Austin,[58] and

55. Music-industry policy initiatives concerning other, outlying areas of Merseyside also raised the question of power relations between centre and margins: in this case, relations between the city and its periphery.
56. Bianchini and Parkinson (1993), p. 155.
57. See John Street, '(Dis)located Rhetoric, Politics, Meaning and the Locality', in *Popular Music: Style and Identity. International Association for the Study of Popular Music: Seventh International Conference on Popular Music Studies*, ed. Will Straw *et al.*, Montreal, Centre for Research on Canadian Cultural Industries and Institutions, 1995, pp. 255–63.
58. See Barry Shank, *Dissonant Identities: The Rock 'n' Roll Scene in Austin, Texas*, Hanover, Wesleyan University Press, 1994.

has been intensified by the way in which urban regeneration strategies have encouraged a rivalry between cities), I have suggested that the rhetoric has had a particular resonance in Liverpool – which again points to the specificity of cities.

Liverpool's music-industry policy initiatives also point to the specificity of music, popular music and the music business. This chapter has suggested, for example, that as an aesthetic, symbolic form music poses problems for policies with strictly economic aims. As a cultural industry, music also seems to pose problems for city policy-making because of its specific structure and organisation (e.g., the breadth and diversity of city-based music scenes and industries and the centralisation of the national music industry) and its distinctive image (e.g., a reputation for an anti-establishment stance and disreputable activity). Finally, while popular music has become symbolic of the global and globalisation, I have shown that it is also closely connected with local identity. Both music and place matter to people and are important sources of meaning and of expressing identity and a sense of belonging. As a cultural form, music has a unique quality that people find particularly suited to expressing their feelings and ideas about themselves as individuals and groups and about their surroundings.[59] Some travel writers and policy-makers have even put forward the notion that cities have a soul and that music is the medium through which this is best expressed.[60] Connections between music and the city are thus held dear, and are fiercely protected and fought over.

59. See Cohen, *Rock Culture in Liverpool*, p. 224, and the same author's 'Sounding out the Place: Music and the Sensuous Production of Place', in *The Place of Music*, ed. Andrew Leyshon *et al.*, Guilford Press, New York, 1998, pp. 269–90.
60. For example, see Shank (1994), p. 210, in reference to Austin.

11

Learning to Crawl: The Rapid Rise of Music Industry Education

Mike Jones

Introduction

I find it symbolically apposite that the symposium at which this chapter originated as a paper fell almost exactly at the climax of the first year of the delivery, at the University of Liverpool, of an MBA in Music Industries (MBA MI), a degree for which I act as Course Director. This particular MBA is the first of its kind in the world. 'The first of its kind in the world': this phrase cannot but sound like an advertising slogan, and an archaic one at that (at least in terms of the accelerated history of popular culture). It comes with an almost irresistible connotative 'pre-echo': 'Roll up, roll up, see the first MBA of its kind in the world.' Indeed, the first year of the degree owes a debt, if not to P. T. Barnum himself, then certainly to the circus. There have been death-defying high-wire acts, leaps from one trapeze to another, bareback rides, flaming hoops and custard pies – much as there inevitably are whenever any new venture is undertaken. In short, the course 'on the page' is not the course in the lecture theatre, since, from the outset, there has been a constant need to adjust learning methods and teaching goals to the needs of students. There has also been a need to make a Popular Music Studies perspective on the music industry harmonise with, or at least exist alongside, an orthodox management approach to teaching business. Taking all factors together, and within a much wider context of novelty, there have been tensions around exactly what needs to be taught as the 'music industry' and why. In this chapter I want to review not so much the teaching experience itself, nor even (necessarily) the goals of the course. Rather, my main aim is to isolate and examine the source of these (arguably general) tensions in the emergent area of music-industry education. My reason for choosing this aim is driven by my own sense of unease that arises from having the responsibility to deliver a coherent, working understanding of music-industrial practice. As music teachers, we are all present at the birth of music-industry education – and already, confusions and misconceptions about how business is conducted in and by the industry can be seen, arguably at least, to be apparent. As the new discipline spreads throughout and beyond tertiary and higher education, it is vital to track down the sources of confusion and misconception – the better not only to vanquish them but also to create new understandings about how music is originated, disseminated and received.

Popular music teaching is a phenomenon of the very recent past. Whether at secondary, tertiary, graduate or postgraduate level, qualified teachers have begun to appear only in the past decade. As a subset of popular music education, courses in the music industry are of still more recent origin. In both instances, the creation of courses is driven by a combination of social, cultural and economic forces, wherein music-industry education can be argued to be especially and acutely a product of that combination of forces. In view of the bearing that this will have on later remarks, it is necessary first to outline in some detail the contextual dimensions of the emergence of music-industry education:

The Context(s) of the Emergence of Music-Industry Education

The education system has been subject to a series of pressures in recent decades. Almost all of these are traceable to changes (for which read 'reductions') in local and central government funding. There has been a plethora of responses to funding cuts at every level of education, from nursery through to postgraduate. This has not been an entirely negative experience, since the British education system could arguably be claimed as long overdue for root-and-branch reform. Where the changing status of music-industry education is concerned, we need to consider especially the following five points.

First, in higher education, the initial cuts in central government financial support in the early 1980s led to recognition on the part of universities that a proportion of income needed to be self-generated. What then intensified this new and challenging operating context was the upgrading of the former polytechnics into universities in the early 1990s. Today, there are many more universities than there were in 1980, but these institutions now compete for a falling number of students. In this context, the creation of courses that might be attractive to potential students, regardless of any former institutional antipathies to given subject areas, is a brute necessity. The gradual spread of courses in popular music is but one index of this largely needs-led sea change.

Second, the cuts in government expenditure associated with Margaret Thatcher's term of office as Prime Minister were extremely uneven. For ideological reasons (the assertion of 'monetarism' over Keynesianism), they were aimed primarily at the Welfare State and at the nationalised industries. Further, in a reversion to a national rather than a social characterisation of 'Britain', a revival in economic prosperity was made dependent on the reassertion of managerial and entrepreneurial skills, as against the preservation of the rights of workers or a sense of collective, social responsibility for health, housing, the social adversity of disadvantaged groups or education. For the purposes of these remarks, then, a further consequence of the triumph of monetarism has been to valorise business education as never before. In this context, the MBA MI 'marriage' of popular music and business education in the pursuit of a new student cohort was an event simply waiting to happen.

Third, in roughly the same period (and driven by the same ideological project) further education lost its 'traditional' student base in day-release courses and the provision of a narrowly vocational education. At the same time, the sector became subject to 'incorporation' – at once removing the cost of maintaining colleges from the council tax bill and simultaneously forcing further education (FE) to re-market itself both as an attractive 'alternative' to school (for students who might not otherwise have gone on to take Level Three courses) and, almost, as an extension of the local job centre through its involvement in successive schemes designed to address youth unemployment. In such cities as Liverpool and Sheffield – where not only once flourishing apprentice systems have gone but the entire traditional economic infrastructure (docks, steel-making and metal-finishing) has all but disappeared – the local FE system is forced increasingly to 'stand in' for the absence of employment opportunities for young people. 'Super colleges' have emerged through amalgamation of the patchwork of vocationally oriented providers of the past. These, in turn, have impacted on the 'adult' and 'community' education system that FE once staffed and/or supported. Today all Further Education Funding Council (FEFC) income is tied to 'outcomes': essentially, if a course cannot be demonstrated to yield a qualification of some kind, it will not be funded. Even when a fit with existing qualification structures can be engineered, older, traditional users of the system baulk at the need to complete (for example) an OCN, B.Tec or GNVQ qualification in what, for them, was intended to be a pastime. Consequently, both FE and the more informal 'community' education sector now look to courses that will attract 'customers', who are almost always young people inclined to reject the more formal structures of education, but who can be encouraged to submit to some form of assessment pattern in order that the 'host' institution may continue to attract government funds. Courses in the media and popular music have been the great beneficiaries of this change.

Fourth, in some cities and regions existing community provision in popular music courses has been repositioned advantageously as a result of the developments outlined above. Again, Liverpool and Sheffield can be taken as examples of cities in which local-authority-led initiatives in popular music infrastructural support have actually **benefited** from (rather than been penalised by) changes forced on local and community education. Both Merseyside and South Yorkshire have been recipients of strong support for economic regeneration by the European Community, for the most part through the awarding of grant aid by the European Social Fund, the ESF. As the administrative bodies of the two large cities lying at the heart of these regions, both with a strong (though differently informed) Labour Movement heritage, the city councils of Liverpool and Sheffield had already given support to community schemes that brought popular music activities to areas of social deprivation. Sheffield, especially, enjoyed considerable local authority support for such initiatives. Usually funded by youth or employment services (rather than by the Education Department as such), such schemes as Red Tape Studios and Darnall Music Factory, both located in Sheffield, proved vulnerable to cuts in local authority spending but, equally, could fulfil many of the criteria (and offer 'match-funding' capability) for significant ESF grant aid. In Liverpool ESF funding encouraged the creation of the Merseyside Musicians Development Agency (MMDA). Taken as a whole, community-based or community-rooted projects offering popular music support for local musicians have proliferated and consolidated themselves in the relatively recent past, with a consequent effect on the provision of music-industry education.

Finally, within the national school system music is by now taught largely in the guise of 'pop music'. At a recent prize-giving ceremony at my son's secondary school, year awards were interspersed with musical performances by pupils. I was surprised to encounter an almost entirely unbroken sequence of pop material throughout the evening. I will (clearly) need to return to the issues raised by my response to this programme; here, the key point is that, if children and young adolescents are taught music almost entirely through the medium of pop, this then justifies in and of itself an extension of music teaching into music-industrial areas within the tertiary system.

The music industry has been subjected to an enthusiastic embrace by the incoming Labour government. The roots of this embrace are threefold:

- The music industry has at last been recognised as a successful export industry and as a major domestic employer.
- The basic product of the music industry is information: musical goods are 'symbolic' ones, whatever the attractiveness of their carrying formats and associated packaging. On this basis, the industry is now equally enthusiastically embraced as an exemplar of the (apparent) emergence of the 'knowledge economy', the new 'industrial revolution'.
- For the most part (if not exclusively), the music industry continues to rely on the conversion of the musical efforts of a few young people into musical products received by many more young people. This continued engagement with the young is of great social significance when, as a consequence of the lack of job opportunities, it is the very same young people who are most likely to become disengaged from society and to evolve patterns of behaviour contrary to ones represented as 'acceptable' by those with the power to define behavioural standards.

Taken as a package, 'New Labour's' manifestations of enthusiasm for the music industry have had direct and indirect consequences for the rise of music-industry education. Directly, the government has created a national framework for instruction in music-industrial practices in the form of the 'New Deal for Musicians' (NDfM), together with a national network to support the scheme. Indirectly (and for these same purposes), the new rapprochement with the industry has had the effect of legitimising courses in music-industry education, to the extent that an MBA in Music Industries is now considered a viable and respectable degree.

Finally, the music industry itself has become more 'visible', and this in three main ways.

First, a concomitant of New Labour's enthusiasm for the music industry has been the latter's (perhaps more guarded) public enthusiasm for itself, at least where government involvement is concerned. Labour has had an intermittent, and never very successful, relationship with pop acts since the 1960s, stretching from Harold Wilson's award of MBEs to the Beatles to the botches of the 1980s, when, to mangle Marx, farce followed upon tragedy, since neither Red Wedge nor Neil Kinnock's appearance in a Tracy Ullman video brought electoral success. In each of these instances, Labour's practice was largely opportunistic: aimed at stimulating electoral support among young voters by connecting with an ideological dimension of pop. For Wilson, this was its 'working-class' nature; for Red Wedge, its 'radicalism'; for Kinnock, its sense of 'youthfulness' and 'fun'. In all of these cases, Labour omitted to trumpet the 'success' of the business processes behind pop, since this was still strictly 'Old Labour', with its (supposed) antipathy to capitalism, in pursuit of the 'people's' dimension of 'popular' music.

The accession of Chris Smith to Minister for National Heritage and the rapid renaming of his department as that of Culture, Media and Sport were followed by the creation of the Music Industry Forum. The measure came not without a trace of opportunism, especially in Prime Minister Blair's media-friendly 'open night' at Downing Street, organised for, among others, Alan McGee and Noel Gallagher. However, from the outset there has been no doubt that it is the music industry's (successful) **business** practices that form the basis of New Labour's interest in pop. Industry response has been guarded, but the participation of record and publishing industry figures in the Forum, together with the willingness and need of the record industry's trade association, the British Phonographic Institute (BPI), to support government initiatives in anti-piracy and e-commerce has drawn attention to the extent and centrality of the business infrastructure in the creation of pop success.

Second, during the 1990s there were moves from within the industry itself to engage with education. In 1991 the BPI helped to create the 'BRIT School' in Croydon. This school is a 'City Technology College' and, as such, falls within the tertiary sector, offering B.Tec and

GNVQ qualifications. Indirectly, the BPI's search for funding for the initiative led to Paul McCartney's part in the founding of the Liverpool Institute for Performing Arts (LIPA) in 1994. LIPA offers degrees in Performing Arts and in Music but also allows specialisation in 'Enterprise Management'. The existence of both institutions has had the effect of giving a music-industry 'seal of approval' to the principle of music industry education, although the above-mentioned courses, ironically, may arguably have **contributed** to the 'tensions' referred to earlier.

Finally, the video-led and satellite-led 'globalisation' of pop can also be viewed as having drawn the attention of the public to pop's infrastructure (albeit in a stage-managed and mediated way) through coverage of 'awards' ceremonies. For example, the two key British events are now 'The Brit Awards', organised by the BPI, and the 'Mercury Music Awards'. Both are products of the early 1990s and receive live television coverage on the evening of the respective ceremonies after weeks and sometimes months of speculative advance publicity. Similarly, the MTV awards (also of fairly recent date) sit comfortably alongside the 'Emmy' and 'Grammy' award ceremonies at a domestic (US) level. Because of the 'global' reach of satellite broadcasting, they can pretend to the status of the 'Oscars'. Obviously, awards ceremonies are extremely useful marketing devices (usually of a particularly saccharine kind) and, as such, misrepresent the industry every bit as much as the music press and wider news media have always done. Even so, there is a sense in which they raise the issue of the importance of organisational practices in the creation of pop success. In general, the industry is no more (or no less) accessible than it has ever been, but 'access' of however controlled a nature can arguably be said to have encouraged scrutiny. To a limited extent, music-industry courses are a response to this heightened interest in the business of pop.

Context, Content and Expectation

In different forms, at different levels and across a wide range of sites of delivery, music-industry education has very recently emerged. At best, it is the product of the slowly dawning realisation that the music industry is a vital, and interesting and rewarding, area of economic and cultural activity and therefore of study; at worst, it is a comparatively opportunistic response to the need to massage unemployment figures, to boost student enrolments and to draw down European funding. However, for whatever reason an initiative is taken, any and all popular-music and music-industry courses can claim validity through the sheer scale of applications to them. For example, the newly created Nottingham 'super college' has over seven hundred popular-music students; Red Tape Studios in Sheffield has a permanent waiting list of two hundred applicants for its courses; Napier University in Edinburgh has created an entire Popular Music department from scratch (within a newly designated 'Cultural Industries' faculty); meanwhile, Liverpool's MBA MI has doubled its intake in the first year of its existence. Even so, 'quantity' cannot be made to stand for 'quality'. We need to ask hard questions about what is being taught under the billing of 'the music industry': by whom, with what methods, from what perspectives, with what goals, through what conceptions and concepts, and with what resources and support? These questions need to be 'hard', because the music industry is itself 'hard' in both colloquial senses: in being difficult to understand and in being a tough and ruthless environment in which to make music.

The MBA MI is organised jointly by the Institute for Popular Music (IPM) and the Liverpool Institute for Public Administration (LIPAM). My own responsibilities are to co-ordinate the teaching contribution of the IPM and to ensure the completion of dissertations that are required to be based on research into music-industry practices. Where my own teaching is concerned, I deliver my modules through a combination of lectures and discussion around course materials supplemented by contributions from guest speakers. I organise the course and teach from the perspectives gained through the theorisation of my experience as a pop songwriter and pop record maker. My goal, above and beyond the students' achievement of a postgraduate degree, is to 'empower' them: to give them a set of survival skills, precisely because I conceive the music industry to be the 'hard' place referred to above. My resources are a combination of my theorised experience and music industry contacts, and in my endeavours I am supported by my immediate colleagues at the IPM, together with the further support I, and we, derive from participation in the wider, international forum for PMS, the International Association for the Study of Popular Music (IASPM). This combination of, first, personal experience and, second, dialogue and discussion with music industry practitioners and popular music (and other) academics is clear, coherent and continuous. What coheres less well and less convincingly (so

far) is the attempt to import theoretical concepts derived from Popular Music Studies as a broad body of work into the fundamental areas
of music-industrial practice that form the core of the MBA: hence the
circus metaphors in the introduction to this chapter.

Put more simply, it is only **my** conception that the music industry is a
'hard' place, since in none of the justifications surrounding the expansion in music industry education – whether issuing from the DCMS,
HE, FE and community course prospectuses or from the BPI itself –
is this conception of the industry reflected. Rather, the reverse is true.
Take, for example, the reassuring words of Chris Smith himself when
speaking to the Recording Industry Association of America (RIAA) in
1997: 'We have a complex home market which is under-exploited,
and there is much for A and R (Artists and Repertoire) funding to find
and develop, coupled with our plans for a National Endowment to
support talent and our emphasis on music in schools.'[1] Or this
description of the role and nature of the BRIT School from the BPI's
Web site:

> The British record business believes the continued success of this cre-
> ative industry relies on the discovery and development of new talent
> throughout the country. The BPI has a strong commitment to education
> and actively supports initiatives which emphasise the importance of
> music in schools and community projects. As part of our commitment
> to education and training the BPI offers funding to the BRIT School in
> Croydon, South London [...] dedicated to education and vocational
> training for the performing arts, media and the technologies that make
> performance possible.[2]

In both instances, the role of education is to provide more efficiently
the 'raw materials' for the music industry: 'talent' or 'new talent'.
Where music industry education is concerned, we can consider this
from LIPA's current Web site: 'Enterprise Management equips you
with a vital toolbox of highly pertinent and dynamic skills enabling
you to take your place at the forefront of the managerial revolution
sweeping the performing arts world.'[3] Or this from London's City

1. Published in Chris Smith, *Creative Britain*, London, Faber and Faber, 1998,
   p. 84.
2. Downloaded in August 2000 from Internet site
   http//: www.brit.croydon.sch.uk/.
3. Downloaded in August 2000 from Internet site
   http//:www.lipa.ac.uk/lipa/tell/tell_index.htm.

University current brochure for its 'Music Industry and Cultural Industries Training Courses': 'A toolbox of part-time courses [...] An accredited programme [...] to enable you to [...] update your skills and knowledge in a fast moving business sector [...] improve your effectiveness in a highly competitive environment.'[4] Or this from the well-established 'Generator' community music support facility in Newcastle:

> A package of short training courses have [sic] been designed specifically to help musicians, songwriters and start-up or young SMEs understand how the business side of music operates. Each course will help people develop their management, marketing and financial skills, assess their market potential, understand legal and financial structurings [sic] and realise their creative potential through a professional approach.[5]

In all of these instances, music-industry education is conceived only in terms of a bundle of 'skills' that, while requiring periodic updating, are unproblematic in themselves. But the music industry is a far from unproblematic business environment. As Chris Smith himself points out in the **same** speech to the RIAA: 'The business is high risk. On average, 80–90 per cent of artists signed to record companies will not succeed.'[6]

Or, as the BRIT School points out on its Web site under 'Music Performance Careers – Some Advice!': 'Do note that of the 1,000 bands that get signed to record companies every year only 2% actually get anywhere and less than 10% make the charts at all! It's a lottery!'[7] There are many other instances where the extremely high failure rate among pop acts signed to record labels (implicitly, to **major** labels) is cited. Yet beyond the use of these unverified figures as admonition to the vast sea of hopeful pop acts that they must not **expect** success, there is little comment on, and almost no research into, the implications of this carnage. Still, even these cursory mentions of the enormous failure rate among signed pop acts should cause us to ask some of those 'hard' questions referred to previously (especially when such figures are quoted by champions of the industry rather than by its detractors). Further, the questions that we need to ask of the industry itself (rather than, immediately, of courses offering instruction in its methods) are

4. Downloaded in August 2000 from Internet site http//: www.city.ac.uk.conted/.
5. *Generator Newsletter*, Vol. 40 (November–December 1999), p. 3.
6. Ibid., p. 81.
7. Loc. cit.

the following. What is the actual rate of failure, and why is it an industry constant? Why is it a failure rate that affects pop acts but not music-industry companies or their employees? What does it mean for 'business efficiency' if ninety per cent of products fail to make a profit? How are business practices inflected by the knowledge that ninety per cent of products will fail to make a profit? How do music industry operatives conduct their working lives when the 'products' of the music industry are **people** rather than inanimate objects?

My own research is guided exactly by the recognition that the majority product of the music industry is failure – in the strict sense that most signed pop acts have records released that fail to recover the costs of their production.[8] What frames this research is a strong sense that what lies at the heart of all music-industrial practice is human activity organised expressively as 'musical talent', which can become **popular** musical talent only if a complex combination of actions is undertaken so as to lead to the successful commodification of the original musical activity. From this standpoint, I do not doubt that the practices of music-industrial workers **adds value** to the work of musicians; but what I believe is demanded of researchers into the business of music is that they analyse the methods through which the 'value-adding' activities of the music industry are prosecuted. In the absence of this research, and in the absence of the application to music-business practices of concepts that derive from this research, we are left with the rapidly forming status quo of music-industry education: one in which, arguably, instruction is preceding understanding. This has the threefold effect that key debates may be stifled before they have truly been broached; that graduates from whatever level of award may be **disempowered** because they will have been instructed in a narrow **know how** rather than a more useful **know why**; and that management studies will have missed entirely the opportunity to rethink key concepts through engagement with the demanding field of music-industrial production.

Popular Music Studies and Management Science

On the evidence of delivering the MBA MI, there exists a tension between the methods and perspectives of Popular Music Studies and

---

8. Mike Jones, *Organising Pop: Why So Few Pop Acts Make Pop Music*, unpublished PhD thesis, Institute of Popular Music, Liverpool University, 1997.

those of 'Management Science'. This tension is one that can be traced
not so much to an absence of theory in the practice of the latter as to
the nature of its theorisation. Clearly, this is a generalisation, but at
least where some of the standard models and formulations of management theory are concerned – the BCG Matrix, Porter's Generic
Strategies and the Ansoff Matrix, for example – there is a complete
absence of any sense that what making, distributing and consuming
products involves is the conscious activity of individual human beings
– often in their millions. This appears not to be the case where marketing literature is concerned – until we realise that humans are present only as categories, defined by bundles of demographic or
'lifestyle' characteristics. What the IPM brings to the degree is the
interdisciplinary, even **multi**disciplinary, reality of Popular Music
Studies (PMS), wherein, for the purposes of this argument, the business of popular music (what companies actually do) is difficult to separate from the origination of popular music by pop composers and
pop acts, and equally from the active production of meaning intrinsic
to the reception of popular music. This being so, to teach the music
industry either from a strictly management-science perspective, or
from a skills-centred 'vocational' perspective (and to seek only this
type of teaching as a student), is not only to miss the multilayered
richness of the experience of making, mediating and using popular
music but also to create partial (and thereby misleading) **mis**understandings of how pop works as a 'product' and as an 'industry'.

In order to illustrate this last point, it may prove more useful to
consider how the application of theoretical concepts developed
through, or adapted (and thus developed) by, PMS can lead to new
and higher understandings of what are, apparently, business dimensions of popular music.

Alternative Approaches to Teaching Panayoitou and Others *versus* Sony Music Entertainment (UK) Ltd, 1994

Panayoitou *versus* Sony Music Entertainment (UK) Ltd is better known
as 'the George Michael case'. Very briefly, Michael sued Sony Music
for 'Restraint of Trade' in 1993 on the dual basis that his contract with
them (one that Sony had inherited from CBS Records after its takeover
of that company in 1988) was restrictive – in that it required him to
record eight albums for the company over a fifteen-year period – and
also that it had failed to support the release of his most recent album

('Listen Without Prejudice, Volume 1'). After eight months in the High Court, the Judge, Lord Justice Parker, found for Sony for a combination of reasons: (1) that Michael had renegotiated the 1988 agreement; (2) that he had requested a royalty advance under the terms and conditions of the agreement; (3) that, in general, it was reasonable that the record company be given a lengthy period to recoup and enjoy its investment in him; (4) that Michael had received legal advice at every stage of negotiation and renegotiation. Where this argument is concerned, Lord Justice Parker's further judgement is of particular relevance. Against Michael's accusation that Sony had failed to promote and market the 'Listen Without Prejudice' record effectively, the judge argued that it was untenable that a record company would fail to make every effort to sell a product in which it had invested. On this basis, Michael had no grounds to attribute the comparative failure of the record (it sold ten million fewer copies than the previous release, 'Faith') to actions taken or not taken by Sony.

The George Michael case is a landmark in the development of music industry legal relations for a host of reasons. For example, and in the first instance, the judgement in the case broke a sequence (beginning with Schroeder *versus* Macaulay in 1974) in which judges had found for the pop act or songwriter against a music-industry company. More than this, the judgement in the Michael case acted to preserve the essentials of the record contract system, to the almost audible relief of record companies everywhere. Where my teaching on the MBA MI is concerned, the case is pivotal to a discussion of the contract system as a whole (including publishing, management and live performance, as well as recording agreements) for the way in which it allows an insight not only into the legalities that structure creativity but also into how these enshrine the 'added value' that music industry practitioners bring to the agreement with writers or performers of music aspiring to popularity. For example, the fact that all contracts involve 'consideration' opens up discussion of what it is reasonable that pop acts should promise to write and record, and for what degree of remuneration in the form of royalties and advances against royalties. Similarly, the range of 'definitions' allows insight into how, for example, compositions and recordings are defined for the purposes of legal agreement, and so on. All of this is certainly fascinating and useful, but learning about music industry contract law **away from** the processes of the origination of music and the active reception of music by the audience (rather than the misleading and

passive 'consumption') can be viewed as a distortion of our understanding of how popular music works in practice.

Let us consider the Michael case more closely. My own research into
the interactions between popular music acts and those intermediary
figures who help to commodify those acts and their music pivots on the
notion that, together, the act and the succession of music industry
intermediaries with whom they connect in the commodification
process constitute a *de facto* 'organisation' for that period. What all
parties are working towards is popular music or, more accurately,
recordings of music that sell in huge quantities. Since no one can predict with any real certainty whether a recording will achieve this goal,
it is reasonable to argue that the parties, individually and collectively,
will have differing views about how the recording should sound, and
how the recording (and therefore the act that makes the record) should
be brought to the attention of the public. For these reasons, record-
making is inherently conflictual, all conflicts taking place through language or, more accurately, through discourse and discursive practices.
Essentially, discursive struggles are struggles of and for power: the
power to define courses of action – from compositional and record
production decisions through every subsequent music-industrial
dimension of the commodification, sales and marketing process
(whether, how and where to play 'live'; when and how to seek representation through the mass media; what to discuss and how to appear,
dress and behave during those encounters, and so on). Once we recognise this, we need to begin to draw on the wider resources offered by
the incomplete but developing field of PMS in order to explain why
some acts make successful records, while so many fail to do so.

In the case of George Michael's dispute with Sony, our understanding of his grievances (and of Sony's objection and reaction to
them) can be illuminated if we consider, for example, his construction
of fresh identities – musically and visually – around his previous
records, and how the mediation of, and public response to, these previous incarnations inflected the creative decisions he took with regard
to the record 'Listen Without Prejudice'. Similarly, we might consider
that his challenge to the terms of his contract came only after Sony
had taken over CBS Records, a fact that raises issues about Michael's
conception of his role as an 'artist' signed formerly to a 'sympathetic'
– even 'authentic' – record company. When these dimensions are
absent from teaching, the likelihood is that two simultaneous effects
will be encouraged in the student body.

First, their own prejudices about music will go unchallenged. The wider and more intractable problem here is one of what constitutes 'knowledge' about popular music. If 'knowledge' continues to be regarded merely as what is learned through media representations of popular music-making and shaped through fan discussions about pop that draw only on this mediated 'resource', the now 'qualified' students, when they come to interact with pop acts in business, will expect pop really to be made in the ways, and enjoyed for the reasons, that they have 'learned' through the inexactitudes of media representation and through their own discussions of media-represented pop music, and they will make ill-informed decisions as a consequence.

The second effect of delivering courses in popular music that are restricted to, or attempt to emulate, a narrowly defined 'management science' approach will be the intensification of an existing instrumentalism in students. An MBA is viewed as a necessary stepping stone to a career rather than as an end in itself (as, perhaps, an MA qualification might be regarded). Under these circumstances, students are already predisposed to seek 'know how' rather than 'know why': they have paid (handsomely) to learn how the music industry 'works'. By his failure, as in the example of the George Michael case, to interrogate his actions through a wider body of concepts derived from studies of music and making and recording music and also from the mediation of popular music and the use of music by audiences, there is a strong likelihood that the analysis that is employed will be restricted, in the student's understanding, to the dimension of the development of 'skills' (in the way that most music-industry education is presented). The question thus becomes 'So this is how and why a contract is formulated' rather than 'So this is why there are disputes between pop acts and intermediaries, because relationships develop, and contingencies arise, that contracts cannot specify'. Again, to encourage a belief that 'knowledge' is about 'how' processes work rather than about 'why' actions repeat in processual ways is to create the conditions for misunderstanding the collection of practices identifiable as 'the music industry'. The irony here is that, with a little more theory, George Michael might not have ventured to bring the case that he did!

If we return to Lord Justice Parker's judgement that a record company is unlikely to fail to promote and market a product in which it has invested, we arrive unannounced at perhaps the central dilemma that faces pop acts in the commodification process: how to monitor, assess and control the actions of others taken in their name. In the discursive contest that defines the commodification process, acts are forced constantly to take intermediaries, quite literally, 'at their word'. What further weakens the pop act is that so many different actions are taken at the same time, often in diverse locations. Further, for the most part, acts rely on their managers to monitor and interpret events for them – without pausing to reflect that a manager may have an agenda and a related set of discursive practices through which to pursue his or her own career goals. Taken as a whole, pop acts are structurally disempowered in and by the pop commodification process. However, this does not necessarily make them 'victims' of the music industry. It is rather the case that if, at the outset of their careers, they were encouraged to reflect on how business is conducted – through discussion that is eventually enshrined, still in very general terms, in the form of a series of contracts (with record companies, publishers, managers, promoters and so on) – they might also be encouraged to reflect that 'discussion' is where so much is lost, rather than gained. To elucidate this rather cryptic point we need to consider the recent work of Philip Tagg.

Canons to the Left of Us, Canons to the Right ...

In a keynote address to the UK IASPM conference in 2000, Tagg, a pioneer of PMS, expresses his concern that, as a consequence of its increasing academic purchase, negative as well as positive characteristics have developed within the emergent discipline. He presents, in tabular form, a 'historical comparison between the institutionalisation of classical music and PMS'. This makes interesting and quite grim reading. As Tagg concludes:

> The table shows striking similarities and differences between the two institutionalisation processes. The similarities concern the establishment of musical heritage, with tendencies towards conservation and canonisation, both of musical styles and of intellectual discourse about them. Both processes clearly relate to a contemporary global hegemony, and both justify their establishment by association with notions of subjective liberties in relation to an old and unjust order.[9]

9. Philip Tagg, 'High and Low, Cool and Uncool, Music and Knowledge – Conceptual Falsifications and the Study of Popular Music' (unpublished Keynote Address to IASPM Conference, Guildford, July 2000), p. 9.

What is interesting about Tagg's observation is the notion that 'institutionalisation' (in this instance in academia) expresses itself, in part,
through a process of canonisation that is justified through equally
canonical forms of 'intellectual discourse'. In a further observation
Tagg connects this process with the consolidation of power by a rising
class that, in replacing the old order, demonstrates its distinctiveness,
and its power to distinguish and to convey distinction, through
exactly these processes:

> From the table you can also see how the growth of conservatories and
> music departments in the nineteenth century accompanied the defini-
> tive establishment of industrial capitalism and the abandonment of the
> working classes after the bourgeois revolution, the original notions of
> liberté, égalité and fraternité becoming little more than empty slogans.
> That relationship of institutionalised music studies to that process of
> increasing class difference and exploitation is of course ambiguous:
> while propagating humanist ideals in music and while promoting
> notions of sonic beauty, the same values also provided a cultural veneer
> of respectability for the new ruling class.[10]

During the time that I spent on writing this chapter I attended several
popular music events. Over a two-day period I attended a performance by Johnny Marr's Healers at the Leadmill in Sheffield, followed by attendance at an Oasis concert in Bolton at the Reebok
Stadium. I was invited to attend these events by Marcus Russell, the
manager of both Oasis and Johnny Marr. Russell, a very old friend, is
the former manager of my former band, Latin Quarter. During the
Leadmill performance I reflected on how similar his behaviour had
been when Latin Quarter had played the venue fourteen years before:
he gave the performance a frowning concentration, brightening at
moments and aspects that pleased him and grimacing at those that did
not. What was different was a dimension entirely new to me. Such has
been the scale of the success of Oasis that Russell has become one of
the most successful managers in British pop history. Because of his
position, and because, in addition, Johnny Marr had earlier been the
co-leader of the Smiths, one of the most successful British bands of
the 1980s, Russell had ensured the attendance of five major record
labels at the performance, together with other influential music-
industry figures. As each in turn made contact with him and

---

10. Loc. cit.

exchanged words about the event itself, the encounters struck me as very like (in fact uncomfortably like) those between clerics of different faiths. In their non-verbal behaviour the exchanges were reverent and solemn, since one of the recent 'greats' was playing, and this demanded the respect of all. At the same time, matters of great import were clearly in the air, since, whatever his former stature, Johnny Marr no longer qualified automatically for a record deal. In this way, business was the issue but music was the focus of discussion.

How this experience resonated with Tagg's paper lay in the way in which it connected my own analysis of music-industrial practices – as a series of discursively driven power struggles that define pop commodification – with the kinds of encounter I had witnessed around me on that night in Sheffield (and had been witnessing for decades). It occurred to me that the institutionalisation of the music industry, with all its inequalities of wealth and power, also involves and draws power from canonisation; except that, in this case, business decisions are reached (and are masked) through discourses about music – where canons and the discourses of canonisation are used to justify whether to sign or not to sign an aspirant pop act, whether to prioritise a signed pop act or not, and so on. In this instance, business judgements about the commercial potential of an act (or, in the case of George Michael, about a record) are expressed through, and draw their 'authority' from, canons and discourses of canonisation that operate not so much as a 'veneer of respectability' (although they achieve this as well) but as a system of 'naturality'. Through this process, the responsibility for quite savage commercial decisions and for often incompetent practices within the commodification process are transmogrified into the natural consequences of (identifiable and canonically verifiable) qualities of music or the performances of musicians.

Viewed in the above light, it is no wonder that a judge could not imagine that a record company would 'under-perform' in the selling of a record. Yet George Michael's instinctive supposition was probably an accurate one. For whatever set of 'political' reasons, it is conceivable that the effort required to make a success of 'Listen Without Prejudice' was not forthcoming on the part of Sony Music: the problem for George Michael lay in **proving** this. Again, even a star of his magnitude would find it difficult to monitor and audit the actions of the intermediary figures who stand between his compositions and the mass marketplace for recordings of those compositions. However, if Michael's practice as a songwriter and performer had been informed by theories of popular music-making that anticipate the strategies and strategic modes of intermediary business figures, he could well have been better prepared to survive changes in the business environment that followed on his actions or the actions of others.

Conclusion

The first year of the MBA MI has been a fascinating one. It has proved to be more of an engagement with theory than might have been expected by students – but in a manner that did not lose sight of human, social agency in the the making, disseminating and using of popular music. As an individual, I find it a positive experience to be able to teach and discuss popular music within higher education, and I find it equally positive to interact with talented individuals who may go on to help create the popular music of the future. What is less welcome is the realisation that music industry education as a whole may already have become resistant to the vital activity of generating theory about music-industrial practice. My discomfort when attending the year awards ceremony at my son's school was to witness, and to be expected to enjoy, the praxis of the institutionalisation of popular music: ABBA songs, Eric Clapton's *Layla*, Andrew Lloyd-Webber show-tunes and Whitney Houston ballads all glazed with the hope and expectation that someone, somewhere, would give this 'talent' a 'chance'. As the BRIT School Web site has it, 'It's a lottery!' – but lotteries, human contrivances though they are, rest on natural forces: ping-pong balls in a swirl of hot air in the case of the weekly National Lottery. Pop success, on the other hand, is created by and through industrial processes. It is wrong to encourage young people to sing or play their hearts out without also encouraging them to learn not just how the music industry works but also why it is the way the way that it is. Unless they gain an informed sense of music-industrial practices, young, aspirant pop musicians will be, in the manner of one of P. T. Barnum's infamous scams, queuing to see the 'egress' long after the pennies have dropped for everyone else involved in their careers.

Index of Personal Names

Editor's note

Alphabetisation follows the word-by-word system (thus 'Da Silva' precedes 'Dale'). The letter 'n.' after a page reference indicates the number of a footnote occurring on that page. When a name appears both in the main text of a page and in a footnote on (or beginning on) the same page, only the former is indicated.